Wakefield Press

'Roaming Freely Throughout the Universe'

'Roaming Freely Throughout the Universe'

Nicolas Baudin's Voyage to Australia and the Pursuit of Science

Edited by
JEAN FORNASIERO AND JOHN WEST-SOOBY

Wakefield Press

Wakefield Press
16 Rose Street
Mile End
South Australia 5031
www.wakefieldpress.com.au

First published 2021

Copyright © this collection Jean Fornasiero and John West-Sooby, 2021
Copyright in individual chapters remains with the respective authors

All rights reserved. This book is copyright. Apart from
any fair dealing for the purposes of private study, research,
criticism or review, as permitted under the Copyright Act,
no part may be reproduced without written permission.
Enquiries should be addressed to the publisher.

Cover designed by Liz Nicholson, Wakefield Press
Typeset by Jesse Pollard, Wakefield Press

ISBN 978 1 74305 827 5

A catalogue record for this book is available from the National Library of Australia

Wakefield Press thanks Coriole Vineyards for continued support

Contents

1	Nicolas Baudin, François Péron and the Changing of the Guard **Jean Fornasiero**	1

PART ONE: Scientific Voyaging in Context

2	Constructing the Scientific Voyager **John West-Sooby**	11
3	The Pacific as a Laboratory for Natural History **John Gascoigne**	28
4	François Péron and the Invention of the Nineteenth Century **Jean-Luc Chappey**	39

PART TWO: François Péron as Chronicler of the Scientific Voyage

5	The Manuscripts of François Péron in the Natural History Museum of Le Havre **Gabrielle Baglione and Cédric Crémière**	69
6	The Journals of François Péron and the *Voyage de découvertes aux Terres Australes* **Margaret Sankey**	89
7	The Products and Perils of François Péron **Stephanie Pfennigwerth**	104

PART THREE: The Scientific Record of the Voyage to the Southern Lands

8	An Episode from the Baudin Expedition to the Southern Lands: the Return of the *Naturaliste* to France **Michel Jangoux**	125
9	The Unpublished Reports of Jean-Baptiste Lamarck and the Fate of the Invertebrate Collection from the Southern Lands **Michel Jangoux**	152

10	François Péron as an Ornithologist: Identifying his 'New' Bird Species from the Baudin Expedition **Philippa Horton, Justin J.F.J. Jansen and Andrew Black**	**180**
11	François Péron's Notes on the Albatross **Justin J.F.J. Jansen**	**220**

PART FOUR: François Péron's Fellow Voyagers

12	Jacques Félix Emmanuel Hamelin: A Reluctant Scientific Voyager? **Jean Fornasiero**	**249**
13	A Scientific Voyager in Limbo: Théodore Leschenault's Return to Imperial France **Paul Gibbard**	**267**
14	An Emotional Voyager: Stanislas Levillain (1774–1801), Trainee Zoologist on the Baudin Expedition **John West-Sooby**	**286**
15	Louis Freycinet at Port Jackson: 'Race', Colonialism and the Figure of the French Scientific Traveller, 1802–1839 **Nicole Starbuck**	**302**
	Bibliography	**318**
	Contributors	**331**
	Index	**333**

Chapter 1

Nicolas Baudin, François Péron and the Changing of the Guard

Jean Fornasiero

The Baudin expedition, which was long considered a controversial episode in French maritime history, has been progressively losing its reputation as a contested history. It was certainly time to review the historical record, coloured as it was by extravagant tales of incompetence and brutality.[1] If present-day scholars are decidedly more inclined to engage with the historical records of the expedition than with the legend, they nevertheless encounter a dilemma when it comes to framing the discussion.

In its early historiography, the expedition was seen as a tale of personal conflict, a struggle for dominance between two of the strongest personalities on board: its commander, the renowned scientific voyager, Nicolas Baudin, and François Péron, the trainee zoologist who became the expedition's leading scientist.[2] Since it was Péron who came to write the official account of the voyage, as a consequence of Baudin's premature death, his misrepresentations of key aspects of the voyage came invested with institutional authority.[3] When the commander's own account of his voyage was rediscovered in the twentieth century,[4] and made known through the work of successive generations of scholars, the worst charges of incompetence and misconduct against him were progressively lifted.[5] Baudin's voice was finally heard and Péron's narrative increasingly challenged.

However, it was not simply Péron's narrative which had caused the expedition, along with its commandant, to fall so deeply into disrepute. The reasons for this fall from grace are complex, but a significant part of the explanation lies in the new political situation that greeted the expedition upon its return in 1804. The scientific observations and collections amassed by Baudin and his team were no longer of prime concern to the French government, which was now more preoccupied by the upheavals of Empire than by the advancement of human knowledge.[6] Other scholars have pointed to the links between changes in the scientific world and the deepening of the disgrace of the commander. Ralph Kingston suggested that scientific rivalries undermined the voyage from the outset.[7] For his part, John West-Sooby affirmed that Baudin's disgrace foreshadowed the demise of the type of scientific voyager that he represented,[8] while Jean-Luc Chappey saw Baudin's bad reputation as a sign of future changes in the way scientific voyaging would be conducted.[9]

The time thus seems ripe for further scrutiny of the competition for authority between the two voices of the expedition. With much archival material now available for analysis, historians can move on from simply pitting Péron's words and actions against those of Nicolas Baudin and changing one narrator for another. Besides, to read the expedition through the metaphor of the duel of two 'damned souls',[10] although the stuff of a fine story, and indeed a fitting metaphor for the ultimate fate of the protagonists, is to ignore other differences that separated Nicolas Baudin from François Péron, differences that were as professional as they were personal. In fact, their story occupies a privileged place within the political, social and scientific debates of the early nineteenth century. To persist in seeing their situation otherwise is not just to overdramatise the conflictual nature of working relations on the expedition but also to trivialise the outcomes of the voyage itself. Just as these outcomes were indisputably scientific, so too was the nature of the difference that separated one scientific voyager from the other. François Péron, in writing the narrative of the expedition on his own terms, was not simply accomplishing an act of retribution, he was also donning the mantle of the scientific voyager, and the mantle he chose was of a distinctly different cut from Baudin's. However, before we can come to an understanding of Péron's success in establishing his own position of scientific authority over the expedition, and in acquiring his status as a pivotal figure in scientific voyaging of the nineteenth century, we need to see how Baudin's eclipse came to pass and why a changing of the guard became inevitable.

This outcome was scarcely predictable in 1800 when the voyagers left Le Havre. Nicolas Baudin carried with him the expectation that he would rival in his achievements the greatest of French scientific navigators – Louis Antoine de Bougainville, no less.[11] Louis-François Jauffret, the secretary to one of the expedition's sponsoring scientific institutions, the Society of the Observers of Man, publicly ranked Baudin alongside James Cook.[12] François Péron had himself penned a few lines of verse to that effect.[13] The celebrated scientist Jean-Baptiste Lamarck had commented glowingly on Baudin's discernment as a natural history collector in his own right.[14] A thoughtful and well-connected man, Baudin had reason to covet the mantle of philosophical traveller. Indeed, his writings are revealing on that point.[15] The journals and correspondence that relate to his expedition to Australia, and the narrative of his voyage to the Carribbean, all give evidence of a conscious attempt to take on the persona of the enlightened voyager, prone to musing on the events he witnessed and developing a world view.[16]

As commander of the voyage of discovery to New Holland, Baudin derived great pride from the collections that he and his scientific team collected in the field, a pride that is reflected in his correspondence with Antoine-Laurent de Jussieu, then director of the Paris Museum. Indeed, the collections from the Australian voyage were as large as they were novel. Even if the commander did complain that Péron and his companions preferred to speculate and theorise about their findings with one another, while keeping him in the dark about what they had found, he was content with their achievements. In a melancholy and particularly lucid letter, he conjectured either that he was not a man of science in the eyes of his scientists – or at least not one whose science resembled theirs – or that they feared he would claim their work for himself and steal their glory as collectors and aspiring scholars.[17] In fact, they did believe the former and probably the latter as well, judging from their later accusations according to which Baudin had attempted to steal the expedition's collections. For Baudin, both ideas were scandalous and, from the tone of his letter, deeply distressing, but he recognised that they were too deeply entrenched be be remedied.

This was no doubt so, because Baudin's approval had ceased to be of interest to his young scientists. If they had embarked upon the voyage thanks to the recommendation of the professors of the Museum, it was in the hope of one day joining their ranks. Their work was as much their own as the nation's and they intended to benefit from it. They did not see themselves as collectors in the sense that Baudin's fellow travellers on his earlier Carribbean voyage had been. The gardener Anselme Riedlé and the zoologist René Maugé were long-standing employees of the Museum, who did not, or could not, aspire to a different status. These experienced collectors understood that their role was to provide carefully chosen specimens that would enable the Museum professors to draw conclusions as to their significance. Baudin's view was similar, in that he believed that the duty of the scientific staff was less to lay claim to scientific discoveries than to collect for the voyage's sponsoring institution. It was his incomprehension of his scientists' aspirations, as much as their lack of understanding of his own role, that led to a siloing effect within the shared workspace of their 'floating laboratory'.[18]

When zoologist Bory de Saint-Vincent had first cast doubt on the commander's ability to lead a scientific expedition, he had made at least one statement that rang perfectly true. He had insisted that Baudin could only feel at ease with the type of collector that he called a 'ramasseur': a derogatory term in this context, since etymologically it implies a more random and less discerning form of gathering than collecting.[19] Yet Baudin was also right when he complained to Jussieu that Bory, Péron and their companions considered that they were above those whom Bory himself may have considered mere 'ramasseurs',[20] and that they would neither assist them in their duties, as Baudin did, nor take any advice from the commander. As an experienced scientific voyager, Baudin clearly thought he could make a contribution to the education of all the young men in his charge, and in his instructions for the voyage he was cast in the role of a paternal figure.[21] Péron had initially been docile in this respect and Baudin stated in dispatches that he was pleased with his work. However, the young scientist whose apprenticeship was greatly aided by the expertise of the seasoned collectors such as Maugé, and who intially acknowledged it, eventually treated the captain's friends with the same disrespect as did Bory. Baudin complained bitterly of this attitude: he gave this disdain as the reason why the scientists would not help him write an epitaph in Latin for the tombstone of the gardener, Riedlé, who died during the first stopover in Timor.[22] But more was to come. Péron would eventually claim Maugé's discoveries of new specimens for himself, carefully crossing out the older zoologist's name on his manuscripts and replacing them with his own or that of his friend Lesueur.[23] Baudin was not to know this, but it may not have surprised him, since this corresponded to the careerist attitude that he deplored on several occasions. Yet, this attitude brought its rewards: in the few years following his return, Péron achieved the scientific recognition he sought.[24] In contrast, a defunct collector had, by definition, nothing more to contribute. Baudin's cause was consequently abandoned by his former protectors within the Paris Museum, in particular Jussieu, who, in the troubled years of the Empire, could perhaps do no more than protect his own interests. Georges Cuvier, then Péron's mentor, was in the ascendant. His support was crucial in persuading the government to publish the official account of the voyage, and hence in establishing François Péron's credentials as both a scientist and a scientific voyager.

Baudin's reputation had thus lost out in a battle of scientific and institutional influence to Péron, who had, in the careerist sense, collected more wisely than he. In this context, the conflict between Baudin and the new breed of scientific voyagers represented by Péron takes on far greater significance than the story of personal animosity and character assassination to which the Baudin expedition has so often been reduced. The voyage took place at a pivotal point in terms of the role and nature of the scientific voyager and, in its dramatic turns of fortune, can be seen as a difficult changing of the guard. Although Baudin's fall from the pedestal of revered scientific traveller is a personal catastrophe, and intrinsically interesting because of all the circumstances that conspired to produce it, it is now a story that is widely known. It is also, and was so even in its day, a story belonging to the past of scientific voyaging, to the eighteenth century, that Baudin's values and practices so clearly represented.[25] That being so, it is time for the pendulum to swing back to Péron's story, not as Baudin's nemesis, but as a voyager more attuned than his commander to new modes of scientific enquiry, and to their effects on documenting, reporting and voyaging for the emerging group of scientific travellers of the nineteenth century.

The aim of this volume of essays is thus to explore the ways in which Péron and his companions conducted themselves as they went about their work or positioned themselves in their journals and other writings as scientific voyagers. The kind of work they produced and its significance are also a focus of a number of contributions to this volume. If special attention is paid to the central figure of François Péron, it is because his rapid personal and professional development best encapsulates the ideological and institutional churn of that turbulent time.

Notes

1. For an analysis of the layers of storytelling that contributed to the construction of the expedition's bad reputation, see Jean Fornasiero and John West-Sooby, 'Doing it by the Book: Breaking the Reputation of Nicolas Baudin', in Jean Fornasiero and Colette Mrowa-Hopkins (eds), *Explorations and Encounters in French*, Adelaide: University of Adelaide Press, 2010, pp. 135–164.
2. For a description of François Péron's rise to prominence in the final stages of the expedition and his struggle to publish the account of the voyage and its scientific results, see Frank Horner, *The French Reconnaissance: Baudin in Australia 1801–1803*, Carlton: Melbourne University Press, 1987, chapters 15 and 16.
3. François Péron, *Voyage de découvertes aux Terres Australes, exécuté par ordre de Sa Majesté l'Empereur et Roi, sur les corvettes le* Géographe *et le* Naturaliste *et la goëlette le* Casuarina *pendant les années 1800, 1801, 1802, 1803, et 1804, Historique*, vol. 1, Paris: Imprimerie impériale, 1807. François Péron and Louis Freycinet, *Voyage de découvertes aux Terres Australes, Historique*, vol. 2, Paris: Imprimerie royale, 1816.
4. Nicolas Baudin, *The Journal of Post Captain Nicolas Baudin, Commander-in-Chief of the Corvettes* Géographe *and* Naturaliste, translated by Christine Cornell, Adelaide: Libraries Board of South Australia, 1974.
5. For an account of the expedition's historiography, see Margaret Sankey, Peter Cowley and Jean Fornasiero, 'The Baudin Expedition in Review: Old Quarrels and New Approaches', *Australian Journal of French Studies*, vol. 41, no. 2, 2004, pp. 4–14.
6. Horner, *The French Reconnaissance*, pp. 343–344.
7. Ralph Kingston, 'A not so Pacific voyage: the "floating laboratory" of Nicolas Baudin', *Endeavour*, vol. 31, no. 4, 2007, p. 145.
8. John West-Sooby, 'Baudin, Flinders and the Scientific Voyage', in Serge M. Rivière and Kumari R. Issur (eds), *Baudin-Flinders dans l'océan Indien, Voyages, découvertes, rencontre/Travels, Discoveries, Encounter*, Paris: l'Harmattan, 2007, p. 191.
9. Jean-Luc Chappey, 'Le capitaine Baudin et la Société des observateurs de l'homme: Questions autour d'une mauvaise réputation', in Michel Jangoux (ed.), *Portés par l'air du temps: les voyages du capitaine Baudin*, special number of *Études sur le XVIIIe siècle*, vol. 38, 2010, p. 155.
10. Oskar Spate used the expression 'âmes damnées' when discussing the relationship between the two protagonists: 'Ames damnées: Baudin and Péron', *Overland*, no. 58, 1974, pp. 52–57.
11. Antoine-Laurent de Jussieu made this claim in support of Baudin's project for a round-the-world voyage in 1798. In a letter to the Minister of Marine dated 20 juillet 1798, and quoted by André-Pierre Ledru, *Voyage aux îles de Ténériffe, la Trinité, Saint-Thomas, Sainte-Croix et Porto-Ricco* [sic], *exécuté par ordre du gouvernement français, depuis le 30 septembre 1796 jusqu'au 7 juin 1798, sous la direction du capitaine Baudin, pour faire des recherches et des collections relatives à l'histoire naturelle; . . . par André-Pierre Ledru*, Paris: Arthus Bertrand, 1810, vol. 2, pp. 307–308, Jussieu refers to Baudin as 'l'un des voyageurs qui ont le plus mérité de l'histoire naturelle' ('one of the voyagers who have earned the greatest merit in natural history').

12 Louis-François Jauffret, cited by Jean-Luc Chappey, *La Société des Observateurs de l'Homme (1799–1804). Des anthropologues au temps de Bonaparte*, Paris: Société des études robespierristes, 2002, p. 162.
13 Péron had made the same flattering comparison in a poem he had written in Baudin's honour before the expedition's departure. See Horner, *The French Reconnaissance*, pp. 36 and 80.
14 Jean-Baptiste Lamarck, 'Rapport sur la collection d'histoire naturelle du citoyen Baudin', in Ledru, *Voyage*, vol. 2, pp. 297–303.
15 In 'The Acquisitive Eye? French Observations in the Pacific from Bougainville to Baudin', in John West-Sooby (ed.), *Discovery and Empire: The French in the South Seas*, Adelaide: University of Adelaide Press, 2013, pp. 69–97, Jean Fornasiero and John West-Sooby argue that Baudin's writings place him in the lineage of predecessors such as La Pérouse and Bougainville.
16 Fornasiero and West-Sooby, 'The Aquisitive Eye?', p. 95.
17 Nicolas Baudin, Letter to Citoyen Jussieu from Port Jackson, 20 Brumaire Year 11 (11 November 1802), Muséum national d'Histoire naturelle (MNHN), Bibliothèque centrale, ms 2082, pièce no. 5.
18 Kingston, 'A not so Pacific voyage', p. 150.
19 Jean-Baptiste Bory de Saint-Vincent, *Voyage dans les quatre principales îles des mers d'Afrique, fait par ordre du gouvernement, pendant les années neuf et dix de la République (1801 et 1802), avec l'histoire de la traversée du capitaine Baudin jusqu'au Port-Louis de l'Île Maurice*, Paris: Chez F. Buisson, 3 vols, 1804, vol. 1, p. 189.
20 Baudin, Letter to Jussieu, MNHN ms 2082, pièce no. 5.
21 Pierre-Alexandre Forfait, Minister of Marine, Instructions to Nicolas Baudin, 29 September 1800, cited in Jacqueline Bonnemains (ed.), *Mon voyage aux Terres Australes: Journal personnel du commandant Baudin*, Paris: Imprimerie nationale, 2000, p. 98.
22 Bonnemains (ed.), *Mon voyage*, p. 392.
23 Michel Jangoux, 'L'expédition du capitaine Baudin aux Terres australes: les observations zoologiques de François Péron pendant la première campagne (1801–1802)', *Annales du Muséum du Havre*, vol. 73, 2005, p. 3.
24 As his early biographers point out. See, for example, Marie Joseph Louis Alard, *Éloge historique de François Péron, redacteur du voyage de découvertes aux terres australes, lu à la Société Médicale d'émulation de Paris, séant à la Faculté de médecine, dans la séance du 6 mars*, Paris: Imprimerie de L.-P. Dubray, 1811.
25 Fornasiero and West-Sooby, 'The Aquisitive Eye?', p. 95.

Part 1

Scientific Voyaging in Context

Chapter 2

Constructing the Scientific Voyager

John West-Sooby

The Age of Exploration undoubtedly paved the way for European conquest and the expansion of trade, but science was also a major beneficiary. Indeed, such was the link that developed between science and travel that by the second half of the eighteenth century it had become customary to appoint naturalists to all voyages of discovery.[1] The botanist Philibert Commerson, for example, accompanied Louis-Antoine de Bougainville during his circumnavigation of the globe in 1766–1769. A cosmopolitan group of scientists, featuring the English botanist Joseph Banks, the Swedish naturalist Daniel Solander and the Finnish naturalist Herman Spöring, sailed with James Cook on his first Pacific voyage in the *Endeavour* (1768–1771). The pattern was set. It reached its zenith at the end of the century with two French expeditions: Napoleon Bonaparte's Egyptian campaign (1798–1801), which had both military and scientific objectives and involved the participation of 167 savants, engineers and artists; and the voyage of discovery to the 'Southern Lands' led by Nicolas Baudin (1800–1804), which had an unprecedented contingent, for a maritime expedition, of 22 naturalists and artists – 24 if we add the two young artists Baudin hired to illustrate his personal journal (Charles-Alexandre Lesueur and Nicolas-Martin Petit). Included in that voyage was an aspiring young naturalist, appointed as a trainee zoologist with special responsibility for comparative anatomy, François Péron.

It might at first glance seem perfectly logical and even indispensable for scientists to go and study natural phenomena *in situ* in order to gain a proper understanding of them, but this view was not universally shared. There were some, such as Péron's patron, Georges Cuvier, who considered that 'it is only really in one's study (*cabinet*) that one can roam freely throughout the universe'.[2] The field naturalist, he argued, may have the advantage of observing things 'in their natural surroundings, in relationship to their environment', but he did not have at his disposal the full range of specimens from the different parts of the earth that would allow him to make meaningful comparisons. These were only available back home, in museums or private collections. The travelling naturalist's observations were thus condemned to being 'broken and fleeting'.[3] The hardships of the voyage and the emotions generated by the immediacy of first-hand encounters with objects and living things were also said to mitigate against dispassionate study. Of course, as Diarmid Finnegan reminds us, the 'sharp lines drawn by Cuvier between the study and the field' were 'blurred in practice': if field sites were by nature 'transient and unstable', the institutional spaces in which Cuvier worked were likewise 'fluid and composite rather than stable and univocal'.[4] The distinction was nevertheless a powerful one. True to his principles, Cuvier famously declined the invitation to go to Egypt with Bonaparte.

Cuvier was in a sense drawing on a long tradition of sedentary naturalists working on the objects brought back to metropolitan centres by field collectors. This had begun in somewhat random fashion, as the collecting practices of the various merchants, sailors, missionaries and government envoys who made those early voyages were driven in many cases by nothing other than simple curiosity. Around the middle of the seventeenth century, the Curator of the Royal Society in London, Robert Hooke, realising the need for a more systematic approach, began to put the case for instructions to be drawn up to guide travellers and those occupying the outposts of empire in what they collected and how they recorded their observations. Responding to this call, the Anglo-Irish scientist Robert Boyle published in 1665–1666 his 'General Heads for a Natural History of a Countrey, Great or Small', which specified for the first time the natural phenomena to which travellers should pay particular attention in the best interests of science.[5] During the following decades, instructions of a similar nature began to appear in other European countries, and in ever-growing numbers. This kind of direction even extended to the more culturally focused guidebooks for travellers which offered advice on what to see and how to behave when visiting other countries. These experienced a sharp rise in popularity during the eighteenth century as the Grand Tour became the obligatory rite of passage for young Europeans from the upper classes seeking to become acquainted with Europe's rich artistic and cultural heritage.[6] In keeping with the spirit of the age, the curiosities of the natural world drew increasing attention in such publications, as it came to be understood that some familiarity with natural history was essential to a well-rounded education for the well-to-do.[7]

It was with a very different audience and purpose in mind, however, that, in 1759, the Swedish scientist Carl Linnaeus (1707–1778) published his influential *Instructio peregrinatoris*, an 'instruction for travellers' aimed at providing direction for his 'apostles', as his students were known, when they undertook scientific work in foreign lands.[8] This was a *vade mecum* for the budding naturalist which, as its title suggests, offered firm directives rather than gentle advice and guidance. Linnaeus's foundational text not only signalled a more systematic and methodical approach to scientific field work, it also established parameters – relating to skills, training and temperamant – intended to form a basis for selecting those who were competent to undertake it. In both of these respects, it heralded a major shift in the nature and role of the scientific voyager – a shift that gathered pace during the second half of the eighteenth century as the enlightened amateur gave way to the trained specialist. While travellers of all ilks continued to collect curiosities, a more programmatic approach to the practice of field science – a practice informed by expert knowledge and requiring formal instruction – was gradually establishing itself as the norm.

Specialist savants and naturalists were at this time taking part in a variety of expeditions with particular scientific aims. Linnaeus himself had travelled to Lapland early in his career (1732) in the hope of finding new animals, plants and minerals. In 1736 Pierre Louis Moreau de Maupertuis likewise visited Lapland, with the aim of measuring the length of a degree of arc of the meridian. The second prong of this French Geodesic Mission was an expedition to Ecuador to make the same measurement of a degree of arc, in this case at the equator. It was led by the astronomers Charles Marie de La Condamine, Pierre Bouguer and Louis Godin. At stake in these twin expeditions was the question of whether the earth was oblate (flat at the poles), as Maupertuis had calculated, or prolate (egg-shaped), as his rival Jacques Cassini predicted. The experiment, which confirmed that the circumference of the earth was greater at the equator ('horizontally') than around the poles ('vertically'), settled the controversy in Maupertuis's favour.

Another of these early European missions with an exclusively scientific agenda was Carsten Niebuhr's Danish Arabia Expedition (1761–1767), which visited Egypt, Syria and Arabia, including the little-known Arabia Felix (present-day Yemen), with the primary aim of elucidating the Old Testament. The team of six, of which only Niebuhr survived the journey, included one of Linnaeus's apostles, Peter Forsskål (1732–1763). The Professor of Arabic and Hebrew at the University of Göttingen, Johann David Michaelis, had compiled a list of 99 questions to guide their work, which was to cover geography, cartography and the natural sciences, but also the language and customs of the peoples they encountered.[9] Injunctions to note the appearance and way of life of the locals had also featured in Linnaeus's *Instructio*. Ethnography was on the way to becoming a science in its own right.[10]

The appointment of trained naturalists to voyages of discovery was thus symptomatic of a general trend towards a more specialised type of scientific voyager. As John Gascoigne notes of Joseph Banks's participation in Cook's *Endeavour* voyage, the task of rendering natural history 'fruitful' 'required more than the random notes which a naval officer such as Cook was likely to produce'.[11] There was nevertheless an important difference between the status of Banks and that of his French counterparts. In France, where science had been institutionalised for a considerable period and was in a sense 'professionalised', naturalists on scientific expeditions were appointed and funded by the state;[12] Banks, in contrast, was a wealthy private citizen who paid his own passage on Cook's *Endeavour*. He and his companions, Solander and Spöring, were scientifically educated and well credentialled, but they were not professional scientists in the way we understand that term today. A sign of their particular status is the quaint term Cook used to refer to them: the 'experimental gentlemen'. Matthew Flinders, during his *Investigator* voyage which circumnavigated Australia in 1801–1803, similarly referred to his naturalists as the 'scientific gentlemen'.

The difference in their status notwithstanding, these European savants were all well-trained and highly specialised scientific voyagers whose exploits earned them notoriety and respect. As the example of Cuvier illustrates, however, the alternative paradigm of the sedentary savant working in a metropolitan centre of knowledge on specimens gathered by less well credentialled – albeit discerning – field collectors had by no means been supplanted. This was indeed the model that prevailed over Nicolas Baudin's voyage to the West Indies in the *Belle Angélique* in 1796–1798. The aim of this expedition was to recover (and augment) the collection of natural history specimens that Baudin had amassed during his earlier travels and that circumstances had obliged him to leave for safe-keeping in the Spanish-held island of Trinidad. To assist him in this task, the professors of the National Museum of Natural History in Paris appointed a small contingent of naturalists: the botanist André-Pierre Ledru; the zoologist René Maugé, whose interest in the study of animals had led the Museum to grant him an associate position; the gardener Anselme Riedlé, an employee of the Museum with an intimate knowledge of its botanical collections; and the mineralogist Alexandre Philippe Advenier, from the School of Mines. All four were given the title of 'aide-naturaliste' – a sign of their modest status. In addition, the surgeon Valentin Truffet had some training in zoology and several other members of the expedition had the unofficial status of 'amateurs d'histoire naturelle', among them Stanislas Levillain, who served as Baudin's secretary. Selected for their knowledge and zeal, the naturalists, as specified in the minutes of the meeting of the Museum professors on 12 July 1796, were 'to provide the savants with precious observations on the state of this land [Trinidad]'.[13] There was thus no confusion regarding their role: these were field naturalists working to collect specimens for detailed examination by the savants back in Paris.

Baudin, for his part, was delighted with this arrangement. In the course of his travels, he had developed a penchant for natural history and had become an astute collector, but he had no claims to scientific expertise beyond that. The appointment to his expedition of this small group of knowledgeable but unpretentious and practical-minded naturalists was in perfect harmony with his own pragmatic approach to scientific voyaging. In the event, Baudin was well served by this dedicated group. On arrival in Trinidad, he discovered that the island had been taken over by the British. Despite carrying a passport delivered by the authorities in London recognising the neutrality of his voyage, Baudin was refused permission to recover his natural history collections by the island's obdurate governor, Thomas Picton. He therefore made for the Danish-held island of Saint Thomas before moving on to Porto Rico, where he and his team spent nine months compiling a completely new collection of tropical plants and animals. Despite the various obstacles and hardships they had to endure, this proved to be a highly productive undertaking, made possible in large part by the spirit of solidarity and the assiduity of his naturalists.[14] On arriving back in France, Baudin's collections of live tropical plants were paraded through the streets of Paris on the occasion of the 'Fête de la Liberté' and he himself was acclaimed as a national hero.

This experience is of particular relevance to our understanding of Baudin's next expedition, the voyage of discovery to the Southern Lands, which left the Normandy port of Le Havre on 19 October 1800. The various rifts and resentments that developed as the journey unfolded between the commander and a number of his scientists, and indeed among some of the naturalists themselves, of course had various causes, but they can to an important extent be attributed to conflicting conceptions of the role and nature of the scientific voyager. For Baudin, the principal aim of the work in natural history during the voyage to Australia was to record observations and collect specimens – primarily those that were new or less well known.[15] He was supported in this by three of the naturalists who had accompanied him to the West Indies and who again constituted the core of his team for this new venture, Maugé, Riedlé and Levillain. Their unassuming and almost self-effacing approach to their work was not shared, however, by the other scientists, many of whom saw in the voyage an opportunity to pursue their own agenda and make a name for themselves. What Baudin had failed to grasp, in imagining he could recreate the collegial atmosphere of his *Belle Angélique* voyage, was the importance of the ideological and institutional shift that had occurred between 1796 and 1800 with the change in political regime from the Directory to the Consulate – that is to say from a collective form of government (by committee) to one nominally run by three consuls but in reality dominated by the imposing figure of Napoleon Bonaparte. The republican spirit that had characterised the organisation and conduct of Baudin's voyage to the West Indies had given way to a mindset in which individual ambitions were newly legitimised.

No-one embodies this shift in mentalities better than François Péron, whose rise from the humble position of trainee zoologist to that of leading naturalist and spokesman for the Baudin expedition owed as much to personal ambition and drive as it did to circumstance (namely the departure of seven members of the scientific contingent at Mauritius during the outward journey, the premature deaths of four others – among them Baudin's three trusted companions from the *Belle Angélique* voyage – and the death of the commander himself during the journey home).[16] A protégé of Cuvier, whose influence had secured him a position on the expedition, Péron was well aware of the career opportunities that new research and the publication of its results might afford him. By the same token, however, he was still very much a novice when he left France. An aspiring savant, Péron had first to earn his stripes as a collector and observer. In some notes he compiled after the voyage, he presented this as a virtue – his work in the field, he argued, had given him a distinct advantage over the savants of Europe (and especially the English):

> On these shores [...] so rich in animals of all species, the English had still done almost nothing, and the successive studies of Broussonet, Pennant, Shaw, Fabricius, Chemnitz, Collins and Schmidt had been limited to the description of a few species of mammals, birds, insects, fish and shells [...]. Moreover, as most of these naturalists had not travelled to these locations, and had no choice but to work on animals that were dried or preserved in alcohol, they had not been able to provide sufficiently complete descriptions. In this respect, the studies conducted by Monsieur Péron on the very sites themselves and almost always on living animals could not fail to have, for these two reasons, a particular advantage over those of the naturalists we have just mentioned.[17]

As Péron's use of the third person might suggest, these were notes he was compiling for others to use on his behalf, more specifically for the report that the professors of the Museum in Paris were to present on the work he and his friend Lesueur had conducted during the Baudin expedition. Given that this report was to be presented by none other than Cuvier himself, whose views on the superiority of the work of the sedentary scientist were presumably well known to all, it is perhaps not surprising that Péron deleted from later drafts this claim to the advantages of work in the field.[18]

The expedition to Australia was thus a necessary rite of passage which offered Péron the opportunity to conduct field work that would not only supplement his training but also provide him with a rich store of material for subsequent analysis. His published account of the voyage reveals an attempt to sit astride the supposed divide between the field scientist and the accomplished savant or 'philosophical traveller', and to position himself as mastering both roles. The tensions and inconsistencies in narrative voice evident in that account suggest that he had difficulty in reconciling the two postures. It would take the charismatic figure of Alexander von Humboldt to transcend what Nigel Leask describes as the 'invidious distinction between the "sedentary naturalist" working in the metropolitan "centre of calculation" and the field collector who merely supplied the former with raw material'.[19] In his travel writing in particular, Humboldt achieved what Charles Darwin considered to be a 'rare union of poetry with science', particularly 'when writing on tropical scenery'.[20] Humboldt, whose voyage to South America (1799–1804) coincided with that of Péron to Australia (1800–1804), certainly had time to hone his craft: the 30 volumes of his *Voyage aux régions équinoxiales du Nouveau Continent* were published between 1807 and 1834; Péron, in contrast, died in 1810, just three years after the first volume of his *Voyage de découvertes aux Terres Australes* was published.[21]

Baudin's expedition to Australia thus took place at a pivotal point in terms of the role and nature of the scientific voyager. Indicative of a certain state of flux in that regard are the instructions provided to travelling scientists on state-sponsored French expeditions during the 1790s. Those given to the naturalists who travelled on Bruni d'Entrecasteaux's voyage in search of La Pérouse at the beginning of the decade, for example, were highly prescriptive and reveal an attempt to exert central control over the work that was to be conducted in natural history. As Hélène Richard has noted, the Society for Natural History (Société d'histoire naturelle), which had instigated the expedition, was well aware that the information gathered by travelling scientists could be fragmentary. Its members therefore provided d'Entrecasteaux's savants with very precise models of observation to frame their work.[22] Independently, the Academy of Sciences passed on to d'Entrecasteaux just prior to his departure the memoir it had prepared for the naturalists on the La Pérouse expedition – a comprehensive document covering all domains of scientific enquiry (anatomy, zoology, mineralogy, botany, chemistry, astronomy, geography, meteorology . . .). It was this latter document, which was more comprehensive than the Society's guidelines, that d'Entrecasteaux tried to insist his naturalists should adhere to. Irrespective of which set of instructions ultimately served to guide their work, it is clear in both cases that the metropolitan based scientists were attempting to harness and control the work of their travelling counterparts.

By the same token, however, the Society recognised the importance of acknowledging the value of the work the travellers would conduct in the field and sought to promote their status as specialist savants in their own right. In an address to his colleagues, the botanist Louis Claude Richard argued that the Society should invite to its meetings all the naturalists appointed to accompany d'Entrecasteaux, and grant them associate status.[23] Another member, the deputy inspector of mines, Alexandre-Charles Besson, highlighted the unique advantage they would have over their metropolitan colleagues who, for the most part, 'have only worked in their cabinets from memoirs or books [. . .] without being able to judge the value of the observations made by others, through lack of contact with nature, having not seen or studied it or undertaken their own observations and research'.[24] This was a ringing endorsement of the value of field work – although, in keeping with his practical, no-nonsense approach, Besson also cautioned the travellers against falling into the trap themselves of indulging in theoretical speculation.

A further sign of the autonomy afforded d'Entrecasteaux's naturalists – and thus of the respect they enjoyed as scientists – is the fact that it was left to them to decide who would take responsibility for which branch of research. As one of their number, Claude Riche, reported in a letter to d'Entrecasteaux, it was only at the Cape of Good Hope that they settled on their roles: 'You know, Sir, that through an agreement established between M. Labillardière, M. Deschamps and me, I have taken particular responsibility for ornithology, helminthology and mineralogy during the voyage.'[25] The disciplinary specialisation that would emerge at the end of the decade was evidently not a source of dispute for this group at this point in time. While some of the duties they assumed corresponded to established interests – it is no surprise, for example, that Labillardière ended up with botany – it is clear that the scientists considered themselves capable of covering all branches of natural history. This is not to say that they did not consider their work to be specialised. On the contrary, they were fiercely protective of their rights and status as savants. As d'Entrecasteaux reported to the Minister of Marine from the Cape, the naturalists complained bitterly to him about the collecting being done by others such as the surgeons, who in their view were not qualified to do so.[26] It is clear, then, that d'Entrecasteaux's scientists saw natural history, in general terms, as their exclusive preserve.

The situation changed radically for the naturalists who accompanied Baudin to the West Indies five years later. While their instructions were just as detailed, and reveal a similar intention to exert central control over their work, they were not afforded the status or autonomy enjoyed by the scientists who accompanied d'Entrecasteaux. As already noted, these employees and associates of the Museum were explicitly appointed as collectors, not savants.[27] The Director of the Museum, Antoine-Laurent de Jussieu, was at pains to point this out, explaining to the Minister of Marine that the role of the naturalists would be strictly confined to 'collecting with discernment the objects that might enrich the Museum's collection' – and thus provide its professors with new objects for study.[28] This was also made clear in the general and individual instructions Jussieu compiled. The mineralogist Advenier, for example, was to 'collect mineral samples in sufficient quantity for the Museum to share with [the School of Mines] the product of his work'.[29] The word 'collect' – 'recueillir', in French – occurs repeatedly in Jussieu's instructions. Even the important task of recording observations was subordinated to the need to gather specimens. In his instructions for the botanist Ledru, Jussieu wrote:

> as he will be pressed for time, and as this time will be best employed in collecting rather than describing, he will be well advised to shorten his descriptions, simply recording the ephemeral characteristics which disappear when the plant dies, and not bothering with those traits which subsist in the dried specimen and which can be studied long afterwards.[30]

Furthermore, although the naturalists were all enjoined to help one another, if and when the need should arise, their roles were all clearly defined and delineated. Each of them was directed to collect 'the objects that are within his remit'.[31] There was indeed to be no confusion regarding their particular duties. The zoologist Maugé, for example, after preparing the animals for conservation and removing their skins, was instructed to 'pass on the body to the anatomist', but not before asking those who could draw 'to sketch the shape and common posture of each animal so that these drawings could assist the Museum to give the stuffed animals the most natural appearance possible'.[32] As this level of direction makes clear, Baudin's small team did not have anything like the degree of autonomy that was extended to d'Entrecasteaux's savants.

For the voyage to Australia at the end of the decade, Baudin received a large and varied array of instructions covering everything from research on smallpox to the operation of the cooking stoves.[33] Of particular note are the two sets of instructions concerning anthropology compiled by Cuvier and Joseph-Marie Degérando.[34] Those of Cuvier focused on comparative human anatomy, whereas Degérando was primarily interested in questions of culture and social organisation, including language and other means of communication – a novel approach requiring a level of dialogue and interaction that would prove difficult to achieve during the mostly brief shore encounters.[35] Complementary rather than competing, the two detailed documents compiled by Cuvier and Degérando were groundbreaking in their scope and detail. In contrast, the instructions concerning natural history were, as Michel Jangoux has described them, 'woefully banal'.[36] The mineralogists, it is true, were provided with a reasonably detailed list of questions to guide their work – 37 in total – but zoology and botany received scant attention – four and five questions respectively, and of a very general nature, such as: 'What are the dominant species of birds?'[37] There is nothing here to match the precision and fastidious detail that characterised the instructions compiled for the naturalists on the d'Entrecasteaux and *Belle Angélique* voyages. Moreover, and again in contrast to the two previous expeditions, the brief notes pertaining to natural history contain no mention of the scientists themselves. Apart from the fact that some were appointed with the status of 'chef' and others that of 'élève' (trainee) or 'garçon' (the gardeners), their role, their personal conduct and the nature of their work were left entirely unspecified. Did the government and the Museum professors consider them to be, as Jangoux has put it, 'actors' or 'agents', that is to say scientists capable of autonomous research and reflection, or collectors working in the service of the specialists back home?[38] Baudin and Jussieu, who was then at the height of his power within the political and institutional context of the Paris Museum, were of one mind in this regard: the main objective of the expedition, in terms of natural history, was to enrich the collections of the Museum, thus providing its professors, Jussieu chief among them, with an expanded store of materials for study.[39] This was a tacit understanding, however; the instructions were silent in this respect.

It is hard to imagine that an ambitious young naturalist such as Péron, not to mention his more well-credentialled colleagues, would have accepted to remain confined to the relatively 'humble' role of collector that was embraced by the likes of Maugé, Riedlé and Levillain. As we have noted, the ideological and institutional climate had changed in significant ways compared to the 'republican moment' of the mid 1790s. This is perhaps one reason why Jussieu did not issue the detailed general and individual instructions he had compiled for the naturalists on the *Belle Angélique* voyage. Despite his expectations and intentions, he may have felt wary about going too far. The sheer number of scientists appointed might also have mitigated against such detail. Whatever the reason, this void opened the way for a profound misunderstanding to develop between Baudin and several of his scientific staff. It also left the path open for the pursuit of agendas that conflicted with that of the commander – as exemplified by Péron's repeated assertion that he had received private orders that prevented him from performing some of the duties that his captain requested him to undertake: 'You have surely not forgotten', Baudin wrote to him, 'that you have told me, more often than I would have liked to hear it, that Monsieur Cuvier, at whose request you were embarked, had given you private orders, and not the government.'[40] The commander eventually gave up the fight.

Baudin's expedition to Australia thus constitutes a particularly compelling case study in terms of the figure of the scientific voyager, the evolution of which had reached a critical point. The prevailing fluidity of this role, which was compounded by the dearth of detail in the scientific instructions, proved to be a major problem for Baudin; conversely, these same factors provided François Péron with the opportunity to mould the role to his own purposes. The irony is that, notwithstanding the pretensions of some of Baudin's savants, the expedition ultimately proved to be a record-breaking exercise in collecting, returning to France with a staggering number of natural history specimens – well in excess of 100,000. François Péron himself had amassed many of these items – albeit, according to his captain, in often indiscriminate fashion.[41] The wishes of Jussieu and the other Museum professors were thus fulfilled to a degree they could scarcely have imagined. And yet their scholarly exploitation of this treasure trove, while more significant than is often recognised, failed to match the scale of what was placed at their disposal. Perhaps the very volume itself of the material gathered mitigated against the type of detailed analysis that was needed to produce new theories and syntheses. Did the Baudin expedition, then, in compiling such an extensive collection, reveal the limits of a policy dedicated to the principle of accumulation, thereby undermining the role of the collector? That would be the ultimate irony.

Notes

1   The link between science and colonisation is not our subject here, but it was just as strong, as demonstrated in the case of pre-Revolutionary France by François Regourd and James McLellan, *The Colonial Machine: French Science and Overseas Expansion in the Old Regime*, Turnhout: Brepols Publishers, 2012.
2   Cited in Dorinda Outram, 'New Spaces in Natural History', in Nicholas Jardine,

James A. Secord and Emma C. Spary (eds), *Cultures of Natural History*, Cambridge: Cambridge University Press, 1996, p. 262.
3   Outram, 'New Spaces', pp. 259–260.
4   Diarmid A. Finnegan, 'The Spatial Turn: Geographical Approaches in the History of Science', *Journal of the History of Biology*, vol. 41, no. 2, 2008, p. 379. On this question, see also Marie-Noëlle Bourguet, 'La collecte du monde: voyage et histoire naturelle (fin XVIIe siècle – début XIXe siècle)', in Claude Blanckaert *et al.* (eds), *Le Muséum au premier siècle de son histoire*, Paris: Éditions du Muséum national d'Histoire naturelle, 1997, pp. 163–196.
5   Robert Boyle, 'General Heads for a Natural History of a Countrey, Great or Small', *Philosophical Transactions*, vol. 1, 1665–1666, pp. 186–189. This was later expanded and published as a book: *General Heads for the Natural History of a Country, Great or Small, Drawn out for the Use of Travellers and Navigators*, London: printed for John Taylor, 1692.
6   Lorelaï Kury, 'Les Instructions de voyage dans les expéditions scientifiques françaises (1750–1830)', *Revue d'histoire des sciences*, vol. 51, no. 1, 1998, pp. 66–67.
7   On this scientific or philosophical turn in travellers' guides, see Pierre Laubriet, 'Les Guides de voyages au début du XVIIIe siècle et la propagande philosophique', *Studies on Voltaire and the Eighteenth Century*, vol. 32, 1965, pp. 269–325.
8   This was actually the disssertation of one of Linnaeus's students, Erik Anders Nordblad, but it was clearly a synthesis of the master's views and is conventionally attributed to him. An English translation of the text is given in Lars Hansen *et al.* (eds), *The Linnaeus Apostles: Global Science and Adventure*, Whitby: IK Foundation, 8 vols, 2007–2012, vol. 1, pp. 201–211.
9   Johann David Michaelis, *Fragen an eine Gesellschaft Gelehrter Männer, die auf Befehl Ihro Majestät des Königes von Dännemark nach Arabien reisen*, Frankfurt am Main: Johann Gottlieb Garbe, 1762. The same publisher produced a French translation in 1763, entitled *Recueil de questions, proposées à une société de savants, qui par ordre de Sa Majesté danoise font le voyage de l'Arabie*. A second French translation was published in Amsterdam in 1774.
10 On this subject, and on the role of scientific instructions more generally, see Silvia Collini and Antonella Vannoni (eds), *Les Instructions scientifiques pour les voyageurs (XVIIe–XIXe siècle)*, Paris: L'Harmattan, 2005.
11 John Gascoigne, *Encountering the Pacific in the Age of Enlightenment*, Cambridge: Cambridge University Press, 2014, p. 280.
12 An important caveat to this portrayal of the situation of scientists in France, as Roger Hahn points out, is that most members of the Paris Academy of Sciences could not survive solely on the funding provided by the state: 'A serious gap [thus] existed between what historians refer to proudly as funded government sponsorship of French science, and the life of the individual scientist.' R. Hahn, 'Scientific Careers in Eighteenth-Century France', in Maurice Crosland (ed.), *The Emergence of Science in Western Europe*, London: Macmillan, 1975, p. 131.
13 Archives Nationales de France (ANF), série Muséum, AJ 15/580. Reproduced in Nicolas Baudin, *Journal du voyage aux Antilles de La Belle Angélique (1796–1798)*, édition établie et commentée par Michel Jangoux, Paris: Presses de l'Université Paris-Sorbonne/Académie royale de Belgique, 2009, p. 30.
14 On the 'republican' nature of this voyage, see Jean Fornasiero and John West-Sooby, 'Voyages et déplacements des savoirs. Les expéditions de Nicolas Baudin entre Révolution et Empire', *Annales historiques de la Révolution française*, vol. 385, no. 3, 2016, pp. 23–46 (article also available in English translation).
15 As Michel Jangoux has pointed out, this focus on collecting was the basis of Baudin's relationship with the Director of the Paris Museum, Antoine-Laurent de Jussieu. For Baudin, collecting was an end in itself. This suited Jussieu, who considered that the specimens gathered would serve as a basis for his research

and for that of his Museum colleagues. See Michel Jangoux, 'Les zoologistes et botanistes qui accompagnèrent le capitaine Baudin aux Terres australes', *Australian Journal of French Studies*, vol. 41, no. 2, 2004, pp. 55–78.

16 Ten scientists and four artists (two of whom were officially appointed, the other two recruited by the commander) embarked on Baudin's ship the *Géographe*; nine scientists and one artist sailed in his consort ship the *Naturaliste*. Seven scientists left the expedition at Mauritius, one from the *Géographe* (the astronomer Frédéric Bissy) and six from the *Naturaliste* (the zoologists Jean Baptiste Bory de Saint-Vincent and Désiré Dumont, the botanists André Michaux and Jacques Delisse, and the gardeners Jean François Cagnet and Michaux's black slave Merlot). The three officially appointed artists also disembarked at Mauritius: Jacques Gérard Milbert and Louis Lebrun from the *Géographe*, and Michel Garnier from the *Naturaliste*. Of the 12 scientists who remained with the expedition after Mauritius, four died relatively early, from dysentery and tropical fevers contracted at Timor following the exploration of the western Australian coast (the gardeners Anselme Riedlé and Antoine Sautier; and the zoologists René Maugé and Stanislas Levillain). The astronomer Pierre-François Bernier died on 6 June 1803, following the second stay in Timor. Those who completed the expedition's exploration of Australia were thus: the zoologist François Péron, the botanist Théodore Leschenault (who remained in Timor due to illness in June 1803 but who eventually made his way back to France, in 1807); the geographers Charles Pierre Boullanger and Pierre Auguste Faure; the gardener Antoine Guichenot; and the mineralogists Joseph Charles Bailly and Louis Depuch (though the latter died at Mauritius on 3 February 1803 during the homeward journey on the *Naturaliste*). The artists Lesueur and Petit also completed the voyage.

17 Muséum d'Histoire naturelle, Le Havre, Collection Lesueur, 22 012. Pierre Broussonet was a French naturalist and politician who worked in London under the tutelage of Joseph Banks and others on the fish specimens collected during Cook's Pacific voyages; Thomas Pennant was a Welsh naturalist who described the bird specimens that Banks collected during his voyage with Cook in 1769–1770; George Shaw was an English naturalist who published the first *Zoology of New Holland* in 1794; Johan Christian Fabricius was a Danish entomologist and student of Linnaeus who worked in London on the collections of Banks and others; Johann Hieronymus Chemnitz was a German clergyman and conchologist with strong Danish connections who studied the shells from Australia and New Zealand collected during Cook's first Pacific voyage; David Collins was a British naval officer who travelled to Botany Bay with the First Fleet and whose well-known description of the early years of the settlement, *An Account of the English Colony in New South Wales* (1798), included some notices on 'rare and curious objects' of Australian fauna; the Schmidt in question may be the German conchologist Frédéric-Chrétien Schmidt (1755–1830).

18 Dossier 22 of the Lesueur Collection in the Le Havre Museum contains several drafts of this text. The final version of the report was reproduced as a kind of preface to the first volume of Péron's *Voyage de découvertes aux Terres Australes*.

19 Nigel Leask, 'Darwin's "Second Sun": Alexander von Humboldt and the Genesis of *The Voyage of the Beagle*', in Helen Small and Trudi Tate (eds), *Literature, Science, Psychoanalysis, 1830–1970: Essays in Honour of Gillian Beer*, Oxford: Oxford University Press, 2003, p. 22. Mary Louise Pratt has argued that Humboldt sought 'to reframe bourgeois subjectivity, heading off its sundering of objectivist and subjectivist strategies, science and sentiment, information and experience' (*Imperial Eyes: Travel Writing and Transculturation*, London: Routledge, 1992, p. 119).

20 From Charles Darwin's *Diary*. Quoted in Leask, 'Darwin's "Second Sun"', p. 22.

21 François Péron, *Voyage de découvertes aux Terres Australes, exécuté par ordre de Sa Majesté l'Empereur et Roi, sur les corvettes le* Géographe *et le* Naturaliste *et la*

goëlette le Casuarina *pendant les années 1800, 1801, 1802, 1803, et 1804, Historique*, vol. 1, Paris: Imprimerie impériale, 1807. François Péron and Louis Freycinet, *Voyage de découvertes aux Terres Australes, Historique*, vol. 2, Paris: Imprimerie royale, 1816.

22 Hélène Richard, *Le Voyage de d'Entrecasteaux à la recherche de Lapérouse*, Paris: Éditions du CTHS, 1986, p. 61.
23 'Adresse à la Société d'histoire naturelle de Paris au sujet de l'expédition à la recherche de la Peyrouse, par Richard (17 janvier 1791)', Muséum national d'Histoire naturelle, ms 46 (dossier I).
24 'Observations sur le choix des minéralogistes et leurs recherches pendant le voyage projetté pour la recherche de M. de la Peyrouse, lues à la Société des naturalistes de Paris le 18 fevrier 1791 par M. Besson Sous Inspecteur des Mines et de la Société', Muséum national d'Histoire naturelle, ms 46 (dossier IV). He was particularly scathing in his criticism of those whose theories on the history of the earth had, in his view, little or no practical basis.
25 Riche to d'Entrecasteaux, 29 July 1792, ANF, série Marine, 5JJ 6A.
26 D'Entrecasteaux to the Minister of Marine, 13 February 1792, ANF, série Marine, 5JJ 6A. The commander, while acceding to some of their demands, had little sympathy for the naturalists: in his view, natural history, like the air we breathe, was open to everyone.
27 This was understood and accepted by the appointed naturalists. In responding to the invitation to join the expedition, the botanist Ledru modestly wrote: 'in accepting the mission you have offered me, I have consulted my zeal for botany more than my limited understanding of this charming field of our knowledge'. Ledru to Jussieu, 4 Vendémiaire Year V (25 September 1796), ANF, série Muséum, AJ 15/569, fol. 40.
28 Jussieu to the Minister of Marine, 3 Fructidor Year IV (20 August 1796), Service Historique de la Défense (SHD), Archives centrales de la Marine à Vincennes (Mar.), BB4 995, fol. 253 sq. Reproduced in Michel Jangoux's edition of Baudin's *Journal du voyage aux Antilles de la Belle Angélique (1796–1798)*, Paris: Presses de l'Université Paris-Sorbonne and Académie royale de Belgique, 2009, pp. 30–32.
29 Jussieu, 'Instructions', 28 Fructidor Year IV (14 September 1796), SHD, Mar., BB4 995; Jangoux, *Journal du voyage aux Antilles*, p. 36.
30 Jussieu, 'Instructions'; Jangoux, *Journal du voyage aux Antilles*, p. 34.
31 Jussieu, 'Instructions'; Jangoux, *Journal du voyage aux Antilles*, p. 33.
32 Jussieu, 'Instructions'; Jangoux, *Journal du voyage aux Antilles*, p. 35.
33 All of these instructions are reproduced in Jacqueline Bonnemains's edition of Baudin's personal journal, *Mon voyage aux Terres Australes*, Paris: Imprimerie Nationale, 2000, pp. 47–73.
34 Georges Cuvier, 'Note instructive sur les recherches à faire relativement aux différences anatomiques des diverses races d'hommes', reproduced in Jean Copans and Jean Jamin (eds), *Aux origines de l'anthropologie française: les mémoires de la Société des Observateurs de l'Homme en l'an VIII*, Paris: Le Sycamore, 1978, pp. 171–176; Joseph-Marie Degérando, 'Considérations sur les diverses méthodes à suivre dans l'observation des peuples sauvages', in Copans and Jamin, *Aux origines*, pp. 127–169 (published in English translation by F.C.T. Moore as *The Observation of Savage Peoples by Joseph-Marie Degérando*, London: Routledge and Kegan Paul, 1969). The permanent secretary of the short-lived Société des Observateurs de l'Homme, Louis-François Jauffret, also provided Baudin with notes to guide in the choice of objects for a mooted special museum. See Copans and Jamin, *Aux origines*, pp. 187–194; English version in Nicolas Baudin, *The Journal of Post Captain Nicolas Baudin, Commander-in-Chief of the Corvettes* Géographe *and* Naturaliste, translated by Christine Cornell, Adelaide: Libraries Board of South Australia, 1974, pp. 594–596.
35 On the originality of these instructions, see Jean-Luc Chappey, 'Le capitaine

Baudin et la Société des observateurs de l'homme: Questions autour d'une mauvaise réputation', in Michel Jangoux (ed.), *Portés par l'air du temps: les voyages du capitaine Baudin*, special number of *Études sur le XVIIIe siècle*, vol. 38, 2010, pp. 145–155.
36   In French, 'd'une affligeante banalité'. Michel Jangoux, *Le Voyage aux Terres Australes du commandant Nicolas Baudin: Genèse et préambule (1798–1800)*, Paris: Presses de l'Université Paris-Sorbonne, 2013, p. 306.
37   See Baudin, *Mon voyage*, pp. 49–50.
38   'Mais étaient-ils acteurs ou exécutants?' Jangoux, *Le Voyage aux Terres Australes*, p. 308.
39   See Jangoux, *Le Voyage aux Terres Australes*, pp. 308–309.
40   Baudin to Péron, 12 Messidor Year X (1 July 1802), Muséum d'Histoire naturelle, Le Havre, Collection Lesueur, 63 018.
41   'Citizen Péron [. . .] will be able to write a volume on worms and molluscs. He has one or two cases of broken shells, for in several places along the shore one can shovel them up.' Baudin, *Journal*, p. 494.

Chapter 3

The Pacific as a Laboratory for Natural History

John Gascoigne

The Varieties of Natural History

Drawing the Pacific into the European map of the world was largely accomplished in the second half of the eighteenth century. It was, above all, the work of Cook but it was, nonetheless, a cosmopolitan achievement in which the warring European nations co-operated to a remarkable degree. Much of the co-operation sprang from a sense that all would benefit from the promotion of science in an age when the Enlightenment emphasised the merits of science. This integration of the Pacific into the European model of the globe was occurring at the same time as new forms of science were coming to maturity, particularly those linked with that protean enterprise, natural history. Such a conjunction meant that the Pacific became, *par excellence*, the laboratory for new forms of natural history – a phenomenon established in the late eighteenth century but with a continuing tradition which reached its acme with Darwin's *Beagle* voyage of 1831–1836.[1]

By origin, natural history simply meant a description of the way in which nature in all its myriad forms operated. For Francis Bacon, accurate natural histories were the foundation on which science, in the sense of a theoretical body of knowledge, could be built. He envisaged natural history as in some senses the subordinate activity, leaving the task of discerning fundamental patterns and laws of nature in the data thus diligently collected by the natural historian to the more sophisticated analysis of the natural philosopher. For Francis Bacon, the natural historian produced the grapes which the natural philosophy turned into wine or, as he wrote in the *Advancement of Learning* (1605): 'For NATVRAL HISTORY describeth the *varietie of things*: PHISICKE [natural philosophy] the CAVSES'.[2] This ambition of producing large-scale natural histories as a basis for scientific enquiry informed the work of the Royal Society of London, which took Bacon as its presiding genius. One way in which, from its beginnings in 1660, the Royal Society sought to promote such goals was through encouraging travellers to unfamiliar parts of the globe to send back reports which could be added to the ever-growing repositories of knowledge at the great centre of calculation, the Royal Society.

But for all its enthusiasm for the Baconian programme of accumulating ever larger mounds of data the Royal Society became increasingly committed to another strand of Bacon's great project for the fruitful study of nature to render it more useful for the 'relief of man's estate', namely the pursuit of experimental knowledge. The worth and potency of experimental knowledge gathered further force when it was combined with mathematics, an approach that Bacon had not embraced with great relish. The result was that natural history – which in Bacon's conception embraced the study of all aspects of nature – shrank more and more to those aspects of knowledge which could not be readily studied by experimental or quantitative methods. Natural history, then, became concerned with the description of the three kingdoms of animal (including the world of humankind), vegetable and mineral. Such a pursuit was given greater scientific dignity by the rise in the second half of the eighteenth century of systems of classification, of which Linnaeus's was the most influential.

The link between Pacific exploration and such an approach to natural history was obvious and pronounced. On Cook's *Endeavour* voyage of 1768–1771, the naturalists, Joseph Banks and Daniel Solander, were both self-declared disciples of Linnaeus and, indeed, Solander had been a student of the great Swedish naturalist. One of the achievements of that and subsequent Pacific voyages was bringing back to the European centres of learning vast quantities of natural history specimens from the Pacific. Such was the object and outcome of the ill-fated Spanish Malaspina expedition of 1789–1794, which sought to 'work towards the advancement of natural history [...] in respect, chiefly, of human nature'.[3] Earlier, when proposing the voyage, Alejandro Malaspina had commented on the way in which the 'noble competition' between the French and British in the scientific exploration of the Pacific had meant that 'The history of human society has thus been founded on much wider research; [and] natural history has been enriched with almost endless discoveries'.[4] Indeed, Malaspina's voyage brought back vast stores of natural history specimens and data, though these scientific riches were to be a casualty of Spanish palace intrigue in the age of the French Revolution. As Bruno Latour has argued, such 'cycles of accumulation' enabled the major European centres of calculation to reconstruct the Pacific from afar and to integrate it into their scientific speculations about the globe as a whole.[5] Possessing the Pacific in this form also strengthened the belief that it was possible to integrate the Pacific into not only scientific but also imperial maps of the world.

The high age of Pacific exploration in the second half of the eighteenth century, then, corresponded with one major development in natural history, namely the rise of classificatory systems which gave order and purpose to the growing mounds of specimens brought back from what was, to European eyes, a new quarter of the globe. This gave the great Pacific voyages a scientific dimension which lifted them above the familiar great power rivalries based on strategic or commercial advantage – though such goals and tensions were never absent and the promotion of science itself became another arena in which to pursue national glory. Along with this strand of natural history, which might be described as 'purposeful collecting', there was also another which was more pronounced in France than in Britain with its strong Baconian traditions. This was an approach to natural history which regarded it as more of a science in its own right rather than, as Bacon had viewed it, a platform on which to erect science. For one way in which the Scientific Revolution had transformed the traditional pursuit of natural history was to promote more historically based understandings of nature. Intimations of this view of natural history as having an historical logic which could serve as a form of scientific explanation can be found as early as the Hermetic philosophers of the Renaissance but it achieved its most influential early theoretical explication in Descartes's *Principles of Philosophy* (1644),[6] in which he attempted to develop an historical explanation of the way in which the earth and the solar system more generally had developed.[7]

Appropriately, it was another Frenchman, Georges-Louis Leclerc, comte de Buffon, who, in the mid eighteenth century, reanimated this historical understanding of nature in his immensely influential *Histoire naturelle, générale et particulière*, the first volume of which appeared in 1749 and which thereafter appeared regularly until his death in 1788. A further eight volumes were published posthumously up to 1804, completing the 44 volume set, which was replete with illustrations.[8] The first volume opened with a theoretical preface 'On the manner of studying and dealing with natural history', which, in a manner reminiscent of Descartes's principles of philosophy, laid out the theoretical approach which was to inform his vast masterpiece. In this he urged the need to rise above the study of particular examples in order 'to combine observations and to generalise from facts', thus arriving at an understanding of the more general effects enabling us to 'compare Nature with herself in her great operations'.[9] Not only did Buffon shape the development of natural history with his widely read work but he also promoted such a view of natural history during his long reign as superintendent of the Jardin du Roi (King's Garden) from 1739–1788. This royal precinct was, under the shadow of the Revolution, to be transformed in 1793 into a more truly national institution, the Muséum national d'Histoire naturelle,[10] but the extent of continuity both in personnel and intellectual aspirations was remarkable.[11]

Buffonian Natural History and the Pacific

The development of such fruitfully variant approaches to the study of natural history left its mark on Pacific voyaging, particularly in France, though it had reverberations elsewhere, and notably in Germany. The Buffonian programme of the 'history of nature' was adopted by that formidable father and son duo, Johann Reinhold and Georg Forster, the naturalists on Cook's second voyage and avowed disciples of Buffon. They in turn helped shape the intellectual horizons of Alexander von Humboldt, with his attempt to explore the interrelated workings of all aspects of Nature. In turn, Darwin was an admirer of Humboldt and like him drew particularly on close study of the natural history of the Pacific coast of South America.

Even before France had become a major force in Pacific exploration with the pioneering and influential voyage of Louis-Antoine de Bougainville (1766–1769), the importance of the scientific agenda – and, in particular, that established by Buffon, which such voyages could promote – was being enunciated. In a work which did much to spur French Pacific exploration, 'Lettre sur le progrès des sciences' (1752), Maupertuis, in the manner of Buffon (whom he cites approvingly), speculated on the way in which natural history could be made 'a true science' by moving beyond the examination of particular case studies to 'the general processes of Nature'.[12] This approach extended to the study of humankind and Maupertuis envisaged the scientific benefits that would flow from encounters with fellow human beings in the hitherto largely unknown quarter of the globe encompassed by the South Seas. For it took the globe to realise fully the grand Buffonian vista of nature and to study the processes of Nature. One could not travel back in time but one could travel the earth to see the record of the way in which the historical processes of Nature had shaped different environments and the way of life of the different living things they supported, including different human societies. Venturing into the Pacific, then, provided natural historians with a laboratory which could test and develop hypotheses about large-scale historical processes of the sort which did not lend themselves to the laboratories which were doing so much to develop the physical and chemical sciences in the same period. When providing advice to the naturalists on the d'Entrecasteaux voyage, the geologist Déodat Dolomieu acknowledged the importance of Buffon's influence when expiating on how the voyagers could study the way in which 'the ancient history of the globe was written in the first strata of the earth'.[13] This advice was provided on behalf of the Society for Natural History, an informal body which played a major role in transforming the Jardin du Roi into the Museum.[14]

Part of the reason for Buffon's success was his ability to promote a belief in both the scientific fascination of natural history and its utility. The latter consideration particularly helped to strengthen state support through institutions such as the Jardin du Roi, which had a tradition of promoting expeditions that widened the reach of its collections and the domain of natural history.[15] Such utilitarian considerations were reflected in the instructions from the Ministry of the Marine to La Pérouse in regards to botany: the way in which voyages had 'enriched botany by the discovery of a multitude of plants' was welcomed but his voyage was urged to devote particular attention to plants serving useful objects such as food or medicine.[16] True to such injunctions, one of La Pérouse's botanists, Robert de Lamanon, followed up his study of the natural history of Tenerife by sending back seeds of a potentially useful variety of white bean.[17]

Natural History and the Baudin Expedition

These different impulses within the fast growing field of natural history – the urge to classify and order; the quest for a broad, indeed global, canvas, on which to depict the historical processes of Nature; and the pursuit of utility – all left their mark on the Baudin expedition, and more particularly on the scientific agenda pursued by François Péron. Within the Jardin du Roi and the Muséum national d'Histoire naturelle, the classificatory impulse remained important and was given a particularly French signature with the work of the Jussieu dynasty and their challenge to Linnaean principles. The zoological advice given by the Society for Natural History to the d'Entrecasteaux voyage included caution about classifying according to 'arbitrary principles', which had been criticised by Buffon and his assistant (and fellow officer of the Jardin du Roi), Louis Jean-Marie Daubenton. Instead, the instructions urged the expeditioners to base classification 'on the unchanging correspondence of the mechanical structure evident in animals'.[18] Nationalism and the scientific critique of what was viewed as the artificial form of classification adopted by Linnaeus coalesced in such comments as those made in the 1806 report reproduced as preface to Péron's account of his Pacific voyage by the Institut de France, which wrote disparagingly of 'A mistaken method of description, introduced into science [...] especially [by] belonging to the Linnaean school', adding, reassuringly, that 'M. Péron knew how to avoid this error'.[19]

In fruitful tension with this emphasis on accurate description, those associated with the Jardin du Roi and the Muséum national d'Histoire naturelle also promoted the Buffonian wide vista with its approach which might be termed a 'history of nature', to distinguish it from other forms of natural history.[20] While taking classes at the Museum during the course of his medical studies, Péron may well have imbibed such a wide remit for natural history. This broad Buffonian view seems to be reflected in his

1800 pamphlet, 'Observations on Anthropology', in which he writes of the need to place the study of humankind in the widest possible context by setting goals such as: 'To determine the physical nature of the climate, to seek and pinpoint its influence on the organic constitution of the people who live in it'.[21] Such a perspective seems also to have coloured the approach adopted by the pioneering anthropological society, the Société des Observateurs de l'Homme, after its foundation in 1799, with Georges Cuvier an important common link between the Society and the Museum.[22] Hence the strongly historical approach to the study of the varieties of humankind which Joseph-Marie Degérando urged Baudin to adopt when he wrote in his 'Considérations sur les diverses méthodes à suivre dans l'observation des peuples sauvages' (1800) that 'The philosophical traveller who sails to the extremities of the earth, traverses in effect the sequence of the ages; he travels into the past; each step he takes leaps a century [. . .]. [He] retraces for us the state of our own ancestors and the earliest history of the world'.[23]

Playing the card which was most likely to encourage government to promote such voyages, Baudin had attempted to urge the utility of the study of that branch of natural history which was coming to be known as 'anthropology'. By travelling to the South Seas and studying 'the character and customs of the peoples residing in that part of the globe', argued Baudin, it would be possible to instill a knowledge of the arts and manufactures which France had to offer. Knowledge of the quadrupeds, birds, vegetables and minerals of these regions would also be useful both for the promotion of science and for national commerce.[24] Such sentiments struck a chord with those in charge of the Museum, who saw them in accord with the object of the institution, which was 'to gather all the means of studying nature and to advance science'. This extended to more overtly utilitarian goals such as seeking 'to import animals and plants from foreign countries to let them acclimatise and multiply in France'. In accord with such utilitarian aims, bringing back specimens which were simply curious was discouraged but, interestingly, this was also combined with a reassertion of the goal of making the Museum's collections as complete as possible.

For in a period when the French imperium was expanding across Europe, the desire to promote forms of French universalism extended to science – hence the expressed desire 'to lift this establishment to such a level that it is more important than any other foreign establishment of the same kind'. The Museum professors even rejoiced in the way that France's victories had expanded its collections and looked forward to the time when it had a right of confiscation.[25] The Museum, then, responded both to the political imperative of demonstrating the utility of its work and to the desire to use its collections as a way of promoting its influence and that of France more generally. Expanding its reach to the Pacific gave it a more global presence which could be of benefit both to it and to France in appropriating the products of as much of the earth as possible in ways that could promote both science and possible French influence.[26] Hence the considerable support which the Museum gave to the Baudin expedition and, earlier, the Jardin du Roi to the voyages of La Pérouse and d'Entrecasteaux. This again emphasises the extent of continuity in the relations between the French scientific establishment and the pre- and post-revolutionary regimes. The Revolution did, however, bring with it the imperative to link explicitly the values of science with those which had been used to justify the overthrow of the old regime. The zoologist on board the d'Entrecasteaux expedition, Louis Auguste Deschamps, saw science as the 'mortal enemy of superstition & despotism',[27] while Baudin sought to recommend his proposed voyage by arguing that it would help 'destroy the prejudice of those who had reason to fear the progress of reason and the arts'.[28]

The promotion of scientific universalism did not, of course, preclude the promotion of forms of scientific nationalism and, in particular, the continuation of rivalry in the realm of science with the ancient adversary, perfidious Albion. Thus a report on the Baudin expedition published in 1804 by the director of the Museum commented on the way in which the French naturalists had surpassed the British in the study of the novel specimens from the animal kingdom opened up by the exploration of Australia.[29] This report was later incorporated into a more general evaluation of the expedition which viewed it as a continuation of a whole series of French voyages which were particularly important since they provided a French foothold in a region in which the British were expanding their empire and seeking to keep for themselves any lucrative commerce.[30] Such sentiments were in keeping with those of

Péron, who expressed himself with particular vigour in an 1803 report to Captain General Decaen of Mauritius, the gaoler of Matthew Flinders. For Péron, the English colonisation of Australia was one more chapter in the long rivalry between France and Britain. In his report, Péron claims that it was the desire to prevent such national humiliation that explained Napoleon's decision to authorise the expedition, adding that the promotion of natural history served merely as a convenient pretext for such essentially political goals[31] – though Péron, who clearly valued the promotion of natural history for its own sake, may here have been writing what he thought Decaen wanted to hear.

Pacific voyaging and natural history were, then, close allies. Natural history provided the scientific spur to venture into what was, from a European perspective, a dark quarter of the globe. Such voyaging added to the store of specimens which were being incorporated both literally and metaphorically into the European stores of intellectual capital and which could increasingly be put into ordered systems thanks to the systems of classification that were one of the most characteristic features of the age of the Enlightenment. For the French, particularly, the elastic field of natural history provided another motive for Pacific voyaging: to pursue the history of nature in a global laboratory, the sheer span of which provided an opportunity to observe the workings of nature over space and time. Persuading governments to provide the large sums necessary to fund such expeditions often meant recourse not only to the scientific worth of natural history but also to its potential economic benefits. The involvement of governments in an age of intense national rivalry necessarily brought with it some reference to the national advantages to be obtained by outpacing rivals, whether through greater access to natural resources or – what was of particular importance in the highly charged ideological atmosphere of the Revolutionary period – through claims to greater rationality as exemplified in the patronage of the promotion of knowledge. The elastic character of natural history, then, provided a pliable garment to clothe the arguments for Pacific voyaging and for the expansion of the European scientific map of the world. But such an expansion was to change natural history, too, as the sheer volume of information brought back from around the world, and the Pacific particularly, meant that natural history became not one but many pursuits as its different sub-disciplines came increasingly to the fore – among them the field of anthropology, which Péron was one of the first to define as a separate field. Voyages to distant parts of the globe changed Europe's perception of the maps of knowledge as well as of the globe, for natural history both influenced Pacific voyaging and was influenced by it.

Notes

1. Roy Macleod and Philip F. Rehbock, 'Introduction' to *Darwin's Laboratory: Evolutionary Theory and Natural History in the Pacific*, Honolulu: University of Hawaii Press, 1994, p. 4.
2. Francis Bacon, *The Advancement of Learning*, in Michael Kiernan (ed.), *The Oxford Francis Bacon*, Oxford: Oxford University Press, vol. 4, 2000 – Oxford Scholarly Editions Online, 2012, p. 82.
3. Alejandro Malaspina, 'Introduccion', in Andrew David, Felipe Fernández-Armesto, Carlos Novi and Glyndwr Williams (eds), *The Malaspina Expedition 1789–1794*, London: The Hakluyt Society, 3 vols, 2001–2004, vol. 1 (2001), p. lxxxi.
4. Alejandro Malaspina, 'Plan for a Scientific and Political Voyage Around the World', in David et al., *The Malaspina Expedition*, vol. 1, p. 312.
5. Bruno Latour, *Science in Action. How to Follow Scientists and Engineers through Society*, Cambridge, Mass.: Harvard University Press, 1987, pp. 220–222.
6. René Descartes, *Principia Philosophiae*, Amsterdam: Ludovicum Elzevirium, 1644.
7. Phillip R. Sloan, 'Natural History, 1670–1802', in Robert Olby, Geoffrey Cantor, John Christie and Jonathon Hodge (eds), *Companion to the History of Modern Science*, London: Routledge, 1996, pp. 297–298.
8. Georges-Louis Leclerc, comte de Buffon, *Histoire naturelle, générale et particulière, avec la description du Cabinet du Roi*, Paris: Imprimerie royale, 44 vols, 1749–1804.
9. Numa Broc, *La Géographie des philosophes, géographes et voyageurs français au XVIIIe siècle*, Paris: Éditions Ophrys, 1975, p. 192.
10. Dorinda Outram, 'New Spaces in Natural History', in N. Jardine, J.A. Secord, and E.C. Spary (eds), *Cultures of Natural History*, Cambridge: Cambridge University Press, 1996, p. 257.
11. Carol E. Harrison, 'Projections of the Revolutionary Nation: French Expeditions in the Pacific, 1791–1803', *Osiris*, vol. 24, no. 1, 2009, p. 35.
12. Pierre Louis Moreau de Maupertuis, 'Lettre sur le progrès des sciences', *Œuvres*, Lyon: J.M. Bruyset, 4 vols, 1756, vol. 2, p. 422.
13. Déodat Dolomieu, 'Notes communicated to the Naturalists [on the] voyage to the South Sea [. . .]', 29 July 1791 [Printed], Service Historique de la Défense (SHD), Archives centrales de la Marine à Vincennes (Mar.), BB4 993, (p. 1).
14. Harrison, 'Projections of the Revolutionary Nation', p. 38.
15. Michael S. Reidy, Gary Kroll and Erik M. Conway, *Exploration and Science. Social Impact and Interaction*, Santa Barbara: ABC Clio, 2007, pp. 44–45.
16. 'Mémoire pour La Pérouse', SHD, Mar., BB4 992, p. 380.
17. 'Chev. De Lamanon to My Lord', 26 August 1785, John Dunmore (ed.), *The Journal of Jean-François de Galaup de la Pérouse*, London: Hakluyt Society, 2 vols, 1994–1995, vol. 2, pp. 455–457.
18. Philippe Pinel, 'Sur les progrès que la zoologie attend des voyages de long cours', SHD, Mar., BB4 993.
19. François Péron and Louis Freycinet, *Voyage of Discovery to the Southern Lands*, translation of the second edition (1824) by Christine Cornell, Adelaide: The Friends of the State Library of South Australia, 2 vols, 2006/2003, vol. 1, p. lvi.
20. Phillip Sloan, 'Natural History', in Knud Haakonssen (ed.), *The Cambridge History*

of *Eighteenth-Century Philosophy*, Cambridge: Cambridge University Press, 2 vols, 2006, vol. 2, p. 911; Phillip Sloan, 'The Gaze of Natural History', in Christopher Fox, Roy Porter and Robert Wokler (eds), *Inventing Human Science. Eighteenth-Century Domains*, Berkeley: University of California Press, 1995, pp. 112–151.

21 François Péron, cited in Jacqueline Bonnemains, Elliott Forsyth and Bernard Smith, *Baudin in Australian Waters. The Artwork of the French Voyage of Discovery to the Southern Lands 1800–1804*, Melbourne: Oxford University Press, 1988, p. 26.

22 Jean-Luc Chappey, *La Société des Observateurs de l'Homme (1799–1804). Des anthropologues au temps de Bonaparte*, Paris: Société des études robespierristes, 2002, p. 471.

23 Joseph-Marie Degérando, cited in Bonnemains *et al.*, *Baudin in Australian Waters*, p. 38.

24 Baudin to Minister of Marine, SHD, Mar., BB4 999.

25 Professor Administrators of the Museum of Natural History, Paris, 18 Thermidor Year VI (5 August 1798), SHD, Mar., BB4 993.

26 Michael Osborne, 'Applied Natural History and Utilitarian Ideals: "Jacobin Science" at the Muséum d'Histoire naturelle, 1789–1870', in Bryant Ragan and Elizabeth Williams (eds), *Re-creating Authority in Revolutionary France*, New Brunswick: Rutgers University Press, 1992, pp. 124–126.

27 Louis Auguste Deschamps, 'Journal du voyage sur *La Recherche*', Natural History Museum, London, Botany Library, 110.

28 Baudin to Minister of Marine, SHD, Mar., BB4 999.

29 Antoine-Laurent de Jussieu, 'Notice sur l'expédition à la Nouvelle Hollande entreprise pour des recherches de Géographie et d'Histoire naturelle', *Annales du Muséum national d'Histoire naturelle*, vol. 5, 1804, pp. 8–9.

30 [Jean-Baptiste Lesueur], *Notice sur l'Expédition française aux Terres australes, ordonnée en l'an VIII, et exécutée par les deux corvettes de l'État, le Géographe et le Naturaliste, parties du port du Havre le 17 Brumaire, An IX*, Brochure in-8°, Rouen: Imprimerie des Arts, 1804 – copy held in the National Library of Australia (NLA), MS 7445, pp. 1, 3.

31 Péron, Report to Decaen, 20 Frimaire Year XII (12 December 1803), Bibliothèque Municipale de Caen, Papiers Decaen, tome 92 (transcript held in NLA, Hélouis transcripts, MS 11/4, File 28, item 2, p. 2).

Chapter 4

François Péron and the Invention of the Nineteenth Century

Jean-Luc Chappey

François Péron occupies a special place in the canonical history of French anthropology. In the last decades of the nineteenth century, he was presented by the champions of physical anthropology (associated with Paul Broca in the Société d'Anthropologie de Paris) as the instigator of new rules for the study of man and for the analysis of societies. His observations of Australia's indigenous populations – based on measurements of strength made with Régnier's dynamometer – had indeed appeared to legitimise the methodological assumptions behind the classification of the various races of humanity. It gradually became accepted that Péron, in the early years of the nineteenth century, had contributed to the formalisation of a science of races that was based on physical or biological criteria.[1] Historians of French anthropology thus came to consider him to be the primary, if not central, player in the major change of direction given to the epistemological and methodological foundations of anthropology at the turn of the nineteenth century. The choice to view indigenous peoples through the lens of their physical strength was indeed seen as signalling the end of a certain ideal of the Enlightenment and the beginning of a new era of affirmation of white and European superiority.

This idea of a radical shift, and of Péron's association with it, is strongly affirmed by Jean Copans and Jean Jamin in their book, *Aux origines de l'anthropologie française*:[2] Péron is presented by them as the figure who led nineteenth-century French anthropology down the medical and biological path at the expense of the social and cultural approach. As Copans and Jamin assert, Péron's work constitutes:

a break, a major shift in perspective with respect to representations of 'primitive' man, who, although still seen as primitive, as a man of nature, is no longer valued in this capacity or for this relationship with the natural world, and who is no longer favoured by a physical perfection or power that were thought to derive from that relationship. Péron argues instead that the 'primitive' man's excessive closeness to nature weakens his body and adversely affects his intelligence.[3]

In this context, Péron appears as a renegade, if not a traitor, who is alleged to have denied, during his voyage to Australia, the principles of an approach to anthropology that was concerned with observing and transforming indigenous societies – an approach that united the members of the Société des Observateurs de l'Homme (1799–1804).[4] In his account of the voyage, published in 1807,[5] he indeed seems to turn his back on the very principles he presented in the *vade mecum* of anthropology that he wrote in 1800,[6] the aim of which was to legitimise the role of this branch of scientific endeavour as part of the work to be carried out by the scientists accompanying Captain Baudin.

Nevertheless, while it is indisputable that Péron embodies an essential transformation in French anthropology, we need to consider more closely the nature of this transformation and also to qualify it. In order to do that, we must begin by reminding ourselves of the context in which the first edition of his narrative account was produced and received. This offers the possibility of (re)discovering a figure whose position is much more complex than is often acknowledged. By examining more specifically the conditions of his return to Paris following the Baudin expedition, and the issues that were at stake in his portrayal of distant peoples, both in his *Voyage de découvertes* of 1807 and in the secret report he compiled on his return to Paris in 1804 for the Councillor of State Antoine-François de Fourcroy,[7] we will see how Péron's practices as an observer and a writer reflect the ambiguities that characterise the political and intellectual transition that was taking place during the imperial period (1804–1815). For this reason, Péron must be considered as a pivotal player in the transition from the eighteenth to the nineteenth century.

Writing a Travel Account and Describing Indigenous Peoples

When he published the first volume of his travel account in 1807, François Péron was still trying to reap the rewards of his perilous journey to Australia. Following his return to France in 1804, he had succeeded in building his reputation, thanks, in particular, to the scientific collections that had enriched the Muséum national d'Histoire naturelle in Paris. However, in the context of the competition being waged by the surviving members of the Baudin expedition, it is important to note that Péron was not the first to publish an account of his observations. In this race for recognition that was being run by the young scholars who had embarked with Baudin, Jean-Baptiste Bory de Saint-Vincent had taken the lead by publishing in 1804 a first account of the expedition.[8] It is particularly important to take into consideration this competition for control of the scientific narrative because Péron had been chosen by the scientists of the Institut national and by members of the Société des Observateurs de l'Homme to undertake the critical mission of observing indigenous peoples.

When the expedition returned to France, Péron was immediately hailed by various scholars of the Museum for his work as a collector. As early as 1804, scientific newspapers informed their readers of the importance for various natural history collections of the objects he had brought back. In 1807, the publication of his travel account served further to enhance Péron's reputation. However, this account, which featured his observations of indigenous peoples, was designed first and foremost to allow him to claim a position as a scientist, as opposed to being seen as a mere collector – that is, as someone considered to be a simple agent remotely controlled by the sedentary scientists in Paris.[9] The publication of his *Voyage* was thus intended to allow Péron to claim a certain autonomy from the professors of the Museum. More particularly, at a time when there was no longer any institution specialising in the observation of man and human societies, the narrative of his voyage would allow him to position himself as an anthropologist and to affirm his status as such. Furthermore, his narrative aimed to make his status as scientist known not only to scholars but also to a wider audience. We must therefore pay particular attention to the various modes of writing that are put to use in the construction of his travel account.

Péron's comments about Pacific peoples address contrasting subjects and are grounded in a dual system of writing and reading. On the one hand, there is the travel account published in 1807 and printed by the imperial printing presses, giving it official status. On the other, there is the long report addressed to Fourcroy, member of the Council of State, a report that sheds light on the political and diplomatic implications of scientific voyages. Whereas the official narrative features descriptions of indigenous peoples, the confidential report concentrates instead on the populations of European origin and on the analysis of colonial societies. These two texts are not compiled according to the same criteria and do not address the same readership. If the *Voyage* is intended for an audience comprising both scientists and the wider public, the report is intended only for the diplomatic offices. We therefore need to be especially attentive to the contrasting rhetorical strategies deployed in these two texts.

Particular consideration has to be given to the scientific nature of the descriptions of 'savage' peoples presented by Péron in his travel account. It should likewise be noted, however, that, as in all such publications, which were intended for a wide readership, the *Voyage* of Péron uses narrative devices which aim to arouse curiosity and inspire the imagination. Péron was thus juggling with competing narrative imperatives. We should recall that one of the purposes of the instructions given to the members of Captain Baudin's expedition was to establish conditions for observation and writing that would preserve against the prejudices or the effects of the imagination which rendered many travel narratives unreliable. The soundness of such accounts, and of the observations they contained regarding the peoples encountered, relied not only on the author's claim to the status of witness, but also on techniques of validation to be found within the accounts themselves. This imperative was all the more compelling as, by 1807, the theoretical and institutional foundations for anthropology proposed by the Society of the Observers of Man, and even the general science of man elaborated by the 'Idéologues' of the 1790s, had become outdated. The reorganisation of the scientific world that had been taking place since the end of the Consulate favoured new divisions of knowledge which rendered null and void the principles underpinning the type of anthropology to which Péron was meant to devote himself during his voyage. The kind of readership and readerly expectations which had prevailed at the moment of Péron's departure from France had thus disappeared by the time he came to compile his account. Péron's task was thus twofold: on the one hand, he had to convince the scientific community, especially the doctors and naturalists, of the validity of his observations; at the same time, however, and at the risk of skewing the reality of what he had observed, he had to compile an effective narrative that appealed to a more general and worldly audience. It should not be forgotten that during the imperial period, scientific careers were forged in the salons as well as within scientific institutions!

Publishing a travel account was not a simple matter during the imperial era. Such narratives had in fact become the subject of much criticism since the close of the eighteenth century, their commercial success only serving to weaken their scientific status. At a time when the very basis for the general study of man and of human societies was being criticised by many theorists, Péron had to find the rhetorical tools necessary to convince his reader and to establish the 'truthfulness' of his account. It is now known that Péron did not hesitate to falsify his account or to deform some of his descriptions. We might suppose, for example, that, for narrative purposes, he did not hesitate to blacken certain descriptions of indigenous peoples in order to make them appear even more 'savage' and different. Nevertheless, while it was important for him to mark these differences and to draw from these picturesque descriptions certain contrived effects intended to titillate the curiosity of the public, Péron also needed to establish the validity and the exactitude of an account intended simultaneously for scientists.

From this point of view, the presentation of the results obtained by Péron's experiment with the dynamometer – an instrument designed to measure physical strength – can be regarded as a strategic narrative device aimed at establishing the legitimacy of his observations on native populations, and thus of his account more generally.[10] Through the use of measurements of muscular strength, Péron was conforming to the new constraints of scientific writing: such observations henceforth had to be supported by facts and figures. By including tables of figures within his narrative and granting his measurements such an important role, Péron could thus be distinguished from the poets and the philosophers and present himself in the guise of a 'true' scientist.

It should indeed be remembered that, during the Empire, scientists had to defend the legitimacy of their writings in the face of attacks launched by men of letters. The new regime, having reorganised the space of intellectual activity at the expense of the encyclopædic mode of organisation set up under the Directory, favoured the emergence of a new type of writer figure who constructed his persona in large part by attacking that of the scientist. Scientific writing became the target of particularly violent attacks on the part of writers who claimed that literature should serve as a rampart against the 'degradation' of man. The tables resulting from Péron's measurements served to mark a distinct contrast with literary writing. By that means, Péron sought above all to reinforce his legitimacy as a scientist and to guarantee the validity of his observations.

In this respect, far from turning his back on them, he conformed perfectly to the standards of observation recommended by Joseph-Marie Degérando and Georges Cuvier in their 'travel instructions' written in 1800.[11] Both warned against the dangers of the imagination. Both called on travellers to write precise and exact descriptions. These 'Observers of Man' were anxious to change the way indigenous peoples were looked at and to improve the way they were described. This is not to say that their instructions were entirely the same in nature. Whereas Degérando defended the model of the traveller-philosopher, and of the observer-participant who bases his observations on meetings and exchanges with indigenous peoples, Cuvier defended that of the traveller-collector and the technical work of gathering scientific specimens (crania, in particular). If, in 1800, the Society seemed to lean towards the former (by publishing Degérando's 'Considérations'), it should be noted that in fact Péron fulfilled perfectly the mission conferred by Cuvier: by basing his observations of indigenous peoples on measurements, he indeed seemed to have brought back to France exact and irrefutable data.

Whereas the theories of Franz Joseph Gall on craniology were the subject of much debate, it seems that Péron sought to align himself with the new standards for the study of man, which had to be based on measurements. What was at stake was not insignificant in a context where many questions had arisen relating to the distinction between the sciences and other fields of intellectual activity and, within the scientific community, between the various sciences themselves – those that were officially recognised and those that were not. As I have shown elsewhere, this figure of the 'modern' traveller is constructed at the expense of that of the traditional voyager, which is incarnated in particular by Nicolas Baudin.[12] We can interpret the criticisms that Péron directed at his commander as an additional means by which he sought to convince the reader of his status as 'scientist': in broad terms, his account establishes a rift between the traveller of the nineteenth century (who measures and who thus conforms to the required standards of exactitude) and the 'traveller-philosopher' incarnated by Baudin.

This does not prevent Péron's travel narrative from also being an account addressed to a larger audience, an account which obeys the rules of the genre: 'heroisation' of the narrator, surprise 'effects' and the use of various narrative techniques which make it possible to engage his readership. Should these strategies be seen as a justification for certain exaggerations in the description of situations or in the portraits he paints? As objects of science, savage peoples were also objects of curiosity (as in the case of the Hottentot Venus). That would explain the differences between observations written in the field, in notebooks, and the descriptions finally published in the travel account. It might also explain certain particularly unpleasant passages relating to 'savage' peoples. In short, it can rightly be considered that Péron, who unquestionably wished to build a reputation for himself in the eyes of a large audience, sought to arouse the reader's curiosity and did not hesitate to spice up his narrative with picturesque details. The problem lies in the fact that these descriptions often became fossilised and were used as a basis for the 'science of races' throughout the nineteenth century . . .

Without wishing to reduce everything to narrative or rhetorical strategies, it appears necessary to consider the effects that the writing of his travel account had on the gaze Péron came to cast on remote populations. The voyage and the encounter with savage peoples seem for Péron to have turned into a disappointing experience. Covering vast geographical distances allowed him to travel back in time, but he did not meet the long awaited 'handsome' savage. In his account, Péron continually highlights the gap between his ideals, which resulted from 'books', and the reality of his observations in the field. Of his first meeting with the inhabitants of Van Diemen's Land, he writes:

> We had been much moved by the general harmony of the family and the kind of patriarchal life that we had witnessed; I saw with inexpressible pleasure the realisation of those brilliant descriptions of the happiness and simplicity of the natural state, whose seductive charm I had so often relished in my reading . . . I was very far from suspecting at that time the full extent of the privations and miseries of such an existence . . .[13]

Responding in anticipation to the criticisms frequently levelled at travel accounts, Péron presents himself as a scientist, thus justifying the 'cold' gaze he casts on native peoples: his observations, supported by measurements, make it possible to verify that, contrary to the idealised portraits which had for so long been made of him, savage man is instead characterised by his 'physical debility' and his 'moral and intellectual deprivation'.[14] This is far removed from the 'inalterable health' of savage man that Péron himself had evoked the day before his departure for the Southern Lands: 'Is it not in savage man alone that we can still find traces of the robust majesty of natural man: everything that travellers and doctors tell us about the development of physical strength in non-civilised peoples, and of the actions which derive from it, is truly a subject of wonder . . .'[15] Nonetheless, it is important to consider what is at stake in this change of attitude. Does the acknowledgement of the 'weakness' of savage man in 1807 constitute a disavowal of the ideas defended by the same Péron in 1800?

We need in particular to consider Péron's understanding of the notion of 'civilisation', a concept which was the subject of significant debate during the imperial period. It is clear that Péron embodies a reductionist approach to the observation of man. Contrary to men such as Degérando or the Abbé Grégoire, he ignores problems related to language or communication with savage peoples. And yet, in spite of this, Péron was not entirely a precursor of the biological study of human races.

Péron and Civilisation

Péron fits into a theoretical configuration which associates travel in space with travel in time: to move away from the shores of Europe is, so to speak, to journey back into the past. According to the thesis of the stages of civilisation, savage peoples appear as the vestiges or the monuments of the most developed civilisations, in particular that of Europe. This thesis of the various stages of civilisation, which had spread since the middle of the eighteenth century by means of the Scottish Enlightenment, became topical again under the Empire. It caused much debate and was at the heart of a new polemic which opposed the 'heirs' and the adversaries of the Enlightenment at the beginning of the nineteenth century. It seems to me – and this point is open to discussion – that Péron falls within a theoretical framework based on this notion of stages in the age and progress of humanity. In this respect, Péron seems to fit within the framework of the legacy of the Enlightenment.

Contrary to the partisans of polygenism, who began to find voice as early as the Consulate when they set about justifying the re-establishment of slavery, Péron defends the idea that there is only one human race. According to him, human societies are at different stages of development, determined by natural conditions, political institutions and social organisation. As a soldier, then as a student at the School of Medicine, Péron was strongly influenced by practical and hygienist medicine (he took courses given by Jean-Noël Hallé, for instance). Travellers, like doctors, had as their mission to investigate the living conditions of populations. Furthermore, the function of such investigations was to transform the living conditions of these populations and to facilitate their improvement. It is from this point of view that the observation of remote societies opened the way to an anthropology or general science of man.

The measurements carried out by Péron with Régnier's dynamometer enabled him to establish a kind of hierarchy and to hypothesise with respect to the apparent physical weakness of savage peoples.[16] Far from being satisfied with noting these differences and measuring them, Péron sought to understand the reasons for this weakness that he associated with the natural state of man. This observation enabled him to reverse the propositions he had made in 1800: contrary to his first assumptions, savages are on the contrary 'weak'. At a distant remove from civilisation (and excluded from the bonds created by trade), these populations seem indeed to be condemned to a state of physical as well as moral weakness. Admittedly, Péron is not the first to have overturned the idealised portrait of savage man. The comte de Buffon, basing himself on the observations made by travellers in the eighteenth century, was thus able to assert that 'the savages of the New World are less robust, less sensitive, more timorous and more cowardly than Europeans. They have no liveliness, no activity in the soul'.[17]

The observations of Péron relate to several savage peoples (the Diemenese, the New Hollanders, the Timorese) who, according to him, correspond to different stages of development: 'In passing from Van Diemen's Land to New Holland, we have (so to speak) risen imperceptibly from the lowest level of the savage state to the one immediately above it'.[18] The measurements he carried out are compared with those conducted on the English in the colony and on the French sailors. For him, there is no doubt that Europeans are placed much higher than savage peoples. According to these measurements, the Tasmanians, who were closest to 'un-social man' and who were 'children of nature par excellence', represented the very bottom rung of the ladder of civilisation, one step below the mainland Australians. The Europeans were of course on the top. And indeed, the physical strength of each group of subjects, scientifically measured and recorded in detailed tables for all to see, varied in direct relation to their degree of civilisation. The conclusions of the experiments are well known: 'the development of physical strength is not always directly proportional to the absence of civilisation; it is not a constant product or necessary consequence of the savage state'.[19] How was he to explain this observation, which discredits the portrait of the 'noble' and 'beautiful' savage that was current in the collective imagination? Let us not forget that this portrait of the 'noble' savage reappeared with force at the time of the Empire.

According to Péron, the explanation for the muscular and physical weakness of savage peoples does not lie in their natural conditions: even the 'weakest' peoples benefit from favourable conditions in order to procure food. In his view, weakness comes firstly from inaction, from 'idleness' ('apathy and indifference'), from the lack of activity and work. The inferiority of the savages must therefore also find an explanation in political and cultural causes. For Péron, civilisation is thus regarded as the condition for good public health. This is exactly the opposite position to the one he defended in 1800 in his 'Observations on anthropology . . .' In that document, Péron had been particularly critical of the effects produced by the 'progress' of civilisation. He therefore denounced the 'appalling cohort of diseases of all types which have no other source than the very progress of our civilisation' and called for a return to the past and to savage peoples in order to find remedies for the various evils (urban overpopulation, suicides or other moral vices . . .) that characterise civilised societies ('free humanity, I say, from all of those ills that are necessarily unknown to less civilised peoples; how much less than ours is the sum of their infirmities!'[20]).

Under-emphasised by historians, this criticism of the effects of civilisation expressed in 1800 by a young man representing the scientific community is quite original and shows the existence of certain reservations with respect to the ideology of progress. However, by 1807, these reservations and criticisms on Péron's part had completely disappeared. From now on, he considers it important, on the contrary, to affirm the benefits of civilisation, which is a necessary condition for both moral and physical progress. The hierarchy that he establishes between peoples is based not on any racial essentialism, but on the varying degrees of civilisation: the more individuals are isolated and live 'at a distance' from civilisation, the more they are 'weak'. Péron thus transformed himself into a paragon of 'progress'. In order to understand this about-face, it is necessary to take into account the general transformations taking place in the political context at the time.

Published in 1807, Péron's travel account can be regarded as a defence of the idea of civilisation against adversaries who, supported by various newspapers, were increasingly active under the Empire: 'I am content to have been the one to carry out the first observations in this field and to have set direct tests and much factual information against that opinion – too commonly held, possibly too dangerous and most certainly too exclusive – that *ascribes man's physical degeneration to the advanced state of civilisation . . .*'[21] It seems that these descriptions of savage peoples made it possible to answer the 'detractors of the social order':

> The product of, and companion to, vigorous health, physical strength would indeed constitute one of the prime claims to superiority; and if it truly were the exclusive – or even the more particular – attribute of the native state, civilisation would (it must be admitted) have robbed us of one of the most certain indications of happiness. And so the detractors of the social order have directed their most eloquent oratory at this sort of decline of civilised man and have endeavoured to establish it as a principle.[22]

During the imperial era, many theorists, who were hostile to the French Revolution and who were the descendants of the enemies of the Enlightenment, called into question the idea of the progress of civilisation. Moreover, this offensive went hand in hand with a criticism of 'the empire of the sciences' and of the scientists. Civilisation, which was symbolised by the 'monstrous' city, was in their view the cause of a 'degeneration' that was marked, in particular, by the rise in the number of suicides . . . and divorces. This attack on the idea of regeneration and civilisation is to be seen in the context of the Catholic revival. Such attacks were particularly numerous in the columns of a newspaper called *Le Spectateur français du XIXe siècle*, to which François-René de Chateaubriand and Louis de Bonald contributed, among others.

It seems to to me that Péron's *Voyage* constitutes something of a counter-offensive to this movement of Catholic revival – a riposte, moreover, that was supported by the authorities. Indeed, Péron becomes the spokesman not only for the champions of science, but also for all of those 'modern' thinkers who refuse to denounce the misdeeds of progress and to idealise the past. Whereas the idea of 'progress' is attacked and 'prejudices' are put forward as an alternative model to scientific reason, Péron affirms that the progress of civilisation is the only condition for moral and physical perfectibility in human societies. In the context of the political struggles and intellectual debates which characterised the imperial period, it seems that the more the portrait of savage peoples was pejorative and degrading, the more effective was the defence of the progress of civilisation. As shocking as it may seem, it appears that the defence of civilisation caused the downfall of the savage.

It should be recalled that Péron's *Voyage* was published about the same time as Doctor Jean-Marc Gaspard Itard's study on the young savage of Aveyron. Although the two works relate to different objects, they can nevertheless be read in parallel. On the one hand, both authors acknowledge their illusions regarding their initial approach to the savage. On the other, their account is that of an experience of disappointment: their work showed that savages were unhappy people characterised by physical and moral weakness. The two works tend on the other hand to underline the benefits of civilisation. Happiness cannot be found in proximity with nature. This defence of civilisation is a further justification for the pedagogical and colonial mission, which is in keeping with the desire to lead savage peoples out of their present unhappy state.

The position that Péron defends regarding the progress of civilisation thus makes it possible for him to ponder another phenomenon: colonisation and its effects. This time, it is less a question of analysing savage peoples than of examining colonial society and the European populations which comprised it. This study of the consequences of the establishment of European populations in the Southern Lands constitutes the principal subject of the report addressed to Fourcroy. If economic and political matters take pride of place in this document, the question of civilisation nevertheless remains omnipresent.

Péron and Colonisation

Published only three years after the independence of Haiti, Péron's *Voyage* is also read as an authoritative account of the English colonial experiment. Beyond the gaze he casts on the indigenous inhabitants, Péron is particularly attentive in his narrative to those who have migrated and to the experiment of settling Europeans in the Southern Lands. Nevertheless, it is in his confidential report intended for Fourcroy that

Péron presents the conditions which made it possible for the English colony to reach a 'level of magnificence and prosperity that we could not even imagine in Europe, and especially not in France'.[23] This document offers a substantial reflexion on the colonial venture undertaken by the English in the southern seas and presents a very precise picture of the geostrategic interests and power relations in the region. Péron's objective is to mobilise the French authorities in the struggle against English dominion in the Pacific. And, given this intention, he does not hesitate to idealise somewhat his description of these English colonies.

After denouncing the effects of France's isolation, caused by the Revolution, he applauds the new conditions put in place by the regime that was established in France in 1799. In his report, Péron focuses on one particular goal: to analyse 'the state of the English' and the 'resources' being developed in the colony. 'Savage' populations are thus pushed into the background and Péron's observations are intended to be put to use for training the officers and administrators who might take over the running of the colony from the English authorities.[24] The objective is indeed clearly stated: it is a question not only of expelling the English from these lands, but of taking possession of them so as to continue the development of the colony: 'Now, supposing that an attack might be made on these colonies, does it not become vital for you to be better informed about all of the principles that form the basis on which the colonies are organised, so that, in your instructions, you might ratify those principles you feel should be preserved and modify those that might seem to lend themselves to being changed?'[25] What is at stake in this conquest is not just the military exercise, but a more ambitious colonial undertaking. In the imperial context, Péron must indeed try to impose another model of colonisation on France.

Péron repeatedly stresses the 'exact' nature of his observations: he recalls that he was in direct contact with the English population in the colony and that his observations are the result of first-hand experience. Here again, he needs to affirm his legitimacy as a scientist who justifies his mission of espionage. He then examines, in a systematic and detailed manner, the various English settlements established in the Southern Lands (Botany Bay, Port Jackson, Sydney, Parramatta ...) using modes of description that derive from medical and statistical surveys: the natural settings that constitute the 'environment' (the topography – rivers, mountains, climate, geographical situation . . .) are followed by descriptions of the 'natural resources' and the various economic developments (crops, plantations . . .). He dwells in particular on the Hawkesbury River whose valley is compared with that of the Nile. This overview of the 'specificities of the physical characteristics of the land' enables him to present the possibilities available to the English colonists, but also the constraints within which they have to operate. After describing the English colonies, Péron recounts the discoveries that were made on the west coast of New Holland during the time of the Baudin expedition and the settlements planned by the English for that region, while reminding his reader of the competition presented by the expedition led by Captain Matthew Flinders. He thus highlights new possibilities for colonisation. He then describes in detail the settlements established in Van Diemen's Land and in New Zealand, which is presented as the pivotal site for English trade in the region, and all of the other settlements in the Pacific. He particularly stresses the cynicism of the English with respect to indigenous populations, a cynicism which has enabled them to reinforce their domination:

> They start wars themselves, only then to act as peace-makers; they pretend to appear just and benevolent in order to obtain increasingly greater rights to the trust of these peoples, until they have become powerful enough to be unjust; they can then successfully cast aside the mask of intrigue and safely seize the exterminating sword.[26]

After drawing this 'picture' of the English possessions, Péron describes the administrative and commercial state of the colonies. This is important in order to understand the conditions that are favourable to their progress and rapid development. Péron thus insists on the role of political and administrative institutions, considered as factors that can have a greater or lesser degree of influence on the development of human societies. Several factors testify to the success of the colonial venture undertaken by the English: not only has the number of people in the colony increased, but so has their quality, thanks to the decision of certain respectable families to remain there rather than returning to Europe. It is this regeneration of the population that seems to Péron to be the most important factor: the English colonies, in particular Botany Bay, are presented as laboratories in which the government has managed to improve individuals.

For Péron, the process of colonisation, as it was put into practice in the Southern Lands, is particularly favourable to the process of civilising people and their behaviour. The secret report intended for Fourcroy can be read as a treatise on the conditions for the improvement of men. As Margaret Sankey has already noted, it is no accident if Péron devotes particular attention to criminals and the conditions of their rehabilitation.[27] In this respect, Péron fits within a long tradition of voyager-naturalists who, far from limiting themselves to the simple observation of natural phenomena, extend their interest to areas such as poverty or delinquency. The various missions undertaken by the voyager-naturalists who followed the armies of the French Republic into France's neighbouring States under the Directory come to mind here. The observations that André Thouin brought back from his mission to Belgium and the United Provinces between 1794 and 1795 would be a case in point.[28] The philanthropic dimension of the scientific voyage should not be forgotten. These voyages, the observational methods adopted and the objects observed, all fall under the same regime of knowledge as the statistics on the French 'départements' which had come back into fashion thanks to François de Neufchâteau. This is, moreover, the perspective that the members of the First Class of the National Institute adopted in placing particular emphasis on the scope of Péron's observations, as illustrated by the following example:

> The transformation of England's most fearsome brigands and most shameless thieves into honest, peaceful citizens and hard-working farmers, the effecting of the same change in the vilest prostitutes, and compelling them by infallible means to become decent wives and excellent mothers; the rearing of the new-born population, its most careful preservation from the contagion of its parents, and the preparation in this way

of a more virtuous generation than that which gave birth to it – such is the moving spectacle presented by the new English colonies.[29]

Following the same line of questioning as that of the Observers of Man, Péron wonders about the potential for improving populations. What are the most favourable conditions for the 'civilisation' of populations? According to Péron, two factors were necessary in the case of these new English colonies: the fear caused by laws and the justice system, but also the possibilities given to people to improve their living conditions:

> On the one hand, there are large numbers of soldiers, always armed, watching over each individual; wherever you look gallows have been erected; prisons and cells have been established in all parts of the colony; there are irons and chains, an active police force, terrible punishment for the slightest misdemeanours, death for more serious crimes. On the other hand, there is the hope of freedom, the reduction of time spent in slavery or even its complete termination, the certainty of soon being able to take their place in society through good behaviour, of obtaining grants of land and being served in turn by other convicts, of being able to enjoy in peace all of the pleasures of domestic life, even of achieving wealth and respect, of one day being able to return to Europe to enjoy the fruits of one's labour and industry.[30]

Péron wonders more particularly about the condition of the indentured servants and of those who were condemned and deported to these colonies. Seeing them as dependent and deprived of freedom, and thus placed in a position of subjugation, he analyses the means necessary to mend their ways and to help them achieve the status of free men – to use the vocabulary of regeneration. One of the conditions for the success of the colonial venture relates to the role played by the government, which manages the undertaking and then steps back in order to leave room for private initiative. The property holders amongst the colonists receive the assistance of the authorities and for several years are provided with the means required for the expansion of the farm (food, tools, but also women for marriages . . .). At the end of this time, private individuals are thus able to repay the loans granted by the government, which in turn bequeaths the land as a freehold title in exchange for a licence or rent. While equipping the colony with establishments necessary for education and health, the government takes particular responsibility for defending the properties against brigands. Moreover, the government facilitates social fluidity within the colonial settlements by allowing repentant criminals to join the community of free men. Respect for the law and hard work thus make it possible to ensure a profound renewal of society:

> good conduct has its reward. When a convict shows himself to be honest, active and hard-working, when he performs some special deed or makes a discovery that is useful to the colony, then the government has the power to pardon him and to declare him free. In some instances it simply reduces the period of slavery. In every case, when his sentence is terminated, the convict is welcomed back into society and regains all of the rights this entails; land is granted to him; slaves are assigned to him to help him clear his land; he receives implements and food; in a word, he enjoys all the benefits that the title of landholder brings with it. Having learned through long periods of misfortune that crime and wrongdoing will be punished and that honesty alone can make man happy, and, above all, having been thoroughly convinced that penalties and physical punishment await them should they commit fresh offences, whereas well-being and respect will be the reward for the change in their behaviour, these men, when freed in these circumstances from their shackles, almost always prove to be extremely honest and prudent. The work habit that they were inevitably obliged to acquire during a long period of captivity gives them a kind of superiority over the free men who have come to these lands; the clearing of their lands is usually

conducted in a more methodical and intelligent manner, and they are generally noted to be very good farmers; the same can be said of those who devote themselves to a craft and to commerce; almost all of them are successful, and I would go so far as to assert that, within less than 30 years, most of the wealth in this colony will be in the hands of these criminals.[31]

Thanks to the encouragement and guidance given by the government, the conditions for the improvement of the lowest social categories (robbers, prostitutes ...) are put in place. For Péron, the success of the colonial undertaking can be explained precisely because it is based on this kind of population:

> Indeed, if we note that, in all countries, prostitutes belong to the fairest and most robust section of the population; if we note that such a profession and the various opportunities it entails necessarily produce heightened expectations, and that this is even more true of the callings of highwayman and city thief that demand strength, skill and a kind of audacity that is not the preserve of ordinary men; it must follow that, both physically and mentally, the children of such couples are not as badly off as we might think.[32]

The creation of schools and the maintenance of a coercive force thus make it possible for the English government to create the conditions that are favourable to economic expansion and social stability. For the most recalcitrant and 'irremediable' cases, Péron almost comes to the point of legitimising their suppression (in the name of 'purification'). This is one of the limits to the theory of 'regeneration':

> Whenever it decides to found a new settlement in a particular location, it is the most disreputable men, the most hardened convicts who are employed for the first land clearings. They are the ones who are given the

most arduous tasks and often they do not survive. Other, more worthy families soon enjoy the fruits of this labour, which could only be completed through the sacrifice of a few individuals, and it is probably better for this sacrifice to have been made by these profoundly depraved men who have been sullied by the most heinous of crimes and who are destined to be held in public contempt for the entire course of their existence.[33]

Another reason for the success of colonisation lies in the fact that the government has, so to speak, encouraged social intermingling: along with criminals, the English government has also deported political prisoners (Irish in particular) who often come from the social elites, and who gradually come to mix with the lower social categories. Consequently, a colony such as Botany Bay has become attractive, even for 'free and honest' families 'who have come to take advantage of government largesse and to reap the benefits of the climate and the soil'.[34] From this point of view, slavery seems, on the contrary, to be presented as harmful: the fact that it takes the masters away from work causes a degeneration in them related to their inactivity.

In keeping with the positions adopted by other contemporaries, such as the Abbé Grégoire, Péron's vision of the savages reveals a complexity and an ambiguity that are likewise related to this construct of the history of civilisations. He is not a promoter of polygenism: he considers that there is only one human race. He insists on the fact that these populations are 'inferior' but that it is not impossible that they might 'progress'. Péron differentiates himself from many theorists and scientists who, from 1802, and following in the footsteps of Pierre-Victor Malouet and Jean Barré de Saint-Venant, take part in a veritable campaign for the legitimisation of slavery. He does not give up on the idea of human perfectibility, but, contrary to a Jean-Joseph Virey, he does not defend a polygenist or creationist theory.[35] According to him, societies are capable of progress. If he justifies the colonial enterprise, he absolutely does not legitimise slavery.

If Péron marks a turning-point in the history of the figure of the traveller, we can see how in his case the figure of the 'traveller-collector' and that of the 'traveller-philosopher' coexist.³⁶ Whereas the first is the subject of the greatest praise on the part of Georges Cuvier, the second should nevertheless not be overlooked. The various obituaries that were published in 1811 set Péron up as a true 'hero' of science. His *Voyage* seems indeed to play a part in the battle being waged against the adversaries of the Enlightenment and of civilisation. As noted by the author of one of those obituaries:

> We may reproach Péron with having at times used in his account of the *Voyage to the Southern Lands* a luxurious style which is not suited to the simplicity of narrative; but no voyager, with the exception of George Forster, has taken so much trouble to identify the physical and moral characteristics that distinguish different peoples from one another, or to highlight the relationship to be found between their social organisation, their customs and their intelligence, and he has over the English naturalist the advantage of having protected himself from the constraints of theory. There are in this work descriptive passages that are of a remarkable beauty and are worthy of the pen of Buffon, the depiction of the savages of Van Diemen's Land, among others.³⁷

It is no doubt true, as Bronwen Douglas has highlighted, that François Péron marks an important stage in the formalisation of the racial approach to remote populations and consequently breaks with a certain ideal of the Enlightenment.³⁸ His eurocentric gaze and the prejudices expressed against such populations constitute without a doubt a departure from the principles established by the anthropological project of the Observers of Man. Yet, as I have argued, Péron cannot be reduced to being the grave digger of Enlightenment ideals. His observations on indigenous peoples testify to the ambiguities which characterise the transition from the eighteenth to the nineteenth century.

Appendix

Péron's Endangered Heritage: a Letter to the Minister of the Interior, 1811[39]

[...] The friendship that bound me to the unfortunate Péron, my desire to see his memory honoured and, above all else, the interest I have in the publication of the results of the Voyage to the Southern Lands, prompt me to write to you in confidence to inform you of certain facts which I do believe you might consider worthy of your particular attention. [...] He saw the greater part of his work unpublished. He thought that following his death his enemies and those who were jealous of his fame would attempt to appropriate his many treasures, or at least misrepresent his findings. He often discussed these sad details with me and, by acquainting me with the people of good faith about whom he entertained the strongest doubts, he also spoke to me of those whom he believed to be the most fit to continue the work he had begun, or to publish descriptions of the numerous collections that the government had acquired thanks to his efforts. [...] M. Péron had so clear an idea of M. Leschenault's incompetence that he would never have credited him with the intention of wanting to continue any part of his works. [...] M. Leschenault, the botanist of this expedition, was left behind because of illness on the island of Timor about a year before the corvettes returned to port in France. He subsequently remained for three or four years on the island of Java. [...] I have great difficulty believing everything that has been reported to me on this matter: would it not indeed seem very strange that, rather than dealing with the task of publishing his own works (which is an essential obligation for him), M. Leschenault would have sought on the contrary to request that he work on the publication of those of M. Péron, which are more or less unfamiliar to him?

As for those whose influence and ambition M. Péron had even more reason to fear, I list for Your Excellency the names of M. Cuvier, one of the perpetual secretaries of the Class of Physical and Mathematical Sciences of the Institute; M. Duméril and M. Geoffroy, both of the Institute. The great erudition that M. Péron had acquired, the incredible number of animals and objects of all kinds that he had collected with his friend and collaborator Lesueur, had excited envy, jealousy and enmity among most of those who should have been, above all others, his admirers. According to what M. Péron told me on several occasions, I can be in no doubt that the scholars whose names I have just mentioned to Your Excellency were among their number. M. Péron spoke to me several times of the distress that their jealousy and their animosity caused him. He was so convinced of the unfortunate attitude of these scholars towards him that he was tempted on several occasions to destroy his manuscripts in order to prevent them falling into their hands.

M. Péron counted among his close friends a scholar who was as modest as he was respectable and who had once been a fellow student: M. Duvernois merited his entire confidence and had obtained it. He was the one whom M. Péron had designated before his death as his successor for the publication of his works in natural history, in collaboration with M. Lesueur. [. . .]

As for the continuation of the narrative of his voyage, M. Péron hoped to be able to complete this glorious task himself. [He nevertheless chose] M. Kéraudren, a doctor and inspector in the health services of the navy [. . .].

French Text

[...] *L'amitié qui me liait à l'infortuné Péron, le désir que j'ai de voir honorer sa mémoire et par-dessus tout encore, l'intérêt que je prends à la publication des résultats du Voyage aux Terres australes, m'engagent à vous écrire confidentiellement pour vous faire connaître divers faits qui, j'ose le croire, vous paraîtront dignes d'une attention particulière. [...] Il voyait la majeure partie de ses ouvrages non encore publiés. Il pensait qu'après sa mort, ses ennemis et les jaloux de sa gloire chercheraient à s'approprier ses nombreuses dépouilles, ou du moins les dénaturer. Il m'a souvent entretenu de ces tristes détails, et en me faisant connaître les personnes de bonne foi desquelles il avait le plus à douter, il m'a aussi parlé de celles qu'il croyait les plus propres à continuer les travaux qu'il avait commencés, ou à publier les collections nombreuses d'histoire naturelle que le gouvernement avait acquis par ses soins. [...] M. Péron avait une [si] nette idée de l'incapacité de M. Leschenault qu'il ne lui eût jamais prêté l'intention de vouloir être le continuateur d'aucune partie de ses ouvrages. [...] M. Leschenault, botaniste de cette expédition, fut abandonné malade sur l'île de Timor, environ un an avant le retour des corvettes dans les ports de France. Il demeura ensuite trois ou quatre ans dans l'île de Java. [...] J'ai bien de la peine à croire les rapports qui m'ont été faits à cet égard: ne paraîtrait-il pas bien étrange en effet que M. Leschenault, bien loin de s'occuper du soin de publier ses propres travaux (ce qui est pour lui un devoir indispensable) voulût au contraire solliciter de travailler à la publication de ceux de M. Péron qui lui sont plus ou moins étrangers?*

À l'égard des personnes dont M. Péron redoutait avec bien plus de raison l'influence et l'ambition, je citerai à votre Excellence, M. Cuvier, l'un des secrétaires perpétuels de la Classe des physiques et mathématiques de l'Institut; M. Duméril et M. Geoffroy, tous deux de l'Institut. La haute instruction que M. Péron avait acquise, la quantité incroyable d'animaux et d'objets de toute espèce qu'il avait recueillis conjointement avec son ami et collaborateur Lesueur, lui avaient fait des envieux, des jaloux et des ennemis de la plupart de ceux qui, plus que d'autres, auraient dû être ses admirateurs, d'après ce que m'a dit M. Péron à diverses reprises, je ne puis douter que les savants que je viens de nommer à votre Excellence n'aient été de ce nombre. M. Péron m'a entretenu plusieurs fois du chagrin que lui faisaient éprouver leur jalousie et leur animosité. Il était tellement convaincu de la fâcheuse disposition de ces savants à son égard que plusieurs fois il a été tenté de détruire ses propres manuscrits pour empêcher qu'ils ne tombassent entre leurs mains.

M. Péron avait au nombre de ses amis particuliers un savant aussi modeste qu'estimable qui avait été jadis son compagnon d'études: M. Duvernois méritait toute sa confiance et il l'avait obtenue. C'est lui que M. Péron désignait comme son successeur pour la publication de ses travaux d'histoire naturelle conjointement avec M. Lesueur avant de terminer ses jours. [...]

Quant à ce qui est [de] la continuation de l'historique de son voyage, M. Péron espérait pouvoir remplir lui-même cette tâche glorieuse. [Il choisit néanmoins] M. Kéraudren, docteur en médecine, inspecteur du service de santé de la marine [...].

Notes

1 Mondher Kilani, *L'Invention de l'autre. Essais sur le discours anthropologique*, Lausanne: Payot, 1994.
2 Jean Copans and Jean Jamin (eds), *Aux origines de l'anthropologie française: les mémoires de la Société des Observateurs de l'Homme en l'an VIII*, Paris: Le Sycomore, 1978.
3 Copans and Jamin, *Aux origines de l'anthropologie française*, p. 32.
4 For a full account of this society, see Jean-Luc Chappey, *La Société des Observateurs de l'Homme (1799–1804). Des anthropologues au temps de Bonaparte*, Paris: Société des études robespierristes, 2002.
5 François Péron, *Voyage de découvertes aux Terres Australes, exécuté par ordre de Sa Majesté l'Empereur et Roi, sur les corvettes le* Géographe *et le* Naturaliste *et la goëlette le* Casuarina *pendant les années 1800, 1801, 1802, 1803, et 1804, Historique*, vol. 1, Paris: Imprimerie impériale, 1807. His death in 1810 prevented Péron from finishing the second volume. It was completed by Louis Freycinet and published in 1816.
6 François Péron, 'Observations sur l'anthropologie, ou l'histoire naturelle de l'homme, la nécessité de s'occuper de l'avancement de cette science et l'importance de l'admission sur la flotte du Capitaine Baudin d'un ou plusieurs naturalistes spécialement chargés des recherches à faire sur cet objet', Paris: Stoupe, 1800. Reprinted in Copans and Jean Jamin, *Aux origines*, pp. 177–185.
7 François Péron, 'Mémoire sur les établissements anglais à la Nouvelle-Hollande, à la terre de Diémen et dans les archipels du grand océan Pacifique, Au citoyen Fourcroy, Membre du Conseil d'État', Muséum d'Histoire naturelle, Le Havre, Collection Lesueur, dossier 12. I thank John West-Sooby for allowing me to read his transcription of this long report. This document has been published in French by Roger Martin, in 'Le Rêve australien de Napoléon. Description et projet secret de conquête française', *Revue de l'Institut Napoléon*, vol. 176, no. 1, 1998, pp.x4–187, and in English by Jean Fornasiero and John West-Sooby, in *French Designs on Colonial New South Wales*, Adelaide: Friends of the State Library of South Australia, 2014, pp. 125–286.
8 Jean-Baptiste Bory de Saint-Vincent, *Voyage dans les quatre principales îles des mers d'Afrique, fait par ordre du gouvernement, pendant les années neuf et dix de la République (1801 et 1802), avec l'histoire de la traversée du capitaine Baudin jusqu'au Port-Louis de l'Île Maurice*, Paris: Chez F. Buisson, 3 vols, 1804.
9 For the distinction between a 'savant sédentaire' (sedentary scientist) and a 'voyageur collecteur' (traveller-collector), see Marie-Noëlle Bourguet, 'La collecte du monde: voyage et histoire naturelle (fin XVIIe siècle – début XIXe siècle)', in Claude Blanckaert *et al.* (eds), *Le Muséum au premier siècle de son histoire*, Paris: Éditions du Muséum national d'Histoire naturelle, 1997, pp. 163–196.
10 See Christian Licoppe, *La Formation de la pratique scientifique*, Paris: La Découverte, 1996. The use of the dynamometer was recommended by the physicist Charles-Augustin Coulomb (1736–1806), a member of the Institute and of the Academy of Sciences.
11 Georges Cuvier, 'Note instructive sur les recherches à faire relativement aux différences anatomiques des diverses races d'hommes', reproduced in Copans

and Jamin, *Aux origines*, pp. 171–176; Joseph-Marie Degérando, 'Considérations sur les diverses méthodes à suivre dans l'observation des peuples sauvages', in Copans and Jamin, *Aux origines*, pp. 127–169 (published in English translation by F.C.T. Moore as *The Observation of Savage Peoples by Joseph-Marie Degérando*, London: Routledge and Kegan Paul, 1969).
12 Jean-Luc Chappey, 'Le capitaine Baudin et la Société des observateurs de l'homme. Questions autour d'une mauvaise réputation', in Michel Jangoux (ed.), *Portés par l'air du temps: les voyages du capitaine Baudin*, special number of *Études sur le XVIIIe siècle*, vol. 38, 2010, pp. 145–155.
13 François Péron (continued by Louis Freycinet), *Voyage of Discovery to the Southern Lands*, Adelaide: The Friends of the State Library of South Australia, translation of the second edition (1824) by Christine Cornell, 2 vols, 2006/2003, vol. 1, p. 184.
14 Copans and Jamin, *Aux origines*, p. 31.
15 Péron, 'Observations sur l'anthropologie', p. 183.
16 Péron, *Voyage de découvertes*, vol. 1, chapter XX; *Voyage of discovery*, vol. 1, chapter XX.
17 Georges-Louis Leclerc, comte de Buffon, cited by Michèle Duchet, *Anthropologie et histoire au siècle des Lumières*, Paris: Albin Michel, 1971, p. 247.
18 Péron, *Voyage of Discovery*, vol. 1, p. 356.
19 *Ibid.*, p. 360.
20 Péron, 'Observations sur l'anthropologie', p. 183.
21 Péron, *Voyage of Discovery*, vol. 1, p. 370.
22 *Ibid.*, pp. 351–352.
23 Péron, 'Mémoire', chapter 1, p. 1.
24 The use of the term 'savage man' in this discussion is a translation of the French terminology 'homme sauvage', which was in common use at the time.
25 Péron, 'Mémoire', chapter 2, p. 1.
26 *Ibid.*, chapter 1, p. 11.
27 Margaret Sankey, 'François-Auguste Péron: le mythe de l'homme sauvage et l'écriture de la science', *Cahiers de sociologie économique et culturelle*, vol. 9, 1988, pp. 37–46.
28 Ferdinand Boyer, 'Le Muséum d'Histoire naturelle à Paris et l'Europe des sciences sous la Convention', *Revue d'histoire des sciences*, vol. 26, no. 3, 1973, pp. 251–257. See also Madeleine van Strien-Chardonneau, *Le Voyage de Hollande: récits de voyageurs français dans les Provinces-Unies, 1748–1795*, Oxford: Voltaire Foundation, 1994.
29 Georges Cuvier, 'Rapport fait au gouvernement par l'Institut Impérial sur le Voyage de Découvertes aux Terres Australes', *Procès-verbaux des séances de l'Académie, Classe des Sciences physiques et mathématiques*, vol. 3 (séance du lundi 9 juin 1806), 1807, pp. 363–367. Reproduced in Péron, *Voyage de découvertes*, vol. 1, pp. xi–xii; English translation in Péron, *Voyage of Discovery*, vol. 1, p. lxi.
30 Péron, 'Mémoire', chapter 2, p. 2.
31 *Ibid.*, chapter 2, p. 6.
32 *Ibid.*, chapter 2, p. 8.
33 *Ibid.*, chapter 2, p. 8.
34 *Ibid.*, chapter 2, p. 11.
35 See Yves Benot, *La Démence coloniale sous Napoléon*, Paris: La Découverte, 2006, pp. 211 *et seq.*
36 This position adopted by Péron goes some way to explaining the difficulties that came to mark his relationship with Cuvier and that are evident in the letter reproduced at the end of this article.
37 Marie Joseph Louis Alard, *Éloge historique de François Péron, redacteur du voyage de découvertes aux terres australes, lu à la Société Médicale d'émulation de Paris, séant à la Faculté de médecine, dans la séance du 6 mars*, Paris: Imprimerie de L.-P. Dubray, 1811, p. 162.

38 Bronwen Douglas, 'Seaborne Ethnography and the Natural History of Man', *The Journal of Pacific History*, vol. 38, no. 1, 2008, pp. 3–27; 'Slippery Word, Ambiguous Praxis: "Race" and Late-18th-Century Voyagers in Oceania', *The Journal of Pacific History*, vol. 41, no. 1, 2006, pp. 1–29.
39 Archives Nationales de France, série F, demandes de places, de secours et de pension: F 1dII/P/5 – Dossier Péron. Extract from a letter addressed to the Minister of the Interior, Jean-Pierre de Montalivet, on 21 January 1811, by a friend of Péron whose signature is illegible. Translation by Jean Fornasiero.

Part 2

François Péron as Chronicler of the Scientific Voyage

Chapter 5

The Manuscripts of François Péron in the Natural History Museum of Le Havre

Gabrielle Baglione and Cédric Crémière

The Museum of Natural History in Le Havre holds in its Lesueur Collection many of François Péron's manuscripts relating to Baudin's voyage to the Southern Lands, as well as a number of zoological notes written between 1804 and 1810. These manuscripts offer an overview of the diverse themes taken up by the 'trainee zoologist', anatomist and anthropologist as early as 1804. They also confirm that Péron's role in the voyage was not confined to zoology: he was seeking to summarise and synthesise the world. Inch by inch, step by step.

Our intention is to give an account of the work being undertaken on these manuscripts, that is, to look at all of the steps being taken to ensure that these precious source documents are made as widely available as possible, a process which will result in the transcription, translation and interpretation of these manuscripts. Our first step is to provide a summary of Péron's manuscripts: the subjects they cover; the volume they represent as a proportion of the manuscripts in the Lesueur Collection; their current condition. We then propose to examine more closely the themes developed by Péron, using a numerical summary which will indicate both the nature of the documents and their present availability. A number of the manuscripts have been transcribed, but much remains to be done. This overview will serve to give us a better idea of the work that has been completed and of what remains to be done.

To contextualise this analysis, it is important to note that the Museum of Le Havre intends to make the entirety of the manuscripts in the Lesueur Collection available on its website once they have been photographed, transcribed and translated into English. This work on transcription and translation is a long-term project which has already involved several researchers, notably the members of the international team of the Baudin Legacy project.[1] However, let us clarify from the outset that our summary only takes into account the transcriptions that we have at our disposal at the Museum of Le Havre, which do not currently include those of the Baudin Legacy project.[2] Jacqueline Bonnemains, the former curator of the Lesueur Collection, transcribed a considerable number of Péron's manuscripts but also those of Nicolas Baudin and Charles-Alexandre Lesueur.[3] At her instigation, several others took on the task of transcribing certain of Péron's manuscripts, in particular Jean-Marc Argentin, graphic designer at the Museum of Le Havre, but also researchers such as Geneviève Amourette, Gérard Breton, Claire Bustaret, G. Coat, Edward Duyker, Jacqueline Goy, Michel Jangoux and Roger Martin.[4] We should note, however, that these transcriptions were undertaken using a variety of methodologies. Establishing a methodology is in fact a challenging task, as it involves a complex set of choices. Should a text be transcribed exactly as it appears, with its crossings-out, its errors in syntax and spelling, its multiple repetitions? Or, conversely, should one transcribe the essence of the text, focusing on its meaning and putting aside questions of form and the various issues these raise?

Leaving aside that question for the time being, what follows is an overview of the manuscripts in the Lesueur Collection, which also sets out the projects that the Museum of Le Havre has developed around them.

1. Presentation of the Manuscript Collection
An original classification system and the methodology behind it
It took ten years to produce the inventory that was established with great rigour by Jacqueline Bonnemains. Indeed, it was no simple task to classify such a diverse set of manuscripts, where different subjects are sometimes grouped on the same page and might belong to different periods (sometimes an interval of several years can separate the contents of the front and back of a manuscript page).

In the numerical system of the Bonnemains inventory, the numbers do not always cover the same material reality. Sometimes a number will correspond to a short note on a piece of paper that measures a few square centimetres; at other times a number designates a notebook of a few dozen pages. In short, a number in the inventory does not always

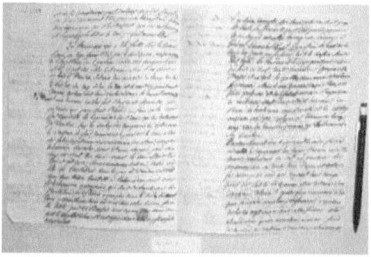

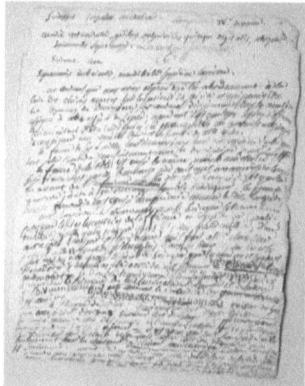

Sample pages from various manuscripts in François Péron's hand.

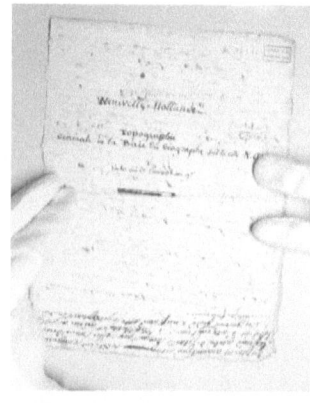

correspond to a single page – far from it. In order to establish an overview relating to the processing of these manuscripts, therefore, it is more pertinent to use the number of pages as a basis for our summary, rather than the inventory numbers.[5] That said, the very word 'page' can equally be applied to quite different sets of material realities, ranging from the short three-line note on paper measuring a few square centimetres to the page measuring 35 x 20 cm covered with writing on both sides. Taking this into account, we have calculated that there are 4,239 manuscript pages in Péron's hand in the collections of Le Havre.

The manuscripts: form, decipherability, state of conservation

Before evoking the contents of the manuscripts, we need to provide a description, however brief, of their form. As we have indicated, the item that we shall refer to here as a 'manuscript page' can cover a range of quite different material realities. A short note comprising a few words is taken as constituting a manuscript page. A sheet measuring 35 x 20 cm with writing on both sides and across two columns (a part of which might be crossed out) is also a manuscript page. In the case of a brief note, it might only take three minutes to transcribe its contents. In the case of a double-sided page with writing across two columns, several days may be required, and the result might not satisfy expectations: the transcriber may be forced to leave blank spaces because certain words remain a mystery.

We must point out in this regard that, although Péron's handwriting is in the main very elegant, it remains particularly difficult to decipher. The enthusiasm that we can experience when broaching a manilla folder whose contents are written in an exquisite hand, whose form is well defined and whose meaning seems equally clear, is easily shattered when we are confronted with a few pages that are more problematic than others. The photographs speak for themselves. The task of transcribing requires much better eyesight than one might reasonably assume: as those who have undertaken this task are well aware, the terms 'patience' and 'perseverance' take on new meaning when it comes to dealing with certain pages.

When confronted with a thin sheet of paper that is only written on one side, a reading remains possible, even if it sometimes requires making hypotheses and using guesswork. But when there is handwriting on both sides of the paper, establishing a reading often becomes complicated, if not impossible.

To the difficulty of deciphering certain documents must be added the challenge of preserving them. It is a museum's mission to attempt

A manuscript page showing the high visibility of writing on the reverse side.

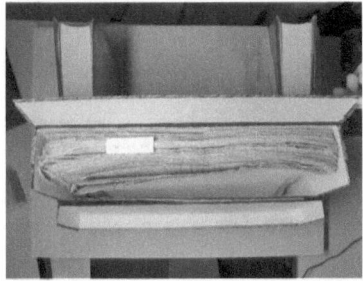

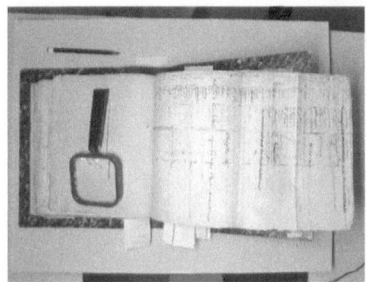

Manuscript storage box.

to give the objects within its care the longest life expectancy possible. In the case of certain manuscripts in the Lesueur Collection, however, this mission is compromised. In some instances the paper is particularly thin, a problem which is compounded by the use of corrosive ink. Two centuries later, these inks have acidified and burnt the cellulose. Where there are crossings out or large blobs of ink (for example, in flourishes, which occur quite frequently), this can cause that part of the paper to disintegrate.

In addition to material questions such as these, problems can sometimes arise due to the methods used in the nineteenth century to house these manuscripts. The documents from the Voyage to the Southern Lands, along with certain zoological manuscripts, were stored in boxes which were specially created to house them and which resembled luxury editions of books (leather binding, fine gold lettering on the spine). The format of these boxes was standardised. Some documents turned out to be greater in size. Not *much* larger, but large enough for the constraints of the box to cause some pages to become dog-eared at the top, on the bottom or on the sides. The manuscripts are no longer housed in such boxes, but the damage to certain documents is irretrievable. Fine paper, corrosive ink and folds, all of these can lead purely and simply in the long term to the loss of parts of a page. When the top, bottom and/or side of a page are missing, certain narratives become hard to follow. Other pages, such as those in dossier 65,[6] were assembled into books, that is, mounted on guards and grouped in the same set. These pages, just like any others, come in all possible sizes. Some are thus folded over several times to fit into the binding.

The classification and conservation systems outlined above have obviously had some impact on the state of the collection, but we must also acknowledge that they have prevented or limited the loss of documents, and we can only pay tribute to those who initiated them. Today, the task of conservation involves asking different questions, requiring a different set of solutions. This is an ongoing process: we have as yet no fixed notion of the extent to which these manuscripts might be restored. We know we cannot expect miracles. Photographing each document, which was the mission we chose and which is now well advanced, can in itself prove to be a means of conservation for a certain number of documents. Those manuscripts that will go untouched for years before finding the person who commits to transcribing them will at least acquire in this way a virtual duplicate of themselves. This will include small pieces of paper that are condemned to disappear in the long term.

Bound manuscripts with pages of varying sizes.

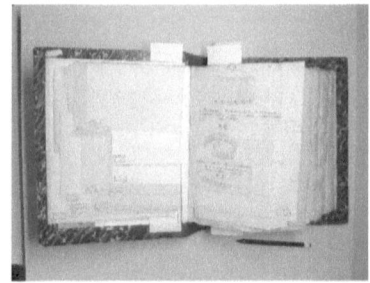

Looking beyond these material questions, we should also mention the specific case of certain zoological manuscripts written in Latin, whose transcription requires the skills of both a Latin specialist and a zoologist.[7] Before transcribing such a text, one would therefore need to be interested in Péron, have good eyesight, possess historical and zoological knowledge and master the rudiments of Latin.

2. The Manuscripts of the Voyage to the Southern Lands

We have identified 301 manuscripts of Péron on this theme, ranging from the preparation of his narrative of the voyage to the publication of its scientific results (bibliographical research included). These manuscripts comprise exactly 2086 pages, representing about half of the manuscript material in Péron's hand within the collection. Of these, 610 pages have been transcribed, that is, a little under 30% of his writings related to the Voyage to the Southern Lands.

Contents of Péron's notes relating to the Voyage to the Southern Lands

Like many scholars of the period, Péron, whose role during the expedition was that of trainee zoologist, anatomist and anthropologist, was involved in a variety of scientific pursuits. He also took a keen interest in politics. The manuscripts concerning the preparation of his voyage account reflect this diversity of interests. They also reveal a Péron who worked hard and was alert to future opportunities. His documentation includes: notes on the objectives of the expedition to the Southern Lands and on those who participated in it; notes on different expeditions from the sixteenth to the nineteenth centuries; a bibliography on a variety of subjects (such as zoology, medical observations, deep-sea ocean currents, and the temperature and phosphorescence of the sea). His preparatory notes give a partial indication of the research that he intended to cover in his voyage account and demonstrate that his research interests were extensive. This group of documents on the preparation of his narrative of the expedition comprises 81 manuscripts, for a total of 343 pages.

Péron's notes on the natural sciences from the voyage constitute a total of 93 manuscripts and 894 pages. Zoology, botany, mineralogy, geography, meteorology, the temperature and phosphorescence of the sea ... these are some of the fields covered in more or less depth in the manuscripts, and classified by geographical zones corresponding to the stages of the expedition's itinerary. Several manuscripts are in fact notebooks (a number of pages of which may be blank), which have a title that generally gives a very clear idea of the contents. The mention 'Voïage aux Terres Australes' and the content headings are an indication of Péron's structured classification system.

Some of these notes on the natural sciences were made by Péron on a daily basis during the voyage. They also convey details of how the expedition unfolded. In these notes, most of the scientists are regularly mentioned, with Péron describing the work they undertook and their discoveries. There is information on such topics as the general state of health of the crew, including the episode of zoologist Stanislas Levillain's death (manuscript no. 07 013), the events that took place at the Ile de France (Mauritius) in a political context marked by tension between France and England (15 024), or the expedition's chance meeting with Matthew Flinders (09 015).

Péron made notes on many of the people he encountered during the Voyage to the Southern Lands, but, when it came to indigenous peoples, he adopted a different approach. The Museum of Le Havre has in its collections narratives of encounters with first peoples that include studies of their social and religious customs (for example, at Maria Island, in Tasmania – 18 040),[8] as well as physical studies. The 'Hottentot apron' (the deformation of the labia minora of certain South African women) as well as steatopygia (a highly developed curve of the buttocks) were of particular interest to Péron.[9] The stopover at the Cape of Good Hope during the voyage home gave him the opportunity to reflect on this subject, which had been a source of interest in Western society for three centuries. Using his credentials as an anatomist he requested privileged access to the local hospital in order to find women who presented the two deformations identified. Accompanied by Lesueur, who was given the task of drawing the specific anatomical parts of these women, Péron wrote up his observations in minute detail; two papers on this topic, which are held at Le Havre, were read to the Institut de France in 1805.[10]

Diseases and their cures were also a legitimate subject of interest for Péron as a medical student. Before his departure, he had already made notes on diseases that frequently occurred on board ships engaged in expeditions. In particular, he looked into the methods adopted by James Cook during his three Pacific voyages in order to determine what means might be adopted to avoid common ship-board illnesses such as dysentery and scurvy. During the different stopovers and long periods spent in port, in Tenerife, Mauritius, New Holland and at the Cape, Péron took note of diseases and how to treat them. For example, he recorded in his notes the vaccine introduced at the Cape to combat smallpox (19 001). His interests were not confined to questions of a purely physical nature, however; he also described certain practices of indigenous peoples that were related to trade, to arts and crafts, and to pastoral and agricultural activities. In short, everything seemed to excite Péron's curiosity.

One of the distinctive features of his published voyage account is the interest Péron takes in relations with the British. A whole dossier, no. 12 in the Le Havre collection, is devoted to it. Of the total of 44 manuscripts contained in this dossier, 14 (264 pages in all) are in Péron's hand. The Voyage to the Southern Lands took place during a moment of heightened tensions between France and Britain. The Amiens peace treaty was signed on 25 March 1802. However, the period of peace it brought would only be fleeting; it collapsed in 1805. The historic rivalry between the two nations had found expression through the establishment of colonies around the world. The British colony of Port Jackson had been in existence since 1788, that is for 14 years, when the Baudin expedition came to sojourn there for several months during the southern winter and spring of 1802.[11] Almost all of the scientists on the voyage expressed their admiration for the prosperity that this colony had achieved in so short a time. So did several of the officers. Pierre-Bernard Milius, the second-in-command on Baudin's consort ship the *Naturaliste*, could see the benefits that would flow from colonisation and slavery in terms of increased wealth.[12] Péron, on the other hand, adopted a geopolitical point of view, analysing England's position, firstly in the context of its broader colonial holdings, and secondly in relation to the interests of other colonising nations, more specifically Spain and France. He made a comprehensive assessment, which included England's strengths and weaknesses in various domains. He established the same type of analysis for Spain's colonies in the Americas, particularly South America. While

Péron's political reflections are not exceptional for the time and for intellectuals of his status, they remain nonetheless of great interest.[13]

The scientific results of the voyage

Péron took on the task of synthesising the scientific results of the expedition. His involvement is immediately apparent in the very form of the manuscripts held in the Museum of Le Havre: his writing is on all the folders in which the manuscripts are classified, and his desire to impose on the presentation of the results a structure and clarity is palpable. It was Péron who established the numerous lists and tables of items collected: 29 manuscript documents (of the 70 that make up the relevant dossier – no. 21) are in his hand, comprising a total of 199 pages. Péron also established lists of collections given to Baudin's scientists by people who were not part of the expedition (for example, the list of objects donated by Monsieur Ravelet at Mauritius – 21 023, 21 035, 21 037).

Péron was concerned with ensuring the proper conditions for the conservation of these natural history collections. Five manuscripts (12 pages) were exclusively devoted to issues related to the conservation of the samples collected. During the voyage, Péron himself requested Baudin's authorisation to change the rum in all of the jars to ensure the conservation of the specimens they contained (21 030). He also produced a document describing the state of the 53 crates of specimens on board the *Géographe* when it returned to France, and stipulated whether the contents were to be put 'in a dry place', whether they were 'fragile' or whether the mode of conservation was 'immaterial' (21 025). In addition to listing the collections made by the scientists of the expedition or donated to them, Péron described the live animals brought back to France on the *Géographe*, where room had been found to house them (21 012). Lastly, there are two sets of documents in this series concerning the items which were intended for the Museum of Rouen (21 100–21 122) and for the high school at Moulins near Péron's native village of Cérilly (21 130–21 133).

2.e classe

Oiseaux.

N.os des espèces	Genres	Espèces.	Connues ou Nouvelles	Lieux où elles se trouvent.	Dessins	Observations Générales.
6	Psittacus	Lacepedii... mas.	S.N.	Détroit Dentrecasteaux	....	
7	P.	id. ... Femin.	id.	id.	....	
8	P.	Lamanon.	id.	id.	....	
9	P.	Insula Maria.	id.	Ile Maria.	....	
10	Cuculus	Gasteroxanthus.	id.	Détroit Dentrecast.x	....	
11	C.	Diemenensis.	id.	id.	....	
12	Lanius	Rostr-oculo-pedifloreus	id.	id.	....	
13	Muscicapa	Bivittatorufa.	id.	Côte S.O. de N.Hol.	....	
14	M. Grisonea	Grisonea	id.	Dét. Dentrec.x	....	
15	M.	Vindulosa	id.	id.	....	
16	M.	Gasteroxantha.	id.	Côte S.O. de N.Hol.	....	
17	Muscivora	Guthuri fulva.	id.	Dét. Dentrecast.x	....	
18	M.	Bitæniofulvoptera.	id.	id.	....	
19	Turdus	Epirufus.	id.	id.	....	
20	T.	Guloflavus.	id.	id.	....	
21	Tanagra	Lilaccoeloo.	id.	id.	....	
22	Loxia	Bas-our-erythra.	id.	Ile Maria.	....	
23	Corvus	Australis.	Sp. Lin.	Dét. Dentrecast.x	....	
24	Parus	chlorocephanotus.	S.N.	id.	....	
25	P.	Sophia.	id.	id.	....	
26	Glaucopis	Cinerea.	Sp. Lin.	id.	....	
27	Certhia	Flavoptera	S.N.	id.	....	
28	Alcedo	Cristata.	S. Lin.	id.	....	
29	Sterna	Melasoma	S.N.	mer australe. 1/2 lat	....	
30	S.	Caspioides.	id.	id.	....	
31	Larus	Melapterus.	id.	mer aust. 43.°	....	
32	Sula	Whytensis.	id.	Terre de Whyt.	....	
33	S.	Sanwensis.	id.	Iles Sanw.	....	
34	S.	Diemenensis.	id.	Terre de Diemen	....	
35	Ardea	Banksiana	id.	Détroit de Bank.	....	
36	Tantalus?	Melaloptrus.	id.	Iles Formeux?	....	Tantaus et ne seft aurais
37	Tringa	Nivea.	id.	Détroit Dentrecast?.	....	
38.						

Page from Péron's list of birds collected during the voyage. Muséum d'Histoire naturelle, Le Havre – manuscript no. 21 003-1CR.

The publication of Péron's voyage account

The publication of the expedition's narrative and scientific achievements was entrusted to Péron and Lesueur. Péron was in charge of operations. He had not only demonstrated that he possessed all the qualities required for this undertaking but he was also one of the few scientists (in any case the only zoologist) to have survived the expedition. He was certainly eager to undertake the task: 20 manuscripts are petitions addressed to the Minister of Marine, to Napoleon and to Joséphine de Beauharnais, in which Péron tried to convince them of the absolute necessity of publishing what he described as the splendid results of the voyage (dossier 22, notably nos 22 062–22 067).

The publication of course required funding and this took some time to materialise. In his pitch to the authorities, Péron did not hesitate to raise the issue of Franco-British rivalry and its relevance to the publication of the expedition's work, in particular that relating to geography (improved knowledge of the Australian coastline). He did in the end win out: the Atlas of maps was published in 1811, well before Flinders was able to publish his maps and voyage account.[14]

Among the various documents relating to the voyage account, there are preparatory drafts of a number of sections (11 manuscript documents in total). The study of these documents provides an insight into the way in which the narrative gradually took shape.

Aside from the manuscripts, Péron's influence on the drawings is also particularly noteworthy. Further work on the portraits of indigenous people by Nicolas-Martin Petit was undertaken upon the expedition's return, by Petit himself before his death in 1804 or by Jacques Milbert, who had abandoned the expedition in May 1801 before rejoining it upon its return to Mauritius in 1803. Milbert thus had to rework motifs that he had not observed himself. The reworking of these illustrations had two objectives: to finalise the drawings done in the field, adding colours to them; and to rework them for the purposes of publication. This is clearly where Péron's input became essential. He knew that the number of engraving plates would be limited – much more limited than he would like. But his ambition was to say all there was to say, and to show all there was to show. He thus had no other choice than to assemble on a single plate elements that had initially been intended for separate individual

Aborigines lighting a fire. Nicolas-Martin Petit. Muséum d'Histoire naturelle, Le Havre – no. 20 045-1.

engravings. The necessity of making a synthesis implied (or led to) the bringing together of motifs (people, landscapes, objects) which had not necessarily been seen together. Thus the engravings sometimes display images that appear to be snapshots of real scenes but that were in fact carefully composed.

It is instructive to read some of the remarks that Péron inscribed on the drawings. On a sketch of Aborigines from New Holland lighting a fire (20 045-1), he wrote: 'we could reduce this plate and complete it with other objects, for example place them in front of huts [...] from New [South] Wales'. On a drawing of a 'Hottentot apron' (19 036), Péron wrote: 'nos 1 and 2 combined on a single plate which will be engraved in black'. Péron justified the choices he made to modify certain drawings, taking full responsibilty for deliberately transforming a drawing which had been done in the field, and which we might assume would correspond as closely as possible to reality. For example, he wrote on a portrait of a woman from Van Diemen's Land: 'take care to maintain the general shapes, but touch up the essential flaws; as the thin shapes of the limbs are a characteristic of this race, they must be respected with great care'. On a drawing of the 'apron' of a Hottentot woman, he wrote: 'plate to be composed in black [and white] – we shall have to reduce the size of the thighs which could cost too much to engrave – perhaps they could even be drawn with a single-line'. Clearly, anatomical precision could be sacrificed for the sake of material constraints. On the portrait of a Malay man Péron has written: 'we must take care to respect the thin and weak shapes of the trunk and limbs, but we can correct the essential flaws'. Such subjective commentary can be quite surprising.

Arra-Maïda, woman from South Cape, Tasmania. Nicolas-Martin Petit. Muséum d'Histoire naturelle, Le Havre – no. 20 022-3.

Apart from those remarks that have an impact on the very meaning of the drawing, some of Péron's commentary is often simply descriptive, and no doubt intended to describe a zoological species in words or to assist with the illustrated description. For example: '*Doris? tetraptera* – De Witt's Land – 1867 – 1590 – slightly tawny colour, dotted all over with small brownish and bright sky-blue spots – the foot underneath a dirty white' (65 695). One particular text shows how Péron sought to occupy centre stage, and highlights the high regard he had for himself and for the work done during the expedition:

> it is especially in zoology that its [the expedition's] triumph is truly prodigious; and what is most admirable in all this, is that just two men, through their steadfastness and their dedication, brought about this resounding success. Of the five zoologists nominated by the government, only M. Péron remained after the 1st campaign. He joined forces with a young man who embarked on his ship with no title, but who was very capable of showing his zeal and becoming his collaborator and his friend. (22 019, transcription Jacqueline Bonnemains)

In his defence, the lack of interest that was shown in the expedition inevitably spurred him on to justify his achievements. The captain and many of the scientists had not survived the journey; it was thus logical and legitimate for Péron to take on the role of defending the voyage to the hilt – at the risk, as we know, of transforming History to some extent, even to a high degree. But this is not our subject here; other scholars have dealt with this aspect of Péron's persona.[15]

3. The Zoology Manuscripts

Numerous manuscripts by Péron make up almost the entirety of the dossiers strictly devoted to the different zoological groups (apart from ornithology). A large number of these manuscripts were prepared in collaboration with Lesueur. Generally speaking, Péron would give a written description of a new species and, alongside it (in the same notebook, for example), Lesueur would do an illustration. We can thus see just how artificial a division it would be to separate the documents into texts and drawings, into Lesueur's work and that of Péron, or any other sub-groupings.

As a general rule, Péron established the methodology behind the inventory for the group of living species and Lesueur followed his lead. Lesueur would spend the rest of his life pursuing to a significant extent the work he had done with Péron. The work on the medusae was undoubtedly the most representative and the most accomplished example of this close collaboration: the quality and detail of Lesueur's drawings assisted Péron in his descriptions of the specimens collected and in the formulation of hypotheses.

In one of the manuscripts, Péron outlined a method for dealing with various zoological groups, describing what should usefully be noted down in a publication. The following is an extract:

> With frogs, draw a distinction between frogs themselves, which usually live in water, tree frogs, which live for the most part in the woods, toads, which live on dry land in damp places, salamanders, which live in salt water [...].
> With fish, it would be impossible to go into every detail. Make do with indicating whether the [illegible] is full of fish, whether this is at all times of the year, point out the species which are the most remarkable, the most useful, the commonly used fishing practices, the different modes of preparing fish, etc... Whether there are some which are extremely beautiful in terms of their colours and very unique by way of their form [...].
> For seabirds, indicate with care the latitudes and longitudes where they appear, at what distance from land, etc...
> These observations should be applied to all types of marine animals and are very important, given that the number of species is limited, that they appear in particular regions, and that their presence can differ [...].
> (65 005, transcription J. Bonnemains)

On the practical level, Péron described in detail the dredging operations that were carried out during the voyage in order to harvest marine specimens.[16] He also undertook bibliographical research on many of the zoological fields in which he was involved. In keeping with the approach he took to the expedition as a whole, he considered that the work of his predecessors formed the basis, the foundation stone for his own reflections. He described all of the species collected and systematically specified which were the new species in a genus. The place where the observation was made and/or the specimen taken is usually indicated. He indeed attached great importance to the habitat of animals. In manuscript 65 018, we find the first appearance of the notion of ecology, a constant preoccupation of Péron's, as Jacqueline Goy has noted:[17]

> The habitat of animals is without question one of the oldest and most important parts of their history.
> Habitat is the element on which all of the most essential circumstances of their existence depend. It is related to every detail of their food, their mating, their generation, their sedentary life, their migrations. It must necessarily cast a light on the connections between these aspects of their existence and, while it does not constitute the essential foundation for how they function, it can, at least, almost always provide valuable data, especially for the determination of species.
> Without a precise knowledge of the habitat of animals how can one propose the general hypotheses without which detailed information is deprived of its value and its principal source of interest. (65 018, p.1, transcription J. Bonnemains)

Péron named a certain number of species after the scientists from the expedition, in keeping with tradition. In particular, he named after Lesueur a species of boa taken on King Island, specifying that his companion, 'each day, through his obliging nature, is ever more worthy of recognition' (78 091). He sought out specimens, classified them, and learnt to preserve them. He set up the entire process. Lesueur followed the master, learning at his side how to collect samples and stuff animals, among other techniques. This was knowledge that he put into practice during the rest of his life, in the United States and in France.

In the dossiers strictly devoted to zoology, we have identified 1055 manuscript documents in Péron's hand, comprising a total of (exactly!) 2153 pages. Of the entire collection of Péron's manuscripts held in the Museum of Le Havre, two thirds are strictly concerned with zoology. This amounts to half of the manuscript pages in Péron's hand.

Conclusion

A brief numerical summary:
- number of manuscript documents in the Le Havre Museum's collection: 2239;
- number of manuscript documents within the collection by Péron: 1532;
- number of pages in Péron's hand: 4239;
- almost 70% of the manuscripts in the collection are Péron's work;
- about 11% of these manuscripts have been transcribed.

The future creation of a website at the Museum of Le Havre, containing multiple resources, will require choices to be made on how to organise Péron's manuscripts. A technical choice based on conservation may involve regrouping the manuscripts. Creating such a site would also imply making choices about the priorities that would apply when it comes to digitising and transcribing manuscripts and thus making them available online. But above all, choices will have to be made about how much value-adding in the form of interpretation would need to be undertaken for these manuscripts. Into what overall structure would Péron's work need to be placed in order for the public to gain access to these resources?

In commencing this task, our first priority has been to engage with the theme of the 'Southern Lands' in order to prepare a major exhibition, backed up by a research project with our Australian colleagues.[18] Henceforth we intend to pool all of our collective means in order to provide access not only to the archival documents themselves but also to the precious resource that is the interpretation of these sources. In order to achieve this goal, we are pursuing a partnership with the Archives Nationales de France, the Muséum national d'Histoire naturelle in Paris, and other institutions. In this way, researchers seeking to understand Péron's work in its entirety will be able to call not just upon the manuscripts but upon the full range of documentary material relating to the expedition – the artwork of Lesueur, Petit, Milbert and others, but also the objects collected during the voyage. This in turn will provide for a shift in focus, in our analysis of Péron and his work, from the biographical to the thematic, from his personal story to the Voyage to the Southern Lands itself.

Notes

1. The Baudin Legacy project was sponsored by the Australian Research Council from 2005 to 2009. Its mission was to transcribe and translate into English the essential archival documentation relating to the Baudin expedition to Australia (1800–1804), and to post this material on a dedicated website. The chief investigators on this project are Margaret Sankey (University of Sydney), Jean Fornasiero and John West-Sooby (University of Adelaide), and Michel Jangoux (Université libre de Bruxelles and Université de Mons-Hainaut, Belgium). Url: https://baudin.sydney.edu.au/.
2. At present, the Baudin Legacy site contains transcriptions and translations of documents from a number of sources, including the Archives Nationales de France, the Bibliothèque Nationale de France, the State Library of New South Wales and the Muséum national d'Histoire naturelle in Paris.
3. In addition to the numerous transcripts she made or acquired 'for internal use', to assist researchers using the Lesueur Collection, she published several significant manuscripts held in other collections, for example, the personal journal of Nicolas Baudin (*Mon voyage aux Terres Australes*, Paris: Imprimerie nationale, 2000) and, with P. Hauguel, the journal of Pierre-Bernard Milius (*Récit du voyage aux Terres australes par Pierre-Bernard Milius*, Le Havre: Société havraise d'études diverses, 1987).
4. Some transcripts made by these researchers, occasionally in collaboration with Jacqueline Bonnemains, were published as articles or catalogues, often within the *Annales du Muséum du Havre* but also in other outlets. For example: Michel Jangoux, 'L'Expédition du capitaine Baudin aux Terres australes: les observations zoologiques de François Péron pendant la première campagne (1801–1802)', *Annales du Muséum du Havre*, vol. 73, 2005, pp. 1–35; Roger Martin (ed.), 'Le Rêve australien de Napoléon. Description et projet secret de conquête française', *Revue de l'Institut Napoléon*, vol. 176, no. 1, 1998, pp. 4–187; Jacqueline Goy, *Les Méduses de Péron et Lesueur: un autre regard sur l'expédition Baudin*, Paris: Éditions du CTHS, 1995.
5. While respecting this principle for our summary, we nonetheless quote inventory numbers whenever this is required in order to identify a specific manuscript for the purpose of analysing or describing its contents.
6. This is the dossier named 'Mélange de groupes zoologiques' (Miscellaneous Zoological Groups).
7. See, for example, Justin Jansen's chapter in this volume, which features the transcription of Péron's notes on the Albatross (79 089-1, 79 089-2, 79 090). These notes include passages in Latin copied from Gmelin (1789). In other documents, Péron writes notes directly in Latin.
8. This document was published in English translation by N.J.B. (Brian) Plomley,

The Baudin Expedition and the Tasmanian Aborigines, 1802, Hobart: Blubberhead Press, 1983, pp. 80–95.
9   These studies are to be found in dossier 19.
10 These two papers were subsequently published: François Péron and Charles-Alexandre Lesueur, 'Observations sur le tablier des femmes hottentotes', *Magasin encyclopédique*, vol. 3, 1805, pp. 195–197; François Péron, 'Réponse de M. Péron aux observations de M. Dumont sur le "Tablier des femmes hottentotes"', *Magasin encyclopédique*, vol. 5, 1805, pp. 298–310.
11 The two expedition ships were reunited in Port Jackson in early July 1802 and stayed there until 18 November.
12 This view was contained in the report Milius wrote for the governor of Mauritius, General Decaen, during the voyage home: 'Brief Overview of the English Settlements in New Holland and on the Portuguese colony in China. Naval Action to Damage English Trade in the Indian Sea, etc., 1803', in Jean Fornasiero and John West-Sooby, *French Designs on Colonial New South Wales*, Adelaide: Friends of the State Library of South Australia, 2014, pp. 337–342. His journal has been published in French and English: in Bonnemains and Hauguel (eds), *Récit du voyage aux Terres australes par Pierre-Bernard Milius*; and in *Pierre Bernard Milius, Last Commander of the Baudin Expedition: The Journal 1800–1804*, translated and annotated by Kate Pratt with an introduction by Anthony J. Brown, Canberra: National Library of Australia, 2013.
13 A critical edition and translation of the Péron documents preserved in dossier 12, along with other supporting documentation, can be found in Fornasiero and West-Sooby, *French Designs*.
14 Matthew Flinders, *A Voyage to Terra Australis: Undertaken for the Purpose of Completing the Discovery of that Vast Country, and Prosecuted in the Years 1801, 1802 and 1803, in His Majesty's Ship the* Investigator, London: G. and W. Nicol, 2 vols and Atlas, 1814.
15 See, for example, the study of the Baudin expedition by Frank Horner, in which the extent of Péron's rewriting of the voyage is made clear: *The French Reconnaissance: Baudin in Australia 1801–1803*, Carlton: Melbourne University Press, 1987.
16 Jacqueline Goy refers to Péron's notes on collecting sea animals contained in files 68 501Bv and 68 357 (*Les Méduses*, p. 26). It must be remembered, however, that, although Péron claimed to have pioneered the use of instruments and techniques for collecting marine animals, he had himself been initiated into such methods by experienced zoologists René Maugé and Stanislas Levillain. See Michel Jangoux, 'François Péron, l'émergence d'un naturaliste', *Une petite ville, trois grands hommes. Actes du colloque de Cérilly, 15–16 mai 1999*, Moulins: Pottier, 2000, pp. 137–152; Jean Fornasiero, 'Charles-Alexandre Lesueur: An Art of the Littoral', in Vivonne Thwaites and Jean Fornasiero, *Littoral*, Adelaide: 5 Star Print, 2010, pp. 17–19.
17 Goy, *Les Méduses*, pp. 40–41.
18 This aim was achieved through the travelling exhibition *The Art of Science: Baudin's voyagers, 1800–1804*, which commenced at the South Australian Maritime Museum in 2016 and was subsequently shown in museums in Launceston, Hobart and Sydney, before making its final appearances at the National Museum of Australia in Canberra and the Western Australian Museum in Fremantle in 2018. Details can be found in the exhibition catalogue: Jean Fornasiero, Lindl Lawton and John West-Sooby (eds), *The Art of Science: Baudin's Voyagers 1800–1803*, Mile End: Wakefield Press, 2016. Other research projects with researchers from the University of Adelaide and elsewhere are currently in train.

Chapter 6

The Journals of François Péron and the *Voyage de découvertes aux Terres Australes*

Margaret Sankey

The scientific voyages of the late eighteenth and early nineteenth centuries, inspired by the conjoined Enlightenment beliefs that the rapidly emerging and developing natural sciences would provide true knowledge about the world, had quasi encyclopædic aims. Recording these voyages was of prime importance for the future analysis and dissemination of the scientific data. To this end, both officers and scientists kept written records of their observations and findings.

In accordance with naval regulations, each ship had a logbook in which the officer of the watch recorded measurements of the winds, distance covered, direction taken and other matters connected with the mechanics of sea voyaging. The officers also kept their own personal journals, in which they recorded the same information as well as their own commentary on events. Both species of record were in a form laid down by naval regulations. The scientists, on the other hand, although they did in fact sometimes keep daily journals, were not constrained by naval discipline. Their task was to record, in a way that they determined, their scientific observations. This was accomplished in a variety of genres: reports of excursions undertaken, documentation of specimens collected, illustrations of natural phenomena, collections of data and analysis of this material.

Departing from Le Havre for New Holland on 19 October 1800, the expedition, commissioned by Napoleon Bonaparte and planned and led by Nicolas Baudin, was the most ambitious scientific voyage undertaken up to that point. All the known sciences – botany, zoology, mineralogy, cartography, astronomy and also the new science of anthropology – were covered. There were 22 scientists and 32 officers on board, and a high degree of collaboration was necessary for the success of the voyage. A vast amount of written material was generated during the expedition – logbooks, journals, maps, scientific reports, notes and correspondence – presenting diverse points of view and covering a wide range of knowledges.

In a voyage of this type, the commander, since he had oversight of the voyage and the requisite experience and expertise, would normally have been responsible for the official account of the expedition, prepared for publication on return to France. He would have had the duty of overseeing the preparation of the atlases of maps and illustrations. Captain Baudin was meticulous in the writing of his own daily journal – his '*journal de mer*' (sea log)[1] – and, in the expectation of the future publication of the voyage account, had begun to prepare his '*journal historique*' (fair copy) that he described as an edited version of the sea log.[2] In it, he included reports from the officers and scientists, as well as illustrations by the artists of the expedition, Charles-Alexandre Lesueur and Nicolas-Martin Petit.

The death of the captain at the Île de France (Mauritius) on the return journey put paid to that scenario. Instead, surprisingly in such a context, the young zoologist, François Péron, was entrusted with the task of writing up the narrative of the voyage. Under the patronage of Georges Cuvier,[3] a comparative anatomist at the Muséum national d'Histoire naturelle in Paris, Péron, who had been studying at the École de Santé, had written a pamphlet entitled 'Observations sur l'anthropologie et l'histoire naturelle de l'homme ...' ('Observations on anthropology and the natural history of Man ...') in support of his request to participate in the expedition.[4] The study of natural man was indeed to be one of the projects of the expedition and Péron's pamphlet was complementary to the document prepared by Joseph-Marie Degérando of the Société des Observateurs de l'Homme. Degérando's work, entitled 'Considérations sur les diverses méthodes à suivre dans l'observation des peuples sauvages' ('Considerations on the various methods to be followed in the observation of savage peoples'),[5] laid out the principles for studying natural man, based on dialoguing with him and observing him in his social context. As well as carrying out his duties as a zoologist, Péron embraced the nascent science of anthropology enthusiastically, and made it one of the principal focuses in his published account of the expedition.

The first volume of the account, *Voyage de découvertes aux Terres australes* (*Voyage of Discovery to the Southern Lands*), was published in 1807.[6] When Péron died in 1810, he left the second volume unfinished. It was completed by one of the officers, Louis Freycinet,[7] and published in 1816.[8]

The circumstances in which Péron came to publish the official account have been well documented.[9] On the return to France without its leader, the expedition was considered to have been a failure, mainly because of the advance unfavourable commentary by the naturalist Jean-Baptiste Bory de Saint Vincent concerning the captain's management of the expedition.[10] Bory had left the expedition at the Île de France on the outward journey, when already signs of conflict had begun to emerge between Baudin and his officers and scientists, and had returned to France before the arrival there of the expedition's ships. Napoleon's oft-quoted comment 'Baudin did well to die: on his return I would have had him hanged',[11] set the tone for the prevailing attitudes of the time and was supported on the return of the voyage by the criticisms of Baudin made by officers such as the Freycinet brothers.

In such a climate, there was certainly no great interest in publishing the account. Yet, objectively, under the leadership of Captain Baudin, much had been accomplished. It was Baudin, fired with enthusiasm for the advancement of science after his successful expedition in *La Belle Angélique*,[12] who had planned the expedition. The accomplishment of this new project was, however, fraught because of the unforeseen, contradictory demands of naval discipline and the free-wheeling agenda of the enthusiastic scientists, particularly Péron. This dynamic and the imbalance in numbers between officers and scientists created resentments and frustrations which undermined Baudin's authority in all sorts of intangible ways. Alliances formed between scientists and officers against Baudin, and his decisions and strategies were constantly questioned.

In the final event, it seems to have been the ambitious Péron alone who was eager to publish the account of the voyage. Normally after the death of the captain, it could have been expected that one of the officers would undertake the gathering together of the material and the writing of the narrative. It is not hard to understand, however, that in such an unfavourable context, none of the officers would have been willing to do so. Why associate themselves any further with what they and others now perceived as having been a failed and flawed expedition?

I have already mentioned Baudin's preparation for the writing of the official narrative, his sea log providing the *avant-texte* (pre-text) for the final account of the voyage, his fair copy, which he was writing in parallel. If one of the other officers had taken on the task of writing the official account, it could have been expected that the starting point would be both the captain's journals and that officer's daily journal, as well as the ships' logbooks.[13] Instead, the untried and untrained Péron offered himself for the task.

What records did Péron use as a basis for his writing of the *Voyage de découvertes*? The naturalist's account is quite idiosyncratic in various ways. One of the most notable features of his narrative is his virtual writing out of Captain Baudin and the failure to name him or to quote his journals. Péron's account is also driven by a quite personal agenda, insofar as the voyage of scientific discovery is concerned. Manuscript journal records, if they existed, might shed some light on the evolution of his perceptions of the captain and of the voyage as it unfolded. In the collections of the French National Archives and the Muséum national d'Histoire naturelle in Paris, where the majority of the Baudin expedition journals are held, there was no notebook that could be identified as a daily diary kept by Péron.[14] Looking further, I did, nevertheless, discover traces of journal writing in the numerous fragmentary documents in Péron's hand in the Lesueur Collection in the Muséum d'Histoire naturelle in Le Havre. I propose here to discuss the nature of these documents and in what ways these writings might have contributed to, or influenced, Péron's writing of the *Voyage de découvertes*. We can deduce from the evidence of these fragments that Péron did in fact keep records akin to journal material during the expedition, at least some of the time. He may even have been more systematic than it would appear from the loose-leaf, disorganised papers which survive in the Lesueur Collection.

After Péron's death, Louis Freycinet, in order to complete the second volume of the *Voyage de découvertes*, would have had access to Péron's papers. This is to say that Péron's papers would have been re-used first by himself in the preparation of his narrative account, and then by others after his death. The present fragmentary and unsystematic nature of the documents might indicate Péron's general mode of working, from jottings on loose leaves of paper, but could also be an artefact of their subsequent handling.

Most of Péron's papers were retained finally by the artist Lesueur, Péron's particular friend, who bequeathed them to the Le Havre Museum together with his own drawings and the material he subsequently collected during his later sojourn in America.[15] The material remained unclassified until Jacqueline Bonnemains, the curator of the Lesueur Collection between 1977 and 2003 made an inventory, ordered and catalogued the material from the expedition, and made transcriptions of certain passages. Sifting through the material at Le Havre, I was impressed by the great effort that has gone into making some sense of the pile of disparate documents, running from mere scraps of paper to small notebooks. The added difficulty in the case of Péron's work is his execrable handwriting, often in pencil and on occasion overwritten by himself.

Péron's papers in Le Havre are of several different types. Firstly, there are his scientific notes and reports, some in the form of letters. Secondly, there are drafts of Péron's narrative of the voyage. Thirdly, there is a large number of miscellaneous notes and jottings. These writings are on various loose leaves of paper of different sizes, sometimes folded to make up small notebooks. It is among these latter two categories that I sought 'journal' material.

The second category is composed of drafts of chapters, or parts of chapters, for the *Voyage de découvertes*. Sometimes there are several drafts of a particular section, indicating considerable reworking and editing of the material by Péron himself, and sometimes by others. These documents appear to be based on journal entries, but represent a later stage, or indeed sometimes a succession of stages in the narrativisation process leading to the official account. As such, the material contains sections and commentaries which do not appear in the final printed version, and which reveal other aspects of Péron's interests. In the third category are to be found notes clearly written by Péron in the immediacy of the moment, on a day-to-day basis. Sometimes these contain the sort of information to be found in the *'journal de bord'* (logbook) of the officers, with some measurements, but they do not include detailed log tables. In other jottings in this category are to be found Péron's personal musings, as well as texts in Latin and translations.

I shall look now at the form and content of Péron's 'journal' material in the second and third categories described above, according to the chronology of the voyage, to explore what light they might shed on Péron's writing of the *Voyage de découvertes*.

There are several documents concerning the beginning of the voyage, from Le Havre to Tenerife.

1.1 The first of these documents in chronological terms is a draft of eight manuscript pages of Chapter 2 of volume 1 of the *Voyage*, written in two columns in black ink, relating the crossing from Le Havre to the Canaries and the stay in Tenerife, with the beginning of a description of the Canary Islands.[16]

1.2 The second document, a later version of one part of the first, consisting of six large manuscript pages, recounts the part of the voyage from Le Havre to Cap Finisterre in Spain.[17] In this draft, the text is on the left-hand side of the page, with Péron's comments and additions on the right. The text is considerably edited, with crossings out and corrections in Péron's hand. Both this and the previous text contain material, such as Péron's problem with seasickness, not to be found in the final published account.

1.3 The third document from the same period, of eight manuscript pages, evokes the journal genre with the dating of entries and the immediacy of its commentary.[18] It is, however, reminiscent of the *'journal intime'* (diary), rather than the logbook of the officers which, while incorporating the possibility of commentary on the voyage, allows little room for more personal impressions. In this document, Péron speaks of his sadness at abandoning his mother. He then discourses in a philosophical vein, with comments about his interactions with his fellow voyagers, interspersed with Latin quotations. The naturalist also speaks of his seasickness and describes poetically his melancholy, aggravated by the blackness of night in the Tropics. The immediacy of this writing, and at the same time its literary and subjective nature, display both his erudition and his sensitivity, and offer a contrast with the reworked and edited versions of the voyage narrative above. This document finds no place in the *Voyage*.

1.4 The fourth text from the same period, entitled 'Nuit des Tropiques' ('Tropical Night'), consists of three manuscript pages.[19] A poem is followed by Péron's description of his sadness at leaving his love, Sophie.[20] The naturalist then gives a lyrical description of the tropical night:

> What profound calm reigns in the sky, in the air and on the waves . . . how imposing, how majestuous is this vast silence of nature! Weary from the daytime heat, how she breathes with delight the salutary freshness of the night . . .[21]

None of this material is directly used in the published voyage narrative. It is clear in the case of the first two of the four extant documents concerning this part of the voyage that at this stage of writing Péron was consciously preparing a text for publication, and that the material is in fact a draft of one of the chapters in the *Voyage de découvertes*. Given its nature, the writing could be the reworking, on Péron's return to France, of earlier documents, perhaps of journal material now lost. But it is also possible to hypothesise that Péron did not in fact keep complete records of the voyage and that he relied on his friends among the officers for the chronological outline and sequencing of events in the *Voyage de découvertes*. The third and fourth manuscript documents above belong to a quite different genre. It would appear from them that, during this early period of the voyage at least, Péron also kept a diary, recording his immediate, emotional responses to the surroundings as well as his feelings and thoughts. None of this more personal material appears in the *Voyage de découvertes*.

Each of the next four 'journal' documents, in chronological terms, deals with a different period of the voyage, and there is only one version in every case.

2.1 The first of these is entitled 'Passage du Tropique de Capricorne' ('Crossing the Tropic of Capricorn') and covers chronologically the first ten days of the Republican calendar month of Nivôse Year 9 (22 December 1800 – 1 January 1801), a period in which the expedition was en route from Tenerife to the Île de France.[22] The document is in the form of a notebook of 56 pages (28 folios) and is in a poor state, with pages torn out. Much of it is in pencil and is very difficult to decipher. It is a hybrid document: in some respects it resembles the officers' logbook, but it also has characteristics of the diary. It appears to be an attempt on Péron's part to follow naval practice in keeping a journal, since it contains some meteorological readings. It departs from naval practice, however, as it also contains Péron's philosophical musings and personal observations. For example, he expatiates on the nature of beauty at some length, speculating on the relationship between the 'agréable' and the 'utile' (what is pleasing to the eye and what is useful).

2.2 The next document is of the same type as the previous one and covers the period from 13 November 1801 (22 Brumaire Year 10) to 12 January 1802 (22 Nivôse Year 10).[23] During this time the expedition, after its first stay in Timor, sailed to Van Diemen's land (Tasmania). The daily journal is in the form of a notebook of 23 pages and its appearance suggests that it was either torn out of a larger book or that loose leaves were sewn together in a perfunctory fashion. As well as numerous meteorological records, it contains observations about the animals captured and observed, and gives details of the naturalist Levillain's illness and death.[24] Some of this material would be used in the first volume of the *Voyage de découvertes*.

2.3 The next body of documents covers the period from 10–28 Germinal Year 10 (31 March – 18 April 1802).[25] This material consists of 25 pages of varying sizes, grouped together by Péron to constitute a journal and numbered by him. The entries are in both ink and pencil and the journal is difficult to read. Most of the pages are written on both sides. Some of the pages have been recycled from previous use.[26] For example, written on the back cover are the words 'Les Amours/d'Enée et de Didon/traduction du IVe livre de l'Énéïde' ('The Love Affair of Aeneas and Dido/translation of Book IV of the Aeneid'). The form of the entries in this mini-journal is reminiscent of the officers' logbook. On the left-hand side of the page, Péron records the winds and weather and other details, although he is much less systematic in his recording than most of the officers. Since there was no template for the journals of naturalists on scientific voyages, it is possible that Péron, as the voyage progressed, had recognised in the method of recording of the officers a useful chronological frame with which to contextualise his own scientific reports and notes, as he does here. During the period covered, the voyagers were travelling towards the west from Wilson's Promontory. Thus the journal covers the encounter with Flinders at Encounter Bay and the survey of the north coast of Kangaroo Island, and finishes with the exploration of Spencer Gulf. Although he still includes comments on his colleagues and shipboard life, uppermost now for Péron is his role as scientific explorer and his main focus is on natural phenomena. He records his observations on the flora and fauna of New Holland, comparing and contrasting them with the other areas of the country visited by the expedition.[27] Such a document would have served as preparatory notes both for the official account and for his scientific reports.

3.1 In another, later document, Péron describes the events at King Island from 17 to 19 Frimaire (8–10 December 1802).[28] The *Naturaliste* left the island on 8 December to return to France, leaving the *Géographe* and the *Casuarina* to complete the reconnaissance of the coast.

All the documents described above, both legible and illegible, are ample evidence of Péron's constant writing during the voyage. Some, as we have indicated, are simply fragmented notes or musings, but enough of the remaining documents demonstrate that Péron was maintaining some kind of journal writing during the voyage. Even if he did not keep a daily journal, he clearly did do so at certain times. The examples listed here are the only ones to be found in the Le Havre collection, and are probably part of much more extensive record keeping on Péron's part, of which the present whereabouts are unknown.

Curiously, there are almost no papers by Péron in journal form to be found in the Le Havre archive for the return journey – except for the above fragment concerning King Island. Given the paucity of extant draft documents for the *Voyage de découvertes*, it would seem probable that other such documents, as well as other 'journal' items produced by Péron during the voyage, have simply gone missing.

What part did Péron's 'journal' fragments play in his overall written production? As we have indicated, Péron does not appear to have kept a journal in any systematic way throughout the journey and given his other activities, such as his specimen collecting and report writing, and based on the evidence above, we can assume that he had bursts of 'journal' writing. From this, we can surmise that the activity of writing a journal was not considered by him as an end in itself but as both preparatory notes and a framework for his reports. His more private record, a sort of diary, although often to be found side by side with journal items recording the voyage, was a place for him to express his feelings, try his hand at literary composition and indulge in philosophical speculation. This contention would be supported by the sheer illegibility of most of these 'journal' documents, which militates against their being read easily by others.[29]

That Péron intended this material for future use is demonstrated by his numbering of the documents he had created – the 'journal' fragments, as well as his other writings of various types (scientific reports, correspondence, copies of the scientific work of others). The numbers are usually written in red ink and were probably added after the voyage. Thus we find, for example, the following numbering:

2934–8: 'Nuit des tropiques'
2941–6: Tenerife
3233–51: Wilson's Promontory – Spencer Gulf
3286 to 3324: 'Passage du Tropique de Capricorne'
3987: Other musings

From these examples, we see that each number corresponds usually to a paragraph, so that particular episodes are covered by a sequence of numbers. Generally, but not always, as can be seen above, the numbers increase in accordance with the chronology of the voyage. Gaps in the numbering of the 'journal' fragments could indicate missing documents, but it is also possible that the missing numbers correspond to scientific reports or other writing that Péron was doing during that period. Reconstructing Péron's numbering system, tracing through the content that corresponds to the sequence of numbers, will perhaps shed light both on his way of working and on his method of composition.

I return now to my question concerning the relationship between the *Voyage de découvertes* and Péron's 'journal' writing. It appears from the evidence above that Péron did not keep a journal in any regular or consistent fashion and, as we have suggested, probably relied on the journals of others such as the Freycinet brothers to fill in the gaps. It is clear also that Péron was not the ideal or even an appropriate person to write the official version of the expedition if the aim of such an account was to synthesise all aspects of the voyage. The young, untried scientist did not have the training and discipline which would have enabled him to provide an overall dispassionate account of the expedition in all its complexity.

We have spoken about the subjectivity of much of Péron's 'journal' writing, akin more to the diary than to the logbook. He was writing in an age when natural science was emerging from speculative natural philosophy and his interest in philosophical speculation and in the literary expression of his feelings and impressions characterises much of this writing. In his pamphlet, 'Observations sur l'anthropologie ou l'histoire naturelle de l'homme ...', mythical thinking, inspired by Rousseau's Second Discourse,[30] inspires his attitude to native peoples. The questions to which he will seek answers during the Baudin expedition clearly express the parameters of this enquiry:

> 1. Must not moral perfection be in inverse relationship to physical perfection?
> 2. Does not this physical perfection exclude not only moral sensibility but also physical sensibility itself?[31]

The strong ideological as well as mythical component of Péron's thinking is carried into his voyage narrative, and is indeed one of the structuring principles of the *Voyage de découvertes*. As I have written elsewhere,[32] Péron as narrator of the *Voyage de découvertes* constructs himself as the mythical scientific voyager-hero on a quest for knowledge and truth, casting Captain Nicolas Baudin as the anti-hero who hinders the intrepid scientist – Péron – who overcomes this opposition to reach the truth.

The *Voyage de découvertes*, structured by the quest narrative, is permeated by Péron's nostalgic search for the perfect physical specimen of the 'uncivilised' native living in a naturally idyllic state, and by his disappointment at not finding what he is seeking in the Aborigines of Van Diemen's Land and New Holland. Yet there is a disjunction at the heart of Péron's text. His descriptions of encounters and interactions with the Aborigines in Van Diemen's Land, where he is captivated and entranced by the native women, are in jarring contrast with his later negative conclusions concerning the Aborigines, based on his measurements of their strength with the dynamometer. These latter records contain no commentary on the interaction that occurred during the experiments with the dynamometer between the French scientist and his experimental sujects, the Aborigines. Apart from naming certain of the experimental subjects, there is no personalisation of the indigenous people involved, and the only records of the encounters are the numerical tables.[33]

Péron was an ambitious young man, anxious to make his mark and seal his reputation as a scientist. Participating in the Baudin expedition and then being entrusted with the writing of the official account of the voyage gave him the ideal opportunity to accomplish these aims. During the four years between 1800 and 1804 during which the voyagers had been away from Europe, the Enlightenment ideals of the brotherhood of man had given way to a focus on European superiority. In the three years from the return of the voyagers to the publication of the first volume of his account in 1807, Péron had time to assimilate the winds of change and to fashion his narrative to suit the prevailing ideologies. His dynamometer experiments, in 'proving' that the strength of non-Europeans was inferior to that of Europeans, set the scene for the focus on, and the development of, physical anthropology, at the expense of social anthropology, and were eagerly taken up by those justifying colonialism and the reinstitution of slavery.[34]

In conclusion, the 'journal' records Péron kept during the voyage played an important part in shaping both the form and content of the narrative of the *Voyage de découvertes*. The fragmentary nature of his 'journals' would have given Péron infinite possibilities for ordering, seen as both an aesthetic and ethical choice. With his multiple notebooks and jottings, the naturalist could organise the raw material in the most advantageous way in order to achieve his aims. Likewise, his philosophical musings provide a window on his thought, and show his constant questioning and the evolution of his thinking during the voyage.

Our study of Péron's 'journal' material has shed some light on how the naturalist saw his role as a scientific voyager, on his recording methods, and on the composition of the *Voyage de découvertes*. Deciphering most of this 'journal' material is a difficult task, requiring persistence and patience, and it is to be hoped that in the future Péron's manuscripts will yield more of their secrets.

Notes

1. Nicolas Baudin, *The Journal of Post Captain Nicolas Baudin, Commander-in-Chief of the Corvettes* Géographe *and* Naturaliste, translated by Christine Cornell, Adelaide: Libraries Board of South Australia, 1974. The manuscript of this journal (or sea log) in five volumes is to be found in the Archives Nationales de France (ANF), série Marine, 5JJ 36–39 and 40. It has not to date been published in French.
2. This journal (the fair copy) is in four volumes: ANF, série Marine, 5JJ 35, 40B, 40C, 40D. It was edited by Jacqueline Bonnemains as *Mon voyage aux Terres Australes: Journal personnel du commandant Baudin*, Paris: Imprimerie nationale, 2000. It covers the period preceding the departure of the voyage to the end of the first stay in Timor (March 1800 to November 1801). Once the voyage has commenced its entries lag behind those of the sea log.
3. Cuvier had also written anthropological instructions for the expedition, principally concerned with accurate drawings and measurements of the natives observed: 'Note instructive sur les recherches à faire relativement aux différences anatomiques des diverses races d'hommes', reprinted in Jean Copans and Jean Jamin, *Aux origines de l'anthropologie française: les mémoires de la Société des Observateurs de l'Homme en l'an VIII*, Paris: Le Sycomore, 1978, pp.171–176.
4. François Péron, 'Observations sur l'anthropologie, ou l'histoire naturelle de l'homme, la nécessité de s'occuper de l'avancement de cette science et l'importance de l'admission sur la flotte du Capitaine Baudin d'un ou plusieurs naturalistes spécialement chargés des recherches à faire sur cet objet', Paris: Stoupe, 1800. Reprinted in Copans and Jean Jamin, *Aux origines*, pp. 177–185.
5. Joseph-Marie Degérando, 'Considérations sur les diverses méthodes à suivre dans l'observation des peuples sauvages. Extrait des procès-verbaux des séances de la Société des Observateurs de l'Homme ... Certifié conforme, à Paris, le 28 fructidor an 8 ...', [Paris]: Société des Observateurs de l'Homme, [1800]. Reprinted in Copans and Jamin, *Aux origines*, pp. 127–169. Published in English translation by F.C.T. Moore as *The Observation of Savage Peoples by Joseph-Marie Degérando*, London: Routledge and Kegan Paul, 1969.
6. François Péron, *Voyage de découvertes aux Terres Australes, exécuté par ordre de Sa Majesté l'Empereur et Roi, sur les corvettes le* Géographe *et le* Naturaliste *et la goëlette le* Casuarina *pendant les années 1800, 1801, 1802, 1803, et 1804, Historique*, vol. 1, Paris: Imprimerie impériale, 1807.
7. Both Louis Freycinet and his brother, Henri, were officers on the expedition. For the return journey, Baudin purchased an additional ship, the *Casuarina*, in Sydney, of which he made Louis captain.

8   François Péron and Louis Freycinet, *Voyage de découvertes aux Terres Australes, Historique*, vol. 2, Paris: Imprimerie royale, 1816.
9   Frank Horner, *The French Reconnaissance: Baudin in Australia 1801–1803*, Carlton: Melbourne University Press, 1987, pp. 330 *et seq.*
10   Jean-Baptiste Bory de Saint Vincent, *Voyage dans les quatre principales îles des mers d'Afrique, fait par ordre du gouvernement pendant les années neuf et dix de la République (1801 et 1802)*, Paris: F. Buisson, 3 vols, 1804.
11   Horner, *The French Reconnaissance*, p. 338.
12   See Nicolas Baudin, *Journal du Voyage aux Antilles de* La Belle Angélique *(1796–1798)*, édition établie et commentée par Michel Jangoux, Paris: Presses de l'Université Paris-Sorbonne/Académie royale de Belgique, 2009.
13   It is interesting in this context to quote Baudin's comments on Péron, after the stay in Timor: 'Citizen Péron, who wished to take on various areas of natural history, will most likely provide me with an interesting memoir, but I fear it will be incomplete, as he will not have limited himself to the type of work that is in keeping with his talents and even his knowledge'. See Baudin, *Mon voyage*, p. 398. This appraisal of the young scientist's way of working, the condescension of which might explain Péron's hostility to the Captain, would appear to have a certain justification.
14   Diaries exist within these collections for other naturalists, such as Théodore Leschenault and Stanislas Levillain (ANF, série Marine, 5JJ 56 and 5JJ 52 respectively).
15   After his period in America, Lesueur was appointed the first director of the Muséum d'Histoire naturelle of Le Havre in 1845, though bureaucratic delays prevented him from actually taking up his duties before his death in 1846.
16   Muséum d'Histoire naturelle, Le Havre, Collection Lesueur (henceforth Collection Lesueur), 07 003, 35cm x 22.5cm.
17   Collection Lesueur, 07 002, 37cm x 23cm.
18   Collection Lesueur, 07 005, 35cm x 22.5cm.
19   Collection Lesueur, 07 006, 20cm x 14cm.
20   Anne-Sophie Petitjean, daughter of Pierre-Lazare Petitjean, a benefactor of Péron in his home town of Cérilly.
21   'Quel calme profond regne à-la-fois dans les cieux, dans les airs et sur les flots . . . qu'il est imposant, qu'il est majestueux ce vaste silence de la nature! Fatigué de la chaleur du jour, comme elle respire avec délices la fraîcheur bienfaisante de la nuit . . .' (Collection Lesueur, 07 006).
22   Collection Lesueur, 65 008, 11cm x 17cm.
23   Collection Lesueur, 07 013, 20cm x 15cm.
24   Levillain died at sea on 23 December 1801, from the effects of dysentery and fever contracted at Timor.
25   Collection Lesueur, 09 006 to 09 026.
26   For example, lists of tools, an account for bread, a list of food items.
27   Collection Lesueur, 09 025, 17cm x 16cm. Péron also makes several remarks concerning Baudin.
28   Collection Lesueur, 09 005, 22.5cm x 17.5cm.
29   Péron made fair copies of various reports which are perfectly legible. This would support the idea that he did not want his more private documents to be read by others.
30   Jean-Jacques Rousseau, *Discours sur l'origine et les fondements de l'inégalité parmi les hommes*, Amsterdam: Marc Michel Rey, 1755.
31   Péron, 'Observations sur l'anthropologie', in Copans and Jamin, p. 184.
32   Margaret Sankey, 'François-Auguste Péron: le mythe de l'homme sauvage et l'écriture de la science', *Cahiers de sociologie économique et culturelle*, no. 9, 1988, pp. 37–46.
33   It must be noted that Péron's observations and conclusions concerning the

Australian Aborigines, foregrounded by the publication of his *Voyage de découvertes*, are only a fraction of the material collected by the members of the expedition. With a different focus, the journals of Captain Baudin make many observations, as do the journals of the officers and naturalists of the expedition. A large part of this material is to be found in the transcriptions of journals from the expedition, available on the Baudin Legacy Project web site https://baudin.sydney.edu.au/. Likewise, the bibliography provided on the Project website lists many articles on the subject of contacts between members of the Baudin expedition and Australian Aborigines that explore a wide range of points of view. See, for example, Margaret Sankey, 'Les premiers contacts: Les Aborigènes de la Nouvelle Hollande observés par les officiers et les savants de l'expédition Baudin', in Michel Jangoux (ed.), *Portés par l'air du temps, les voyages du capitaine Baudin*, special number of *Études sur le XVIIIe siècle*, vol. 38, 2010, pp. 171–185.

34 Jean-Luc Chappey, 'François Péron et la question de la civilisation aux antipodes', *Annales historiques de la Révolution française*, vol. 375, no. 1, 2014, pp. 139–159.

Chapter 7

The Products and Perils of François Péron

Stephanie Pfennigwerth

When François Péron landed on Bernier Island off the western Australian coast in June 1801, he was not overly impressed by the scenery. Despite its 'shrubby trees spread out over the ground like so many immense parasols', he reported that the island, like the mainland, exhibited a 'hideous sterility'. There were relatively few land animals, and most of them, he wrote, were 'unpleasant or harmful'. The sole exception was what he described as 'the smallest and most elegant member of this extraordinary family of New Holland animals', the 'extremely gentle' and 'pretty' banded hare-wallaby.[1] Péron was particularly impressed by the animal's maternal instincts, which he praised even as he also described its bludgeoning to death by his companions. The mother hare-wallabies sought to protect their joeys from the hunters with 'truly admirable courage'. It is worth quoting Péron's description at length:

> when wounded, they fled with their baby in the pouch and only abandoned it if, too overcome with weariness, too exhausted by loss of blood, they could carry it no longer [...]; should the hunter's chase cease or merely slacken, they were immediately seen returning to their nursling; they called to it with a sort of grunt, which is peculiar to them; they stroked it affectionately, as if to reassure it, guided it back into the pouch and, with this sweet burden, sought some new refuge.

He continues:

> The same proofs of intelligence and affection on the part of these poor mothers were again seen, even more touchingly, when they sensed themselves mortally wounded: all their care was directed toward the salvation of their nursling. Far from attempting to escape, they stood still beneath the hunter's blows [. . .]. Noble self-sacrifice, of which so many examples are found in accounts of animals' lives, and which often we can but envy!²

Yet it seems the banded hare-wallabies were not alone in exemplifying an enviable amount of noble self-sacrifice. For Péron's observations and collections on Bernier Island were, he writes, 'the product of many perils and much labour which, on two occasions, almost cost me my life.'³ The first near-fatal incident was when, '[c]arried away by my zeal and by the pleasure of the important discoveries that I was [. . .] making', he got lost in 'this frightful desert'. '[E]xhausted and collapsing through weariness and hunger', he writes, and 'overcome with fatigue and pouring with sweat', he fell to the ground and spent a night 'gripped with deadly cold' before, thanks to his 'companions' generous devotion', he was rescued.⁴ Péron's second and even more dramatic brush with death occurred as he collected 'valuable specimens' on 'a hazardous reef'.⁵ Washed by a wave over the 'fearsome surfaces' of the reef, he found his clothes 'were all ripped to shreds', and he was 'covered in cuts and bruises and bathed in blood'. '[S]ummoning all my strength to escape', he writes, 'I dragged myself on to the shore, where I collapsed, faint with pain and the loss of blood.' Péron's condition was such that when he finally limped back to camp around midnight, 'several of my friends could not help shedding tears'. He must really have been bashed about, for he reports that even 'the Commander himself [the much-maligned Nicolas Baudin] appeared touched by my woeful state'.⁶

In this passage, and many others, Péron seems eager to cast himself as an archetypical culture hero who endures much for the nation. Certainly, his *Voyage of Discovery to the Southern Lands* features enough danger, drama and disaster to fit comfortably within the genre of adventure narrative. As is typical in such narratives, Péron actively maps his European identity in non-European places – the harsher and more hazardous, the better. But on the other hand, Péron's fulsome accounts of his sufferings seem to undermine the genre's standard trope of European physical masculinity as an expression of superiority and conquest. If anything, his account of Bernier Island serves to highlight his physical inferiority and helplessness in a pitiless landscape. Indeed, the Bernier Island account encapsulates many of the characteristics of his *Voyage of Discovery to the Southern Lands*, and of Péron himself: the struggle and sacrifice, the sentimentality, the solidarity of brother voyagers, the back-stabbing of Baudin and, above all, Péron's self-consciousness, self-worth and self-promotion. Such was the esteem in which he was held, Péron seems to suggest, that sub-lieutenant Picquet disobeyed Baudin's orders to abandon him on the island;[7] such was the importance of this Frenchman, this scientist.

In the eulogies that followed Péron's death more than 200 years ago, much mention was made of his particular talents. According to Joseph Philippe François Deleuze, scientist and librarian of the Muséum national d'Histoire naturelle in Paris, Péron 'not only gained the esteem and friendship of all those with whom he lived, he had even acquired an extraordinary influence over them.'[8] Péron's charm was evident during his protracted negotiations to convince his superiors of the value of the now discredited voyage, and of his authority as the person best able to write its account. Perhaps the greatest achievement of this young, provincial trainee zoologist was that, by the time of his death, as chief naval physician Pierre-François Kéraudren notes: 'Academics, savants, people of rank appreciated his worth and loved him for himself. He was admitted by several important officials into their inner circle and they provided him daily with the most profound attachment.'[9] Deleuze declares Péron a 'genius'[10] and in the years that followed, the zoologist's reputation rose still higher. An anonymous reviewer of Émile Guillaumin's 1930s biography calls Péron 'a hero, a kind of saint'.[11] This chapter will explore the techniques Péron used – both subconsciously and, perhaps, deliberately – to establish the superior value of his work and his place in the echelons of the Institut de France.

'This glorious struggle'
There is no reason to doubt the reality of Péron's pains and privations. A landlubber, he worried about the potential psychological toll of his first sea voyage, which was 'Alas! [...] far from my tastes [...], contrary to my inclinations, my manner of living and feeling'.[12] His expedition ship, the *Géographe*, measured around 40 metres long and 10 metres wide[13] and left port packed with some 118 men. As the voyage wore on, the ship would have looked and smelt like a zoo. It sailed back to France with at least 70 live animals;[14] by the end of the voyage, all the scientists and officers had been crammed into the great cabin and gun-room so that the animals could be penned in the cabins. This zoological manifest does not include the usual stowaways to be found on sailing ships at the time. As one of the officers who sailed on Bruni d'Entrecasteaux's expedition, Pierre Roch Jurien de la Gravière, noted: 'The cockroaches had multiplied with such fertility that the corvettes had become infested with them [...], the rats on their side had multiplied with no less success. All these animals caused a nauseating smell'.[15] This kind of aroma was no doubt enhanced by the shellfish buried in buckets of sand and left to decay so their shells could be emptied and cleaned by the scientists. Scurvy-stricken men too 'gave out a fetid smell', writes one of Baudin's medical officers, Hubert Jules Taillefer, 'which, when you breathed it, seemed to attack the very root of life'.[16] The men's water was rationed so that no animal went thirsty, the ship's provisions probably provided little by way of nutrition or palatability, and – *quelle horreur!* – there was a chronic shortage of alcohol.

In addition to the usual physical discomforts, shipboard relations throughout the expedition were characterised by disobedience, insolence and spite. Of the 238 men (not including 11 stowaways and two passengers) who left France in 1800 on the *Géographe* and the *Naturaliste*, more than 60 deserted, defected or died.[17] Ten of the 22 scientists left the expedition before it had even reached New Holland. Only four, including Péron, saw the voyage to its completion.[18] Yet he achieved extraordinary results. Having already sent some 40,000 specimens back to France on the *Naturaliste* in November 1802,[19] Péron complemented the *Géographe*'s menagerie with some 300 living plants and some 200 crates of specimens.[20] It is no wonder he received a rapturous response from the scientific community. Pre-eminent zoologist and comparative anatomist Georges Cuvier, chairman of the Commission of the Institut de France and former teacher of Péron, praised his protégé's 'zeal and dedication'.[21] Cuvier compared the haul of some 2,500 species hitherto unknown to European science to that of Cook's second voyage, which 'did not produce more than two hundred and fifty new species', and to the outcomes of the voyages of Philip Carteret, Samuel Wallis, Tobias Furneaux, John Meares and George Vancouver combined. Péron and the artist Charles-Alexandre Lesueur, he concludes, 'have made known more new creatures than all recent travelling naturalists put together'.[22]

> We are not afraid to declare that such work is infinitely superior to everything of a similar nature that has thus far been performed on expeditions of discovery, whether French or foreign.[23]

Cuvier's words are particularly useful for the way in which they position Péron's work in the cultural and political contexts of the times. They highlight the culture of flattery, usually the preserve of inferiors hoping to cultivate their superiors. But in this example, it is a form of self-aggrandisement, with the flatterer acknowledging his own success as a teacher and scientist by flattering his student, and in doing so showing himself to be a person of sensibility and thus, of social stature. We will say more about this 'feedback loop' of flattery later. Moreover, Cuvier's comparison of Péron's achievements with those of the other voyagers, all of whom were British, demonstrates an environment in which the pursuit of intellectual empire, procured by the supposedly neutral pursuit of scientific knowledge, was a competition if not a combat. This political context is further revealed in the opening statements of Péron's *Voyage*, in which he writes:

> Since the time when scientific discoveries were rightfully placed among mankind's principal claims to glory and prosperity, a noble competition has developed between nations, fresh scope for rivalry between governments has been created [. . .]. English scholars, spread over the

> immense stage of one fifth of the world, were possibly on the brink, in several respects, of deciding the opinion of Europe in their nation's favour. [...] In such a state of affairs, national honour and the progress of science amongst us united to call for an expedition of discovery to the Southern Lands [...].[24]

The connection between national honour and scientific progress – and its resulting strategic and economic advantages – had already been made evident by Napoleon Bonaparte. 'The true power of the French republic must henceforth consist in not allowing there to be new ideas which do not belong to it', he writes in a letter to the Directorate of the Institut after his election to its First Class (the scientific section) in December 1797.[25] This proprietary attitude is echoed in Baudin's instructions from the Minister of Marine and Colonies, Pierre-Alexandre-Laurent Forfait, dated 29 September 1800. Stressing the need for government control over all aspects of the expedition, Forfait writes:

> It is the Republic who is defraying the entire cost of the expedition: it is she alone who must reap the benefit of it. Therefore make it known that whoever disobeys this just prohibition shall be severely and rigorously dealt with [...]. Announce that no one must permit himself [...] to send reports to Europe that could defraud the Government of its right of property over the results of the expedition.[26]

In this heightened – even paranoid – political climate, natural science in little-known places was a form of strategic reconnaissance, and the products of scientific discovery, pure and applied, were to be seized and defended for the Empire. The battle for intellectual territory was especially fierce given that, despite the peaceful veneer of this 'noble competition', the opposing sides were traditional military combatants. Even the smallest gain by the other was a loss to France. Péron describes as a 'sort of national spoliation' the fate of shells collected by some of his companions that had 'passed into the hands of some Englishmen at

Port Jackson' and thence to 'British museums priding themselves upon our own discoveries'. 'In every instance', he adds, 'it must be considered a sort of crime in the eyes of a man of honour to hand over the fruits of these labours to foreigners – even enemies of one's country'.[27]

A veteran of the Revolutionary Wars, Péron was willing to volunteer and then fight for a place in this new campaign.[28] He calls the quest for scientific discoveries a 'glorious struggle' in which 'France alone has been able to challenge [England] successfully in her triumphs and her superiority'.[29] Thus, in addition to the obvious celebration of fraternity that we saw in his account of his salvation at Bernier Island, there is a hint of battlefield reminiscence:

> Dawn was already starting to break when I heard a gunshot in the distance ... This sound filled me with the sweetest emotion; my courage rose, and at about six o'clock I found myself amongst my comrades. [...] M. Picquet, lieutenant commander, [...] had led his men out to look for me.[30]

It is also not insignificant that Péron's discoveries were made on an expedition of two naval ships whose renaming as the *Géographe* and the *Naturaliste* further blurred the lines between martial and scientific endeavour. Péron refers to his later work on King Island as 'special operations',[31] and his eulogist Deleuze, perhaps drawing upon the testimony of Péron's colleagues, writes that 'if he were occupied in some important scientific research, he disposed of those who could assist him as though they were under his orders'.[32] With his specialised training, his esoteric procedures and his endorsement by the future Emperor, Péron was indeed a special agent. There are similarities and slippages between scientific collecting and other intelligence gathering activities: both seek to reveal, analyse and impose authority over information; both can be used to capture and organise, exploit and control. On the expedition and in its literary aftermath, these attributes also provided equal opportunity for Péron to prove his imperialist credentials.[33] Little wonder, then, that the self-proclaimed scientist-spy took it upon himself to gather intelligence at Port Jackson;[34] that his descriptions of Bernier Island, with their careful noting of landing places and of the geology which, he writes, 'could supply masonry with evenly cut building stone',[35] read as a survey of a military installation as much as of a place of scientific fieldwork. And no wonder that with field naturalists deployed like foot soldiers, fighting at the edges of maps and on the frontiers of knowledge, an ardent young patriot like Péron could write of chivalry and valour, and be esteemed for sacrificing blood for the Cause.

Testing Grounds

Nicolas Baudin's sea log provides copious examples of the 'special operations' of these soldier-scientists. On 10 December 1802 he watched as the *Géographe*'s dinghy set off to land on King Island in Bass Strait, carrying not only Péron and his colleagues but also, the Commander grimly notes, 'their knowledge and their baggage, for these gentlemen never move without pomp and magnificence'.[36] The symbolic claiming of territory was worthy of a show, if not of firearms and flags, then of something perhaps just as powerful: expertise, represented by penknives, trowels, ring-nets, vascula, specimen bottles, notebooks and eventually, scientific labels and the voyage account. The scientists' sense of superiority which so irritated Baudin is nevertheless understandable: these cocky young men embodied the aspirations and authority of their teachers and their times. As Tony Ballantyne explains, they were operating in a crucial testing ground for European science – and European people.[37] Exploration in the Pacific shaped emergent scientific disciplines, such as anthropology, and their claims to cultural authority within Europe. Exploration also shaped emergent scientists, who were keen to justify their existence, prove their legitimacy and consolidate their authority. Péron's presence on the voyage had already proved his scientific commitment, but proving his scientific *credentials* – his expertise and ability to do the work in a practical sense – was another matter.

Providing proof was a challenge. Knowledge has a geography as well as a history. As noted by Dorinda Outram: 'Sociologists like Erving Goffman have pointed out that the spaces of scientific knowledge have often determined the degree of credence given to claims of expert knowledge'.[38] The testing ground for these voyaging scientists was a long way away from their controlling hub of knowledge production, the Muséum national d'Histoire naturelle in Paris. Laboratories, lecture theatres and museum galleries manifest and impose structures of authority, influence and access to knowledge; if these literal and symbolic structures do not exist, it is difficult to determine that authority and that influence, and who has access to them. It is even more difficult to lend credence to knowledge derived from a field naturalist moving rapidly through a space, like Péron, rather that dwelling in it, sometimes literally, as Cuvier did in his cabinet at the Museum. In 1807, Cuvier argued that, compared to a sedentary (and ostensibly less heroic) cabinet naturalist such as himself, the observations made by such men of action were 'broken and fleeting.' He writes: 'The field naturalist [...] is struck, one after the other, by a great number of interesting objects and living things. [...] But he can only give a few instances of time to each of them.' By contrast, Cuvier declares:

> If the sedentary naturalist does not see nature in action, he can yet survey all her products spread before him. He can compare them with each other as often as is necessary to reach reliable conclusions [...]. The traveller can only travel one road; it is only really in one's study (*cabinet*) that one can roam freely throughout the universe [...].[39]

Furthermore, the data required for the reliable conclusions so cherished by Cuvier could be compromised by time: the first volume of Péron's account, for example, was released three years after his return to France. What discrepancies would emerge from the raw data when reexamined? How would scribbled notebooks transmogrify into elegant yet accurate prose? Given these factors of space and time, presence and absence, field naturalists and their findings posed something of an epistemological problem: could they be trusted?

David Livingstone believes that 'the circulation of scientific knowledge was an inescapably *social* affair involving judgments about people.'[40] Trust was in large part derived by deploying field scientists with sufficient technical competence to reliably observe and record data. On King Island, Péron was forced to subcontract this competence.

Unable to study first-hand the island's endemic dwarf emu (except for those he ate in a stew), he garnered the birds' behavioural ecology via a 33 point questionnaire with a man he himself considered trustworthy: a sealer by the name of Daniel Cooper.[41] The questionnaire allows the reader to virtually witness not just the species but also Péron at work; Péron's account seems all the more trustworthy because his own credibility gave him the discernment to judge his sources likewise. In a discussion of a partial English-language translation of the questionnaire, Louis Brasil remarks that it 'shows us how carefully these travellers were making their investigations and to what degree of confidence we can accept their observations'.[42]

Péron reiterated his supposed trustworthiness by reminding his readers of the trustworthiness of those who had taught him. In his 'Dissertation on the New Genus *Pyrosoma*', for example, he notes: 'My predecessors had always lacked good texts, but I – a pupil for four years in M. Cuvier's school – I had as a guide, not only his method and principles, but also the handwritten instructions that he had been kind enough to draw up for me upon my departure from Europe.'[43] This is one of Péron's numerous references to his teachers – who, it must be remembered, were also the commissioners and consumers of his work (he notes that 'a fifth position as zoologist had just been granted to me on the recommendation of several illustrious scientists'[44]). Seen in the context of the culture of flattery mentioned earlier, such references can be regarded as a highly conscious payment of dues. (This also suggests that Cuvier was a kind of commanding general, deploying and controlling his scientist in the field.) Another example of Péron's drive to prove the integrity of his observations – and acknowledge the patronage of the Institut – is to be found in his discussion of the 'massacres'[45] of King Island's elephant seals by Daniel Cooper's men: 'this eloquent prediction by one of my earliest and dearest teachers will undoubtedly come true', he writes, before going on to quote from Lacépède's *Natural History of Cetaceans*: 'This great species will [...] disappear from the face of the earth [...]. It will exist only in the memory of men and in works of genius.'[46] By quoting Lacépède in his own account of the seals, Péron includes himself in the company of this scientist and declares the genius of his own work.

Péron's proof of the superior truth-value of his findings was also bound up in his bodily experiences. Returning to his account of Bernier Island, we can see how he used his sufferings to indicate his moral courage – his acceptance, even desire to put his body on the line for the Cause – and to establish his intellectual credibility with his audience. As Livingstone writes: 'Because credibility was invested in the authority of the person, the moral economy of wounds assumed a great importance in calibrating trust'. Suffering is thus a line of enquiry, another kind of witnessing, with 'the signs of truth imprinted in the flesh'.[47] If the credence and authority of knowledge are influenced by, if not embedded in, the place of its creation and dissemination, and if natural history is a kind of strategic reconnaissance, then it was in Péron's own body that the space and place of science – the mental endeavour and the material world – merged.

Other examples of this merging can be found throughout Péron's *Voyage*. Stranded at the Wonnerup Inlet in southwest Australia in June 1801, for instance, Péron reported 'violent colic and abdominal debility, with which I, myself, was attacked during the night' after ingesting the 'very bitter sap' of samphire. Returning to the ship, he was 'in such a state of collapse, that my friends could scarcely recognise me, so greatly had I been tortured by the lack of sleep, exhaustion and the colic brought on by the samphire and the brackish water'. He added: 'there seemed to me no doubt that a few more days of this kind of diet would have been sufficient to kill us all.'[48]

In March 1803, lost and tormented with the gardener Antoine Guichenot and artist Nicolas-Martin Petit in a part of western Australia now called the Peron Peninsula, Péron documents the symptoms of heat stroke:

> Our bodies ran with constant and excessive sweat; our weakness was soon at its height. In vain did we fill our mouths with small pebbles to induce a few drops of saliva – the supply appeared to have dried up; a feeling of desiccation and distressing aridity and an unbearable bitterness made our breathing difficult and somehow painful; our trembling legs could no longer support us;

one or other of us fell at every moment, and it was a long
time before we could get up again.

Along with 'the burning in our mouths' and 'the painful gnawing at our stomachs', Péron notes 'I could barely distinguish objects; my hearing was almost gone; and my withered tongue could not form words'. Then, almost as if turning the lens on a microscope, he changes focus in a footnote with the remark: 'This effect of starvation upon the organs of sight and hearing appears to me to merit the interests of physiologists.' He supports these observations by quoting Jean de Léry, who explored Brazil in 1578.[49] Péron's body was both a specimen for analysis and a laboratory for testing theories and reaching conclusions, as much as any room in the Museum. His accounts of his sufferings demonstrated he had the sensory competence to be trusted. But in addition to being a venue of and for science, could he have also considered himself a *victim* for science?

The Sentimental Traveller

At least two of Péron's eulogies comment on his sensibility. The physician Kéraudren wrote that Péron's 'physiognomy always bore an expression of gentleness and sensibility: the warmth of his intellect, the vivacity of his character were tempered by an extreme kindness that came straight from the heart; to his other attributes was added an extreme modesty'.[50] The Museum's librarian, Deleuze, said he was possessed of 'a lively imagination, an ardent soul and extreme sensibility. These attributes are allied with genius'.[51] Sensibility – in terms of its literal definition of having a capacity for feeling, of being physically and mentally perceptive – was a good trait in a naturalist, guided as he was (or was supposed to have been) by what his senses told him; ostensibly by his experiences and observations alone. It re-confirmed the credibility of his discoveries and voyage account, since they would have been keenly observed and carefully noted. As Livingstone writes, 'the disciplining of the senses and the deprivation of the body were taken as mutually confirming'.[52]

However, and as his eulogists indicate, Péron was also guided by the alternative concept of sensibility. Defined as acute consciousness, delicate and discerning taste, and refined intellect and judgement, this sensibility unites the physical with the moral. It provided the psychological framework for Péron's observations and voyage account – which is perhaps unsurprising for a naturalist who emerged in a Revolutionary philosophical and political climate in which nature and the natural were held as ethical touchstones. Jacobin rhetoric dictated that by illuminating nature and making its order 'visible, accessible and transparent',[53] natural scientists would contribute to the moral uplift and political and civic regeneration of the People. Péron's self-conscious and effusive writing style, with its heavy emphasis on physical, sensory experiences and moral judgements, is perhaps symptomatic of his self-serving need to illuminate and elucidate contemporary concerns. Furthermore, it marked him as a civilised person undertaking civilised acts. But Péron's voyage account also reflects contemporary aesthetic expectations. His positioning of himself as the observing subject of his narrative, constantly reacting to external stimuli and interpreting them for his readers, owes much not only to scientific technique but to sentimental literature, which in Europe reached its height of popularity just before the French Revolution. His eulogist, Deleuze, certainly noticed the difference between Péron's writing and that in the more traditional tomes in the Museum's library, commenting: 'One can [...] reproach him with having sometimes employed a colourful style, ill-suited to narrative simplicity. This shortcoming was the inevitable consequence of a very lively imagination and possibly, also, the stylistic conventions that several writers have adopted today.'[54]

In *Virtue in Distress*, Robert Brissenden dissects François Vernes's *The Sentimental Traveller*, first published in 1786, to discuss these stylistic conventions. In a sequence of episodes or cameos, Vernes's sentimental traveller interacts with a variety of disadvantaged people: an orphan and a crippled soldier; a blind man and his daughter; a man and his five children clustered around the dead body of their mother, and so on. The sentimental traveller, the man of feeling, is the only link between each victim of misfortune. Investing each episode with wider meanings, he reveals his value system, which figures Enlightenment theories of morality. For example, the traveller meets an impoverished butcher who explains that he lost his job because he did not want to kill his friend, his pet sheep. Profoundly moved, the traveller declares that he has always loved the peasantry, 'and in general those whom heaven has created our equals but whom chance has placed beneath us'. Each victim leads the traveller to make similar conclusions and take actions of compassionate solidarity.[55] Although the stories are fiction, the philosophy is not: the link between the sentimental and the political is clear. The reader is encouraged to sympathise with the victims and share the traveller's conclusions because the traveller's observations are founded in his sensibility (in both senses of the word). His subjective experiences are authoritative because they are felt personally and are thus authentic, and because they are interpreted through the appropriate moral lens. Readers who discern and share these views are validated for their own sensibility.

Péron's narrative features several instances in which the narrator demonstrates a similar writing style and reveals a similar value system. We saw earlier his sentimental description of the noble self-sacrifice of the banded hare-wallabies, doing everything to protect their 'sweet burdens'. In another example, the salvation of the hungry and rain-soaked Péron in 1803 thanks to the English sealers on King Island, there is something of the noble savage in his depiction of their leader, 'the honest Cowper' (he meant Daniel Cooper) and his gang. Despite living in what Péron called 'wretched hovels' of wood and bark, being warmed by a 'great fire kept burning day and night with big tree trunks', and wearing clothes made 'by subjecting seal and kangaroo skins to some rough preparation', the sealers nevertheless 'all enjoyed the most vigorous good health'. Péron wrote that 'these good men overwhelmed us with demonstrations of concern and kindness.' He could not resist drawing an ideological conclusion:

> Why is it that this touching hospitality [...] should almost always be shown by men whose roughness of character and miserable condition seem least to oblige them to act in this way!... Alas, rather than our brilliant education and philosophy, it would be more fitting to develop in us that noble and disinterested quality that gives us sympathy for another's troubles![56]

King Island's elephant seals are to Péron, for a few pages at least, yet another group of heroic victims. He pronounced them 'gentle, innocent', 'good, docile', 'intelligent, gentle', 'good', 'peaceful' and 'so powerful, so gentle and so unfortunate'. 'One can wander amongst them without fear; and none of them have ever been seen to lunge at a man unless they were attacked or provoked in the most violent manner.'[57] Most 'gentle and peaceful' were the females who, Péron noted, 'rarely meet violence with violence [...]. If their retreat is cut off, they shake violently; an expression of despair comes into their eyes and they dissolve into tears.' He bolsters this observation with a declaration of his own sensibility:

> I, myself, saw one of these young females shedding copious tears while one of our sailors (a cruel, wicked man) amused himself, every time she opened her mouth, by smashing her teeth with the broad end of one of the oars from our long-boat. This poor animal filled one with pity; her whole mouth was bleeding, and tears streamed from her eyes.[58]

However, this sentimental traveller did not necessarily combine his moral pronouncements with acts of mercy. He did not stop the sailor from torturing the seal, nor had he prevented his companions from slaughtering the vulnerable wallabies on Bernier Island. (Instead, in another example of his ability to coolly switch modes of enquiry, he wrote that the wallabies' flesh 'seemed to us [...] to be rather like that of the wild rabbit, but more aromatic [...]. It is, moreover, the best of the kangaroo flesh that we discovered subsequently'.[59]) Péron's sentimentalism is both obvious and ambiguous. As David Denby writes, sentimentalism can be 'an act of enthrallment, an expression of the power of the dominant to *choose* to behave with humanity towards those placed under them'.[60] Péron's accounts of these episodes emphasise the victims' undeserving torment. This emphasis gives his subsequent conclusion a reason to exist: if Péron had made the sailor stop his attack, he would not have been able to write about the man's cruelty and wickedness, and to thus imply how virtuous he was to have noticed such cruelty (and differentiate himself from the wicked sailor). If he had told his companions to spare the female wallabies with pouch young, he then would have been denied the opportunity to exquisitely emote over the mothers' noble self-sacrifice. Péron needed to describe violence in order to describe his reaction to it, and to again assert his philosophical credentials with sympathetic readers. However, his often startling ability to disengage from an object that he could closely – sometimes almost simultaneously – engage with as a subject allowed him also to retain credibility as an appropriately remote observer drawing rational conclusions rather than choosing to intervene with humane practical action that would have disrupted the natural order of things.[61] This choice to remain aloof is another expression of the power of the dominant and, in this case, the credible. It is interesting to speculate whether Péron deliberately employed the licence of science in these situations to disguise or justify the fatal consequences of scientific collecting and thus avoid – and also spare his sympathetic readers – accusations of moral hypocrisy.

Another reason Péron may have recorded, perhaps even indulged in, such episodes of suffering – and then done nothing to alleviate them – is because as a long-suffering scientist/soldier/specimen, he judged the animals' victimhood useful evidence to prove a personal point. His own experiences of suffering not only allow him to draw moral conclusions about others' torment, but also encourage the reader to draw conclusions about Péron's own – to choose (to paraphrase Denby) to react with humanity towards *him*. In this feedback loop of flattery, a sympathetic reader's virtue was validated and their power, demonstrated by their choice to be sympathetic, acknowledged and confirmed. Péron in turn received validation from his readers, especially his powerful patrons at the Institut, for the worth (and worthiness) of his endeavours. His struggles to overcome his vulnerability in a harsh and heartless environment rendered his outcomes triumphant. For an audience for whom Revolutionary violence was a fresh memory, Péron's sufferings – or his account of them – may have been redolent of the glorious struggle for the new Republic. As we have seen, drawing such parallels may have indeed been Péron's aim. His body and his narrative map imperialist expansion, charting new intellectual territory at the expense of a willing casualty, himself. His victimhood for science was thus justifiable, authentic, credible and virtuous: a politically, technically and philosophically appropriate account of conquest upon which a reader can agonise, marvel and be legitimised without being subjected to such calamities themselves.

Whether through design or circumstance, Péron's 'product of many perils and much labour' proved effective. Collecting possessions for his nation, he himself became a national possession. 'The first volume of the *Voyage* appeared at the beginning of 1807', writes his eulogist Deleuze, 'and from then on Péron's worth could be fully appreciated.' Whether a warrior, a witness, a victim or a young provincial genius desperate for validation, Péron achieved his ambitions. He was someone, as Deleuze concluded, 'to whom science has so great an obligation'.[62]

Notes

1. François Péron (continued by Louis Freycinet), *Voyage of Discovery to the Southern Lands*, Adelaide: The Friends of the State Library of South Australia, translation of the second edition (1824) by Christine Cornell, 2 vols, 2006/2003, vol. 1, pp. 88, 94, 95, 99.
2. Péron, *Voyage of Discovery*, vol. 1, p. 96.
3. *Ibid.*, p. 99.
4. *Ibid.*, p. 100.
5. *Ibid.*, p. 101.
6. *Ibid.*, p. 102.
7. *Ibid.*, p. 100.
8. Joseph Philippe François Deleuze, 'Historical Eulogy of François Péron', in Péron, *Voyage of Discovery*, vol. 1, p. lxxx.
9. Pierre-François Kéraudren, 'Nécrologie'. Cited in Edward Duyker, *François Péron, an Impetuous Life: Naturalist and Voyager*, Melbourne: The Miegunyah Press, 2006, p. 9.
10. For example, see Deleuze, 'Historical Eulogy', pp. lxv, lxvii, lxxvi.
11. Anonymous review, 'Émile Guillaumin, *François Péron*', *Bulletin de la Société d'Émulation du Bourbonnais*, vol. 39, 1936, p. 112. Cited in Duyker, *François Péron, an Impetuous Life*, p. 3.
12. Draft letter, Péron to a friend, Muséum d'Histoire naturelle, Le Havre, Collection Lesueur, 14 047. Cited in Duyker, *François Péron, an Impetuous Life*, p. 45.
13. Frank Horner, *The French Reconnaissance: Baudin in Australia, 1801–1803*, Carlton: Melbourne University Press, 1987, p. 57.
14. *Ibid.*, p. 328.
15. Cited in John Dunmore, *French Explorers in the Pacific*, Oxford: Clarendon, 2 vols, 1965–1969, vol. 1, p. 40.
16. Cited in Dunmore, *French Explorers*, vol. 1, p. 42.
17. Horner, *The French Reconnaissance*, p. 63; Duyker, *François Péron, an Impetuous Life*, pp. 70–71.
18. Georges Cuvier, in his report on the expedition, puts this number at three, but in addition to Péron, the geographer Charles Pierre Boullanger, the gardener Antoine Guichenot, and the mineralogist Joseph Charles Bailly returned to France on the *Géographe*. Three others also completed the exploration of Australia: the botanist Théodore Leschenault (who returned to France in 1807), the geographer Pierre Auguste Faure (who disembarked in Mauritius where he remained till his death

in 1855), and the mineralogist Louis Depuch (who died in Mauritius during the journey home). See Georges Cuvier, 'Report Presented to the Government by the Institut de France on the Voyage of Discovery to the Southern Lands: Extract of the Proceedings of the Division of Physical and Mathematical Sciences Session of Monday 9 June 1806'. English translation in Péron, *Voyage of Discovery*, vol. 1 (see p. lxii). Also cited in Horner, *The French Reconnaissance*, pp. 2–3, 374–376.
19 Péron, *Voyage of Discovery*, vol. 1, p. 329. Commanded by Emmanuel Hamelin, the *Naturaliste* returned to France on 7 June 1803 loaded with sick and 'unfit' humans as well as the preserved specimens and one live emu, one black swan, six other birds, three wombats, two dingoes, two Indian gazelles, a four-horned ram, and a long-necked tortoise (Horner, *The French Reconnaissance*, pp. 251–252, 358).
20 Horner, *The French Reconnaissance*, p. 328; Richard W. Burkhardt, Jr. 'Unpacking Baudin: Models of Scientific Practice in the Age of Lamarck', in Goulven Laurent (ed.), *Jean-Baptiste Lamarck 1744–1829*, Paris: CTHS, 1997, p. 506.
21 Cuvier, 'Report', in Péron, *Voyage of Discovery*, vol. 1, p. lv.
22 *Ibid.*, p. lvi.
23 *Ibid.*, p. lix.
24 Péron, *Voyage of Discovery*, vol. 1, p. 3. In reality, the expedition was Nicolas Baudin's suggestion. See, for example, Horner, *The French Reconnaissance*, pp. 37–40.
25 Napoléon Bonaparte, *Correspondance de Napoléon I*, vol. 3, no. 2392. Cited in Maurice Crosland, *The Society of Arcueil: A View of French Science in the Time of Napoleon*, London: Heinemann, 1967, p. 13.
26 Pierre-Alexandre-Laurent Forfait, 'The Minister of Marine and Colonies to Citizen Baudin, Post Captain, Commander-in-Chief of the Corvettes, *Géographe* and *Naturaliste*', in Nicolas Baudin, *The Journal of Post Captain Nicolas Baudin, Commander-in-Chief of the Corvettes* Géographe *and* Naturaliste, translated by Christine Cornell, Adelaide: Libraries Board of South Australia, 1974, p. 8.
27 Péron, *Voyage of Discovery*, vol. 2, p. 135. His assumption that the specimens were his to take in the first place speaks volumes.
28 He had served for almost three years in the 2nd Allier Battalion of Volunteers, had been wounded in battle, and kept as a prisoner of war in Prussia (Duyker, *François Péron, an Impetuous Life*, pp. 22–36).
29 Péron, *Voyage of Discovery*, vol. 1, p. 3.
30 *Ibid.*, p. 100.
31 Péron, *Voyage of Discovery*, vol. 2, p. 19.
32 Deleuze, 'Historical Eulogy', p. lxxx.
33 'M. Péron particularly set himself to gain sound knowledge of all the details of that vast system of colonisation of the southern lands', Cuvier remarks. 'The entirety of his work in this connection appears bound to be of the greatest interest in every respect to both the philosopher and the statesman.' Cuvier, 'Report', in Péron, *Voyage of Discovery*, vol. 1, pp. lx–lxi. Perhaps Cuvier is here also proving his own credentials.
34 This reconnaissance has been the subject of much discussion, most recently in Jean Fornasiero and John West-Sooby, *French Designs on Colonial New South Wales: François Péron's Memoir on the English Settlements in New Holland, Van Diemen's Land and the Archipelagos of the Great Pacific Ocean*, Adelaide: Friends of the State Library of South Australia, 2014.
35 Péron, *Voyage of Discovery*, vol. 1, p. 92.
36 Baudin, *Journal*, p. 442.
37 See Tony Ballantyne (ed.), *Science, Empire and the European Exploration of the Pacific*, Aldershot: Ashgate, 2004.
38 Dorinda Outram, 'New Spaces in Natural History', in Nicholas Jardine, James A. Secord and Emma C. Spary (eds), *Cultures of Natural History*, Cambridge: Cambridge University Press, 1996, pp. 252–253.

39 Cited in Outram, 'New Spaces', pp. 261–262.
40 David Livingstone, *Putting Science in its Place*, Chicago and London: University of Chicago Press, 2003, p. 153.
41 Péron, *Voyage of Discovery*, vol. 2, pp. 14–15; Alphonse Milne-Edwards and Émile Oustalet, 'Note sur l'émeu noir (*Dromaeus ater V.*) de l'île Decrès (Australie)', *Bulletin du Muséum d'Histoire naturelle*, vol. 5, 1899, pp. 206–214. English language translation of entire questionnaire in Stephanie Pfennigwerth, 'New Creatures Made Known: (Re)discovering the Extinct King Island Emu', MA thesis, University of Tasmania, 2010, unpublished.
42 Louis Brasil, 'The Emu of King Island', *Emu*, vol. 14, no. 2, 1914, p. 94.
43 Péron, *Voyage of Discovery*, Book 5, 2007, p. 4.
44 Péron, *Voyage of Discovery*, vol. 1, p. 8.
45 Péron, *Voyage of Discovery*, vol. 2, p. 40.
46 *Ibid.*, p. 46.
47 Livingstone, *Putting Science in its Place*, p. 152.
48 Péron, *Voyage of Discovery*, vol. 1, pp. 78, 80–81, 81.
49 Péron, *Voyage of Discovery*, vol. 2, pp. 147–148.
50 Kéraudren, 'Nécrologie'. Cited in Duyker, *François Péron, an Impetuous Life*, p. 9.
51 Deleuze, 'Historical Eulogy', p. lxvii.
52 Livingstone, *Putting Science in its Place*, p. 152.
53 Outram, 'New Spaces', pp. 257–258.
54 Deleuze, 'Historical Eulogy', p. lxxvi. It is illuminating to compare Péron's writing with Baudin's matter-of-factness, for example, the latter's account from Kangaroo Island in January 1803 of being 'nearly crushed by a tree that fell in a different direction to the one expected. In coming down, it knocked me over, and I was so entangled in the branches that it took me a long time to free myself. I got off, however, with some cuts on the head and other parts of the body. This fall made me spend the night ashore, where I rested perfectly well, although extremely uncomfortably. We had very fine weather during the day, and overnight there was a slight easterly breeze which made the air very crisp, and even cold.' Baudin, *Journal*, p. 469.
55 See Robert Francis Brissenden, *Virtue in Distress: Studies in the Novel of Sentiment from Richardson to Sade*, London: Macmillan, 1974, pp. 3–23.
56 Péron, *Voyage of Discovery*, vol. 2, pp. 15, 16, 15, 18.
57 *Ibid.*, pp. 38, 42, 38.
58 *Ibid.*, p. 41.
59 Péron, *Voyage of Discovery*, vol. 1, p. 96.
60 David J. Denby, *Sentimentalism and the Social Order in France 1760–1820*, Cambridge, New York: Cambridge University Press, 1994, p. 48.
61 For further discussion of Péron's disengagement from King Island's elephant seals, see Stephanie Pfennigwerth, 'New Creatures Made Known: Some Animal Histories of the Baudin Expedition', in John West-Sooby (ed.), *Discovery and Empire: The French in the South Seas*, Adelaide: University of Adelaide Press, 2013, pp. 180–185.
62 Deleuze, 'Historical Eulogy', p. lxxxiii.

Part 3

The Scientific Record of the Voyage to the Southern Lands

Chapter 8

An Episode from the Baudin Expedition to the Southern Lands: the Return of the *Naturaliste* to France

Michel Jangoux[1]

In early August 1802, during the stopover in Port Jackson, Nicolas Baudin informed Captain Emmanuel Hamelin of his intention to send the *Naturaliste* back to France.[2] The commandant gave several reasons to justify his decision: the mediocre navigational qualities of the *Naturaliste* and its excessively deep draught, which prevented it from drawing close enough to the coast to effect geographical surveys; the conservation of the existing scientific collections, which would thus be spared any misadventures in the next stages of the expedition; the necessary replacement of those crew members from the *Géographe* who had died during the voyage by other crew from the *Naturaliste*; and also the opportunity to send home those 'useless' individuals whose departure, Baudin explained, would be a great relief to him and would greatly decrease the consumption of supplies.[3]

In Sydney, most of the collections made during the first campaign of the voyage were thus embarked on the *Naturaliste*, namely some 48 crates of zoological, botanical and mineralogical specimens, 30 or so live animals and 69 half-barrels of plants in full growth.[4] In a report to the commandant, François Péron gave a detailed description of the contents of the zoological collection.[5]

The *Géographe*, the *Naturaliste* and the *Casuarina* (the additional schooner purchased by the commandant in Sydney for hydrographical surveys) left Port Jackson together on 17 November and sailed in convoy to King Island. They separated on 8 December, the day the *Naturaliste* set sail for France. Hamelin reported that there were 59 crew members aboard (of whom five were in poor health) and three passengers (Surgeon James Thomson, his wife and servant).[6] Apart from the captain, the officers were Lieutenant Jacques Saint Cricq, Sub-lieutenants François Antoine Heirisson and Charles Moreau, and medical officers Jérôme Bellefin and Hubert Taillefer. There were also seven midshipmen (Hyacinthe Bougainville, François-Désiré Breton, Joseph Louis Brüe, Joseph Victor Couture, Étienne Duval Dailly, Antoine Giraud and Jean-Marie Maurouard) and a naturalist, the mineralogist Louis Depuch, who was seriously ill.[7] During the journey home, Hamelin was persuaded in equal measure by the state of health of the invalids and the urgent need to caulk his ship to make a brief stopover at the Île de France (Mauritius), where he stayed from 2 to 10 February 1803. He informed Baudin of this in a letter he left on the island:[8]

> Île de France, at moorings on the Île aux Tonneliers, on this day 19 Pluviôse Year 11 [8 February 1803]
>
> Citizen Commandant,
> Through the journal attached, you will become acquainted with the crossing that I have made and that I sincerely hoped to continue, in accordance with your orders, without calling in to port; I could indeed have completed it if my ship, which suffered heavy strains at sea, was not in urgent need of caulking, from the copper all the way up and also the manger-boards. I am still taking on water through the rabbet of the stem below the waterline, but I shall use the pumps to get to France.
> The only one of your animals I have lost is a turtledove from the Navigator Islands,[9] the rest appear to be in quite good health. I take care of all of them according to the advice you gave me. The plants are in quite good condition. The large tree from Timor is growing well. The New Zealand flax is flourishing. The Norfolk pines, which remained green for a long time, are starting to turn red; I hold great fears for them.
> In the month before our arrival here, M. Depuch was unable to keep down anything he ate, and was suffering

from the most violent attacks of colic; he could no longer walk on deck and would inevitably have died on board if I had not left him ashore.[10]

I also disembarked the old seaman suffering from fever and the novice with dysentery.[11] Two of my people seem to have deserted, the rest are in good health and dance every evening.[12] I am taking on ten men as replacements.[13] The government has given me three passengers;[14] among them is M. Lebas, who will not be in a position to compromise my mission. I was hoping to leave tomorrow, since the caulkers were finishing up today, but I doubt that General Magallon's packets are ready. He is giving me two gazelles and a sheep with four horns to take with me. For the six days I have been here, I have been exclusively occupied with the caulking and with adding to the collections. Yesterday I inspected the entire gun-room; there is not a single crate that is damp or that has been broken into by rats even though I have a lot of them.

I send you my sincere good wishes for the success of the next part of your glorious mission and for your own safety.

With respect and best regards,
Hamelin

I take the liberty of recommending to you my relative, midshipman Brèvedent.[15]

The corvette left Île de France on 10 February. It came within sight of the Scilly Islands on 25 May. During the entire Atlantic crossing, her situation continued to deteriorate: she was taking on two inches of water per hour when she left the French colony, but she took on four on 4 March and up to seven on 21 May; a few days earlier, on 18 May, the mainmast had split above the hounds.[16] Some of the caged birds died (the second turtledove from the Navigator Islands, a small emu, and the goose from Bass Strait), and the long-necked turtle laid several eggs. The plants suffered particularly from the cold and even more so from the rats. On 30 April Hamelin wrote in his journal that 'the rats eat all the buds as soon as they appear. I had sown some seeds and watched them sprout with great pleasure, but the rats have destroyed everything. As soon as a tree has a few leaves, the rats immediately strip them off'.[17] Nearly a month later, on 26 May, when they were offshore from Torquay, the captain hailed a fishing boat and sent across the Thomsons and their servant; this was how they reached England. The Thomsons had barely been gone for an hour when two British ships loomed up in front of the *Naturaliste* and fired a cannon shot at her to make her bring to. Hamelin and the *Naturaliste* were subject to a number of incidents which kept them in Portsmouth until 6 June, the day when, thanks to the intervention of Sir Joseph Banks, they were finally able to leave for Le Havre, where they berthed on 7 June. Hamelin concluded his report, addressed to Charles-Henri Bertin, the Maritime Prefect of Le Havre, in these terms:[18]

> On 18 Prairial [7 June 1803] [. . .] at 11 am we entered the port of Le Havre. The corvette is taking on eight inches of water an hour, most of which is entering through the rabbet of the stem on the larboard. On board I have three prisoners who were a great help to me working the ship; I shall send them to the admiral.[19] I have on board a Spaniard of Indian origin who I believe to be from California, and whom I took on at Botany Bay where he had been left as a prisoner of war.[20] For the Museum, I have brought two black swans, one emu, three wombats, one long-necked turtle, two pigeons, two dogs, one ram with four horns, all living specimens. I also have two gazelles from India, two quails, two other birds whose destination I can reveal to you.[21]

The same day that the *Naturaliste* arrived in Le Havre, the Maritime Prefect informed the Minister: 'She entered port at 9.30 am. Captain Hamelin requested my permission to go to Paris to report to you directly on the circumstances of his voyage; I saw no reason to refuse his request'.[22] Hamelin then disappeared definitively from the scene as far as the expedition was concerned.[23]

The news of the *Naturaliste*'s return spread rapidly. In the minutes of the meeting of the committee of the professors of the Museum, dated 15 June, we read:

> According to the advice we have received concerning the arrival of the *Naturaliste*, sent by Captain Baudin, and concerning the details of the objects, it was determined that a member of the Museum staff would be invited to go to Le Havre to pick them up and that he would request an audience with the Ministers of the Interior and the Marine in order to obtain the letters he would need to accomplish that mission. Several parcels relating to this expedition have been sent to the Museum. It was determined that they would be opened by two ad hoc commissioners. Citizens Thouin and Jussieu were nominated. They will write a report and bring it to the next meeting of the committee.[24]

This was indeed what the commissioners did as soon as the consignment arrived, and the report they made of its contents is attached to the minutes of the committee meeting of 22 June 1803.[25] The consignment was made up of nine parcels: the first three contained a journal and different documents written in the hand of the gardener Anselme Riedlé; the fourth, personal belongings of Riedlé; the fifth, the journal of the assistant gardener Antoine Sautier; the sixth, the journal and drawings of the zoologist Stanislas Levillain; the seventh and eighth, personal belongings of the zoologist René Maugé; and the ninth, the death certificates of Riedlé, Maugé and Sautier, as well as a note about the sums of money found in their possession. The professors thus received confirmation of Riedlé's death and learnt of the death of the three other naturalists: Levillain, Maugé and Sautier.

Naturally, the professors were not the only ones to have been informed of the return of the *Naturaliste*. Jean-Antoine Chaptal, the Minister of the Interior, had also heard about it, and he lost no time in proposing himself, in a letter to Museum director Antoine-Laurent de Jussieu dated 15 June, as the spokesman for Mme Bonaparte:[26]

> Citizen, you are to receive a collection of seeds and exotic plants made by Captain Baudin in the course of his voyage to enrich your establishment. I want you to set aside for Mme Bonaparte all of the objects in this collection that she requests of you. Citizen Mirbel will visit you on her behalf and acquaint you with her intentions, to which I invite and authorise you to acquiesce.[27]

It was also Chaptal who, in a letter to the professors, chose André Thouin, the Professor of Horticulture, to go to Le Havre to assemble the natural history collection and send it to Paris. In his letter, the Minister reminded the professors not to overlook the spouse of the First Consul: 'I am advising you that the two black swans that are part of the collection are reserved for Mme Bonaparte and must be handed over to her as soon as they arrive'.[28] As for Charles-Pierre Claret de Fleurieu, then Acting Minister of Marine,[29] he assured the professors that he intended to do everything in his power to facilitate Citizen Thouin's mission.[30] The same Fleurieu addressed a letter to the Maritime Prefect of Le Havre the following day:

> Upon receiving this letter, Citizen Prefect, kindly give orders for the *Naturaliste* to be decommissioned and for the crew to be given the respite it needs after the long period of navigation it has just completed. I authorise you to grant a period of two months' leave both to the officers and midshipmen and to the other men in the crew.[31]

Moreover, he confirmed Thouin's mission with the prefect and called on him to place himself at Thouin's disposal. It was on 27 June, in the absence of the captain of the *Naturaliste*, that they proceeded to decommission the corvette. At the time, Hamelin was in Paris where he had delivered Baudin's correspondence and the journals of the officers of the *Naturaliste*, as well as the maps, charts, etc, that the commandant had entrusted to him. He had given them to Minister Denis Decrès who had had them sent, on 12 June, to General François Étienne de Rosily, head of the Hydrographic Service of the Marine in Paris.[32] A shrewd administrator, the Minister also made enquiries to the Marine authorities in Le Havre about the state of the accounts of the corvette. The only response of the Acting Prefect Reinaud was to send him a kind of report in which he highlighted what was missing:

> I was given no register or paperwork relative to the accounts for food supplies during the campaign. Citizen Saint Cricq, first lieutenant, of whom they were requested, declared that he had no knowledge of any accounts, and that Captain Hamelin was the only one who could offer any explanation for them. This captain is, indeed, the only one to have signed the registers for the masters' supplies. Your predecessor, Citizen Minister, made the decision at commandant Baudin's request, when the expedition departed in Year 9 [1800], that there would be no accountant on board.[33]

Let us return now to Thouin's mission. Named by the Minister on 16 June, he left Paris on the 19th, arrived in Le Havre on the 20th and immediately went on board the *Naturaliste* to examine the state of the collections brought home by the corvette. The very next day, he made a report to the Maritime Prefect (who was thinking of sending the objects to the Museum by road as far as Rouen and from there by river) insisting on the importance of transferring the collections by water exclusively. The prefect, who was anxious to respect the orders received from the Ministers of Marine and the Interior, immediately accepted Thouin's proposal and responded by saying 'put two lighters at [his] disposal in order to have them sent to Paris'.[34] The next day, 22 June, Thouin made a report to his colleagues at the Museum in a letter whose contents they became acquainted with during their committee meeting on the 29th.[35]

Le Havre, 3 Messidor Year 11 [22 June 1803]
To the citizens and members of the Professors' Committee of the Museum
Citizens and Colleagues,

After leaving Paris on 30 Prairial [19 June], I arrived in Le Havre on 1 Messidor [20 June] at 7 pm. My first concern was to visit the ship, the *Naturaliste*, which had been in port for several days. The living plants on board, which were in half-barrels that occupied most of the space, were the first things that came to my attention, and upon examining them closely I was deeply affected. Everything appeared to me to be dead, or just about. Of the 800 individual specimens collected, both in Timor and in New Holland, 20 or so gave some signs of life and there were only 12 or 15 in full vegetation. The dry conditions, the rats which have overrun the ship, and the lack of proper care are the cause of this truly deplorable loss.

The living animals, whose number decreased during the crossing, seemed to me in good health, particularly the black swans, the possums, a doe from the Ganges, a very small long-necked turtle, the cassowary and the quails from Port Jackson. But some of them are lame and listless. Among them are the Indian stag, the four-horned ram, which they claim to be the species from Kashmir, and the dog from Port Jackson whose back is broken.

The crates of minerals, dried plants, madrepores, shells, insects, birds and quadrupeds seemed to me to be properly packed. They were enclosed in the hold, protected from the humidity, and perfectly intact. Only an examination of the inside of the crates will provide the means of evaluating the state of conservation of this part of the consignment, and you are the ones, citizens, who will enjoy the privilege of opening them.

According to the outward state of the living plants, I had considered that we could dispense with sending to

Paris the half-barrels in which they were contained and where there remained nothing living, and to decrease transport costs by this means. However, given that the soil probably contains a great quantity of seeds from the land where it was taken, and that, on the other hand, that good and unfortunate soul Riedlé will certainly have planted in it the bulbous and tuberous roots that he encountered, and last of all that, according to his instructions, he was required to layer it with some of the seeds that he collected in the same countries, I thought it useful to send all of the barrels.

To this effect, the next day, first thing in the morning, I went to see the Citizen Maritime Prefect of this port, to whom I submitted the letter I was instructed to give him by the Ministers of Marine and the Interior, and I advised him to provide me with the means of effecting the transport of the whole collection to Paris. He had already taken measures to procure a large transport vessel, but as it was held up at Quillebeuf by adverse winds and could be there for another month, he had been unable to commence loading. Once I learned that there were two small boats in Le Havre belonging to the State and suitable for taking the consignment all the way to Paris, without having to trans-ship it at Rouen according to the usual practice, I indicated this to the prefect who immediately gave orders for them to be dispatched. With the enthusiastic assistance of the officers and crew of the *Naturaliste*, we began loading yesterday at midday. Loading continued today, tomorrow it will be completed, and on Thursday morning the two boats, taking advantage of the rising tide, will leave the harbour, enter the Seine and make their way to Paris.

They assure me that the voyage from Le Havre to Paris, all circumstances being favourable, can be done in ten days and that, in the worst case, it can take 30 days at most. If we take the average time, it is probable, citizens, that you will see the consignment reach the the Jardin des Plantes, on the 24th of the present month.

To ensure its conservation during the voyage, I instructed Citizen Lasalle to accompany it and not to let it out of his sight.[36] He will cultivate the living plants and tend to them in accordance with detailed instructions that I shall leave for him. He will keep watch over these objects to ensure that not a single one in his care is lost, and that they are well ventilated and kept dry during the entire journey.

The master gunner of the *Naturaliste*[37] is entrusted by the Maritime Prefect with the supervision of the live animals on these two boats. The attention he lavished on them during the crossing from New Holland to here is a certain guarantee of the care he will take to ensure their conservation until they reach their destination. I shall send by coach the crates of seeds that it is possible for me to identify, which is not an easy task since many of them are not labelled with the names of the objects they contain. As for the insects and birds that I intended to send by public coach, after seeing the lack of care they take when loading such things I was put off from using this means because it is risky for all fragile objects.

When the boats are on their way, I myself intend to leave and arrive in Paris around the 8th of the present month.

It is with great satisfaction, Citizen colleagues, that I write to assure you of my devotion and my fond and respectful regards.

Thouin.

Then, with Lieutenant Saint Cricq, Thouin drew up the inventory of the natural history objects transported by the *Naturaliste*[38] before they were loaded on to the two lighters of the Republic, the *Porte Faix* and the *Porteuse* which, as early as 23 June, were to commence the journey up the

Seine that would take them to Paris. The inventory mentions 64 crates:
- 14 labelled 'mineralogy';
- 15 labelled 'zoology' (five of which bore the initials F.P., two others contained the skins of kangaroos and swans, and two were filled with flasks);
- 10 labelled 'birds' (they contained either birds, or birds and quadrupeds, one of them even contained zoophytes and lithophytes);
- 12 without labels (all contained plants, two were marked 'Leschenault', four were marked 'R.F.' and one, containing marine plants, was marked 'Maugé');
- 12 others without labels (one of which contained insects, one shells, one devoted to Natural History was marked 'Maugé', two were marked 'R.F.', and one, sent by coach, contained seeds);

and one last crate containing eggs and other objects.

Apart from these, Thouin listed 18 billets of wood from Port Jackson, three barrels of wood samples, 50 pieces of wood of different species and sizes collected as firewood in New Holland, two wooden shields used by indigenous people, two wooden vases used as pails by indigenous people and collected in New Holland, a pair of spears used as oars for their canoe, a pair of red copper watering cans from the Museum in Paris, and a tinplate syringe. He listed 69 half-barrels containing plants, a large number of which were dead, and 20 live animals (a four-horned ram, two guinea fowls, two gazelles, three wombats, one emu, two dogs, one turtle, two swans, two pigeons with golden wings, two rails, and two little quails).[39]

The collections aroused a great deal of interest not just among the professors, but also in the press: the *Moniteur Universel* published an article on the first results of the expedition[40] and this same journal, together with the *Décade philosophique*, printed the letter of the mineralogist Charles Bailly to Senator Grégoire,[41] a letter which had been brought back by the *Naturaliste* and which provided information on the events of the voyage.[42]

Bass Strait, King Island, 16 Frimaire Year 11 [7 December 1802]

You will surely have heard of the results of the expedition (of Captain Baudin) since our departure from Île de France. You will have seen that following our 40-day sojourn in Île de France, we left for the coast of New Holland, that we travelled from Cape Leeuwin to Shark Bay. This entire coastline, which is sandy and almost entirely without fresh water, is practically uninhabited. The few inhabitants who live there are still as savage as in Dampier's time.[43] They are closer to the state of nature than any other people, and they are also in a wilder state and possess no technical skills, except that of sharpening sticks to defend themselves against their enemies or to obtain the means of subsistence with which hunting and fishing can provide them.

After leaving this coast we went to Timor, one of the islands to the south of the Moluccas. There we found a gentle and cheerful people who enjoyed a partial state of civilisation. Through trading with the Dutch, those who inhabit the coast have become hospitable towards strangers, but those who live inland, and for whom a European face is still unknown, are often cruel to men who dare venture into their territory.

From Timor we went to Van Diemen's Land. This island has inhabitants of a different race from the people of New Holland. The latter have long, black hair, like the peoples of Asia, even though their skin is as black as that of the African negro, whereas the former have frizzy woolly hair like the inhabitants of the Congo. Moreover, they have other characteristics that differentiate them still further: the latter, who have been accustomed for a while now to see European vessels occasionally land on their coast, are less savage than the other peoples of this country.

From Van Diemen's Land we went on to Port Jackson to make a stopover. This nascent colony is the first one where the indigenous inhabitants have had no call for complaint against Europeans. They are treated here with every kind of consideration, but they have always refused to conform to any form of civilisation. Although they have been living for 15 years with the English, they have not yet adopted any of their customs. The need for clothing is still superfluous for them. While they might wear something to protect them from the cold on a rare occasion, they never do so to hide their nudity.

In the 15 years since they have settled here, the English have already developed their agriculture to a degree that is ever surprising. It is no longer ancient forests, but fields of wheat which prosper there prodigiously. You can already see towns and villages where everything we have in Europe, even when it is surplus to needs, can be found in abundance. The population amounts to about 8,000 inhabitants and there are no slaves. I am sending you a sample of the wool from the sheep of this country. They originally came from Peru, Paraguay, the Cape of Good Hope and Bengal. They have already been remarkably improved and every day they promise to improve still further. Those from Bengal, which only had fur, already produce lambs with a luxuriant fleece. A five-month sojourn allowed me to travel through the whole region. We have just departed in order to continue our reconnaissance of New Holland. The commandant is sending the *Naturaliste* back to France with the collections that we have made up till now. I left this ship to embark on the *Géographe* where I am replacing my colleague and friend Depuch, whose health is forcing him to return to France.

Bailly, mineralogist

Strangely enough, this letter was silent on the difficulties and even the dramas that the expedition had experienced: Bailly did not mention the many officers and naturalists who had abandoned the expedition at the Île de France, nor the naturalists who died during and after the stopover of the corvettes in Timor. The news of the death of the gardener Riedlé had nonetheless already reached France. Lieutenant Sainte Croix Lebas, who had left the expedition in Timor, had written from Batavia to inform the Minister of Marine of this, among other matters.[44] Decrès then gave the news to the professors in a letter whose contents became known to them during their meeting of 4 May 1803.[45] As we have previously noted, it was only when the *Naturaliste* arrived back in France that the authorities of the Museum and the Ministry of Marine learned of the deaths of the zoologists Levillain and Maugé and of the assistant gardener Sautier.

The richness and diversity of the collections that were delivered had reassured Jussieu, the director of the Museum (who was also the 'patron' of the voyage), as to the smooth functioning of the scientific activities of the expedition and hence the soundness of its organisation. Thus Jussieu wrote, on 16 July 1803, to the botanist André-Pierre Ledru:

> the 2nd vessel [the *Naturaliste*] has returned with all of the collections that have already been made. There are many beautiful and rare things of different types. [...] Baudin is now engaged in further research; [...] we hope that the bad rumours about Baudin, which have already calmed down since the arrival of the first ship, will dissipate entirely when he himself appears.[46]

The bad rumours that Jussieu mentioned resulted from the injurious criticisms made by certain officers who had abandoned the expedition at Île de France. For example, Lieutenant Pierre Gicquel wrote to his friend Charles-François Beautemps-Beaupré: 'M. Baudin is without any qualities, either moral, or social. He is neither a naturalist nor a sailor! His hair stands on end with fear at the slightest squall and he frightens everyone. [...] We cannot now hide the fact that this expedition is far beyond the forces of Captain Baudin'.[47] Gicquel left Île de France on 16 October 1801 carrying with him a letter addressed to Fleurieu from the astronomer Frédéric Bissy. He arrived in Nantes on 19 January 1802 and the letter must have reached the addressee at the beginning of the month of Pluviôse (around 21 January). In it we can read: 'I dare not pride myself,

Citizen, on having inspired in you the interest required to hear the story of the grievances that we must air against Baudin; but if you wish to find out, Citizen Gicquel will speak to you more knowledgeably about it than I can.[48] And Gicquel must have spoken about it, in particular, during the audience he was granted with the First Consul on 4 February.[49]

The *Porte Faix* and the *Porteuse* reached the Museum around mid-July 1803. During the committee meeting of 20 July, Geoffroy Saint-Hilaire, Professor of the Zoology of Quadrupeds and Birds, announced that the objects sent by Captain Baudin were very numerous and required to be promptly prepared and repaired. The committee determined that Citizen Geoffroy would employ artists from outside the institution to start work immediately on the conservation of these precious objects, and that there would be discussions with the Minister of the Interior in order to obtain the necessary funding for this important operation. As for Thouin, he reported on the current state of the plants that had arrived from New Holland; of the 800 on board, only 30 were in a healthy state of vegetation. However, the professors were also obliged to satisfy the demands of Mme Bonaparte. In this regard, the letter that Minister Chaptal sent in early July is a model of double meaning:

> I authorised you, Citizen, to hand over to Citizen Mirbel for Mme Bonaparte's garden everything that is not absolutely necessary for the establishment which is under your direction. You know as well as I what care Mme Bonaparte lavishes on the cultivation of plants and the rearing of rare animals. It is in the interest of science and the glory of France to encourage these distinguished tastes and I invite you to offer support to her plans and mine by all the means at your disposal.[50]

And so Mme Bonaparte received several live animals.[51] The professors also sent her 289 packets of seeds from the expedition. Others, like Citizen Pierre Marie Auguste Broussonet, also received some. He had become the director of the Jardin des Plantes at Montpellier and was sent a selection of 175 species of seeds. A similar selection was also sent to the Botanical Gardens in Lyon and to the Empress Dowager of Russia (through Mme Bonaparte).[52]

The *Naturaliste* also brought back many skins of mammals and birds captured by the zoologists. During the professors' committee meeting of 4 June, Geoffroy Saint-Hilaire revealed that the corvette had brought back 32 species of mammals (79 individuals) and 206 species of birds (599 individuals).[53] In the minutes of the following meetings (from 10 August 1803 to 21 March 1804), that is, until the arrival of the *Géographe* at Lorient was announced (23 March 1804), discussions regularly took place about the vellums and the mountings of animals brought back by Captain Hamelin. This information, as given below, comes from notes entitled 'Operations of the Zoology laboratory', which were regularly compiled by the naturalist Louis Dufresne.[54]

Operations of the Zoology laboratory [extracts][55]

Meeting of 22 Thermidor Year 11 (10 August 1803)
The following were mounted: a phalanger of the white variety,[56] a water rat, a black quoll with white spots, a brushtail possum, a small water rat, the giant kangaroo; all these animals were brought back by the corvette the *Naturaliste* on Captain Baudin's expedition in Year 11. In a crate labelled zoology that we thought to be filled with shells, we found, in accordance with your catalogue, 78 birds making up 19 species; 26 were put aside to be mounted for the Museum. We also found two crates with botanical specimens, under the label of zoology. They were sent to Citizen Deleuze.[57] Opening the crates of molluscs and putting them away in accordance with the requirements of the zoology stores also took up a great deal of our time.

Meeting of 29 Thermidor Year 11 (17 August 1803)
Mounted in the laboratory were: [...] a large kangaroo, a brown brushtail possum, two small brushtail possums, a rat, a brown albatross, a large petrel, from Captain

Baudin's expedition. Today Félix gave the laboratory a dog from New Holland;[58] it died yesterday. You will find in your meeting room 64 birds from captain Baudin's voyage: 14 turtledoves mounted by Mlle Charpentier, 20 by Lalande, father and son, 30 mounted by Mme Dufresne,[59] 64 [in total].

Meeting of 6 Fructidor Year 11 (24 August 1803)
I am pleased to inform you that the following have been mounted in the laboratory since last week: three platypuses, a black brushtail possum, a male dog which died in the menagerie, a white-tailed rat, two small brushtail possums, another species was mounted after having been preserved in spirits, all from New Holland and sent by Captain Baudin. The order to be established in the zoology stores, as well as the unpacking of shells and other objects from New Holland, also occupied some of our time.

Meeting of 13 Fructidor Year 11 (31 August 1803)
From the 6th of this month were mounted in the laboratory: a large wombat, eight bats, a black swan, two small honey eaters, from New Holland.

Meeting of 20 Fructidor Year 11 (7 September 1803)
Were mounted this week: [...] a white eagle, a frigatebird, [...] a black swan, from New Holland.

Meeting of 27 Fructidor Year 11 (14 September 1803)
The following were mounted this week: [...] a totally white bird of prey, [...] a sparrowhawk, a buzzard, from New Holland. You entrusted 100 birds from New Holland to Mme Dufresne to be mounted for the Museum. On 15 Thermidor she returned 30 to you, on 29 Thermidor 30, today 27 Fructidor 40, 100 [in total]. You will find attached the note about the 40 birds delivered today.[60]

Meeting of 5 Vendémiaire Year 12 (28 September 1803)
This week were mounted an echidna from New Holland (Citizen Geoffroy exchanged this rare species with Citizen Faujas),[61] [...] an eagle, a species of osprey, a sparrowhawk, from New Holland [...]. Jointly, Citizen Geoffroy and I chose for Mme Bonaparte 117 birds from the Southern Ocean sent by Captain Baudin. Around 20 individuals come from the voyage he made to the Americas in Year 7; these 20 birds were part of the collection brought back by the unfortunate Maugé. (The committee will receive the catalogue when we send the birds to Mme Bonaparte.) In the cabinets of the laboratory there are now 164 birds from Captain Baudin's last consignment that have been mounted and more than 50 mammals. Plus, in Year 12, [...] a guinea fowl which died in the menagerie, a species of opossum, from New Holland.

Meeting of 3 Brumaire Year 12 (26 October 1803)
I am pleased to announce that the following were mounted this week: [...] 4 shorebirds, an owl, a barn owl, a drongo, a golden-breasted starling, a red kite, from New Holland [...]. We also worked on restoring the collection of crustaceans that recently arrived from New Holland.

Meeting of 10 Brumaire Year 12 (2 November 1803)
You will probably recall that, when we unpacked the objects sent by Captain Baudin, a large number of the crustaceans had been greatly damaged while in transport. I restored them to the best of my ability. I added the other species from the expedition and am pleased to present them to your committee so that you can see for yourselves the numerous species produced by the seas of New Holland. [...] I am pleased to announce that the following were mounted in the laboratory since the last meeting: an albatross, a large petrel, a seagull, a hobby, a

cardinal, a species of blackbird, all from Captain Baudin's consignment, New Holland.

Meeting of 17 Brumaire Year 12 (9 November 1803)
I am pleased to announce that the following were mounted this week in the Zoology laboratory: [...] two species of grey shrike and two red kites from Timor, another bird of prey, a warbler, a barn owl, from New Holland.

Meeting of 24 Brumaire Year 12 (16 November 1803)
Mounted this week: [...] an eagle, a sparrowhawk, four ducks, from New Holland.

Meeting of 8 Frimaire Year 12 (30 November 1803)
Mounted: a sparrowhawk, a duck, a small cormorant, two other ducks [...] from New Holland.

It was during the meeting of 8 Frimaire (30 November 1803) that Jean-Baptiste Lamarck, Professor of Zoology in charge of insects, worms and microscopic animals, presented to his colleagues the 'catalogue of the animals in his specialisation that were in the last consignment from Captain Baudin'. This type of inventory, drawn up by Citizen Pierre-André Latreille,[62] presented several new genera and many species unknown to naturalists.

Operations of the Zoology laboratory [extracts, continued]

Meeting of 15 Frimaire Year 12 (7 December 1803)
The following were mounted this week in the laboratory: two ducks, a purple swamphen, a curlew, a shoveller,[63] a small heron, three swallows, two flycatchers, two wheatears, a honey eater with yellow whiskers, female, [in total] 14, all from New Holland sent by Captain Baudin.

Meeting of 22 Frimaire Year 12 (14 December 1803)
Mounted this week were: a cormorant, a bittern, a gannet, two *Fringilla*,[64] two *Muscicapa*,[65] a budgerigar, two nighthawks, [in total] 10 from New Holland.

Meeting of 29 Frimaire Year 12 (21 December 1803)
This week the following were mounted: a wombat, two ducks, a white gull, a brown gannet, a godwit, a gull, another gull with a black mantle, a grey curlew, a common tern, an ibis, a night heron, a green pigeon, a small chiffchaff, three *Muscicapa*, an owl, a red duck, a swallow, [in total] 20, all from New Holland.

Meeting of 13 Nivôse Year 12 (4 January 1804)
This week the following were mounted: a large white egret, a white spoonbill, a golden plover, a black headed tern, three warblers, a red *Loxia*,[66] five flycatchers, a honeyeater, five shrikes, a chiffchaff, [in total] 20, all from New Holland sent by Captain Baudin in Year 11.

Meeting of 20 Nivôse Year 12 (11 January 1804)
I have the pleasure of announcing that this week there were mounted: [. . .] a bee-eater, two shrikes, a flycatcher, a figbird,[67] two species of *Loxia*, one species of *Motacilla*,[68] a small collared plover, a speckled shrike, a tridactylous quail, two grey shrikes, [in total] 16, New Holland. You may announce to the meeting, Citizen, that we have just finished mounting all the mammals and birds that you have chosen for the galleries from the collection sent from New Holland by Captain Baudin: 56 mammals and 334 birds of all sizes.

Meeting of 16 Ventôse Year 12 (7 March 1804)
Mounted this week were: [. . .] a speckled gannet from New Holland done feather by feather [. . .]. Mlle Charpentier has had 12 birds to be mounted for the Museum for some

time; she delivered them today to the laboratory; they are all from the expedition of Captain Baudin, and were brought back by the corvette, the *Naturaliste*, in Year 11.

Meeting of 23 Ventôse Year 12 (14 March 1804)
Mounted a cockatoo from Port Jackson. It was in such a state that we were forced to mount it feather by feather.

Meeting of 7 Germinal Year 12 (28 March 1804)
This week we started restoring the *Asterias*[69] sent from New Holland by Captain Baudin.

All of this work mounting and cataloguing the Australian specimens was accompanied by the production of drawings and paintings on vellum by the artists of the Museum. For example, during the month of Frimaire (November-December 1803), several such works were presented at the meetings of the professors' committee: a vellum of unknown insects from the Baudin expedition, painted by Oudinot[70] and presented by Lamarck; two vellums of non-described insects of the same origin, presented by Dufresne (the name of the artist is not indicated); two vellums painted by Wailly,[71] one of which features the dog of New Holland sent back alive by Captain Baudin; and, lastly, a vellum presented by Bernard Germain de Lacépède, the Professor of the Zoology of Reptiles and Fish, which was also painted by Wailly and represents the long-necked turtle sent by Captain Baudin. All of these vellums were deposited in the collections of the Museum's library. The specimens brought back by the *Naturaliste* were also the object of several publications in the *Annales du Muséum*.[72] The sustained activity of preparing and studying the collections of the *Naturaliste* became of secondary importance as soon as news broke of the arrival of the *Géographe* at Lorient, on 25 March 1804.

Shortly after the return of the *Géographe*, Fleurieu, at the request of Minister Decrès, informed him that he would accept the task of dealing with the papers brought back by the *Naturaliste*. Decrès then sent him the following letter:

Paris, 14 Ventôse Year 12 of the Republic [5 March 1804][73]
The Minister of Marine and the Colonies
To Citizen Fleurieu, Councillor of State, President of the Section of Marine

Citizen Concillor, I received your response of the 3rd of this month, and I am pleased to send you not only the pieces that you wished to assemble, but several other pieces which may help to clarify your thoughts. Consequently you will find included:

1° The instructions that were given to Captain Baudin and that, back then, you were kind enough to undertake to write.

2° A letter from Captain Baudin dated 4 Floréal Year 9 [24 April 1801], containing details of the voyage, from his departure from Europe until his arrival at Île de France.

3° A letter from the same captain, dated from Kupang 13 Vendémiaire Year 10 [5 October 1801], in which he reports on his first operations in New Holland.

4° Another letter from Captain Baudin, dated from Port Jackson 20 Brumaire Year 11 [11 November 1802], containing the narrative of his later operations and the instructions given to Captain Hamelin, commandant of the *Naturaliste*, for his return to France. *NB* In my office there exists no other letter from Captain Baudin relating to the scientific part of his expedition.

5° A letter from Captain Hamelin dated from Port Jackson 22 Floréal Year 10 [12 May 1802], to which is attached a chart on which is traced the route taken by this captain along the east coast of Van Diemen's Land.

6° A note written by Captain Hamelin on the British establishments in the southern seas and on several other islands in those seas.

As for the journals, logs, maps or charts from this voyage, all of these objects were sent by my orders to the Hydrographic Service of the Marine on the arrival in France of the *Naturaliste*, and I invite General Rosily to make available to you for consultation those that you consider relevant. You will find attached a note that will enable you to make your choice in advance.

The return of Captain Baudin, that I deem to be quite imminent, will enable you to obtain several supplementary details, and they will be sent to you as well.

Accept my thanks for the kind attention that you will give to your response to my invitation, it can only add to my personal debt of gratitude and to that which every navigator owes you.

With respectful greetings,
Decrès

[Note attached to the letter of 14 Ventôse][74]
- two notebooks making up the Journal of Hamelin, commandant of the *Naturaliste*.
- two parcels covered in cloth containing the logbooks of the *Naturaliste* for the Years 9 and 10, plus seven notebooks of log tables, from 1 Vendémiaire to 18 Prairial Year 11 [23 September 1802 – 7 June 1803].
- four notebooks in a single parcel of papers intended to be used in the construction of the map of the south-west coast of New Holland.
- Journal of Saint Cricq, lieutenant on the *Naturaliste*.
- three notebooks containing the Journal of the voyage, from the departure from Île de France until to Timor and from Timor to Sydney.[75]
- Journal of [blank] from Vendémiaire Year 9 until 1 Prairial Year 11 [October 1800 – 21 May 1803].[76]
- three notebooks by Maurouard, midshipman: in the first, a logbook for Year 10 [September 1801 – September 1802], in the second, a journal for Year 11 [1802 – 1803], and in the third, a journal containing work on the maps.
- eight notebooks of the journal of Bougainville, midshipman on board the *Géographe*, with the last notebook containing bearings taken on the south-west coast.
- Journal of Breton, midshipman on board the *Géographe*, from 9

Vendémiaire Year 9 [1 October 1800] up to Prairial Year 11 [May-June 1803].

Journal of Couture, midshipman on board the *Naturaliste*, from Vendémiaire Year 9 [October 1800] up to Nivôse Year 11 [December 1802 – January 1803].

Journal of Giraud, midshipman on board the *Naturaliste*, during Years 9, 10 and 11 [October 1800 – 1803].

Journal of Duval Dailly from Vendémiaire Year 9 up till 9 Floréal Year 10 [October 1800 – 29 April 1802].

two notebooks of the journal of Brüe, midshipman on board the *Géographe*, finishing at his arrival in Port Jackson.[77]

Some weeks later, Fleurieu received the journals, maps, charts, etc, that were brought back by the *Géographe*. He thus had at his disposal all the journals, official letters and reports (apart from those relating to the natural sciences), and all the charts, maps and coastal profiles established during the course of the voyage. Nothing leads us to believe that he did anything other than consult them.[78]

Notes

1. The author wishes to thank Jean Fornasiero for the English translation of this text.
2. Emmanuel Hamelin, Journal vol. 2, Archives Nationales de France (ANF), série Marine, 5JJ 42.
3. Baudin to the Minister of Marine, dated 20 Brumaire Year 11 (11 November 1802), Service Historique de la Défense (SHD), Archives centrales de la Marine à Vincennes (Mar.), BB4 995.
4. Nicolas Baudin, 'État général des objets [...] embarqués sur *Le Naturaliste* [...]', SHD, Mar. BB4 997, folio 143.
5. Michel Jangoux, 'L'Expédition du capitaine Baudin aux Terres australes: les observations zoologiques de François Péron pendant la première campagne', *Annales du Muséum du Havre*, no. 73, 2005, pp. 1–35.
6. James Thomson was one of the medical officers in the British colony of Port Jackson; with Governor King's permission, he had embarked on the *Naturaliste* to make his return journey to Europe.
7. Hamelin, Journal, vol. 2. Biographical entries on the officers and naturalists embarked on the expedition are to be found in Michel Jangoux, *Le Voyage aux Terres Australes du commandant Nicolas Baudin: Genèse et préambule (1798–1800)*, Paris: Presses de l'Université Paris-Sorbonne, 2013.
8. SHD, Mar., BB4 995, folio 363.
9. The present-day Samoan Islands.
10. Depuch, who had contracted dysentery, did not survive and died in hospital at the Île de France on 26 April 1803.
11. Seaman Fabert and novice Pommel.
12. Seaman Vince and novice Josse.
13. The tender would only give him eight!

14   Sainte Croix Lebas was Baudin's second-in-command on the *Géographe* at the beginning of the voyage but was disembarked on 2 November 1801 – ostensibly because of ill-health, but in reality because he had been involved in a duel and Baudin judged him inapt to continue. He subsequently found his way to the Île de France, where he, his servant and a lieutenant named Lucas, joined the *Naturaliste* as passengers alongside the Thomsons and their servant. The list is completed by a clandestine passenger, a certain Louvigny from Picardy, who was found soon after the departure from the Île de France.
15   Léon Brèvedent du Bocage, who had been appointed second-in-command of the *Casuarina*, was Hamelin's nephew.
16   Hamelin, Journal, vol. 2.
17   Hamelin, Journal, entry dated 10–11 Floréal Year 11 (30 April – 1 May 1803).
18   Report from Captain Hamelin addressed to Bertin, Maritime Prefect of Le Havre, SHD, Mar., BB4 995, folio 355. It should be noted that this text was in Saint Cricq's handwriting, but was signed by Hamelin.
19   Gunners Kleinne and Barbier (accused of theft) and seaman Billiore (for an act of insubordination).
20   In all of the documents I have consulted, this is the only time that the presence of this sailor has been mentioned.
21   They were intended for Mme Bonaparte.
22   SHD, Mar., BB4 996, folio 69.
23   Hamelin was promoted to the rank of post-captain in October 1803 and awarded the Légion d'honneur in February 1804. He subsequently went on to have a brilliant military career. See Jean-Paul Faivre, *Le Contre-amiral Hamelin et la marine française*, Paris: Nouvelles éditions latines, 1962.
24   Minutes of the meeting of the professors' committee held on 26 Prairial Year 11 (15 June 1803), ANF, série Muséum, AJ 15/590.
25   Inventory of the parcels attached to the minutes of the meeting of the professors' committee held on 3 Messidor Year 11 (22 June 1803), ANF, série Muséum, AJ 15/590.
26   Jean-Antoine Chaptal to Antoine-Laurent de Jussieu, letter attached to the minutes of the meeting of the professors' committee held on 26 Prairial Year 11 (15 June 1803), ANF, série Muséum, AJ 15/590.
27   Charles Brisseau de Mirbel was the director of the gardens at Malmaison.
28   Chaptal to the professors, letter attached to the minutes of the meeting of the professors' committee held on 3 Messidor Year 11 (22 June 1803), ANF, série Muséum, AJ 15/590.
29   Denis Decrès was then Minister of Marine but Fleurieu replaced him on occasion. Fleurieu was at that time president of the Marine section in the Conseil d'État. See Jean Tulard, 'Claret de Fleurieu: conseiller d'État et sénateur', in Ulane Bonnel (ed.), *Fleurieu et la marine de son temps*, Paris: Éditions Economica, 1992, pp. 311–316.
30   Fleurieu to the professors, letter attached to the minutes of the meeting of the professors' committee held on 3 Messidor Year 11 (22 June 1803), ANF, série Muséum, AJ 15/590.
31   SHD, Mar., BB2 84, folio 125.
32   Decrès to Rosily, ANF, série Marine, 5JJ 24.
33   SHD, Mar., BB4 995.
34   SHD, Mar., BB4 995. A lighter is a flat bottomed boat.
35   Letter attached to the minutes of the meeting of the professors' committee held on 10 Messidor Year 11 (29 June 1803), ANF, série Muséum, AJ 15/590.
36   A gardener from the Museum.
37   Jean Bertrand Renould.
38   André Thouin, 'Inventaire des objets pris à bord de la corvette *Le Naturaliste* [...]', document attached to the minutes of the meeting of the professors' committee held on 10 Messidor Year 11 (29 June 1803), ANF, série Muséum, AJ 15/590.

39 In his report to the Maritime Prefect of Le Havre (see above), Hamelin mentioned neither the guinea fowls nor the rails.
40 *Le Moniteur Universel*, 14 Messidor Year 11 (3 July 1803).
41 Henri Grégoire (1750–1831), known as Abbé Grégoire, was appointed a senator in 1801. A member of the opposition, he refused to accept the Concordat and voted against the lifetime Consulate and the establishment of the Empire. His ashes were transferred to the Pantheon in 1989.
42 Charles Bailly, 'Copie d'une lettre adressée au C. Grégoire', *La Décade philosophique*, IVe trim., Messidor–Fructidor Year 11 (June–September 1803), pp. 120–121; *Le Moniteur Universel*, 22 Messidor Year 11 (11 July 1803).
43 William Dampier (1651–1715), an English navigator who was the first to map parts of New Holland.
44 In reality, as already indicated (see note 14), Lebas had been sent back to France by Baudin following a duel he had with the engineer François Ronsard.
45 Minutes of the meeting of the professors' committee held on 14 Floréal Year 11 (4 May 1803), ANF, série Muséum, AJ 15/590.
46 Jussieu to Ledru, 16 July 1803, quoted in André Belin, 'André-Pierre Ledru. Sa correspondance à l'occasion d'un voyage aux Canaries et aux Antilles', *La Révolution dans le Maine*, vol. 10, 1934, p. 211. Ledru was the botanist on the expedition of the *Belle Angélique*.
47 Letter dated 7 Floréal Year 9 (27 April 1801), retranscribed by Pierre Gicquel in his journal, ANF, série Marine, 5JJ 55.
48 Bissy to Fleurieu, 10 Vendémiaire Year 10 (2 October 1801), ANF, série Marine, 5JJ 24.
49 The page of Gicquel's journal in which he reported on this interview is definitively lost (it was torn out).
50 Chaptal to the professors of the Museum, letter attached to the minutes of the meeting of the professors' committee held on 15 Messidor Year 11 (4 July 1803), ANF, série Muséum, AJ 15/590.
51 Michel Jangoux, Christian Jouanin and Bernard Métivier, 'Les animaux embarqués vivants sur les vaisseaux du voyage de découvertes aux Terres australes', in M. Jangoux (ed.), *Portés par l'air du temps, les voyages du capitaine Baudin*, special number of *Études sur le XVIIIe siècle*, vol. 38, 2010, pp. 265–282.
52 Minutes of the meeting of the professors' committee held on 10 Brumaire Year 12 (2 November 1803), ANF, série Muséum, AJ 15/591.
53 Document attached to the minutes of the meeting of the professors' committee held on 15 Messidor Year 11 (4 July 1803), ANF, série Muséum, AJ 15/590.
54 Louis Dufresne (1752–1832) was an assistant naturalist in the Zoology laboratory. He was the assistant to the two professors of that discipline, Étienne Geoffroy Saint-Hilaire and Jean-Baptiste Lamarck; he was responsible for the collections which were under their direction.
55 ANF, série Muséum, AJ 15/590 and AJ 15/591.
56 Cuscus or grey phalanger (*Phalanger maculatus*).
57 Joseph Philippe François Deleuze (1753–1835) was at that time an assistant naturalist in the Botany laboratory of Professor René Desfontaines.
58 Probably one of the keepers of the menagerie.
59 Mlle Charpentier was an independent taxidermist; Lalande (or Delalande) father (Adrien-Alexis) and son (Pierre-Antoine) were assistant naturalists for the preparation of animals (attached to the laboratory of Geoffroy Saint-Hilaire); Mme Dufresne, the wife of assistant naturalist Dufresne, was also an independent taxidermist.
60 The note indicates: 'given back to Citizen Geoffroy 40 birds from New Holland at 6 f each; for the 40, 240 f'.
61 Barthélemy Faujas de Saint Fond (1741–1819) was Professor of Geology at the Museum.

62 Pierre-André Latreille (1762–1833) was an assistant naturalist in the laboratory of Lamarck. The catalogue which was established by Latreille and presented by Lamarck was to concentrate only on insects and crustaceans; unfortunately, it was not attached to the minutes of the meeting of the professors of 8 Frimaire.
63 A species of duck.
64 Finches.
65 Flycatchers.
66 Crossbill.
67 Genus of orioles.
68 Wagtail.
69 Starfish.
70 Oudinot was an artist attached to the Museum, specialising in invertebrate animals.
71 Pierre-François de Wailly (1775–1852) was an artist attached to the Museum, specialising in quadrupeds and birds.
72 Jean-Baptiste Lamarck, 'Sur deux nouveaux genres d'insectes de la Nouvelle Hollande', *Annales du Muséum national d'Histoire naturelle*, vol. 3, 1804, pp. 260–265; Étienne Geoffroy Saint-Hilaire, 'Mémoire sur les espèces du genre *Dasyure*', *Annales du Muséum national d'Histoire naturelle*, vol. 3, 1804, pp. 353–363; Bernard Lacépède, 'Mémoire sur plusieurs animaux de la Nouvelle Hollande dont la description n'a pas encore été publiée', *Annales du Muséum national d'Histoire naturelle*, vol. 4, 1804, pp. 184–213; Lamarck, 'Sur une nouvelle espèce de trigonie et une nouvelle espèce d'huître découvertes dans le voyage du capitaine Baudin', *Annales du Muséum national d'Histoire naturelle*, vol. 4, 1804, pp. 351–359; Lamarck, 'Mémoire sur deux espèces nouvelles de volutes des mers de la Nouvelle Hollande', *Annales du Muséum national d'Histoire naturelle*, vol. 5, 1804, pp. 154–160.
73 ANF, série Marine, 5JJ 24.
74 SHD, Mar., BB4 997, folio 132. All of the journals cited in this list are held in the ANF, série Marine, 5JJ.
75 This is the journal of midshipman Heirisson.
76 By elimination and by taking into account the period covered in the narrative, this must be the journal of midshipman Moreau.
77 Brüe, like Breton, Bougainville and Maurouard, was or had been on the *Géographe*; in Sydney they were all transferred by Baudin to the *Naturaliste*, on which they made the return journey to France.
78 Louis Freycinet thanked Fleurieu for his advice in the preface to his major work, *Voyage de découvertes aux Terres australes: Navigation et Géographie*, published in 1815 by the Imprimerie royale in Paris.

Chapter 9

The Unpublished Reports of Jean-Baptiste Lamarck and the Fate of the Invertebrate Collection from the Southern Lands

Michel Jangoux[1]

When the professors of the Paris Museum, who were gathered for a meeting on 31 March 1804, learned that the *Géographe* had docked in Lorient on 2 Germinal (23 March), they designated Geoffroy Saint-Hilaire to go and take delivery of the collections that the corvette had brought back to France. They were all the more impatient to examine the objects that had been collected as their appetites had been whetted by a letter that François Péron had recently sent them from Lorient (25 March):

> I do not know how interesting you would have found the first collection of objects brought back by the *Naturaliste*, but I venture to assure you that the collection we have brought back today seems to me to be infinitely more interesting than the first. Timor alone had provided more than two thirds of the objects initially sent back, and Timor, which is one of the Moluccas, had fewer new or rare objects to offer us. New Holland, on the other hand, with its archipelagos and islands, provided on its own the sizeable collection we are now bringing you. In short, these objects, in almost all classes, are more numerous, better selected and much better organised. I have compiled 15 descriptive journals comprising more than 8,800 descriptions or observations of a very general and consistently uniform nature, along with all the topographical information that should allow them to be clarified or modified. Lastly, more than 370 drawings of

living animals made with great precision by M. Lesueur help to make this work as complete as it is interesting.[2]

The collections arrived at the Museum on 23 April. On 29 May, Jean-Baptiste Lamarck, Professor of Zoology in charge of insects, worms and microscopic animals, made a verbal report on the number and state of the invertebrates in the collection.[3] At the request of his colleagues, he undertook to write down his observations. At the meeting of 8 Messidor (27 June), he presented three preliminary reports: one on the insects (including crustaceans and arachnids); another on the echinoderms; and a third on molluscs. The reports on insects and echinoderms were accompanied by tables; there was no table for the report dealing with molluscs.[4]

1. Report on Insects

Report on the state and number of the crustaceans, arachnids and insects collected during the French voyage of discovery to New Holland by Messrs Péron, Lesueur and Maugé, naturalists embarked on the corvette the *Géographe*.

It might be thought that the classes of animals that occupy the lowest positions in the natural hierarchy of the animal kingdom, which are largely considered by the general public to be of little interest, and whose study is in general less developed than that of the other branches of zoology, would have drawn little attention from the naturalists whose work you are so rightly honouring with your admiration. This view, if you have formed it, will soon be dispelled by the sheer spectacle of what they have done in this regard. These indefatigable men were destined to surpass your expectations. Even if their mission had only had as its objective the study of one of these classes of animals, it would have been perfectly fulfilled.

Various countries of the globe had greatly enriched the entomological section of the national collection; but the more distant regions of the eastern and southern hemispheres had hitherto offered almost nothing. And yet, the products of these distant climates were all the more to be desired as it was felt that they were needed in order to complete and correct the natural method on which our naturalists are now zealously working.

The rough table that I am presenting of the number of species of crustaceans, arachnids and insects brought back by the naturalists who embarked on the *Géographe* will provide much more convincing evidence of the extent of their zeal and efforts than anything I might say.

Thanks to their unrelenting efforts, the Museum now has some 112 species of crustaceans, 36 species of arachnids and 1,035 species of insects, a large number of which comprise multiple specimens in such quantities that the total number of specimens collected exceeds 4,000.

Considered in the light of the advancement of our knowledge, these objects offer us the substance for identifying new generic divisions and approximately 800 new species.

This fine collection has come partly from Timor, partly from New Holland. Some other insects collected on the Barbary coast, at the Cape of Good Hope and at Mauritius have, however, been added to this collection. The specimens from the latter two places were collected by our travellers themselves, and those from the Barbary coast were given to the French mariners by some enlightened friends of Science.

Among the insects collected at Timor, a large number of which are the result of the taxing efforts of the unfortunate Maugé, a certain number are known, this island having many products in common with the Moluccas and with the most western shores of Sumatra.

The collection from Timor is most of all valuable because it contains a large number of butterflies and moths. The National Museum already has a rich collection in this order of insects, but that collection has been augmented to such an extent that it is now unrivalled and will remain so for a long time to come.

The class of crustaceans has also greatly benefited from the results of the work of our naturalists. The renowned Fabricius[5] has described several species of crustaceans, arachnids and insects from New Holland. But, with the exception of these species and some others published in the Memoirs of the Society of London, those that M. Péron has collected in that land are all new.

If someone who was unaware of the details of how this undertaking had been carried out were to cast an eye over the astonishing number of animals that have been discovered, he would be convinced that a large contingent of naturalists contributed to it and that this work consumed a considerable part of their life. What would be his surprise, or rather his admiration, if he were to learn that three men alone, Messrs Péron, Lesueur and Maugé, acquired all of these zoological riches while putting their lives in danger, and all of that in the short space of three and a half years; that, moreover, the first and the second found the time, in Péron's case to observe and describe most of these animals, and in Lesueur's to paint them from life with the most scrupulous precision?

In order to impress upon you that no bias or partiality has had any part whatsoever to play in this report, it should suffice to quote that remarkable pronouncement made by the great entomologist Fabricius who, when he saw our collection of insects and thus the great number of specimens that had escaped his attention, could not prevent himself from turning towards M. Péron and exclaiming: *"Ah, Monsieur, you have distressed me in my old age!"*

Three tables accompany this text; they concern the three zoological groups under consideration. Each table consists of three columns: the second and third record exclusively numbers (the numbers of species and the numbers of specimens, respectively); the first presents a list of names of genera, written in French.[6] While the report is written in Lamarck's hand, the tables are not. It is known that Lamarck did not take a great interest in arthropods; it is therefore likely that, even though he presented these tables himself to his professor colleagues, they were in fact drawn up by Pierre André Latreille,[7] no doubt in collaboration with Fabricius. Lamarck had, moreover, earlier acknowledged that the catalogue of 'animals in his section' brought back by the *Naturaliste* had been established by Latreille.[8]

1.1 Crustaceans

Names of genera	Number of species	Number of specimens
Crab (*Cancer*)	16	50
Box crab (*Calappa*)	3	20
Sponge crab (*Dromia*)	3	8
Ghost crab (*Ocypoda*)	9	15
Lightfoot crab (*Grapsus*)	8	14
A new genus, close to the preceding	1	3
Swimming crab (*Portunus*)	9	18
Long eyed crab (*Podophthalmus*)	1	2
Moon crab (*Matuta*)	1	9
Porcelain crab (*Porcellana*)	4	10
Tiger crab (*Orithya*)	1	1
Pebble crab (*Leucosia*)	5	15
Spider crab (*Maja*)	8	18
Mole crab (*Hippa*)	1	20
Slipper lobster (*Scyllarus*)	2	3
Crayfish (*Astacus*)	6	30
Hermit crab (*Pagurus*)	3	8 to 10
Squat lobster (*Galathea*)	1	6
Spiny lobster (*Palinurus*)	1	8
Palemon (*Palaemon*)	4	10
Prawn (*Gammarus*)	2	5
Water louse (*Asellus*)	16	36
Rock slaters (*Ligia*)	1	1
Wood-louse (*Oniscus*)	4	14
Sea lice (*Caligus*)	2	8
Mantis shrimp (*Squilla*)	2	12
Total	**115** (114)	**344 to 346** (338)[1]

[1] The original totals are sometimes incorrect, as here. Where this is the case, the correct number is given in bold with the original number indicated unbolded in parentheses.

Taking as a reference the *Histoire naturelle des animaux sans vertèbres*,[10] which is the most complete of Lamarck's works in terms of its systematics, we note that only 11 species of crustaceans originating from the places visited by the Baudin expedition are listed in it,[11] as opposed to the 114 species given in the table above. The analysis that Jacqueline Bonnemains and Diana Jones conducted of the drawings of these same crustaceans that were made by Lesueur and that are kept at Le Havre[12] identified 45 species, all collected during the voyage. 15 of these had been classified by pre-Lamarckian authors (Linnaeus, Forsskål, Fabricius, Herbst, Lund and Pallas), one had been classified by Lamarck himself (*Neoxanthias impressus*), 11 by H. Milne-Edwards,[13] and the remaining 18 by individual authors from 1810 to 1959. Several of Lesueur's drawings were reproduced by Jones,[14] by Bonnemains and Jones,[15] and by Bonnemains.[16]

1.2 Arachnids

Names of genera	Number of species	Number of specimens
Scorpion (*Scorpio*)	3	12
Spiders		
Mygale (*Mygale*)	3	4
Spiders (*Aranea*)		
Rug hooker spider	2	2
Mower spider	7	15
Spiny spider	2	3
Crab spider	6	10
Wolf spiders	4	6
Jumping spider	3	5
A large number of egg shells of the St Andrew's Cross spider from the Cape of Good Hope		
Scolopendra[1] (*Scolopendra*)	3	
House centipede (*Scutigera*)	2	
Iulus (*Iulus*)	4	3
Total	**39**	**76**

[1] Scolopendra, Scutigera and Iulus are in fact myriapods, not arachnids.

Only one of the species of spider collected during the expedition is quoted in the *Histoire naturelle des animaux sans vertèbres*.[18] At the Museum in Le Havre, there is a plate of drawings of spiders by Lesueur, but the origin of the specimens represented is not indicated.[19]

1.3 Insects

Names of genera	Number of species	Number of specimens
COLEOPTERA		
Stag beetle (*Lucanus*)	2	11
Passalus (*Passalus*)	2	10
Scarab beetle (*Scarabaeus*)	10	24
Geotrup (*Geotrupes*)	3	4
Dung beetles[1]		
Subgenera		
Dung beetle (*Copris*)	14	25
Aphodius (*Aphodius*)	2	5
Ateuchus (*Ateuchus*)	8	56
Onitis (*Onitis*)	1	3
Cockchafer (*Melolontha*)	22	72
Cetonia		
Subgenera		
Rose beetle (*Cetonia*)	31	79
Trichius (*Trichius*)	4	115
Trox (*Trox*)	3	12
Hister beetle (*Hister*)	4	39
Sphaeridium (*Sphaeridium*)	3	5
Larder beetle (*Dermestes*)	5	12
Carrion beetle (*Silpha*)	2	6
Burying beetle (*Necrophorus*)	1	1
Clerus (*Clerus*)	3	3
Whirligig beetle (*Gyrinus*)	3	21
Hydrophilus (*Hydrophilus*)	1	25
Diving beetle (*Dytiscus*)	5	15
Ground beetles (*Carabus*)		
Subgenera		
Carabus (*Carabus*)	1	6
Panageus (*Panageus*)	2	4
Lebia (*Lebia*)	2	3
Harpalus (*Harpalus*)	10	76
Brachynus (*Brachynus*)	4	28
Anthia (*Anthia*)	3	7
Scarites (*Scarites*)	2	2
Common tiger beetle (*Cicindela*)	4	5
Elaphrus (*Elaphrus*)	1	4
Rove beetle (*Staphylinus*)	4	29
Jewel beetle (*Buprestis*)	24	55

Click beetle (*Elateridae*)	5	6
Soldier beetle (*Telephorus*)	1	1
Melyris (*Melyris*)	1	5
Firefly (*Lampyris*)	2	3
Net-winged beetle (*Lycus*)	5	18
Mylabris (*Mylabris*)	8	164
Blister beetle (*Horia*)	1	1
Zonitis (*Zonitis*)	1	6
Lagria (*Lagria*)	2	26
Cossyphus (*Cossyphus*)	8	16
Diaperis (*Diaperis*)	1	2
Pleasing fungus beetle (*Triplax*)	1	3
Opatrum (*Opatrum*)	5	45
Darkling beetle (*Tenebrio*)	13	31
Chiroscelis (*Chiroscelis*)	1	1
Pimelia (*Pimelia*)	7	10
Sepidium (*Sepidium*)	2	3
Helops (*Helops*)	11	37
Erodius (*Erodius*)	1	2
Mouldy beetle (*Eurychora*)	1	3
Brentus (*Brentus*)	3	7
Prionus (*Prionus*)	4	5
Longhorn beetles		
Subgenera		
Longhorn beetle (*Cerambyx*)	11	46
Lamia (*Lamia*)	16	40
Callidium (*Callidium*)	7	12
Necydalis (*Necydalis*)	1	1
Saperda (*Saperda*)	4	7
Leptura (*Leptura*)	1	2
Stenocorus (*Stenecorus*)	1	3
False oil beetle (*Oedemera*)	4	6
Trogrossita (*Trogrossita*)	1	3
Leaf beetle (*Chrysomela*)	23	82
Galeruca (*Galeruca*)	12	32
Flea beetle (*Altica*)	4	44
Leaf beetle (*Cryptocephalus*)	5	13
Clythra (*Clythra*)	3	4
Weevils		
Subgenera		
Weevil (*Curculio*)	4	50
Calandra (*Calandra*)	3	135
Brachycerus (*Brachycerus*)	1	2

Tortoise beetle (*Cassida*)	2	2
Total (Coleoptera)	**398** (421)	**1687** (1597)
ORTHOPTERA		
Earwig (*Forficula*)	4	16
Cricket (*Gryllus*)	6	20
Locust (*Locusta*)	12	34
Cricket (*Acrydium*)	15	90
Cockroach (*Blatta*)	10	60
Locust (*Truxale*)	1	30
Mantises (*Mantis*)	11	30
Spectrum (*Spectrum*)	3	12
Bladder grasshopper (*Pneumora*)	2	2
Total (Orthoptera)	**74** (73)	**294** (324)
NEUROPTERA		
Dragonfly (*Libellula*)	17	55
Termite (*Termes*)	2	50
Antlion (*Myrmeleo*)	1	14
Ascalaphus (*Ascalaphus*)	1	4
Scorpion fly (*Panorpa*)	1	1
Total (Neuroptera)	**22**	**124**
HYMENOPTERA		
Sawfly (*Tenthredo*)	2	5
Ichneumon wasp (*Ichneumon*)	6	9
Ensign wasp (*Evania*)	1	3
Ant (*Formica*)	17	68
Velvet ant (*Mutilla*)	4	12
Flower wasp (*Thynnus*)	3	15
Mellinus (*Mellinus*)	1	1
Sphex		
Subgenera		
Pompilus (*Pompilus*)	5	5
Sphex (*Sphex*)	12	36
Larra (*Larra*)	3	3
Dorila Fab.[ii] (?)	2	2
Cuckoo wasp (*Chrysis*)	2	3
Wasp (*Vespa*)	23	96
Sand wasp (*Bembex*)	2	2
Bee (*Apis*)	24	63
Small carpenter bee (*Ceratina*)	1	5
Total (Hymenoptera)	**108**	**328**
LEPIDOPTERA		
Sphinx (*Sphinx*)	12	28
Milkweed butterflies		

Subgenera		
Knight (*Equites*)	18	87
Nymph (*Nymphalis*)	82	350
Danaid (*Danais*)	23	192
Plebeji (*Plebei*)	20	124
Skipper butterfly (*Hesperia*)	11	65
Burnet moth (*Zygaena*)	10	45
Silkmoth (*Bombyx*)	30	75
Moth (*Phalena*)	50	104
Yellow underwing (*Noctua*)	18	35
Pyralis (*Pyralis*)	6	12
Clothes moth (*Tinea*)	5	60
Total (Lepidoptera)	**285**	**1177** (1243)
HEMIPTERA		
Leafhopper (*Cicada*)	3	9
Leafhopper (*Cicadella*)	9	13
Scullcap (*Scutellera*)	15	146
Stink bug (*Pentatoma*)	22	55
Bug (*Cimex*)	18	135
Dock bug (*Coroeus*)	13	58
Kissing bug (*Reduvius*)	12	23
Galgulus (*Galgulus*)	1	2
Water measurer (*Hydrometra*)	1	1
Water scorpion (*Nepa*)	3	15
Plate Fab.[iii] (?)	13	29
Membracis (*Membracis*)	3	20
Cochineal (*Coccus*)	3	24
Total (Hemiptera)	**116** (106)	**530**
DIPTERA		
Crane fly (*Tipula*)	4	13
Horesefly (*Tabanus*)	7	19
Robber fly (*Asilus*)	2	3
Bee fly (*Bombylius*)	4	8
Conops (*Conops*)	1	1
Panops (*Panops*)	1	2
Fly (*Musca*)	7	23
Bee fly (*Anthrax*)	1	2
Stalk-eyed fly (*Diopsis*)	1	2
Total (Diptera)	**28**	**73**
Total (Insects)	**1031** (1043)	**4213** (4219)

[i] 'The subgenera here and in the following pages were identified by Messrs Fabricius and Latreille' (original note at the foot of the table).
[ii] A genus proposed by Fabricius but whose description was apparently not published (nomen nudum).
[iii] Idem.

Recapitulation of the Arthropods

	Number of species	Number of specimens
Crustaceans	115 (114)	346
Arachnids	39	76
Insects		
Coleoptera	**398** (421)	**1687** (1597)
Orthoptera	**74** (73)	**294** (324)
Neuroptera	**22**	**124**
Hymenoptera	**108**	**328**
Lepidoptera	**285**	**1177** (1243)
Hemiptera	**116** (106)	**530**
Diptera	**28**	**73**
Total	**1185** (1186)	**4635** (4641)

As already noted, the estimations given in these tables of the numbers of species and specimens collected concern only those brought back by the *Géographe*, the collections from the *Naturaliste* having been the subject of an earlier cataloguing exercise.[23] The lists of genera that are represented make it clear that the collectors in no way overlooked the capture of land invertebrates. While the number of new species suggested by Lamarck (1031 species for insects alone!) is completely unverifiable, it is quite conceivable that the total came to considerably more than half the number he put forward. As indicated above, these tables, which were presented to the meeting of the professors, were most probably compiled by Latreille with the collaboration of Fabricius.[24]

Published information on the insects collected during the expedition is scarce. Some species are presented in Lamarck's *Histoire naturelle*;[25] mostly, however, the species he presents in that work appear to come from material brought back by the *Naturaliste*. He presents, for instance, two species of *Panops* (diptera) and one species of *Chrisoscelis* (coleoptera), but these are in fact species corresponding to the genera he had previously established based on the collections brought back in 1803.[26] Also mentioned among the items from New Holland are two species of *Hymenoptera* belonging to the *Formica* and *Mutilla* genera[27] (are these the specimens that feature in the illustration on vellum submitted by Lamarck to the meeting of the professors held on 1 Frimaire Year

12?),[28] as well as several species of coleoptera: four species of *Helea*, two of which were from Kangaroo Island (and must therefore have figured in the collections of the *Géographe*), one species of *Rhipicera* and four species of *Lamprima*.[29] Unless there are some drawings by Lesueur lying undiscovered in the archives of the Museum in Le Havre or the Paris Museum, the only known illustrations of the insects brought back by the expedition are those published by Lamarck and by Georges Bernardi (see also Bonnemains).[30]

2. Report on the Echinoderms

Report on the echinoderms[31] and stellerids[32] collected by M. Péron during the voyage of discovery

In my previous report I presented to you the general table of objects collected by the naturalists of the voyage of discovery, divided into three classes of invertebrate animals, namely crustaceans, arachnids and insects; I sought to apprise you of the importance of this vast collection, which is without doubt the finest that has been produced by a single voyage and that has ever reached the Museum.

I now draw your attention to the results, which are no less important, relating to the animals in two broad divisions within my class of radiata: the echinoderms[33] and the stellerids.

As you saw in my report on the crustaceans, arachnids and insects collected during the voyage of discovery, the large number of genera provide us with a prodigious quantity of species and specimens. In this new report that I am presenting, the species and specimens may be fewer in number, but they are no less interesting.

The work of M. Péron on ophiuroids and asteroids is truly invaluable. Along the entire length of the coasts that he visited, from the southern cape of Van Diemen's

Land to the eastern shores of the island of Timor, this indefatigable traveller continued to add to his collection, and, over this straight-line distance from north to south of eight to nine hundred leagues, he observed a succession of species, all of which changed at different latitudes, and all of which are equally new and interesting. No such collection had ever been compiled in these southern regions; the work of M. Péron is, as a result, all the more interesting and valuable.

Moreover, as in all the other classes of the animal kingdom, New Holland, which is quite distinctive in this respect, offers nothing but new species on shores that are equally new for us. We might even go so far as to observe that the ophiuroid genus, the species of which appear to be scarce in the other regions of the globe, are precisely those which are the most numerous and the most varied on these distant shores. Their number has now been more than quadrupled thanks to the work of M. Péron, and perhaps a new section for this genus will become necessary, or at the very least a remarkable sub-section within it will need to be established; for the quite sizeable number of cirrigerous ophiuroids[34] brought back by M. Péron display characteristics that are very likely to determine such a division. It will be all the more natural a division because it will be based on a particular conformity of these animals with respect to structure, habits and behaviours, as M. Péron has been able to observe.

In this section of the animal kingdom, therefore, Science has also made new and interesting progress. This progress becomes even more valuable thanks to the care M. Péron has taken in noting the latitudes at which he collected the various species, the precision of the descriptions he has made of them, and the precision, likewise, of the drawings and illustrations that M. Lesueur has taken the greatest care in producing.[35]

2.1 The Echinoderms: Echinoids and Stellerids

Genera	Number of species	Number of specimens
Sea stars	36 (20)[39]	264
Ophiuroids[36]	33 (28)	121
Sea urchins	22 (12)	174
Clypeastroids[37]	5 (3)	22
Spatangoids[38]	4 (2)	10
Total	100	591

Regarding the 65 species considered to be new that are listed above (in parentheses), it is worth noting that only seven of those that Lamarck will describe in 1816 can clearly be identified as coming from the Baudin expedition (three comatulids, two sea urchins, two sea stars and one ophiuroid).[40] It is for these seven species only that Lamarck clearly states or suggests that the specimens come from the collections made by Péron and Lesueur. In the case of the two species of sea star, one is clearly localised (*Asterias calcar*, from King George Sound); the colour of the other (*A. ocellifera*) had been remembered by Lamarck ('M. Lesueur assures me that it was of a beautiful red colour when it was collected'). If we exclude these two species of sea star, no starfish described by Lamarck can be formally identified as coming from the Baudin expedition because either the location mentioned is imprecise ('Inhabits [...] the southern seas?') or else there is no actual location provided. And yet we know that 11 of Lamarck's species of sea star – *Asterias carinifera, A. clavigera, A. cuspidata, A. exigua, A. globifera, A. milleporella, A. multifora, A. obtusangula, A. pentagonula, A. rosacea* and *A. vernicina* – were drawn by Lesueur during the course of the expedition! Moreover, an analysis of Lesueur's drawings, which are kept in the Museum at Le Havre,[41] has demonstrated that no less than 53 different species of sea star are represented and that all but one were new for Science when they were collected.[42] This discrepancy between the wealth of pictorial information (Lesueur's 1804 drawings) and the paucity of published information[43] is all the more disconcerting as Lamarck had been aware of these drawings (he alludes to them in his report) and would therefore have been able to deduce that the specimens came from the expedition. Clearly, the specimens and drawings of invertebrates – both the echinoderms and the arthropods – must have suffered an unusual fate!

At the beginning of the nineteenth century, knowledge of echinoderms was not yet complete. Thus, in addition to the 'cirrigerous ophiuroids', which would prove to be comatulids, the status of sea cucumbers was still uncertain. Lamarck did not classify them as echinoderms (he included them, with sea-anemones and sipunculid, priapulid and echiurid worms, in the 'fistulide' group – which is no longer in use),[44] whereas Cuvier divided them among the two groups of echinoderms that he had established: the pedicellata and the apoda (within the 'apoda', he placed, in addition to certain sea cucumbers, the sipunculid, echiurid and priapulid worms).[45]

Péron had been particularly interested in sea cucumbers during the voyage of discovery, both because of their anatomical features (he described them as 'soft zoophytes') and because of their reputed aphrodisiac properties and their social importance among the peoples of the Far East. On this subject, he wrote: 'Served on the table of the wealthy and important people of the [Chinese] empire, these trepangs are seen both as a source of renewed vigour and as dazzling evidence of the power of the man who uses them'.[46] The fact that Péron, shortly before his death, was working on an article devoted to the sea cucumbers collected during the expedition is further proof of his interest in the subject. The manuscript of this draft article is held in the Museum of Le Havre.[47] Unfortunately, the descriptions contained in this document were never published and consequently the species Péron proposed are not valid (their names are all 'nomen nudum').

No sea cucumber from the Southern Lands is presented in Lamarck's *Histoire naturelle*. However, there is one, *Cuviera agathophytos*, from Cape Leeuwin (the only sea cucumber that Péron had not classified in the genus *Holothuria*), which has an unusual history. Péron dedicated it 'to Citizen Cuvier, Professor at the National Museum of Natural History, as a small token of my respect and gratitude'.[48] Later, Cuvier called it a 'cuvieria' and, as the genus *Cuvieria* was already taken (Cuvier does not seem to have realised that Péron had proposed *Cuviera*, not *Cuvieria*), he reclassified it in the genus *Holothuria* and gave it the species name *Holothuria cuvieria*. This species became official, since it was (summarily) described and depicted by Cuvier in his *Règne animal* (*Animal Kingdom*).[49] Thus, Cuvier's *Holothuria cuvieria*, 1817, came to be self-attributed by its describer, who, in reality, was not the person who described it! There was as a result great taxonomic confusion about this species during the entire nineteenth century and beyond, until such time as its name was finally settled: *Ceto cuvieria* (Cuvier, 1817).[50]

Cuvier's description of *H. cuvieria* is complemented by an illustration drawn by Charles Léopold Laurillard showing the upper side of an organism that must have macerated for some time in alcohol. The animal has two openings: one seems to have a clump of skinny filaments sprouting from it; the other displays five flattened and tooth-like outgrowths.[51] This is a lacklustre drawing compared to Lesueur's almost photographic illustration, which shows the same species in a natural position with its original colours.[52]

Lesueur left France in 1815 to travel around the West Indies with the American geologist William Maclure before heading to the United States in 1816.[53] He stayed there for almost a quarter of a century, finally returning to France in 1838. On his return, he settled in Paris and took possession of his drawings of animals from the Southern Lands. In the summer of 1840, he met the German zoologist Franz Hermann Troschel, who was visiting the Museum to study its collection of star-shaped echinoderms (asteroids and ophiuroids). Lesueur must have shown him his asteroid drawings, as they are mentioned with respect to 15 of the species held in the Parisian collections in the work Troschel published in collaboration with Johannes Müller in 1842.[54] It would not be until 1984, however, that these drawings by Lesueur would become the subject of detailed analysis.[55]

3. Report on the Molluscs

With respect to molluscs, which is a particularly large class, the zealous research conducted by the naturalists who participated in the French voyage of discovery, and notably M. Péron, has earned them no less distinction than their work in the other branches of zoology. They have in fact achieved much more in this regard, and it is for this reason that we have not until now been able to provide a detailed account of this work.

In addition to the many shell-less molluscs that form part of their zoological collections and that we have not yet been able to examine, they brought back such a large number of shells that the total number of specimens greatly exceeds 10,000. These specimens in my view belong to at least 800 species, a great number of which are entirely new for us and were missing from our list of the natural objects that had been observed.

Knowing as we do how extraordinarily passionate Lamarck was about molluscs,[56] this report, however short it may be, allows us to imagine the astonishment and the wonder that this devoted conchologist must have experienced when he came upon such a quantity of new sea-shells! Those specimens which Lamarck called shell-less molluscs (and which are in fact opisthobranch gastropods) were for the most part studied by Cuvier,[57] Lamarck himself being more interested in molluscs with shells. It is known that Lamarck's passion as a collector led him progressively to intermingle the Museum's collection of sea-shells (and thus also that of the Baudin expedition) with his own. An account of that passion, and of its consequences, can be found in Bernard Métivier's article 'Lamarck et les mollusques'.[58]

To what extent did Lamarck make use of the collection of molluscs from the Baudin expedition in preparing his *Histoire naturelle des animaux sans vertèbres*? An analysis of the section devoted to conchifera (the name he gave to bivalve molluscs, which constituted his eleventh class) and to gastropods (which he placed in his twelfth class) is nothing short of astounding. Of the species of bivalves collated by Lamarck in his *Histoire naturelle*, 174 come from a location compatible with the sites visited by the expedition.[59] For 84 of these, the location given is fairly vague (the Seas of New Holland); it is much more precisely indicated in the other cases (Maria Island, Shark Bay, King George Sound, etc). As for the name of the collector (which is generally Péron), it is mentioned for 64 of these 174 species. In short, the list of bivalves in Lamarck's publication appears to be quite a faithful reflection of the diversity of species collected during the expedition.

The same cannot be said for the gastropod molluscs. In the case of the shell-less gastropods, only two marine species ('sea slugs') are presented in the *Histoire naturelle* and no land species ('slugs') are mentioned. Similarly, very few species of land-based or fresh-water testacea (shell-bearing gastropods) are mentioned (two land species and five fresh-water ones). The species of testacea that are mentioned are thus in the great majority marine based (68 species); however, they are much fewer in number than the bivalves.[60] An exact indication of the place where they were collected is provided for only seven of them (for the most part, their origin is simply given as 'Seas of New Holland'). The name of the collector (once again, generally Péron) is noted for 27 of these species.

The number of species from the expedition mentioned by Lamarck in his *Histoire naturelle* (174 species of bivalves and 77 of gastropods) is well short of what he had announced in his brief malacological report (800 species!). The gastropods in particular appear to have been neglected: few species are mentioned and most of those that are have no other locational origin than 'Seas of New Holland'.

Lesueur's gastropod drawings published in 1988 by Jean Gaillard relate to four species;[61] Gaillard provides a list of 16 others that were also drawn by Lesueur. One single drawing of a bivalve mollusc is reproduced by Métivier, who lists five other species that were similarly drawn by the artist.[62] Of the 23 species of molluscs, ten are mentioned in the *Histoire naturelle*, but Lamarck does not refer to Lesueur's drawings for any of these.

Discussion

As Richard Burkhardt has noted,[63] Lamarck's laudatory assessment of the activity and zeal shown by Péron and Lesueur, and of the quality and variety of the collections that were brought back and of the illustrations that were drawn (see the 1804 reports), stands in stark contrast to the sometimes sketchy treatment he gave to these collections in his *Histoire naturelle des animaux sans vertèbres*, which was published between 1815 and 1822.[64] How are we to explain the fact that a significant proportion of the species collected in the Southern Lands and almost all of the drawings were overlooked in this way? Burkhardt speculates that this may have been due to a possible disordering of the collections in the days that followed their arrival in Lorient. It is indeed worth noting that, while Péron had classified the specimens collected according to their geographical origins by noting on the crates and packets that contained them where they were from, these indications were not noted on the jars or packaging in which the specimens themselves had been stored. Péron, who had wasted no time in leaving for Paris, where he arrived on 4 April (the *Géographe* had arrived in Lorient on 25 March), was alerted by a message from Lesueur, who had remained on board, that the Museum's envoy, Geoffroy Saint-Hilaire, had arrived in Lorient and had begun to unpack the objects of natural history to check on their condition. The alarm this caused Péron prompted him to send a letter to Geoffroy Saint-Hilaire on 19 April. This letter is of paramount importance. Following are some of the main passages from it:

> The stage on which [the collections] were compiled is immense, as you know. Stretching from the 9th to the 117th [parallel], New Holland, Van Diemen's Land, their various archipelagos and the seas that surround them provided us with a constant supply of specimens. The location where each object was found was carefully noted by me in my journals, and was done so consistently. We were heading [...] from the southern cape of Van Diemen's Land [...] to the northern cape of New Holland. It was easy to foresee that at such different latitudes the zoological products would be correspondingly varied. [...] The results of my observations were noted in my journals; all of the objects in my collection were carefully labelled and given a number corresponding to the number I used to note my comments about them. In this way, not only is there no specimen whose provenance cannot be rigorously identified, but there is also no significant portion of this southern continent, which we charted, whose products may not be assessed according to the great differences in temperature or exposure. This new means of dealing with my collections seemed to me most likely to produce results that will be as stimulating

for their unusual nature as they might become for their significance. [...]

[I have observed, for example,] that *Haliotis gigantea* does not appear to be found beyond 30° south, at which latitude it is even, so to speak, unrecognisable, as you will see yourself from my various specimens.[65] I have made the same observations regarding the amazing *Bulimus* snail from D'Entrecasteaux Channel and Maria Island [...]. You will see the specimens gradually grow smaller and lose the richness of their colour from the latitude of 44° south up to the St Peter and St Francis Islands where the species is no longer to be found.

[...] The insects were no less a source of interest to me from the point of view I am highlighting here; the entire division of the knights, for example, appears to be excluded from the Southern Lands, as it is from the more northern lands of our hemisphere.[66] [...] All of these modifications become more striking still, and more general, in the families of crustaceans, molluscs, [and] above all worms and echinoderms [...].

I have sought, my dear M. Geoffroy, to ensure that you are fully aware, in advance, of the interest my collections will have if they are maintained in the order in which they were compiled before expressing to you the subject of my fears. This order, as you have seen, is ensured by the number on each crate and by that on each of the packages contained within those crates – all of which numbers correspond to my personal inventories, to my journals, to our numerous drawings. If this numerical order of the crates or objects is changed, the entire fruits of my careful work will be lost. I myself could not find my way around so many different objects collected in so many diverse climates at more or less distant periods of time. The strongest foundations for the zoography of New Holland would be destroyed, and the collections, which were the object of so much care and attention, would be reduced to the common status of second-hand natural history collections. These are my fears, Sir. You will not take offence, I am certain, because your actions have been guided by the interest that my collections inspire and by the desire to conserve them as well as is possible.[67]

Alas, Péron's fears were justified. His letter must have reached Geoffroy between 21 and 23 April; it was no doubt too late, since Geoffroy, in a letter dated 23 April, wrote to his professor colleagues: 'All the crates have been inspected here [and] the damage repaired'.[68] The next day, in a separate letter addressed to Antoine-François de Fourcroy, the director of the Museum, he stated: 'The insects left this morning by coach [. . .]. I have reduced the number of boxes to four packets, or, to be more precise, I have made four packets of the ten boxes of insects'.[69] It is unlikely that Péron's geographical classification survived such a reorganisation. The same applied to the madrepores (or rocky corals), Geoffroy Saint-Hilaire reporting in the same letter that he himself had 'overseen their re-packaging and put each madrepore in a separate box and in cotton, and each box was wrapped in straw appropriate for this purpose'. The collection did admittedly arrive in Paris in good condition, but, for a part of it at least, the specimens were evidently not in the same order as that in which Péron had packed them.

That would not be the end of the story. In a note in May 1804, Louis Dufresne, an assistant-naturalist at the Museum, informed the professors that, 'together with Citizens Péron and Lesueur, we have continued to unpack the crates and set aside what was appropriate for the national collection'.[70] There is an implication here that the remainder of the collection was intended for Mme Bonaparte; but this statement also suggests that the collection of invertebrates, either because of a lack of geographical information or in spite of it, was systematically reorganised in a way that separated out the molluscs, echinoderms, crustaceans, etc, as the format of Lamarck's reports might indicate – a reorganisation that was designed to facilitate the process of counting and cataloguing the specimens.

We should recall that neither Péron nor Lesueur was an employee of the Museum. Consequently, no work space was set aside for them and they were forced to study the specimens in their own residence. This situation created some problems between them and the administrators of the Museum. Dufresne, for instance, was forbidden from lending them specimens unless he obtained prior permission from a meeting of the professors.[71] Moreover, the professors received letters from the Minister of Marine and the Minister of the Interior indicating that Péron and Lesueur had been required to certify that the entirety of the collections made during the voyage had indeed been handed over to the Museum.[72] None of this prevented them from borrowing specimens for (too) lengthy periods. This is what must have led the professors, who were no doubt battle-weary, to appeal to Bernard Germain de Lacépède, their colleague who had become a senator, so that he might put pressure on Péron to return to the Museum the objects of natural history that had been entrusted to him.[73] Confirmation of the tenseness of the situation can be found in the irritated note that Dufresne sent shortly after to the professors:

> Messrs Péron and Lesueur initially returned some orthopteras when we were preparing this family for the galleries. They have now handed back the rest of this family which was still in their keeping and which, unfortunately, they have returned in a poor condition. In the light of this, given that they are leaving in a few days to spend some time in Nice due to M. Péron's state of health, would this not be an opportunity to ask them again for the fish and other objects from their voyage?[74]

Following Péron's death in December 1810, André Thouin, who was then director of the Museum, had his apartment sealed in order to preserve the Museum's property.[75] The seal was removed in April 1811 and the Museum was able to recover the fish, reptiles, insects, molluscs, etc, from the expedition that had been borrowed by the naturalist.[76] Everything suggests, therefore, that the disordering of the collection gathered pace from 1804 to 1810 and that the death of Péron and the subsequent departure from France of Lesueur meant that the geographical origin of many of the species was lost forever. Indeed, for a large number of them, the very fact that they had been collected during the Baudin expedition came to be forgotten! This could no doubt have been avoided if the Museum had kept Lesueur's drawings, but, alas, this was not to be the case.[77] And so, when Lamarck sat down to write his *Histoire naturelle des animaux sans vertèbres*, many of the specimens from the expedition had become divorced from the information on their origins, and the drawings representing them had disappeared. This no doubt explains the fate of the arthropod and echinoderm collections: the species of arthropods from the expedition are only rarely mentioned in Lamarck's work, and the few species of echinoderms that he refers to are often discussed without any details of the precise location where they were found. On the other hand, the molluscs were given a mixed treatment: the bivalves from Baudin's voyage were abundantly referred to, but this stands in contrast to the gastropods, which are dealt with in an incomplete manner. Given Lamarck's great passion for malacology, this difference in treatment is intriguing. The explanation is, in fact, given by Lamarck himself in the foreword that serves as introduction to volume 6(1) of his *Histoire naturelle*: having been reduced to complete blindness by ophthalmia, he had been unable to complete his work (volumes 6(2) and 7 were actually just compilations, made by his daughter, of notes he had previously written).[78]

Burkhardt had pondered the fact that Lamarck, in his considerations on the notion of 'species', referred exclusively to what Péron had told him without making any reference to the specimens the naturalist had brought back to France.[79] He was right to raise this important question, the answer to which is depressing: the collection had lost all connections with its geographical origins. We are left to regret that Péron was not able to undertake his project of writing up the 'Zoography of New Holland'. His observations on the variations in species along gradients of latitude would undoubtedly have led him to consider the processes responsible for their genesis – as Lamarck's note, which Burkhardt refers to, allows us to infer:

> [we may] note that there are often, among the varieties observed, some which are the type for lateral series that lead to other species [. . .]. What we have already seen in this respect clearly shows the basis for this, and I have it

from Péron — that naturalist who is famous for his travels, his observations and his discoveries — that he himself was struck with astonishment when he compared in turn all of the objects he collected.[80]

Notes

1 The author wishes to thank Bernard Métivier for his constructive comments, and John West-Sooby for the English translation of this text.
2 Letter dated 4 Germinal Year 12 (25 March 1804), appended to the minutes of the meeting of the professors' committee held on 21 Germinal (11 April), Archives Nationales de France (ANF), série Muséum, AJ 15/592.
3 Minutes of the meeting of the professors' committee held on 10 Prairial Year 12 (30 May 1804). ANF, série Muséum, AJ 15/592.
4 Lamarck's reports and the accompanying tables are appended to the minutes of the meeting of the professors' committee held on 8 Messidor Year 12 (27 June 1804). ANF, série Muséum, AJ 15/592.
5 Johan Christian Fabricius (1745–1808) was a Danish entomologist. A friend of Pierre André Latreille, a specialist of arthropods, he spent his summers in Paris, at the Museum.
6 The French terms have been translated here, with the Latin equivalent at the time added in parentheses and written in italics.
7 Pierre André Latreille (1762–1833) was at that time an assistant naturalist responsible for the insect collections in Lamarck's laboratory. He would publish, from 1802 to 1805, a 14-volume work entitled *Histoire naturelle des crustacés et insectes* (Paris: Dufart).
8 Minutes of the meeting of the professors' committee held on 8 Frimaire Year 12 (30 November 1803), ANF, série Muséum, AJ 15/590.
9 The original totals are sometimes incorrect, as here. Where this is the case, the correct number is given unbolded in parentheses.
10 Jean-Baptiste Lamarck, *Histoire naturelle des animaux sans vertèbres*, Paris: Deterville, 7 vols, 1815-1822. The arthropods are examined in volumes 3 to 5, published from 1816 to 1818.
11 According to Lamarck (*Histoire naturelle des vertèbres*, vol. 5, 1818), these 11 species belong to the following genera: *Cancer, Gecarcinus, Grapsus, Maia, Palaemon, Plagusia* and *Scyllarus*.
12 Jacqueline Bonnemains and Diana Jones, 'Les Crustacés de la collection C.- A. Lesueur du Muséum d'Histoire naturelle du Havre', *Bulletin de la Société géologique de Normandie et des Amis du Muséum du Havre*, vol. 77, 1990, pp. 27–66. Lamarck alludes to these drawings in his report, but does not subsequently refer to them.
13 Henri Milne-Edwards (1800–1881) occupied the chair of articulated animals (Arthropods) at the Paris Museum from 1844.
14 Diana Jones, 'Crustaceans', in Jacqueline Bonnemains, Elliott Forsyth and Bernard Smith (eds), *Baudin in Australian Waters*, Melbourne: Oxford University Press, 1988, pp. 218–220.
15 Bonnemains and Jones, 'Les Crustacés'.
16 Jacqueline Bonnemains (ed.), *Mon voyage aux Terres Australes: Journal personnel du commandant Baudin*, Paris: Imprimerie nationale, 2000, pl. LXV.
17 *Scolopendra, Scutigera* and *Iulus* are in fact myriapods, not arachnids.
18 *Atypus occatorius*; see Lamarck, *Histoire naturelle*, vol. 5, 1818, p. 105.
19 Jacqueline Bonnemains, 'Les Illustrations du livre de bord du capitaine Nicolas Baudin. Répertoire des documents retrouvés', *Annales du Muséum du Havre*, no. 33, 1986, pp. 1–20.

20 'The subgenera here and in the following pages were identified by Messrs Fabricius and Latreille' (original note at the foot of the table).
21 A genus proposed by Fabricius but whose description was apparently not published (*nomen nudum*).
22 *Idem*.
23 Minutes of the meeting of the professors' committee held on 8 Frimaire Year 12 (30 November 1803), ANF, série Muséum, AJ 15/590.
24 It would surely be of interest to consult the catalogues and archives that these authors may have left. This would allow us to gain a better appreciation of the wealth and diversity of the insect collection brought back by the expedition.
25 Lamarck, *Histoire naturelle*, vols 3 and 4, 1816–1817.
26 Jean-Baptiste Lamarck, 'Sur deux nouveaux genres d'insectes de la Nouvelle-Hollande', *Annales du Muséum national d'Histoire naturelle*, vol. 3, 1804, pp. 260–265. In this article, Lamarck depicts a third species (a member of the Hymenoptera order of the genus *Antophora*) which he does not describe in the text.
27 The genus *Formica* brings together various species of ants; the genus *Mutilla* is a close relative.
28 Minutes of the meeting of the professors' committee held on 1 Frimaire Year 12 (23 November 1803), ANF, série Muséum, AJ 15/590.
29 *Helea* are pie-dish beetles, *Rhipicerida* are cedar beetles, and *Lamprima* is a genus of beetle in the family *Lucanidae* (a group that includes the golden stag beetles).
30 See Lamarck, 'Sur deux nouveaux genres d'insectes'; Georges Bernardi, 'Insects', in Bonnemains, Forsyth and Smith (eds), *Baudin in Australian Waters*, p. 217 (drawings of a pierid butterfly); Bonnemains (ed.), *Mon voyage aux Terres Australes*, pl. LXXVIII.
31 This should be understood to mean 'echinoids' or sea urchins.
32 Star-shaped echinoderms (asteroids, ophiuroids and crinoids).
33 See note 31.
34 These are in fact crinoids that have no stalk, not ophiuroids.
35 Almost all of the echinoderm drawings made by Lesueur represent sea stars!
36 'The great number of ophiuroids brought back by M. Péron will perhaps necessitate a new section of this genus: cirrigera' (note by Lamarck included in the table). We should recall that the cirrigerous ophiuroids are in reality comatulids (crinoids), an interpretation that Lamarck will himself adopt in his *Histoire naturelle*. The common name for ophiuroid is brittle star.
37 Flat sea urchins or sand dollars.
38 Heart sea urchins.
39 The figures in parentheses indicate the numbers of species presumed to be new by Lamarck.
40 Lamarck, *Histoire naturelle*, vols 2 and 3.
41 Archives of the Muséum d'Histoire naturelle du Havre, Collection Lesueur, dossier 74.
42 Michel Jangoux, 'Les astérides (échinodermes) des Terres australes ramenées par l'expédition Baudin', *Bulletin de la Société géologique de Normandie et des Amis du Muséum du Havre,* vol. 71, 1984, pp. 25–56. See also Michel Jangoux, 'Echinoderms', in Bonnemains, Forsyth and Smith (eds), *Baudin in Australian waters*, pp. 221–232, and Bonnemains (ed.), *Mon voyage aux Terres Australes*, pl. LXVI.
43 Lamarck, *Histoire naturelle*, vols 2 and 3.
44 Lamarck, *Histoire naturelle*, vols 2 and 3.
45 Georges Cuvier, *Le Règne animal distribué d'après son organisation*, Paris: Deterville, 4 vols, 1817, vol. 4 (Zoophytes). Note: the priapulids, echiurids and sipunculids were said to be worms because they are vermiform.
46 François Péron and Louis Freycinet, *Voyage de découvertes aux Terres Australes, exécuté par ordre de Sa Majesté l'Empereur et Roi, sur les corvettes le* Géographe *et*

le Naturaliste *et la goëlette le* Casuarina *pendant les années 1800, 1801, 1802, 1803, et 1804, Historique*, vol. 2, Paris: Imprimerie royale, 1816, pp. 247–251. 'Trepang' comes from the Malaysian word 'teripang', which designates a sea cucumber that has been cleaned out and dried. It is in this state that it is commercialised.

47 'Observations sur le genre holothurie: description de dix-neuf espèces de ce genre', Muséum d'Histoire naturelle, Le Havre, Collection Lesueur, nos 65 141–65 190.
48 Péron, 'Observations sur le genre holothurie'.
49 Cuvier, *Le Règne animal*, vol. 4.
50 It was David Pawson who clarified the taxonomy of the species. Pawson was, however, unaware of its 'Péron' origins – that oversight is now corrected! See D. Pawson, 'The Western Australian psolid holothurian *Ceto cuvieria* (Cuvier)', *Journal of the Royal Society of Western Australia*, vol. 54, 1971, pp. 33–39.
51 Cuvier, *Le Règne animal*, vol. 4, pl. 15, fig. 9.
52 This drawing was published in 1988. See Jangoux, 'Echinoderms', p. 232. See also Bonnemains (ed.), *Mon voyage aux Terres Australes*, pl. LXV.
53 George Ord, 'A memoir of Charles Alexander Lesueur', *American Journal of Sciences and Arts*, 2nd series, vol. 8, 1849, pp. 189–216.
54 Johannes Müller and Franz Hermann Troschel, *System der Asteriden*, Braunschweig: F. Vieweg und Sohn, 1842.
55 Jangoux, 'Les astérides (échinodermes) des Terres australes'.
56 Bernard Métivier, 'Lamarck et les mollusques de l'Expédition de Découvertes aux Terres australes', in M. Jangoux (ed.), *Portés par l'air du temps, les voyages du capitaine Baudin*, special number of *Études sur le XVIIIe siècle*, vol. 38, 2010, pp. 253–264.
57 All of Cuvier's notes on opisthobranch molluscs were collected and published in a single volume in 1817: Georges Cuvier, *Mémoires pour servir à l'Histoire et à l'Anatomie des Mollusques*, Paris: Deterville, 1817.
58 See above, note 56.
59 It is interesting to note that of all of these species only six were collected in fresh water.
60 Several species of marine testacea (25 to be precise) had been presented by Lamarck in articles published in 1810 and 1811. See Jean-Baptiste Lamarck, 'Tableau des espèces du genre *Conus*', *Annales du Muséum d'Histoire naturelle*, vol. 15, 1810, pp. 29–40, 263–292, 422–442; 'Description du genre Porcelaine (*Cypraea*) et des espèces qui le composent', *Annales du Muséum d'Histoire naturelle*, vol. 15, 1810, pp. 443–445; 'Suite du genre Porcelaine', *Annales du Muséum d'Histoire naturelle*, vol. 16, 1810, pp. 89–114; 'Suite de la détermination des mollusques testacés', *Annales du Muséum d'Histoire naturelle*, vol. 16, 1810, pp. 300–328 and *Annales du Muséum d'Histoire naturelle*, vol. 17, 1811, pp. 54–80, 185–222.
61 Jean Gaillard, 'Gasteropods', in Bonnemains, Forsyth and Smith (eds), *Baudin in Australian waters*, pp. 209–213. See also Bonnemains (ed.), *Mon voyage aux Terres Australes*, pl. LXII–LXIII.
62 Bernard Métivier, 'Lamellibranchs', in Bonnemains, Forsyth and Smith (eds), *Baudin in Australian waters*, p. 214. See also Bonnemains (ed.), *Mon voyage aux Terres Australes*, pl. LXIV.
63 Richard W. Burkhardt, 'Unpacking Baudin: models of scientific practice in the age of Lamarck', in Goulven Laurent (ed.), *Jean-Baptiste Lamarck, 1744–1829*, Paris: Éditions du CTHS, 1997, pp. 497–514.
64 The part devoted to arthropods was published from 1816 to 1818, the volume on echinoderms appeared in 1816, and the section dealing with molluscs was published from 1818 to 1822.
65 *Haliotis gigantea* is the giant abalone eaten by the natives of Tasmania. See François Péron, *Voyage de découvertes aux Terres Australes, Historique*, vol. 1, Paris: Imprimerie Impériale, 1807, p. 225.

66 The knights are a group of butterflies.
67 Letter appended to the minutes of the meeting of the professors' committee held on 28 Germinal Year 12 (18 April 1804), ANF, série Muséum, AJ 15/590.
68 Letter appended to the minutes of the meeting of the professors' committee held on 19 Floréal Year 12 (9 May 1804), ANF, série Muséum, AJ 15/590.
69 *Ibid.*
70 Report on the activities of the zoology laboratory from 26 Floréal to 3 Prairial Year 12 (16–23 May 1804), ANF, série Muséum, AJ 15/592.
71 Minutes of the meeting of the professors' committee held on 29 Messidor Year 12 (18 July 1804), ANF, série Muséum, AJ 15/592.
72 Letters appended to the minutes of the meeting of the professors' committee held on 16 Prairial Year 13 (5 June 1805), ANF, série Muséum, AJ 15/594. The declaration that they made as a result is reproduced in Jacqueline Bonnemains, 'Origine de la collection "Lesueur" du Muséum d'Histoire naturelle du Havre', *Annales du Muséum du Havre*, no. 49, 1995, p. 592.
73 Minutes of the meeting of the professors' committee held on 7 December 1808, ANF, série Muséum, AJ 15/600.
74 Note appended to the minutes of the meeting of the professors' committee held on 18 January 1809, ANF, série Muséum, AJ 15/601. The orthopteras are a group of winged insects (grasshoppers, crickets, etc.).
75 Minutes of the meeting of the professors' committee held on 26 December 1810, ANF, série Muséum, AJ 15/603.
76 Declaration appended to the minutes of the meeting of the professors' committee held on 17 April 1811, ANF, série Muséum, AJ 15/604.
77 The fate of Lesueur's drawings and the incorporation of a large number of them in the collections of the Museum of Le Havre are recounted by Bonnemains, 'Origine de la collection "Lesueur"'.
78 Lamarck, *Histoire naturelle*, vol. 6, 1819, pp. v–vi.
79 Burkhardt, 'Unpacking Baudin'.
80 Jean-Baptiste Lamarck, 'Espèce', *Nouveau Dictionnaire d'Histoire naturelle*, Paris: Deterville, nouvelle édition, 36 vols, 1816–1819, vol. 10, 1817, pp. 441–451.

Chapter 10

François Péron as an Ornithologist: Identifying his 'New' Bird Species from the Baudin Expedition

Philippa Horton, Justin J.F.J. Jansen and Andrew Black[1]

Introduction

Péron and Freycinet's *Voyage de découvertes aux Terres Australes*[2] contains very little information on the identity of the birds collected during the Baudin expedition (1800–1804).[3] Only 11 of 29 chapters written by Péron refer to birds at all; five of these merely mention some of the birds seen and only three indicate any that were taken as specimens and not just as food. In one (Chapter 11), Péron gives an extended account of seabirds seen, and implicitly collected, during the voyage from Timor to Tasmania from November 1801 to January 1802.[4] In another (Chapter 12), Péron writes that the artist Charles-Alexandre Lesueur collected 12 species of birds at Port Cygnet, Tasmania, on 14 January 1802.[5] Three of these were parrots and another was 'the pretty tit with blue head and collar' (Superb Fairywren *Malurus cyaneus*),[6] but he gives no details of the remaining eight. Later, the expedition moved anchorage to North West Bay, Tasmania, and on 24 January Péron accompanied navigator and cartographer Louis Freycinet on a short exploration of the adjacent North River (now the Derwent). There he observed, in the midst of huge flocks of birds, the Sulphur-crested Cockatoo (*Cacatua galerita*) and Yellow-tailed Black Cockatoo (*Zanda funerea*), as well as hosts of brilliantly coloured parrots.[7] He also recognised seven more species, which he listed with descriptive names, but only one of these is readily identifiable – again the Superb Fairywren. On returning to the ships Péron found that Lesueur had collected, presumably in North West Bay, a further ten species of birds they did not already have, but he gave no details of these.[8]

Péron also reported obtaining on 10 February 1803 a 'new and singular kind of flycatcher' from St Peter Island in Nuyts Archipelago off Denial Bay, Eyre Peninsula, South Australia (32° 15-19' S, 133° 33-37' E).[9] That report, together with an annotated pencil and wash drawing of the specimen by Lesueur, held in the Muséum d'Histoire naturelle of Le Havre, France,[10] led us to identify it as most likely a Rufous Bristlebird *Dasyornis broadbenti*, in contrast with most previous determinations,[11] but we have been unable to locate the specimen or an unpublished description by Péron, despite extensive searches for Baudin expedition bird material.[12]

Yet Péron did not ignore ornithological research entirely, nor was he silent with regard to information on the subject and, included in a series of manuscripts retained in the Le Havre Museum, he described what he believed might be new species. Those manuscripts and other documents written by Péron have the potential to help us identify some of the Baudin expedition's birds and their collection localities.

Material

We have reviewed documents relating to the bird collections of the Baudin expedition, including Péron and Freycinet's *Voyage de découvertes*, the English translation of its revised 2nd edition, and unpublished documents in the Le Havre Museum's Lesueur Collection (MHNH CL).[13] The latter include *Descriptions Zoologiques*,[14] in which Péron listed material in his charge during his return voyage aboard the *Géographe* after leaving Port Jackson, and Péron's *Tableau Général*, the report he made to Baudin when in Port Jackson in June or July 1802, giving his observations on various classes of animals up to that time.[15] The report refers to collections prepared for their return to France aboard the *Naturaliste* and includes brief discussion on the birds of Geographe Bay, Shark Bay and the north-west coast of Australia, Timor, and Tasmania. It also includes a table (Figure 1) of 32 species collected, that Péron mostly could not identify from his reference sources and believed were potentially new. At least 23 of these had been taken by Lesueur following the deaths of senior expedition naturalists René Maugé and Stanislas Levillain, and there are 31 surviving individual manuscripts written by Péron that describe all but one of those 32 species.[16] The manuscript descriptions are written in Latin, with occasional French annotations, and we have transcribed, translated and interpreted them.

Results

Péron's report to Baudin at Port Jackson observed *inter alia* that:

> the head of Port Cygnet and of North [Derwent] River were absolutely covered in [birds]. Citizen Lesueur made a large collection of them and all of the descriptions that I give here are of species he collected and prepared himself. These species seemed to me to be almost all new and I was obliged to consider them such because none of the ornithological works in my possession mentioned them.[17]

He added that 'it is almost certain that most of the species are part of the rich and numerous collection made by Citizen Labillardière and which he is most likely to have published since our departure.'[18]

In his table Péron gave each of the 32 mostly 'new' bird species a number from 6 to 37 and placed them in a taxonomic order that was probably in use at the time. Why the numbering begins at number 6 is unknown. The one species for which there is no surviving manuscript description is the third in the table (number 8), *Psittacus Lamanon* from the Dentrecasteaux Channel. Its identity will remain unknown but it could have been one of a few Tasmanian parrot species (other than Green Rosella and Blue-winged Parrot, both also among Péron's new species), such as Eastern Ground Parrot (*Pezoporus wallicus*), Swift Parrot (*Lathamus discolor*) or Eastern Rosella (*Platycercus eximius*), all of which were collected on the Baudin expedition.[19]

Péron's manuscript descriptions are listed in Table 1. Those with his own numbers are all described as being from the 'Collection du C.[en] Lesueur' ('Collection of Citizen Lesueur'), although numbers 1, 15 and 16 are missing and the number 22 was applied to three separate descriptions. The remainder are unnumbered and are not said to be from the 'Collection du C.[en] Lesueur'. We have identified the species described in most, and some manuscripts are complemented by illustrations of Lesueur's[20] or by specimens retained in the Muséum national d'Histoire naturelle, Paris, or elsewhere.

2ᵉ classe

Oiseaux.

Nᵒˢ des espèces	Genres	Espèces	Connues ou Nouvelles	Lieux où elles se trouvent	Dessins	Observations Générales
6	Psittacus	Lacepedii...mas.	S.N.	Détroit Dentrecasteaux		
7	P.	id. ...Fœmin.	id.	id.		
8	P.	Lamanon.	id.	id.		
9	P.	Insula Maria.	id.	Île Maria.		
10	Cuculus	Gasteroxanthus.	id.	Détroit Dentrecast?		
11	C.	Diemenensis.	id.	id.		
12	Lanius	Rostro-culo-palpebrae	id.	id.		
13	Muscicapa	Bivittata rufa.	id.	Côt. S.O. de la N. Hol.		
14	M. Grisonea	Grisonea	id.	Dét. Dentrec?		
15	M.	Undulosa	id.	id.		
16	M.	Gasteroxantha.	id.	Côt. S.O. de la N. Hol.		
17	Muscivora	Guthri fulva.	id.	Dét. Dentrecast?		
18	M.	Bitaeniafulveoptera.	id.	id.		
19	Turdus	Epirufus.	id.	id.		
20	T.	Guteflavus.	id.	id.		
21	Tanagra	Lilaceocaeso?	id.	id.		
22	Loxia	Das-our-erythra.	id.	Île Maria.		
23	Corvus	Australis.	Sp. Lin.	Dét. Dentrecast?		
24	Parus	Chlorotephronotus.	S.N.	id.		
25	P.	Sophia.	id.	id.		
26	Glaucopis	Cinerea.	Sp. Lin.	id.		
27	Certhia	Flavogastera.	S.N.	id.		
28	Alcedo	Cristata.	S. Lin.	id.		
29	Sterna	Melasoma	S.N.	mer australe. Malh?		
30	S.	Caspioides.	id.	id.		
31	Larus.	Melapterus.	id.	mer aust. 43°		
32	Sula.	Whytensis.	id.	Terre de Whyt.		
33	S.	Sawuensis.	id.	Îles Sawu.		
34	S.	Diemenensis.	id.	Terre de Diemen		
35	Ardea	Banksiana	id.	Détroit St. Paul.		
36	Tantalus?	Melaloptrus.	id.	Îles Pierreuses?		*illegible*
37	Vringa	Nivea.	id.	Détroit Dentrecast?		
38.						

Figure 1 – Péron's table of 32 potentially new species of birds collected on the Baudin expedition – part of his Tableau Général, a report he handed to Baudin in June or July 1802. Muséum d'Histoire naturelle, Le Havre, Collection Lesueur, 21 003.

Table 1

Péron's manuscript documents, describing 'new' species, together with our present identification of them[21]. Also shown are the number of specimens of each species known from the Baudin expedition and, in parentheses, the number recently located, and/or any supporting Lesueur illustration.

The Descriptions

Our transcriptions and translations of Péron's 31 Latin descriptions listed above in Table 1 are given in the Appendix. For the most part the descriptions are beautifully written, Péron having taken particular

MHNH CL ms no./ Péron ms no.	Péron ms name	Present identification	Named locality	Specimens identified	Lesueur image (MHNH CL no.)
79 092/2	*Muscicapa Bivittatorufa*	Uncoloured robin *Petroica* sp.	Southern coast of Australia	0	
79 093/3	*Alcedo Cristata Lin.* or perhaps a new species: *Ceyx Lacepedianum*	Azure Kingfisher *Ceyx azureus* (Latham, 1801)	North West Bay, Dentrecasteaux Channel	3 (2 but both labelled from Timor)	
79 094/4	*Turdus Guloflavus*	Yellow-throated Honeyeater *Nesoptilotis flavicollis* (Vieillot, 1817)	Dentrecasteaux Channel	4 (4)	79 008
79 095/5	*Certhia Flavoptera*	New Holland Honeyeater *Phylidonyris novaehollandiae* (Latham, 1790)	Dentrecasteaux Channel	1 (0)	79 015
79 096/6	*Loxia Basourerythros*	Beautiful Firetail *Stagonopleura bella* (Latham, 1801)	Maria Island	5 (4)	79 011
79 097/7	*Muscivora Gutturifulva*	Satin Flycatcher *Myiagra cyanoleuca* (Vieillot, 1818)	Dentrecasteaux Channel	2 (2)	
79 098/8	*Muscicapa Grisonea*	Dusky Robin *Melanodryas vittata* (Quoy and Gaimard, 1832)	Dentrecasteaux Channel	1 (1)	

79 099/9	*Tringa Nivea*	Ruddy Turnstone (Linnaeus, 1758)	North West Bay, Dentrecasteaux Channel	1 (0)	
79 100/10	*Glaucopis Cinerea* Forst.	Yellow Wattlebird *Anthochaera paradoxa* (Daudin, 1800)	Partridge Island, Dentrecasteaux Channel	2 (1)	
79 101/11	*Parus Chlorotephronotus*	Probable Tasmanian Scrubwren *Sericornis humilis* (Gould, 1838)	Bruny Island, Dentrecasteaux Channel	0	
79 102/12	*Muscivora Bitaeniofulvoptera*	Probable juvenile robin *Petroica* sp. or Grey Fantail *Rhipidura albiscapa* (Gould, 1840)	North West Bay, Dentrecasteaux Channel	0	
79 103/13	*Cuculus Gasteroxantus*	Fan-tailed Cuckoo *Cacomantis flabelliformis* (Latham, 1801)	Dentrecasteaux Channel	3 (3)	79 023
79 104/14	*Corvus Australis* Lin.	Grey Currawong *Strepera versicolor* (Latham, 1801)	Dentrecasteaux Channel	1 (1)	
79 105/17	*Cuculus Diemenensis*	Pallid Cuckoo *Cacomantis pallidus* (Latham, 1801)	North West Bay, Dentrecasteaux Channel	2 (2 but both labelled from Timor)	
79 106/18	*Tanagra Lilaceocolor*	Adult Black-faced Cuckooshrike *Coracina novaehollandiae* (J.F. Gmelin, 1789)	North West Bay, Dentrecasteaux Channel	3 (2)	
79 107/19	*Tantalus Melalophus*	Greater Crested Tern *Thalasseus bergii* (M.H.C. Lichtenstein, 1823)	Furneaux Islands	1 (1)	
79 108/20	*Muscicapa Undulosa*	Immature Black-faced Cuckooshrike *Coracina novaehollandiae* (J.F. Gmelin, 1789)	North West Bay, Dentrecasteaux Channel	3 (2)	

79 109/21	*Turdus Epirufus*	Grey Shrikethrush *Colluricincla harmonica* (Latham, 1801)	Dentrecasteaux Channel	2 (1)	
79 110/22	*Psittacus Lacepedii (Mas)*	Adult Green Rosella *Platycercus caledonicus* (J.F. Gmelin, 1788)	Dentrecasteaux Channel	6 (4)	79 030
79 111/22 . . .	*Lanius Rostroculopediflavus*	Noisy Miner *Manorina melanocephala* (Latham, 1801)	Dentrecasteaux Channel	1 (0)	79 010
79 112/22 bis	*Psittacus Lacepedii (Faemina)*	Immature Green Rosella *Platycercus caledonicus* (J.F. Gmelin, 1788)	Dentrecasteaux Channel	6 (4)	
79 113/23	*Psittacus Insula Maria*	Blue-winged Parrot *Neophema chrysostoma* (Kuhl, 1820)	Maria Island	1 (1)	79 029
79 114/24	*Parus Sophia*	Superb Fairywren *Malurus cyaneus* (Ellis, 1782)	Port Cygnet, Dentrecasteaux Channel	2 (1)	
79 116	*Larus Melapterus*	Probable White-headed Petrel *Pterodroma lessonii* (Garnot, 1826)	Southern Ocean 43° S	0	
79 117	*Muscicapa Gasteroxanta*	Rufous Whistler *Pachycephala rufiventris* (Latham, 1801)	Southern coast of Australia	1 (1)	
79 118	*Sterna Melasoma*	Probable Wilson's Storm Petrel *Oceanites oceanicus* (Kuhl, 1820)	Southern Ocean 41° S	1 (0)	
79 119	*Sterna Caspioides*	Possible Arctic Tern *Sterna paradisaea* (Pontoppidan, 1763)	Southern Ocean 41° S	0	

79 120	*Sula Diemenensis*	Australasian Gannet *Morus serrator* (G.R. Gray, 1843)	Tasmania	≥4 (0)	
79 121	*Sula Whytensis*	Brown Booby *Sula leucogaster* (Boddaert, 1783)	North-west coast of Australia	≥1 (0)	
79 122	*Sula Sawuensis*	Red-footed Booby *Sula sula* (Linnaeus, 1766)	Waters off Savu Islands	≥1 (0)	
79 123	*Ardea Banksiana*	White-faced Heron *Egretta novaehollandiae* (Latham, 1790)	Banks Strait	3 (0)	

care with the texts concerning the 23 birds in Lesueur's collection. Nonetheless his handwriting can be difficult to decipher, particularly in the more hastily written descriptions. Péron tended to add diacritics to some vowels in his descriptions but we have removed these for clarity. In general his spelling seems to have been very good, but he consistently wrote '*fuscescente*' (dark brownish) as '*fucescente*'. In several descriptions he used both the terms '*gula*' and '*guttur*' and we have translated these as 'chin' and 'throat' respectively. In two descriptions, however, he used '*mentum*' for chin and in one of these he used all three terms, so there we translated the first two as 'upper and lower throat'.

The first 23 of the descriptions are of birds included among collections made by Lesueur. Collectors of the last eight are not stated, perhaps from lack of documentation, but might have included other known scientists or officers. Discussion of our identifications follows, beginning with those numbered and named from the 'Collection du C.en Lesueur'.

MHNH CL 79 092 no. 2, *Muscicapa Bivittatorufa*, was a small flycatcher that flew onto the ship, reportedly on 3 April 1802 when the *Géographe* was off the south-east coast of South Australia. Two days earlier Baudin had named Île aux Alouettes after a 'lark' flew onto the ship and it is tempting to link the two and apply Péron's name to the Australian Pipit *Anthus australis* (Vieillot, 1818), and to the specimen MNHN-ZO-2012-720 in the Muséum national d'Histoire naturelle. But Péron had already written elsewhere about that specimen, using the name Alauda-alouette,[22] and it is Vieillot's holotype of that species. The prominent yellow-rufous double wing bars suggest an immature robin, perhaps the Flame Robin *Petroica phoenicea* (Gould, 1837), which was a common post-breeding visitor to that area, although less common in recent decades. The golden yellow soles of the feet that Péron noted are also characteristic of some Australian robins. None of them, however, possesses longer feathers on the head, so the crest-like structure described by Péron is puzzling.

MHNH CL 79 093 no. 3 describes the dark blue upperparts, the rich rufous underparts and the red feet of the Azure Kingfisher. The Tasmanian subspecies is *Ceyx azureus diemenensis* (Gould, 1846). Péron referred Lesueur's specimen to *Alcedo cristata* (= Malachite Kingfisher *Corythornis cristatus*) while considering that it may yet represent a new species, which he named *Ceyx Lacepedianum*.

MHNH CL 79 094 no. 4 describes the grey crown, olive dorsum, yellow throat and yellow spots on either side of the head of the endemic Tasmanian Yellow-throated Honeyeater.

MHNH CL 79 095 no. 5 describes a honeyeater with yellow wings. The four small white markings on each side of the head identify it as a New Holland Honeyeater. The Tasmanian subspecies is *Phylidonyris novaehollandiae canescens* (Latham, 1790).

MHNH CL 79 096 no. 6 (Figure 2) describes a bullfinch with a red bill and rump and partridge-like markings (delicate transverse barring), the Beautiful Firetail. Because Péron made no mention of the black face mask and described the entire body as a reddish-brown colour, it is likely that this bird was a juvenile. Figure 3 shows a surviving specimen of Beautiful Firetail from the Baudin expedition but it is so badly faded that it is difficult to determine if it is a juvenile or not; if it is, then it may be Lesueur's actual specimen no. 6. The nominate subspecies occurs in Tasmania.

MHNH CL 79 097 no. 7 describes the rufous throat and breast and white abdomen of a female Satin Flycatcher. Péron saw the glossy dark blue crown as 'blackish green' and the back as a dark brownish-violet rather than a bluish grey. A female specimen of Satin Flycatcher survives in the Muséum national d'Histoire naturelle (MNHN-ZO-2013-1143) and may be Lesueur's specimen no. 7.

MHNH CL 79 098 no. 8 is of an almost uniformly grey bird with some white markings in the wing. The only Tasmanian species that nears Péron's description is the Dusky Robin, which is dark brown above and

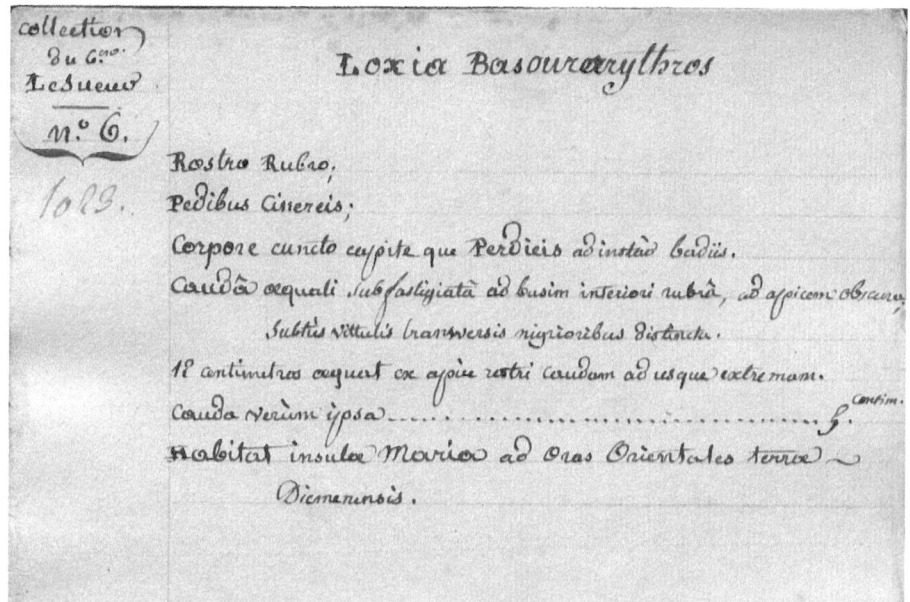

Above: Figure 2 – Péron's manuscript description of Loxia Basourerythros (Beautiful Firetail), no. 6 in the 'Collection du C.en Lesueur'. Muséum d'Histoire naturelle, Le Havre, Collection Lesueur, 79 096.

Below: Figure 3 – Specimen of Beautiful Firetail (Stagonopleura bella) from the Baudin expedition. Muséum national d'Histoire naturelle MNHN-ZO-2014-517. Photo: J.J.F.J. Jansen.

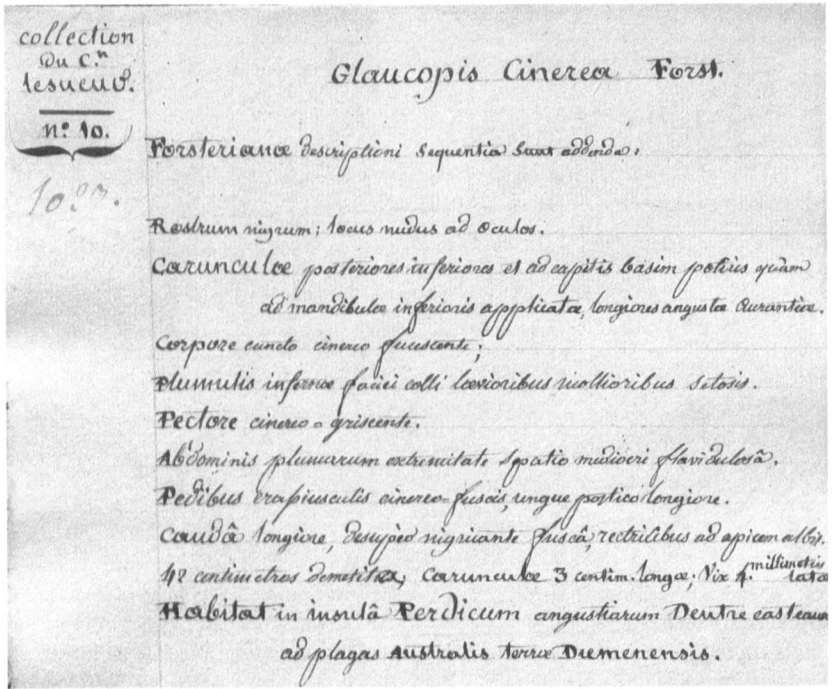

Figure 4 – Péron's manuscript description of Glaucopis cinerea (Yellow Wattlebird), no. 10 in the 'Collection du C.^en Lesueur'. Muséum d'Histoire naturelle, Le Havre, Collection Lesueur 79 100.

lighter grey-brown below, with white in the wing distributed somewhat differently from Péron's assessment.

MHNH CL 79 099 no. 9 describes the short, tapering bill, reddish legs and white abdomen of a Ruddy Turnstone. Péron did not describe distinctive black markings around the chest or rufous colouring on the dorsum, so the bird was in non-breeding plumage. His use of '*pinnatis*' (feathered or feather-like) to describe the feet is puzzling; perhaps he meant '*palmatis*' (like a palm frond or hand).

MHNH CL 79 100 no. 10 (Figure 4): Péron attributed this provisionally to the South Island Kokako or Wattlebird (*Callaeas cinereus*). But he must have considered it as a potentially new species as he added his own characters, such as the long, thin yellow wattles, yellow on the abdomen and white-tipped tail feathers, that identify the specimen as the Yellow Wattlebird. He did not provide his own name for this

Figure 5 – Specimen of Yellow Wattlebird (Anthochaera paradoxa) from the Baudin expedition. Muséum national d'Histoire naturelle MNHN-ZO-2014-433. Photo: P.W. Koken.

new species however. Figure 5 shows the only surviving specimen of Yellow Wattlebird from the Baudin expedition; whether it was Lesueur's specimen no. 10 is not known.

MHNH CL 79 101 no. 11, *Parus Chlorotephronotus*, does not match a Tasmanian bird readily but comes closest to the Tasmanian Scrubwren. It is difficult to know how to interpret its sub-bifurcate tail and greenish-grey back, but Péron may have over-interpreted tail shape from skins and appears to have perceived exaggerated colour tints among other plumages, as in the Satin Flycatcher, Fan-tailed Cuckoo and Black-faced Cuckooshrike. The olive-brown dorsum of the Tasmanian Scrubwren may have appeared to him as rather green.

MHNH CL 79 102 no. 12, *Muscivora Bitaeniofulvoptera*, is a small grey flycatcher with two distinct tawny wing bars. Its size is that of the Pink Robin *Petroica rodinogaster* (Drapiez, 1819), whose uncoloured females and young have the brownest of all wing bars among *Petroica* robins. They are however also the brownest overall, not grey, as described here, although young Scarlet Robins *Petroica boodang* and Flame Robins are almost as brown. The flattened bill and very long tail also suggest a Grey Fantail *Rhipidura albiscapa*, although in juveniles of this species the wing bars are on the coverts rather than on the remiges and are somewhat curved, perhaps not fitting so well with the transversely oblique bands on the black wings that Péron described.

MHNH CL 79 103 no. 13 describes the rufous grey underparts and black and white saw-tooth markings on the tail of the Fan-tailed Cuckoo. This species has a slate-grey dorsum but Péron has described it as greenish violet, one of his most extreme interpretations of colour. The specific epithet he applied, '*gasteroxanta*' or yellow-bellied, suggests further colour confusion, but is explained by a note Péron wrote at the end of his description (MHNH CL 79 117), giving his translation of Greek '*xanthos*' as rufous.

MHNH CL 79 104 no. 14, *Corvus Australis*, is noteworthy on several accounts. At first Péron thought it was a Pacific Ocean corvid described from Tonga, but, apparently considering that it may be a new species, he applied additional details of white wing tips, tail tips and vent that showed that it was undoubtedly a Grey Currawong. He did not, however, provide his own name for it. There is only one known specimen from the expedition (MNHN-ZO-2010-512) and it is evidently the holotype of *Cracticus cuneicaudatus* (Vieillot, 1816), long regarded as a synonym of *Strepera versicolor versicolor* (Grey Currawong from mainland south-eastern Australia), despite 'Entrecasteaux' being written on the underside of its original stand. Yet this very dark currawong may in fact be the Tasmanian representative, the Clinking Currawong *S. v. arguta* (Gould, 1846), and, if so, Vieillot's name would have had priority. This matter cannot be resolved without further examination of the specimen.

MHNH CL 79 105 no. 17 describes the mottled brownish grey colouring and the saw-tooth markings on the wings and tail of the Pallid Cuckoo.

MHNH CL 79 106 no. 18, the lilac-coloured tanager, is, we find, none other than an adult Black-faced Cuckooshrike; its large size and the description of its black face and throat make this clear. Péron's perception of lilac is not so far-fetched if the old vernacular for this bird, the 'blue jay' is recalled. Nevertheless, his finding of lilac colour here and elsewhere is unusual.[23] The nominate subspecies occurs in Tasmania.

MHNH CL 79 107 no. 19 describes a large, white-bodied bird with grey wings and back, black crown and crest, and pointed yellow bill, clearly the Greater Crested Tern. Having noted that it had a rather long, slightly downcurved bill, Péron placed his bird in the genus *Tantalus*, which had been applied variously in the past to ibises, storks and curlews. Later he added a question mark after the genus name both in this manuscript and in the table in his *Tableau Général*; nonetheless it appears that he was not familiar with terns (see MHNH CL 79 118 for further confusion). A specimen of Greater Crested Tern survives in the Muséum national d'Histoire naturelle (MNHN-ZO-2011-143) and may be Lesueur's specimen no. 19.

MHNH CL 79 108 no. 20, *Muscicapa Undulosa*, is a large, pale grey 'flycatcher' with wave-like markings above and paler underparts. Its scissor-shaped tail would suggest a Ground Cuckooshrike *Coracina maxima* which does not occur in Tasmania, and this might be another case where Péron has misinterpreted how feathers appear in a prepared skin. Otherwise the markings suggest that this is a juvenile Black-faced Cuckooshrike or, in view of its adult size, a first-year bird retaining some juvenile features. The facial markings are consistent with this identification. That Péron placed this bird in a different genus from no.

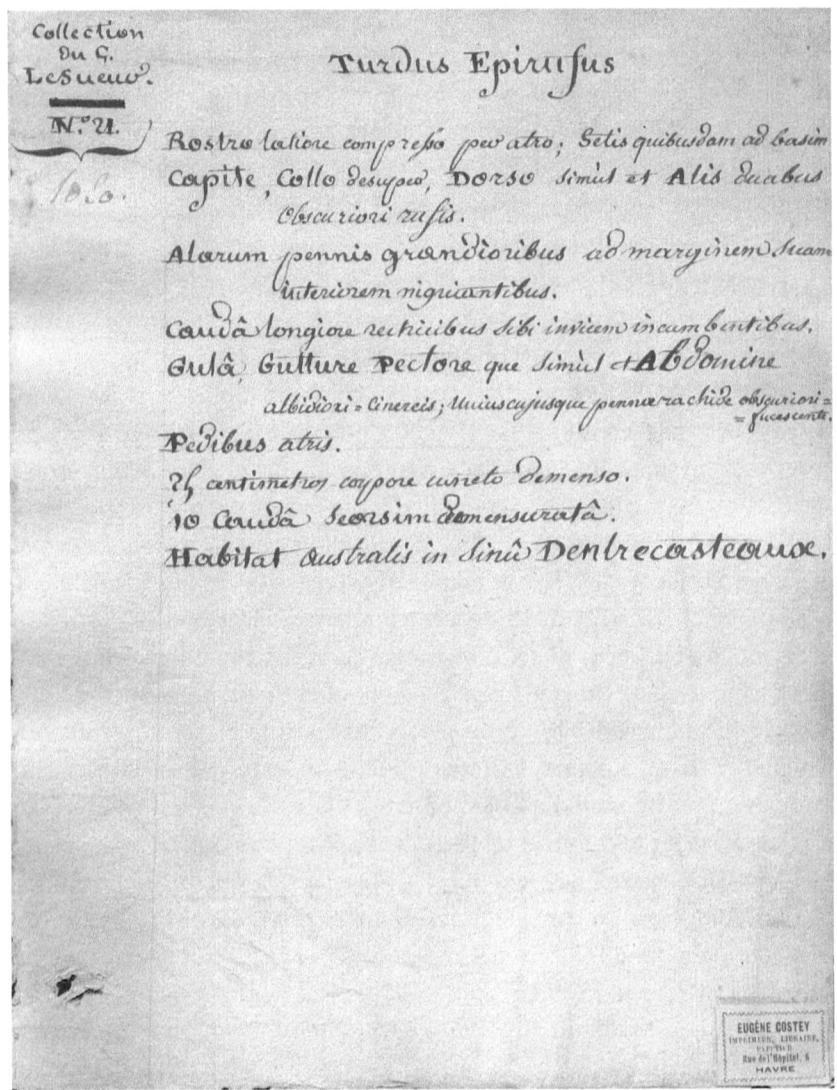

Figure 6 – Péron's manuscript description of Turdus Epirufus (Grey Shrikethrush), no. 21 in the 'Collection du C.^{en} Lesueur'. Muséum d'Histoire naturelle, Le Havre, Collection Lesueur 79 109

Figure 7 – Specimen of Grey Shrikethrush (Colluricincla harmonica) from the Baudin expedition. Muséum national d'Histoire naturelle MNHN-ZO-2014-438. Photo: P.W. Koken

18 reflects the considerable difference in appearance between juvenile and adult Black-faced Cuckooshrikes.

MHNH CL 79 109 no. 21, *Turdus Epirufus* (Figure 6), is a Grey Shrikethrush, the Tasmanian subspecies of which is *Colluricuncla harmonica strigata* (Swainson, 1838). This manuscript is of interest as we had considered it potentially a description of the 'new and singular kind of flycatcher' of St Peter Island, but only if its stated locality of Dentrecasteaux Channel was wrong. Tellingly, however, Péron named the species, with the same locality, in the table in his report to Baudin at

Port Jackson (see Figure 1), written several months before the landing on St Peter Island. There is a further reference to such a bird among those Péron reported seeing on the North (Derwent) River.[24] They included 'le Merle roux' (rufous blackbird or thrush), which we infer to be the same *Turdus Epirufus*, a young Grey Shrikethrush, extensively rufous above and streaked below. An immature bird is shown in Figure 7, the only known surviving specimen of Grey Shrikethrush from the Baudin expedition; it may well be Lesueur's actual specimen no. 21.

MHNH CL 79 110 no. 22 is a good description of the Green Rosella, and the rather yellow underparts indicate that it was an adult bird. Péron dedicated the species to the French zoologist Bernard Germain de Lacépède whom he described as 'one of my first and dearest teachers'.[25]

MHNH CL 79 111 no. 22 ... distinctly describes a Noisy Miner and even Péron's mistaken genus name (*Lanius*, the typical shrikes) alludes to the aggressive behaviour of that species. The Tasmanian subspecies is *Manorina melanocephala leachi* (Mathews, 1912).

MHNH CL 79 112 no. 22 *bis* describes an immature Green Rosella, much greener overall than the adult.

MHNH CL 79 113 no. 23, the Blue-winged Parrot, is one of only two specimens that can be individually associated with collections from Maria Island. The description lacks reference to the parrot's distinctive facial markings and suggests an immature bird, while Lesueur's painting is of an adult.

MHNH CL 79 114 no. 24 is unmistakably of the Superb Fairywren, an adult male. Intriguingly, Péron described the velvet black hind neck, lower back and rump and wing coverts in this species as being of a blackish Prussian blue. It is the nominate subspecies that occurs in Tasmania. In the *Voyage* Péron wrote of the remarkable coloured males of two or three fairywren species.

(MHNH CL 79 115 is a title page, not a description.)

MHNH CL 79 116 is not a description of any gull, despite Péron allocating it to *Larus*, but is consistent with a White-headed Petrel. Péron described the colour of its dark grey wings and grey dorsal mottling as '*atris*', by which he usually seems to have meant 'black', but this can also mean 'dark'. His description of the back pattern of black/dark spots could also suggest a Cape Petrel *Daption capense*, but that species has a dark head and tail and some white in the wings. In addition, Péron was familiar with the distinctive Cape Petrel, having noted that they saw one, 'un Damier' ('checkerboard') on 11 December 1801 at latitude 21°S.[26]

MHNH CL 79 117 describes the slate-coloured dorsum and pale rufous underparts of the Rufous Whistler, either an immature or female specimen. The nominate subspecies occurs in southern Australia. The place and circumstances of this specimen are evident from the stated date: the wind-blown bird was taken aboard the *Géographe* as she sailed south from Nuyts Archipelago ahead of a strong off-shore wind.[27] Greek *xanthos* is usually translated as yellow or blond, but Péron gave his interpretation as rufous.

MHNH CL 79 118: for this tiny seabird Péron used the name *Sterna Melasoma* but he later changed it to *S. melanosoma*, so named 'on account of its black body',[28] and he said it was one of three tern species he saw on 9 January 1802, when the ship was south of the Great Australian Bight at 41°S. However, no tern has a black body and wings with white around the rump and lower abdomen, and this bird is clearly a storm petrel, most likely a Wilson's Storm Petrel, but possibly a Black-bellied Storm Petrel *Fregetta tropica*. The description is very brief, suggesting that Péron did not have a specimen in hand. He made no mention of the bill or feet and so did not describe the diagnostic yellow webbing on the feet of a Wilson's Storm Petrel. Strangely, Péron had said that on 24 November 1801 'we saw storm-birds (*Procellaria pelagica*, Lin.) for the first time',[29] with more seen on 7 December and 1 January. *P. pelagica* is the European Storm Petrel *Hydrobates pelagicus*, similar in appearance to Wilson's, indicating that Péron could recognise storm petrels. His placement of *Melasoma* in *Sterna* is explicable only if the earlier reports of storm petrels were in fact made by others, and Péron himself was not familiar with them. It certainly appears that Péron was not familiar with terns, otherwise he would not have placed this species in *Sterna*; further evidence for this is in MHNH CL 79 107 above.

MHNH CL 79 119, despite Péron's observation, is unlike the Caspian Tern, too small and with a black, not a red bill. It is perhaps most likely to be an Arctic Tern, if Péron saw the grey wings as black or dark. This is one of the three 'tern' species that Péron observed on 9 January 1802 (see MHNH CL 79 118 above).

MHNH CL 79 120 describes well the Australasian Gannet, despite Péron's placement of the buff-yellow colouring on the bill (actually pale blue-grey) and face instead of the head and nape. This inaccuracy and the lack of measurements in his brief description suggest that he did not have a specimen in hand at the time.

MHNH CL 79 121 describes the brown and white plumage of a Brown Booby, and the yellow bill indicates that the specimen was a female. Péron wrote the genus name as '*Sulla*' but in the table in his *Tableau Général* he corrected this to '*Sula*'. He said that the species was 'first seen by us at Witt's Land'[30] in north-west Western Australia and he gave the locality of near King William's River (*sic* = Willem's River), now the Ashburton River.[31] The subspecies occurring in Australian waters is *Sula leucogaster plotus* (J.R. Forster, 1844). This manuscript is unusual in that it was written in haste, perhaps as a draft, and it includes copious notes on the habits of the species; these are not reproduced in the Appendix, however, as they are difficult to read, with many illegible words.

MHNH CL 79 122 describes the blue face and red, webbed feet of the Red-footed Booby. The subspecies that the expedition encountered was *Sula sula rubripes* (Gould, 1838), and Péron included in the *Voyage de découvertes* his detailed notes on when and where the species was encountered, generally within a certain distance of land.[32]

MHNH CL 79 123 describes the bluish-grey plumage and white on the head of a White-faced Heron, another specimen captured when it landed on the ship. Péron named this species after the botanist Sir Joseph Banks.

Discussion

Péron gave the provenance of 19 specimens from the 'Collection du C.en Lesueur' as the Dentrecasteaux Channel, with six of these being from North West Bay, the Yellow Wattlebird from Partridge Island, the Tasmanian Scrubwren from Bruny Island, and the Superb Fairywren from Port Cygnet. Unfortunately he did not give a more precise locality for the remaining ten, despite his probable knowledge of Lesueur's collecting localities. Only the Beautiful Firetail and Blue-winged Parrot are likely to have been taken on Maria Island, as stated, and the Greater Crested Tern was from the Furneaux Islands, with the possible uncoloured Flame Robin collected off the south-east of South Australia. Of the eight unnumbered descriptions, one is of a Brown Booby taken from the north-west coast of Australia before reaching Timor, and four are of seabirds taken during the crossing between Timor and Tasmania, one soon after departing Timor near the Savu islands and three in the Southern Ocean west of, or on reaching southern Tasmanian waters around New Year 1801–1802. The Australasian Gannet was taken on the coast of Tasmania, possibly Port Cygnet where the species was particularly abundant. The Rufous Whistler was another of three land birds collected opportunistically off the Australian southern coast, and the White-faced Heron was taken in Banks Strait, between the north-eastern tip of Tasmania and the Furneaux Islands.

It is noteworthy that all seven of the named birds that Péron said he recognised from the Derwent River[33] are among his 'new' species from Lesueur's collection, and he might well have written them into the *Voyage* after referring to the table in his *Tableau Général*. They are:

- 'le Coucou Xanthogastre' (yellow-bellied cuckoo) = *Cuculus Gasteroxantus* (Fan-tailed Cuckoo, MHNH CL 79 103);
- 'le Merle à collier jaune' (yellow-collared blackbird or thrush) = *Turdus Guloflavus* (Yellow-throated Honeyeater, MHNH CL 79 094);
- 'le Merle roux' (rufous blackbird or thrush) = *Turdus Epirufus* (Grey Shrikethrush, MHNH CL 79 109);
- 'le beau Tanagra couleur lilas' (the beautiful lilac tanager) = *Tanagra Lilaceocolor* (adult Black-faced Cuckooshrike, MHNH CL 79 106);
- 'le Bouvreuil à croupion rouge' (red-rumped bullfinch) = *Loxia Basourerythros* (Beautiful Firetail, MHNH CL 79 096)
- 'le Grimpereau flavoptère' (yellow-winged treecreeper) = *Certhia Flavoptera* (New Holland Honeyeater, MHNH CL 79 095); and
- 'la charmante Mésange à collier bleu' (the charming blue-collared tit) = *Parus Sophia* (Superb Fairywren, MHNH CL 79 114).

Regrettably, many bird specimens from the Baudin expedition have been lost[34] and as can be seen from Table 1 there are no extant specimens of several of Péron's new species. For many others there are still museum specimens, but because their labelling is almost universally inadequate, it is difficult to be certain if they were the actual specimens

Péron used for his descriptions. One of the few that may be linked to a Péron description with any degree of certainty is MNHN-ZO-2014-438 the Grey Shrikethrush; despite being dishevelled and faded, the rufous tints on the dorsum are still visible, indicating that this was an immature individual and therefore quite likely *Turdus Epirufus* (MHNH CL 79 109).

Referring to birds he saw at the Derwent River and the host of others observed elsewhere in the Dentrecasteaux Channel, Péron noted that their natural history 'will be reproduced in detail in our zoological works'.[35] It seems most likely that he also intended to publish his descriptions of new bird species, but he did not do so before his premature death in 1810. Had he published them, a number would have become junior synonyms because he was not able to discover from his reference books that nine of his descriptions were of species that had been described before the expedition left France (see Table 1). They were the New Holland Honeyeater, Ruddy Turnstone, Black-faced Cuckooshrike, Green Rosella, Superb Fairywren, Arctic Tern, Brown and Red-footed Booby and White-faced Heron. Another nine had been named since their departure, as Péron suspected they might, although all but one under the English ornithologist John Latham's authorship and none by Péron's countryman Labillardière.

Nevertheless, Péron had drafted descriptions of nine genuinely new species: Yellow-throated Honeyeater, Satin Flycatcher, Dusky Robin, Tasmanian Scrubwren, Greater Crested Tern, Blue-winged Parrot, White-headed Petrel, Wilson's Storm Petrel and Australasian Gannet. All were later given formal descriptions and were named by others, some even from Baudin expedition specimens. Furthermore, among the species already described prior to or during the expedition, six of Péron's names could still have been in use today had he published them, because they represented subspecies that had not been described. They were: Azure Kingfisher, Grey Shrikethrush and Noisy Miner (all distinct Tasmanian subspecies), Brown Booby and Red-footed Booby (Indian Ocean subspecies), and, had he provided his own name for it, the Tasmanian subspecies of Grey Currawong. Again, all were formally described and published by others, half of them by John Gould.

These 31 descriptions written by François Péron give further insight into his abilities as an ornithologist. In his *Voyage* he gave scant attention to birds and most of his observations were generalised, allowing only a few species to be identified. But in his manuscripts of new species he showed a good grasp of what was required in providing diagnostic descriptions of birds. Many of his descriptions contained as much detail as was customary at the time, and he was able to recognise broad taxonomic groups, although occasionally confusing some such as terns. At a time when no field guides were available, when much of the Australian avifauna was yet to be described, and when his attentions were mainly focused on marine invertebrates, anthropology and other disciplines, he proved to be a competent ornithologist.

One of the most notable aspects of Péron's descriptions is his extreme perception of colour, often seeing shades and intensities of colours that most observers would not. Perhaps this was influenced by the particular lighting conditions under which he wrote the descriptions. Another, unlikely, influencing factor may have been that Péron had suffered from ophthalmic problems for some years and, following war service, had lost the use of his right eye altogether.[36] Regardless of whether this affected colour vision or not, in light of his disability Péron's ornithological achievements are all the more noteworthy.

Appendix

MHNH CL 790 92: Muscicapa Bivittatorufa. Capite, Collo, Dorso, Uropygio que spadiceo-rufescente; Pennis capiti longioribus subcristatis confertissimis. Cauda bifurca, pennis nigricantibus; exteriori ex unoque latere sub albescente. Alis duabus atris; unaquaeque vero duabus et distincta Vittulis propemodum mediis transversis flavidiori-rufis. Genis intensiori cinereis. Gutture pectore que laeviori cinereis, Abdomine vero sordide sub-albidiori. Pedum tarsis spadiceis; Digitis vero subtus aureo-flavis. Habitat ad oras S.O. Hollandiae novae Motacillae minoris proportionibus, e terra effugiens incautus in navem elapsus, fuit apprehensus. 13 ger.al.

Head, neck, back and rump rather rufous chestnut-brown; with the longer feathers of the head almost a compact crest. Tail forked, its feathers blackish; outer [feathers] on each side off white. Both wings black; but each in fact with two distinct small bands almost across the middle, rather yellow-rufous. Cheeks intense ash-grey. Throat and breast rather pale ash-grey, the abdomen in fact a rather dirty off-white. Feet and legs chestnut-brown; the toes actually a golden yellow underneath. Inhabits the south-west coast of New Holland. With the proportions of smaller wagtails, it fled the land and unwarily flew down onto the ship, [where] it was caught 13 Germinal [3 April 1802].

MHNH CL 79 093: Alcedo Cristata Lin. ad genus Ceyx Lacepedianum referenda. Caracteres Linnaeani.
Alcedo Brachyura sub-cristata caerulea; subtus rufa, crista nigro undulata. Habitat in Amboina et insulis Philippinis 5 pol. circit. longa. Caracteribus istis a linnaeo datis sequentes mihi videntur subjiciendi: ad rostri basim plumulae quaedam utrique lateri rufescentes. Genis eodem colore ac ipsa crista. Gula ex rufo alba. Pectoris lateribus sub atris. Pectore verum ipso, Abdomine ipse usque caudae facie inferna intensiori nitidiori que rufis. Dorso nigricante caeruleo nigricantibus et Alis, quibusdam tamen caeruleis pennis immixtis. Ad Alarum Scapulum semi vittula rufa. Pedibus tridactylis rubeolentibus in animale recentius occiso. 17 centimetros vix corpus integrum aequans. Cauda vero seorsim emensa 4 cent. Habitat in portu N.O. angustiorum Dentrecasteaux, ad terram australem Diemen.

May be referred to the species Ceyx Lacepedianum. Linnaean characters. A short-tailed kingfisher, slightly crested, blue; rufous below, crest black, wavy. Inhabits Ambon and the Philippine Islands, about 5 inches long. To those characters given by Linnaeus, it seems to me the following should be added: near the base of the bill some feathers on each side rather rufous. Cheeks the same colour as its crest. Throat, apart from the rufous, white. Sides of the breast nearly black. Yet the breast itself, and the abdomen all the way to the underside of the tail an intense, bright rufous. Back and wings blackish to blackish-blue, nevertheless with some blue feathers intermingled. On the shoulder of the wings rufous half bands. Feet three-toed, reddish in an animal recently killed. The whole body scarcely equalling 17 centimetres. The tail in fact separately measuring 4 cm. Inhabits North West Bay in the Dentrecasteaux Channel, in southern Tasmania.

MHNH CL 79 094: *Turdus Guloflavus*. *Rostro laeviori compressiusculo utrinque emarginato nigro. Vertice obscuriori cinereo. Maculis duabus albidiori-flavis ad basim latera que capitis. Collo Dorso Uropygio obscuriori virescentibus. Alis duabus eodem isto colore sed intensiori; Remigum interiore latere sub atro manente. Cauda longiori-cuneiforme virente, Rectricum Rachide stante nigro. Gula dilutiori flavescente. Gutture Pectore Abdomine que griseo Lini. Pedibus cinereo nigricantibus. 21 centimetros aequante cuncto corpore. Cauda sejunctim emensa 9 centim. Habitat Australis in Canale Dentrecasteaux. Non-ne potius ad Lanios referendus?*

Bill very slightly compressed, on both sides margined black. Crown dark ash-grey. Two whitish-yellow spots near the base and sides of the head. Neck, back and rump dark greenish. Both wings this same colour but more intense; inner sides of remiges remaining near black. Tail rather long wedge-shaped, green, with the shafts of the rectrices remaining black. Chin pale yellow. Throat, breast and abdomen with grey streaks. Feet blackish ash-grey. The whole body equalling 21 centimetres. The tail separately measured 9 cm [sic]. Inhabits southern [parts] in Dentrecasteaux Channel. Could it not rather be referred to Lanius?

MHNH CL 79 095: *Certhia Flavoptera. Rostro nigro, plumulis ad basim utriusque mandibulae per albis. Capite sub-atro maculis quatuor albis duabus scilicet ad rostri basim duabus et aliis oculos pone desuper et ipsos. Corpore obscuro nigricante; Abdomine cinereo nigro que vario. Alarum pennis mediis flavidioribus, flavidis et partim tribus primoribus exterioribus; una vero subatra ipsis et mediis interposita. Interioribus nigricante-fuscis; nigricante quoque extremitate perinarum exteriorum partim flavidularum. Pedibus fuscis. Cauda ad basim latera que sua pari modo flava, reliquo praesertim que ipsius apice nigricante, maculis quibusdam albis extremis. 16 centimetro ex apice rostri caudam usque postremam. Habitat australis in Canale Dentrecasteaux ad Terram Diemen.*

Bill black, feathers near the base of each mandible quite white. Head nearly black with four white spots, namely: two near the base of the bill and two others *behind and above the eyes. Body dark blackish; abdomen variegated ash-grey and black. Middle wing feathers rather yellow, and the outermost primary group partly yellow; but with some that are nearly black and inserted in the middle. The inner ones blackish brown; likewise blackish at the end outside the partly yellow strip. Feet dark brown. The tail towards its base and sides similarly yellow, the remainder and chiefly its end blackish, with some white spots at the ends. 16 centimetres from the tip of the bill to the end of the tail. Inhabits southern [parts] in Dentrecasteaux Channel in Tasmania.*

MHNH CL 79 096: Loxia Basourerythros. Rostro rubro; Pedibus cinereis; Corpore cuncto capite que Perdicis ad instar badiis. Cauda aequali subfastigiata ad basim interiori rubra, ad apicem obscura; subtus vittulis transversis nigrioribus distincta. 12 centimetros aequat ex apice rostri caudam ad usque extremam. Cauda verum ipsa 5 centim. Habitat insulae Maria ad oras Orientales terrae Diemenensis.

Bill red. Feet ash-grey; the whole body and head reddish brown and resembling a partridge. The tail similar, somewhat pointed, towards the inner base red, towards the tip dark; beneath with distinct blackish transverse narrow bands. Equalling 12 centimetres from the tip of the bill to the end of the tail. The tail itself 5 cm [sic]. Inhabits Maria Island on the eastern shores of Tasmania.

MHNH CL 79 097: Muscivora Gutturifulva. Rostro latiore complanato atro; setis ad basim. Vertice virente sub-atro. Collo Dorso Uropygio fucescente-violaceis. Alis duabus obscuriori bruneis. Cauda longiore angusta spadicea. Gula Gutture Pectore rufescente fulvis. Abdomine cuncto candidiore. Pedibus sub atris. 17 centimet. longa. Cauda 7. Habitat australis ad terram Diemen in Dentrecasteaux angustiis.

Bill broadly flattened, black; with bristles at the base. Crown blackish green. Neck, back and rump dark brown-violet. Both wings dark brown. Tail rather long, narrow, chestnut-brown. Chin, throat and breast rather rufous tawny. Abdomen entirely bright white. Feet nearly black. 17 cm long. Tail 7. Inhabits southern [parts] in Tasmania in Dentrecasteaux Channel.

MHNH CL 79 098: Muscicapa Grisonea. Rostro nigricante griseo. Capite Collo Dorso Uropygio Gula Pectore Abdomine intensiori griseis. Alis longioribus sub-atris; Rectricibus 2.da 3.tia margine sua externa per albis; Caeteris omnibus cinereis. Cauda sub-bifurca, atra; inferna sua facie linigrisea. 18 centimetros aequans; 7 cauda. Habitat australis in terra Diemenense ad angustias Dentrecasteaux.

Bill blackish grey. Head, neck, back, rump, throat, breast and abdomen a rather intense grey. Wings long, near black; secondary and tertiary rectrices [he meant remiges] with their outer margin quite white; others entirely ash-grey. Tail slightly forked, black; its underside lined with grey. Equalling 18 centimetres; tail 7. Inhabits southern [parts] in Tasmania in Dentrecasteaux Channel.

MHNH CL 79 099: Tringa Nivea. Rostro teretiusculo longitudine capitis recto compresso subulato nigros [sic]. Naribus nudis linearibus. Capite cuncto Collo Dorso nebulosi cinereo fucescentibus. Gula alba. Gutture Pectoris que anteriore parte dilutiori-fuscis. Abdomine cuncto nivea. Alis duabus obscuriori-cinereis fucescentibus plumulis quibusdam interioribus albis. Cauda breviori subtus alba, desuper fusca. Pedibus pinnatis rubeolis tetradactylis, digito postico brevissimoris ad progressionem inserviente. 20 centimetros corpus integrum aequans. 4 cauda sejunctim emensa. Habitat australis ad plagas ultimas terrae Diemen in angustiis Dentrecasteaux ad fluvium portus N.O.

Bill somewhat tapering, the length of the head, straight, compressed, awl-shaped and black. Nostrils bare, linear. The whole head, neck and back cloudy dark brownish-grey. Chin white. Throat and upper part of the breast a washed-out dark brown. The whole abdomen snow white. Both wings dark brownish-grey, with some of the inner feathers white. Tail short, white below, brown above. Feet feathered/pinnate, ruddy, four-toed, with the hind toe very short and barely serving progress. The whole body equals 20 centimetres. The tail separately measures 4. Inhabits southern [parts] in the most distant regions of Tasmania in Dentrecasteaux Channel at the river of North West Bay.

MHNH CL 79 100: Glaucopis Cinerea Forst. Forsterianae descriptioni sequentia sunt addenda: Rostrum nigrum; locus nudus ad oculos. Carunculae posteriores inferiores et ad capitis basim potius quam ad mandibulae inferioris applicata, longiores angustae aurantiae. Corpore cuncto cinereo fucescente; Plumulis infernae faciei colli laevioribus mollioribus setosis. Pectore cinereo-griscente. Abdominis plumarum extremitate spatio mediocri flavidulosa. Pedibus crassiusculis cinereo-fuscis, ungue postico longiore. Cauda longiore, desuper nigricante fusca, rectricibus ad apicem albis. 42 centimetros demetitus; carunculae 3 centim. longae; vix 4 millimetris latae. Habitat in insula Perdicum angustiarum Dentrecasteaux ad plagas Australis terrae Diemenensis.

To the Forsterian description the following are added: bill black; bare area near the eyes. The wattles posterior and lower, attached to the base of the head rather than to the lower mandible, rather long, slender and golden. The whole body dark brownish ash grey; feathers of the under surface of the neck fairly soft and bristly. Breast ash-grey. Feathers of the abdomen on their outer parts moderately yellow. Feet slightly thickened, dark ashy brown, hind claw rather long. Tail rather long, blackish brown above, rectrices white toward the tips. Measures 42 *centimetres; wattles 3 cm long; scarcely 4 millimetres wide. Inhabits Partridge Island in Dentrecasteaux Channel in the southern regions of Tasmania.*

MHNH CL 79 101: *Parus Chlorotephronotus. Rostro nigro; Superciliis albis; Genis sub-atris. Vertice Dorso Uropygio que viridescente-griseis. Pectore simul et Abdomine flaviduloso-dilutiori cinereis. Pedibus griseo-sub-obscuris; Ungue posteriore crasso longiore. Alis nigricantibus desuper; subtus autem intensiori cinereis. Cauda laevi longiuscula, cinereo-nigricante ad apicem sub-bifida. Longitudine sua corpore cuncto metiente 14½ centim. Cauda separatim emetita 6. Habitat Australis in Insula Bruny angustiarum Dentrecasteaux ad plagas australis terrae Diemen.*

Bill black; eyebrow white; cheeks nearly black. Crown, back and rump greenish-grey. Breast and abdomen pale yellowish ash-grey. Feet fairly dark grey; hind claw stout and rather long. Wings rather black above; below, however, intense ash-grey. Tail slight, a little elongate, blackish-grey, slightly forked at the tip. The length of its whole body measures 14½ cm. The tail separately measures 6. Inhabits southern [parts] on Bruny Island, Dentrecasteaux Channel in the southern regions of Tasmania.

MHNH CL 79 102: *Muscivora Bitaeniofulvoptera. Rostro breve recto depresso nigro, setis ad basim ipsius. Capite Collo Dorso Uropygio plumulis obtectis mollioribus obscuriori cinereis, Rachide sub-albidiori. Gula Gutture Pectore Abdomine sub-albidiori-cinereis. Alis duabus nigris, Vittula duplici fulva transversim obliqua distinctis et ornatis. Cauda sub-forficata longiuscula sub-atra, rectricibus quibusdam ad apicem fulvescentibus. 12 centimetros longa. 7 [sic] cauda seorsim emensurata. Habitat australis ad terram Diemenensem in portu N.O. angustiarum Dentrecasteaux.*

Bill short, straight, flattened, black, with bristles at its base. Head, neck, back and rump covered with rather soft, dark ash-grey feathers, shafts off-white. Chin, throat, breast and abdomen off-white-ash-grey. Both wings black, with distinct and ornate tawny, transversely oblique, double narrow bands. Tail somewhat forked, fairly elongate, near black, with some rectrices becoming tawny at the tips. 12 centimetres long. The tail measuring 7 separately. Inhabits southern [parts] in Tasmania in North West Bay, Dentrecasteaux Channel.

MHNH CL 79 103: *Cuculus Gasteroxantus. Rostro sub-atro; crista nulla. Pedibus sordidiori-lutescente-cinereis. Capite Gula Collo Dorso Uropygio sub-violaceo-virentibus. Gutture Pectore Abdomine Ano que simul cinereo-rufis. Alis duabus spadiceo-nigricantibus. Cauda longior Alis angusta sub-atra, Rectricibus que ad marginem suam albidioris serrato-dentatim maculatis. 26 centimetros aequans ex apice rostri caudam extremam ad usque. Cauda verum ipsa 11 centim. Habitat australis in terra Diemenensi ad angustias Dentrecasteaux.*

Bill nearly black; no crest. Feet dirty yellowish-grey. Head, throat, neck, back and rump somewhat violet-green. Throat, breast, abdomen and vent all ash-grey-rufous. Both wings blackish chestnut brown. Tail rather long, wings narrow and near black, and rectrices spotted along their margins with white saw-tooth marks. Equalling 26 centimetres from the tip of the bill to the tip of the tail. The tail itself 11 cm. Inhabits southern [parts] in Tasmania in Dentrecasteaux Channel.

MHNH CL 79 104: *Corvus Australis Lin. Totus niger; menti pennis laxioribus; Remigibus ex fucescente nigris. Habitat in insulis Amicis maris Australis. 19 pollices longus; cauda 8 pollices longa. Huic descriptioni Linnaeanae sequentia mihi videntur adjicienda. Pennis Menti vix rarioribus; Cauda longa angusta fastigiata, subtus et ad apicem alba. Anus et ipse dealbus. Remigum ad apicem macula alba. Habitat in angustiis Dentrecasteaux terrae Diemenensis.*

Completely black; feathers of the chin loose; remiges from dark brownish to black. Inhabits the Friendly Islands [Tonga], South Sea. 19 inches long; tail 8 inches long. To that Linnaean description it seems to me that the following may be added. Feathers of the chin hardly loose-knit; tail long, narrow, pointed, and white at the tips on the lower surface. The vent itself is white. Remiges with white spots at the tips. Inhabits Dentrecasteaux Channel, Tasmania.

MHNH CL 79 105: *Cuculus Diemenensis. Rostro superne fusco, inferne vero sordidiori-lutescente. Superciliis pallidiori luteis. Capite Collo Pectore Dorso Alarum que facie superna colore generali obscuro-fucescente, striis albidioribus variegato propemodum nebuloso. Abdomine dilutiori cinereo dealbescente. Pedibus cinereo-griseis. Alarum duarum extremitatibus Cauda que simul spadiceo-nigrioribus, rectricibus remigibus que margine sua maculis albis serratulatim distributis. Cauda longior alis 15 centimetros elonga. Corpus autem omne 35 centimetros aequans. Habitat australis ad terram Diemenensem in portu N.O. angustiarum Dentrecasteaux.*

Upper side of the bill brown, but the lower side a rather dirty yellowish. Eyebrow pale yellow. Head, neck, breast, back and upper surface of the wings coloured generally dark brownish, with whitish variegated streaks, almost cloudy. Abdomen pale ash-grey tending to white. Feet ash grey. Ends of both wings together with the tail blackish chestnut-brown, rectrices and remiges with white saw-tooth spots distributed along the margin. Tail rather long, wings 15 centimetres long. The whole body, however, equalling 35 centimetres. Inhabits southern [parts] in Tasmania in North West Bay, Dentrecasteaux Channel.

MHNH CL 79 106: Tanagra Lilaceocolor. Rostro Pedibus que simul atris. Fronte, Mento, gula, Gutture que pariter atris; atris et quoque pennis grandioribus Alarum et Caudae his autem ipsis vittulina circumfusis alba. Reliquo Corpore id est Capitis Vertice, Collo desuper, Dorso, Uropygio, Alarum tectricibus, Pectore Abdomine que tandem dilutiori colore Lilaceo suffusis. Facie tamen inferna Caudae alarum que duarum et Ano stantibus albis. Corpus integrum aequans centimetros 32. Cauda cuneiformis longior seorsim emensa 12. Habitat in portu NO angustiarum Dentrecasteaux.

Bill and feet together black. Forehead, chin and upper and lower throat alike black; and the larger feathers of the wings and tail also black, these, however, with thin bands of white around the edges. Remainder of the body, that is the head, crown, upper side of the neck, back rump, wing coverts, breast, and finally, the abdomen, suffused with a pale lilac colour. However, the lower surface of the tail and both wings and the vent remaining white. The whole body equals 32 centimetres. Tail rather long, wedge-shaped, separately measuring 12. Inhabits North West Bay, Dentrecasteaux Channel.

MHNH CL 79 107: Tantalus? Melalophus. Rostro longiori compresso sub-arcuato subulatim-acuminato, sordide flavo; ad basim suam utroque latere plumulis albis brevioribus setosis obtecto. Mandibulis aequalibus cultratis nequaquam serratis. Lingua angusta ad apicem suum bifida, vix dimidiam rostri longitudinem aequans. Naribus obovalibus longis latioribus nudis. Pedibus nigricante fuscis tarso breviori; Digitis quatuor; tribus anterioribus membrana fusca emarginata per omnem suam propemodum longitudinem unitis; Postico breviore; ungue nullo serrato. Vertice nigro, nigra que simul crista capitis. Gula Gutture Pectore Collo Abdomine, Alarum duarum Caudae que inferna facie niveo per albis nitentibus que. Dorso Uropygio Caudae facie superiore, Alarum tectricibus dilutiori cinereo colore; Alis duabus autem istis caudae longitudinem aequantibus; remigibus nigricantibus. Cauda longiori per angustata, ad apicem acuminata, rectricibus duabus caeteris longioribus prominulis. 48 centimetros corpus aequans omne. Cauda 14. Rostrum 8. Collo breviore. Habitat australis ad insulas Furneaux in angustiis Banksianis.

Bill rather long, compressed, slightly downcurved, pointed and awl-shaped, dirty yellow; at the base of both sides covered with short white bristly feathers. Mandibles similar, knife-like, by no means serrate. Tongue narrow, split at its tip, scarcely equalling half the length of the bill. Nares obovate, long, rather wide, bare. Feet blackish brown, legs short; toes four; the anterior three edged with dark brown membranes [webs] that are united along almost their whole length; hind [toe] rather short; no claw serrate. Crown black, and the crest of the head also black. Chin, throat, breast, neck, abdomen, and the lower surface of both *wings and the tail [appearing] snowy through their glossy whiteness. Back, rump, upper surface of tail, and wing coverts, with pale ash-grey colour; but the two wings equalling the length of the tail; with blackish remiges. Tail rather long, quite narrowed, pointed at the tip, two projecting rectrices longer than the others. The whole body equalling 48 centimetres. Tail 14. Bill 8. With a rather short neck. Inhabits southern [parts] on the Furneaux Islands in Banks Strait.*

MHNH CL 79 108: Muscicapa Undulosa. Rostro per atro sub-trigono ad apicem sub-incurvo; Vibrissis ad nares ipsis que rotundis. Vittula transversim oblonga fusca ad oculos rostri que basim producta; spatio nudo pone oculos. Fronte Vertice Collo Dorso Uropygio que communi colore cinereo-dilutiori, unduloso. Alarum tectricibus cinereis, Remigibus vero sub-atris, exterioribus margine exteriore sua grisea; interioribus omni suo limbo nitidiore sub-albo. Gula Gutture Pectore que simul eodem propemodum colore ac dorsum sed dilutiore. Abdomine dealbescente. Pedibus fuscis, Unguibus atris. Cauda longiore sub-forficata; desuper atra, subtus alba. 30 centimetros aequans, cauda 13. Habitat australis in portu NO. angustiarum Dentrecasteaux.

Bill quite black, rather triangular and somewhat downcurved at the tip; nares round and with whiskers near them. A transverse, oblong, narrow dark brown band extended to the eyes and base of the bill; with a bare patch behind the eyes. Forehead, crown, neck, back and rump generally a pale ash grey colour, wavy. Wing coverts grey, remiges themselves near black, the exterior [ones] with their outer margins grey; the interior [ones] with the whole of their borders bright off-white. Chin, throat and breast together almost the same colour as the dorsum except paler. Abdomen becoming white. Feet brown, claws black. Tail long, somewhat scissor-shaped; above black, underneath white. Equalling 30 centimetres, tail 13. Inhabits southern [parts] in North West Bay, Dentrecasteaux Channel.

MHNH CL 79 109: Turdus Epirufus. Rostro latiore compresso per atro; Setis quibusdam ad basim. Capite, Collo desuper, Dorso simul et Alis duabus obscuriori-rufis. Alarum pennis grandioribus ad marginem suam interiorem nigricantibus. Cauda longiore rectricibus sibi invicem incumbentibus. Gula, Gutture Pectore que simul et Abdomine albidiori-cinereis; uniuscujusque pennae rachide obscuriori-fucescente. Pedibus atris. 25 centimetros corpore cuncto demenso. 10 cauda seorsim demensurata. Habitat australis in sinu Dentrecasteaux.

Bill laterally compressed, quite black; with some bristles at the base. Head, upper surface of the neck, together with the back and both wings, dark rufous. Larger wing feathers on their inner margins blackish. Tail rather long, with rectrices alternately lying upon each other. Chin, throat and breast, together with the abdomen, whitish ash-grey; each one of the feather shafts dark brown. Feet black. The whole body measured 25 centimetres. The tail separately measured 10. Inhabits southern [parts] in Dentrecasteaux Channel.

MHNH CL 79 110: *Psittacus Lacepedii (Mas). Rostro obscuriori-plumbeo; Cera nulla; ad mandibulae Superioris basim vittula angusta transversa intensiori-sanguinea. Ad mandibulae Inferioris basim quoque ex utroque latere, spatium sub-orbiculare, cyaneo-violescens. Vertice sub-virescente flavido. Collo Dorso viridiori nigricantibus, plumarum medio nigricante fusco; limbo verum virescente-rufo. Tectricibus alarum dorsi proximis eodem colore ac dorsum ipsum; anteriori-superioribus sub-atris; anterioribus infernis et externis per vivido colore cyaneo splendidis. Remigibus ad marginem suam exteriorem Purpureo-violaceis; interno latere per atro; Alis duabus subtus atris, anterius tamen plumulis quibusdam cyaneis. Cauda praelonga cuneiformis, per intenso colore viridi propeque modum fucescente desuper; subtus autem rectricibus fastigiatis, maxima sui parte dilutiori colore caeruleo; Gutture Pectore Abdomine que cuncto flavidiori virescente colore; ad Anum colore flavo puriore vividiore; 39 centim. aequat; 19 cauda seorsim commensurata; Habitat coloribus effulgens eximiis, australis terrae Diemenensi in angustiis Dentrecasteaux. Haec a discipulo grata magister habe Parvula Dona. F.P.*

(Male). Bill dark leaden; no cere; with a narrow transverse band of intense blood red near the base of the upper mandible. Likewise, near the base of the lower mandible, a nearly circular sea-blue-violet area on either side. Crown greenish yellow. Neck and back blackish green, the middle of the feathers blackish brown; the borders, however, greenish-rufous. Wing coverts closest to the back with the same colour as the back; the anterior upper ones nearly black; the anterior lower and outer ones a quite vivid colour of gorgeous sea-blue. Remiges on the outer margin purple-violet; on the inner side quite black; both wings black underneath, however some anterior feathers sea-blue. Tail very long, wedge-shaped, with an intense green colour above verging on brown; underneath, however, the pointed rectrices for the most part a pale blue colour; throat, breast and abdomen entirely a yellow-green colour; towards the vent a pure vivid yellow colour; equalling 39 cm; the tail separately measuring 19; glowing with exceptional colours, it inhabits southern Tasmania in Dentrecasteaux Channel. Master, [please] accept these very small, charming gifts from [your] student. François Péron

MHNH CL 79 111: *Lanius Rostr-Oculo-Pediflavus. Rostro sordide flavo ad basim plumulis obtecto griseis. Ad oculos spatio nudo flavo. Capitis vertice nigro vittula que pari colore ex ipso ad Gulam producta. Dorso cinereo fucescente sub-virescente colore. Alarum pennis intermediis virescentibus, caeteris nigricante-fuscis ad apicem albis. Cauda longiore cuneiforme nigricante fusca. Abdomine cinereo grisescente. Pedibus laeviori flavidis. 26 centimetros longitudine sua sub-aequans. 12 cauda seperatim commensurata. Habitat australis in angustiis Dentrecasteaux.*

Bill dirty yellow, towards the base covered with grey feathers. With a bare yellow area near the eyes. Crown of the head black and a band of like colour extending from it to the throat. Back brownish ash-grey slightly tinged green. Middle wing feathers greenish, others blackish-brown with white at the tips. Tail rather long, wedge-shaped, blackish brown. Abdomen ash-grey. Feet light yellow. Nearly equalling 26 centimetres in length. With the tail separately measuring 12. Inhabits southern [parts] in Dentrecasteaux Channel.

MHNH CL 79 112: Psittacus Lacepedii (Faemina). Discrepans a mare dimensionibus paulo minoribus diffet [sic] et sequentibus caracteribus. 1o. Rostrum minus aduncum, utraque mandibula ad apicem sub-albidum, ad basim autem sordidiori-lutescens. 2o. Vittula frontis colore sanguineo magis intenso. 3o. Vertice capitis minime flavo, sed viridi; 4o. Dorsi plumis propemodum penitus viridi colore; 5o. Alarum tectricibus vix quibusdam caerulescentibus et quidem sordide. 6o. Remigum pauciorum extrema margine caeruleo nigricante. 7o. Gutture Pectore Abdomine nequaquam flavis sed viridioribus. 8o. Dimensionibus minoribus corporis 35 centimetros emetitus; 9o. Cauda 15. 10o. Habitat iisdem locis ac mas coloribus egregiis inferior ipsi. Nomen specificum. à Mr. Lacépède professeur au Muséum d'Hist.re nat.elle. Haec a discipulo grata magister habe. Parvula dona. F.P.

(Female). Differing from the male a little in having smaller measurements, and with the following characters.
1. Bill less hooked, with both mandibles off-white towards their tips, at the base, however, dirty yellowish. 2. Frontal band a more intense blood red colour. 3. Crown of the head by no means yellow, but green. 4. Feathers of the back almost entirely a green colour. 5. Some wing coverts scarcely bluish and indeed dirty. 6. Outer margins of a few remiges blackish blue. 7. Throat, breast and abdomen not at all yellow, but greener. 8. Dimensions of the body smaller, measuring 35 centimetres. 9. Tail 15. 10. Inhabits the same localities as the male [but] inferior to the exceptional colours of him. Species name. To Monsieur Lacépède, professor at the Museum of Natural History. Master, [please] accept these very small, charming gifts from [your] student. François Péron

MHNH CL 79 113: Psittacus Insula Maria. Rostro obscuriori-fusco; Mandibula inferior sordidiori-lutea. Narium margine crassata prominente; Vertice obscuriori-virente; Collo Dorso Uropygio, pennis que tectricibus interioribus alarum sub-fusco viridioribus; Gula Gutture Pectore dilutiori viridibus; Abdomine cinereo-viridula. Tectricibus alarum anterioribus cyaneo-violaceis. Rectricibus intensiori nigricante caeruleis. Cauda longiore cuneiformi; desuper obscuriori virente; subtus autem sordidiori-flavidulescente; 7-8 pollices aequans. Habitat australis coloribus ternis in Insula Maria ad oras Orientales terrae Diemenensis.

Bill dark brown; lower mandible dirty yellow. Edge of the nares prominently thickened; crown dark green; neck, back, rump and feathers of the inner wing coverts a rather brownish green; chin, throat and breast pale green; abdomen ash-grey-greenish. Anterior wing coverts sea blue-violet. Rectrices [he meant remiges] intense blackish blue. Tail rather long wedge-shaped; above dark green; below, however, dirty yellowish; equalling 7-8 inches. With three colours [?], it inhabits southern [parts] on Maria Island on the eastern shores of Tasmania. [In saying 'coloribus ternis' Péron may have accidentally used the French word 'ternis' meaning 'tarnished' or 'dull'. As this appears to be an immature bird, 'with dull colours' would be appropriate.]

MHNH CL 79 114: Parus Sophia. Rostro per atro; Pedibus nigricante fuscis; Ungue postico longiore. Vertice cuncto simul et plumulis ad rostri basim speciosissimo vividissimo que colore caeruleo; Collari prussiaco-nigricante; Plumulis quibusdam rufeolis. Dorsi pars anterior eodem isto colore nitidissimo verticis; Pars autem Posterior simul et Uropygium et tectrices alarum eodem colore prussiaco-collaris. Alis utraque facie sua fucescente-cinereis; Cauda longa laevis ad apicem sub-expansa; colore nitidiori-violaceo-caerulescente; Abdomine cuncto cinereo-griseo; 19 centimetros longa; 6½ cauda seorsim aequans. Habitat australis, speciosa in portu Cygnorum angustiarum Dentrecasteaux ad plagas australes Terrae Diemenensis.

Bill quite black; feet blackish brown; hind claw rather long. The whole crown, together with the feathers towards the base of the bill, a beautiful and vivid blue colour; collar blackish Prussian blue; with some feathers rather rufous. The anterior part of back the same most brilliant colour as on the crown; the posterior part, however, together with the rump and wing coverts, the same Prussian blue colour of the collar. The wings on both surfaces brownish-ash-grey; the tail long and light, spreading somewhat towards the tip; colour bright bluish-violet; the whole abdomen ashy-grey; 19 centimetres long; the tail separately equalling 6½. [A] beautiful [bird], it inhabits southern [parts] in Port Cygnet of the Dentrecasteaux Channel in the southern regions of Tasmania.

MHNH CL 79 116: Larus Melapterus. Corpore cuncto per albo. Dorso maculis atris latioribus variegato. Alis duabus atris. Longitudine sua 35=40 centimetros aequans. Cauda aequali alba. Laro Naevio Lin. equidem affinis, nihilominus ab illo distinguendus, reor, cernandus que. Australis gregaria primum apparuit nobis ad 43.ma lat. gradum haud procul caput S. Terrae Diemen.

Voiez mon mémoire intitulé: Animaux observés pendant la traversée de Timor au cap Sud de la Terre de Diemen No. 36.

Entire body quite white. The back patterned with broad black spots. Both wings black. Its length equalling 35-40 centimetres. Tail uniformly white. Certainly related to Larus Naevius Lin., nevertheless it ought to be distinguished from that, I think, and separated. A gregarious [bird] of southern [parts], first apparent to us at latitude 43 degrees not far from the South Cape of Tasmania.
See my paper entitled: Animals observed during the journey from Timor to South Cape of Tasmania No. 36.

MHNH CL 79 117: Muscicapa Gasteroxanta. Rostro ad basim sordidiori-fucescente, ad apicem sub-atro; Capite cuncto, Collo, Dorso, Uropygio ardesiaco generali colore; Alarum tectricibus et remigibus dimidiato-fuscis, exteriori margine stramineis. Cauda sub-bifurca, rectricibus fuscis; Gula, Gutture Pectore naeviis; Abdomine tincta in rufum Vergente Pedibus griseo-fuscis; 17 centimetros longa; Cauda 6. Habitat australis ad oras S.O. Hollandiae-novae 19.a die florealis in navem elapsa nostram plurimis etiamsi secuis [sic] distantem e terris.
Nomen Specificum. e colore rufo Ventris. Radix. [Greek "gaster"] ... Venter ... [Greek "xantos"] ... rufus.

Bill dirty brown towards the base, nearly black at the tip; entire head, neck, back and rump a shared slate colour; wing coverts and remiges half brown, the outer margins straw-coloured. Tail slightly forked, rectrices dark brown; chin, throat and breast speckled; abdomen approaching rufous-tinted. Feet grey-brown; 17 centimetres long; tail 6. Inhabits southern [parts] on the south-west coast of New Holland, on the 19th day of Floreal [9 May 1802] like many [other] carefree [birds] it flew down onto our ship although far from land.
Species name. From the rufous colour of the abdomen. Root. [Greek "gaster"] ... Abdomen ... [Greek "xantos"] ... rufous. [Note: the word 'secuis' cannot easily be translated but may be a spelling error for 'securis', from 'securus' – unconcerned or carefree.]

MHNH CL 79 118: Sterna Melasoma. Corpore nigro, nigris et Alis, Cauda dorso que simul et Pectore, Abdominis que tandem anteriore parte. Uropygio vittula procincto per alba abdominis posteriorem cingente que partem. Australis gregaria 15-20 centimetros aequans, apparuit primo nobis in aequore vasto 19.a die nivose an.o X.o
Voiez mon mémoire intitulé: animeaux observés pend.t notre traversée de Timor au cap S. de la terre de Diemen.

Body black, and the wings and the back of the tail, together with the breast, and

finally the anterior part of the abdomen, also black. Rump and posterior part of the abdomen girded with a white, encircling band. A gregarious [bird] of southern [parts], equalling 15-20 centimetres, first appearing to us in the open ocean 19th of Nivose, Year 10 [9 January 1802]. [According to the next description, this was at 41°S.]
See my paper titled: Animals observed during our journey from Timor to South Cape of Tasmania.

MHNH CL 79 119: Sterna Caspioides. Corpore Cauda Pectore Collo que per albis; Alis duabus atris; atris et Pedibus, Rostro Capitis que Vertice; Reliquo capitis albo. Australis, Gregaria 30-40 centimetros emensa primo nobis apparuit in aequore vasto. 19.a die nivose an X.o ad 41.um lat. gradum.
Voiez mon mémoire intitulé: Animeaux observés pendant la traversée de Timor au Cap S de la terre de Diemen No. 34.

Body, tail, breast and neck quite white; both wings black; the feet, bill and crown of the head also black; remainder of the head white. A gregarious [bird] of southern [parts], measuring 30-40 centimetres, first appearing to us in open ocean 19th of Nivose, Year 10 [9 January 1802] at 41 degrees of latitude.
See my paper titled: Animals observed during the journey from Timor to South Cape of Tasmania No. 34.

MHNH CL 79 120: Sula Diemenensis. Rostro Facie que sulphureo colore. Capite Collo Dorso Uropygio pectore Abdomine Caudae que basi per albis. Extremitate vero Caudae nigra; nigris et alarum apice, margine, inferioris que ipsarum faciei parte. Anatis dimensionibus, australis gregaria propeque modum innumera ad oras terrae Diemen praesertim in rivo Cygnorum angustiarum D'entrecasteaux.
Voiez mon mémoire intitulé: Animeaux observés pendant la traversée de Timor au Cap S de la terre de Diemen No. 39.

Bill and face with sulphur colour. Head, neck, back, rump, breast, abdomen and base of the tail quite white. The end of the tail is actually black; black also the tip of the wings, their edge, and part of their lower surface. The size of a duck [he probably meant a goose], of southern [parts], belonging to flocks of almost immeasurable size, on the coast of Tasmania, especially in Cygnet River [probably either the Huon River or Port Cygnet] of Dentrecasteaux Channel.
See my paper titled: Animals observed during the journey from Timor to South Cape of Tasmania No. 39.

MHNH CL 79 121: Sulla Whytensis [sic]. Ansere paulo minor. Rostro pedibus que sulfureis. Collo Pectore que spadiceo-rufescente. Abdomine verum albo. Dorso *eodem colore ac pectus et collum. Alae longiores superne spadiceae; subtus autem ad articulationem usque secundam albidiores; reliquo spadiceo. Cauda longior fastigiata utraque facie spadiceo-fucescente. Habitatio ... Primo nobis apparuit ad terram Whytensem haud procul e rivo regis Guillemis. Dimensiones. [illeg.] alis duabus expansis [illeg.] 155 cent.met.; ab extremitate vero rostri caudam ad usque extremam [illeg.] 80 cent.met.*

A little smaller than a goose. Bill and feet sulphur-yellow. Neck and breast reddish chestnut. Abdomen actually white. The back the same colour as the breast and neck. Wings rather long, chestnut above; but off-white underneath all the way to the second joint; the remainder chestnut. Tail rather long, pointed, chestnut coloured on either side. Habitat ... first seen by us at Whyte's [sic = De Witt's] Land not far from King William's River. Dimensions. Both wings spread out 155 cm; from the tip of the bill to the end of the tail 80 cm. [This manuscript includes copious notes on the habits of the species, but they are difficult to read, with many illegible words.]

MHNH CL 79 122: *Sula Sawuensis. Corpore cuncto cinerascente griseo, satinaceo-nitente. Rostro fucescente cinereo. Facie intensiori cyanea. Colli Pectoris que plumis imbricatis squammosam superficiem propemodum affectantibus. Alis duabus nigricante-fuscis. Cornea grisea leviori deaurata. Pupilla per atra. Pedibus latiori membrana munitis colore vinaceo rubentibus. Dorso, Uropygio eodem colore ac reliquum corporis, pari que modo satinaceo-fulgidis. Cauda fastigiata intensiori grisea, rectricibus ad basim quibusdam albidioribus. Habitat mollucanus ad insulas Sawu per 125 leucas prosecutus nos.*
Voiez mon mémoire intitulé: Animeaux observés pendant la traversée de l'Ile de Timor au Cap Sud de la terre de Diemen No. 6.7.

The whole body ashy grey, with a satin sheen. Bill brownish grey. Face intense sea-blue. The feathers of the neck and breast almost appearing as an imbricate, scaly surface. Both wings blackish-brown. Cornea [iris] pale golden grey. Pupil quite black. The reddened feet strengthened with a broad, wine-coloured web. Back and rump the same colour as the rest of the body, and giving a similar satin sheen. Tail pointed, intense grey, some rectrices whiter towards the base. Inhabits the Moluccas near the Savu Islands [and] for 125 leagues accompanied us [just under 700 km].
See my paper titled: Animals observed during the journey from the island of Timor to South Cape of Tasmania No. 6.7.

MHNH CL 79 123: *Ardea Banksiana. Rostro nigro longiore robusto recto acuto sub-compresso; sulco e naribus versus apicem exarato; Crista nulla; Naribus linearibus; Lingua acuminata; Capite leviori caerulescente desuper, subtus alba; Collo cinerascente-cyaneo; Dorso eodem isto colore simul et Uropygio; Rectricibus atris; Tectricibus eodem colore ac Dorsum et Uropygium; Cauda sub-atra; Pedibus flavis; ungue intermedio introrsum serrato; Habitat australis dimensioribus Mycticoracis [sic] ad insulas Furneaux in navem nostram delapsa dum navigaremus in angustiis Banksii. Nomen Specificum. A Mr. Banks président de la societé roiale de Londres. Ipsius hic celebrant fluctus terrae que labores. F.P.*

Bill black, rather long, robust, straight, pointed, somewhat compressed; with a furrow from the nostrils extending towards the tip; with no crest; with linear nostrils; tongue pointed; head pale bluish above, white below; neck greyish sea-blue; the back together with the rump also this same colour; rectrices black [he probably meant remiges]; the coverts the same colour as the back and rump; tail nearly black; feet yellow; with the middle claw serrated on the inner side; inhabits southern [parts], the size of a night heron, it flew down onto our ship near the Furneaux Islands while we were sailing in Banks Strait. Species name. To Mr Banks, president of the Royal Society of London. Here the seas and lands do honour the achievements of this man himself. François Péron

Notes

1 We thank Laurent Raty and Tom Burton for help in translating Latin texts and Daniel Philippe and Jean Fornasiero for assistance with French translations. We note however that any errors in translations are our own.
2 François Péron, *Voyage de découvertes aux Terres Australes, exécuté par ordre de Sa Majesté l'Empereur et Roi, sur les corvettes le* Géographe *et le* Naturaliste *et la goëlette le* Casuarina *pendant les années 1800, 1801, 1802, 1803, et 1804, Historique*, vol. 1, Paris: Imprimerie impériale, 1807. François Péron and Louis Freycinet, *Voyage de découvertes aux Terres Australes, Historique*, vol. 2, Paris: Imprimerie royale, 1816. (Henceforth: Péron, *Voyage*.)
3 Erwin Stresemann, in 'Type Localities of Australian Birds collected by the "Expedition Baudin" (1801–1803)', *Emu*, vol. 51, no. 1, 1951, pp. 65–70, commented that any reader of the book expecting to find much information about ornithological matters would be extremely disappointed. The reasons are several, among which was firstly Péron's overwhelming research interest in marine invertebrates followed by his attention to oceanography, anthropology and international politics; in addition, the *Voyage* was intended primarily to describe the journey of discovery, not the science thereof. Finally, Stresemann asserted that neither the zoologist René Maugé nor the artist Charles-Alexandre Lesueur was known to have kept ornithological notes during the Baudin expedition. Péron's limited ornithological records are largely confined to notes and manuscripts, although some, as with several of his published dissertations, are likely to have contributed to details written into the *Voyage*.
4 Péron, *Voyage*, vol. 1, 1807, pp. 209–216. The seabirds are enumerated in François Péron (continued by Louis Freycinet), *Voyage of Discovery to the Southern Lands*, Adelaide: The Friends of the State Library of South Australia, translation of the second edition (1824) by Christine Cornell, 2 vols, 2006/2003, vol. 1, pp. 169–174, and are evidently based on Péron's only known publication on birds, 'Notice d'un mémoire sur les animaux observés pendant la traversée de Timor au Cap Sud de la Terre de Van Diémen', *Bulletin des Sciences, Société philomathique de Paris*, vol. 3, no.95, 1805, pp. 269–270.
5 Péron, *Voyage*, vol. 1, p. 225; Péron, *Voyage of Discovery*, vol. 1, p. 180.
6 Péron, *Voyage*, vol. 1, p. 225 (our translation).
7 Péron, *Voyage*, vol. 1, pp. 246–248; Péron, *Voyage of Discovery*, vol. 1, p. 195.
8 Péron, *Voyage*, vol. 1, p. 248; Péron, *Voyage of Discovery*, vol. 1, p. 196.
9 Péron and Freycinet, *Voyage*, vol. 2, p. 119; Péron, *Voyage of Discovery*, vol. 2, p. 95. See J. Burton Cleland, 'The History of Ornithology in South Australia', *Emu*, vol. 36, no. 3, 1937, pp. 197–221; Stresemann, 'Type Localities of Australian Birds'; Hubert Massey Whittell, *The Literature of Australian Birds*, Perth: Paterson Brokensha, 1954.
10 Muséum d'Histoire naturelle, Le Havre, Collection Lesueur (MHNH CL), 79 041.
11 Alternative identifications of the specimen were evaluated by Andrew Black, Jean Fornasiero, Justin Jansen and Philippa Horton, in 'The "new and singular" bird of St Peter Island', *South Australian Ornithologist*, vol. 42, no. 1, 2016, pp. 1–10.
12 Justin Jansen, in 'Towards the resolution of long-standing issues regarding birds collected during the Baudin expedition to Australia and Timor (1800–1804): specimens still present, and their importance to Australian ornithology', *Journal of the National Museum (Prague), Natural History Series*, vol. 186, 2017, pp. 51–84, reported on what is known of the bird collections of the Baudin expedition and of those specimens that survive to the present time.
13 See also Justin Jansen, *The Ornithology of the Baudin Expedition (1800–1804)*, Grave, The Netherlands: Privately published, 2018, and particularly Tables 3-009 to 3-011 therein.
14 MHNH CL, 21 002.
15 MHNH CL, 21 003.

16 The 31 manuscripts are catalogued in the Collection Lesueur as nos 79 092–79 114 (those numbered and described as from the 'Collection du C.^{en} Lesueur'), plus nos 79 116–79 123 (unnumbered descriptions with no collector stated). They are part of a collection (MHNH CL, 79 053–79 127) of surviving ornithological documents of Péron's from the Baudin expedition.
17 MHNH CL, 21 003.
18 Jacques-Julien Houtou de Labillardière was botanist/naturalist with the d'Entrecasteaux expedition (1791–1794).
19 Jansen, *The Ornithology of the Baudin Expedition*, Appendix 1.
20 MHNH CL, 79 001–79 052.
21 A revision of Tables 3-009 and 3-011 (in part) of Jansen, *The Ornithology of the Baudin Expedition*.
22 MHNH CL, 79 077.
23 He also wrote of gulls on Kangaroo Island, 'a large species of which was distinguishable by the beautiful lilac colour of its back'. Péron and Freycinet, *Voyage*, vol. 2, p. 78; Péron and Freycinet, *Voyage of Discovery*, vol. 2, p. 63.
24 Péron, *Voyage*, vol. 1, p. 247; Péron, *Voyage of Discovery*, vol. 1, p. 195.
25 Péron and Freycinet, *Voyage*, vol. 2, p. 59; Edward Duyker, *François Péron, an Impetuous Life: Naturalist and Voyager*, Melbourne: The Miegunyah Press, 2006, p. 46.
26 Péron, *Voyage*, vol. 1, p. 212; Péron, *Voyage of Discovery*, vol. 1, p. 170.
27 Baudin spent eight days, from 30 April 1802, unable to examine the St Peter and St Francis Islands because of adverse conditions, including hurricane force winds, and therefore turned for Tasmania, ahead of a 'strong north-north-easterly breeze', on 9 May (Péron, *Voyage of Discovery*, vol. 1, p. 265).
28 Péron, *Voyage*, vol. 1, p. 216; Péron, *Voyage of Discovery*, vol. 1, p. 173.
29 Péron, *Voyage*, vol. 1, p. 210; Péron, *Voyage of Discovery*, vol. 1, p. 169.
30 There is no reference in the *Voyage* to any gannet (= booby) being taken during the time the *Géographe* spent in the waters of De Witt's Land. The *Naturaliste* sailed more directly from Shark Bay to Timor, largely bypassing that coast, but Levillain wrote in his journal (MHNH CL, 07 008) that 'during the crossing we caught several seabirds by hand' (translation by Jean Fornasiero). While this booby might be one of them, Péron's detailed account of the specimen and the circumstances of its encounter strongly suggest that it was taken aboard the *Géographe*. Péron had described seeing 'various sorts of gannet' on Bernier Island, Shark Bay (Eendracht Land) (Péron, *Voyage of Discovery*, vol. 1, p. 97), but boobies are not known from so far south. Any 'gannets' seen there are likely to have been Australian Gannets, though they are now no longer found as far north. See Stephen Marchant and Peter Higgins (eds), *Handbook of Australian, New Zealand and Antarctic Birds*, Melbourne: Oxford University Press, vol. 1, 1990. During the expedition's second campaign in De Witt's Land, many seabirds, including 'gannets', were encountered between Barrow Island and the Monte Bello Islands (Péron and Freycinet, *Voyage of Discovery*, vol. 2, p. 157), and Péron listed two booby specimens among those later collections (MHNH CL, 21 002).
31 Péron (*Voyage*, vol. 1, pp. 6, 128) was relying on incorrect information regarding Dutch exploration of the Western Australian coast and thought that Willem's River was named after Willem de Witt. In fact, North West Cape and Willem's (now the Ashburton) River were discovered by Willem Janszoon in 1618. See Rob Mundle, *Dampier, the Dutch and the Great South Land*, Sydney: HarperCollins Publishers Australia, 2015, pp. 54–55. Gerrit Frederikszoon de Witt examined about 200 nautical miles of coastline to the north in 1628 (Mundle, *Dampier*, pp. 93–94).
32 Péron, *Voyage*, vol. 1, p. 209; Péron, *Voyage of Discovery*, vol. 1, pp. 168–169.
33 Péron, *Voyage*, vol. 1, p. 247; Péron, *Voyage of Discovery*, vol. 1, p. 195.
34 Jansen, 'Towards the resolution of long-standing issues'.

35 Péron, *Voyage*, vol. 1, p. 247; the statement is not reproduced in the second edition of the *Voyage*.
36 Duyker, *François Péron, an Impetuous Life*, pp. 15, 23, 26, 29–30.

Chapter 11

François Péron's Notes on the Albatross

Justin J.F.J. Jansen

François Péron has long been hailed as a major figure in the history of science. Early official recognition came from Antoine-Laurent de Jussieu and Georges Cuvier, professors of the Muséum national d'Histoire naturelle in Paris.[1] In their wake, Péron's biographers undertook a work of commemoration of the man and the scientist for much of the nineteenth century. Marie Joseph Alard and Maurice Girard, in particular, devoted many pages to Péron's scientific achievements.[2] Closer to our times, different groups of scientists, in association with Jacqueline Bonnemains, former curator of the Lesueur Collection of the Muséum d'Histoire naturelle of Le Havre, have published detailed catalogues of Péron's work in their own disciplines.[3] More recently, Jacqueline Goy and Michel Jangoux have shown how Péron was in advance of his time in terms of his scientific methods and reflections.[4]

Despite this attention, the full extent of his scientific writings is still not generally known. His early death in 1810 prevented him from finalising and publishing the results of all of the observations and collections he made during the Baudin expedition, with the result that many of his reflections have only survived as archival documents.[5] These documents have been largely preserved within public repositories, with his zoological papers in particular featuring prominently in the Le Havre Museum's Lesueur Collection (MHNH CL).[6] Among these papers are to be found some well consulted documents, such as his work on the *Medusae*[7] and his zoological observations of 1801–1802;[8] but there remains a wealth of papers on diverse subjects, many awaiting closer attention from specialised researchers. One group of papers, which features in dossier 79, is a collection of Péron's ornithological notes. This collection contains a variety of documents, including the record of an interview (with Daniel Cooper, a sealer) on the King Island emu (MHNH CL 79 054),[9] a description of the birds at Geographe Bay (MHNH CL 79 058), and notes on the North Pacific voyage of Joseph Billings (MHNH CL 79 086, 79 087).[10] However, there is also a significant number of short descriptions derived from the study of collected or observed birds. Of these descriptions, one stands out from the others in the amount of detail it provides: this is Péron's description of the albatross (MHNH CL 79 089, 79 090).[11]

The document is of interest from many points of view, but particularly because Péron provides a date on which the specimen was collected, and hence an indication of the collection locality. The precise date of collection is indicated on the first page as 14 January 1801, which situates Péron's work on the albatross as taking place during the crossing from Tenerife to Mauritius and hence during the first campaign of the expedition when Péron was still classified as a trainee zoologist and comparative anatomist. He was thus undergoing his initiation into the practices of scientific voyaging under the supervision of his experienced colleagues, zoologists René Maugé and Stanislas Levillain.[12] Indeed, Péron's place in the hierarchy of the zoological team is reflected in his notes, where he expresses his respect for his senior colleague Maugé and his gratitude for the permission Maugé granted him to proceed with the dissection of the bird's intestines. However, Péron's resulting notes show his familiarity with the genre of scentific description: they demonstrate both his qualities as an observer and his use of scientific literature to support him in his classifications and in his approach to writing up his findings.[13] Maugé was a collector of great discernment, as Péron recognised,[14] and had much to teach the trainee in the techniques of collecting and preserving specimens, but the technique Péron displayed in zoological description was already well developed.[15]

The young scientist owed the acquisition of these skills to a set of fortuitous circumstances which led him from a humble existence in his native village of Cérilly, through the perils of service in the Revolutionary wars, to his studies in the prestigious educational institutions of Paris. The fact that Péron's family was of modest means could well have prevented him from achieving his life's aims, but the foresight of his widowed mother and the benevolence of his fellow villagers combined to ensure he had the education and support he needed to complete his schooling in Cérilly and later to obtain a place as a student of medicine in Paris.[16] While medicine may not have been his first choice as a career,[17] Péron was pragmatic about the possibilities this course of study would open up and threw himself into his studies with great enthusiasm.[18] If he did not complete his training, it was not from a lack of commitment but because, in the wake of a failed romance, he was given an opportunity to commence a new adventure.[19] He applied to join the Baudin expedition and eventually obtained a place, thanks to the support of his professors.[20] He thus embarked as a 'trainee zoologist' on the 'Voyage of Discovery to the Southern Lands' and left France on 19 October 1800. In his 2006 biography of Péron, Edward Duyker listed details of the medical curriculum that was offered in the three years prior to Péron's departure, thus offering an insight into the preparation that had equipped him for his career as a naturalist.[21]

In the early years of the French Revolution, medical education reform, already deemed a political and social necessity, became even more urgent in view of the situation created by the casualties of war and a lack of qualified surgeons. As a result, three medical schools were set up by governmental decree on 4 December 1794, in Paris, Montpellier and Strasbourg. Among the students who applied for a place was the young François Péron. Following an interview in July 1797, he was accepted as a student. Among his teachers in his first semester were Antoine-François de Fourcroy (chemistry and pharmacology), François Chaussier (anatomy and physiology), Raphaël Sabatier (operative medicine), Pierre Lassus (external pathology) and Jean-Nicolas Corvisart des Marets (internal medicine). In his second semester, his teachers included Philippe Pelletan (clinical surgery), Bernard Peyrilhe (materia medica), Philippe Pinel (internal pathology) and Alphonse Leroy (obstetrics). In his third semester, Jean-Noël Hallé (physical medicine and hygiene) became one of his teachers, as did Louis Claude Richard (botany). Richard in particular had a great influence on Péron.[22] He had collected in Guyana, Brazil and the Antilles between 1781 and 1789, evidence of which still survives in the form of eight mounted birds in the collections of the Muséum national d'Histoire naturelle.[23] Richard brought back from his travels vast numbers of natural history items, and no doubt used them in his teachings, showing Péron and his fellow students what it was possible to bring back from far distant lands.

In addition to his medical studies, Péron attended classes at the Paris Museum, identifying several of his teachers as figures of influence. Bernard Germain de Lacépède was a particular source of emulation for Péron, who, in his description of the albatross, warmly acknowledged his teacher's erudition and the rigour of his analyses. Lacépède's contributions to Buffon's *Histoire naturelle, générale et particulière* (1749–1804) formed part of the young Péron's training, as did those of Louis Jean-Marie Daubenton, who undertook detailed anatomical studies of most mammals described within Buffon's encyclopædic work.[24] Lacépède no doubt contributed to awakening his student's interest in marine life, as did Georges Cuvier and Jean-Baptiste Lamarck, the mentors Péron later acknowledged as having recommended that he pay particular attention to the study of molluscs.[25] Péron paid further homage to Cuvier as a source of 'advice' and 'instructions' when referring to his passion for the study of molluscs and zoophytes.[26] In short, with such a range of expertise made available to him, it is little wonder that Péron took his place on the Baudin expedition so well prepared to take up his role as a zoologist.

When we look more closely at Péron's descriptions of the albatross, we can not only see how he used with discernment the scientific literature available to him, but also how he had benefited from his exposure to the different schools of taxonomy. Analysis of his text reveals three elements by which we can evaluate his zoological work: 1° his systematics; 2° his bio-morphological skills; 3° his anatomical skills:

1. It is of particular note that, in his manuscript, Péron used the category of 'subspecies' (*sous-espèce*), which is among the earliest known usages of the term in zoology. There was possibly an early tradition of subspecies usage in Europe at the end of the eighteenth century, but this has not yet been formally established. Although the term 'subspecies' was certainly in use by 1800, its meaning appears to have been much vaguer than it is today.[27]
2. Péron was correct in his description of the age of the albatross

specimen, and in his assessment that albatrosses have different plumages in the different age classes. The specimen depicted in plate 79 046 of the Lesueur Collection shows a bird in a young age class,[28] and the bird in plate 79 045 shows a bird in an older age class.[29] Both birds are either a Wandering Albatross *Diomedea exulans* or Tristan Albatross *Diomedea dabbena*.[30]

3. If we look more closely at his anatomical skills, we are struck by the curiosity he displayed when he put his arm down the throat of the albatross, and when he tasted the liver. We also note that his findings from dissecting the specimen are correct anatomically. However, his understanding of the function of 'protuberances' is debatable. He stated that these served the purpose of holding food inside. We now know that the opposite is true, since they are used for feeding the young and in courtship feeding[31] and they do not therefore constitute an impediment to the regurgitation process.

Overall, the albatross documents show us Péron as an autonomous and enterprising scholar, whose reflections were based on sound analysis and who, even in the early stages of the Baudin expedition, showed signs of being in advance of his time. They give us cause to reflect once more on how unfortunate it is that so few documents giving detailed descriptions such as these have survived the expedition.

François Péron's Descriptions of the Albatross[32]

Document 1

1506 Description of the Albatross[33]
Natural History
Ornithology
Diomedea exulans alba
24 Nivôse Year 9 [14 January 1801]

For several days, as we were drawing closer to the southern tip of Africa, we had been sighting several species of birds, among which we could easily make out a few *petrels* (Procellaria, Lin.), a *gannet* (Sula, Lacep.),[34] and lastly several *albatrosses* (Diomedea exulans, Lin.). Since they had all been flying at a great distance from the ship, we had not been able to catch any, but having encountered one today that was swimming on the surface of the water, and vainly attempting to fly away, it was easy to shoot.[35] As the boat had been sent out, we brought it on board in the best possible condition.

Given that everyone was familiar with this animal, which is very common in this vicinity, it was not difficult to relate it to its genus, and, with the help of *Lacépède*'s methodological table,[36] whose use for the determination of the genus is as simple as it is rigorous, I was soon able, in this case at least, to list the characteristics of the *Diomedea* genus. However, since the table by the illustrious French ornithologist unfortunately does not extend to species, I was obliged to turn to Linnaeus' *Systema Naturae*,[37] a work which I find to be more astonishing and more interesting by the day. With the help of this excellent guide I have no doubt that the species which has fallen into our hands is the *Diomedea exulans alba*.[38]

Nonetheless, even while doing justice to the Danish scholar,[39] we should not fail to pay Lacépède the dues to which he is so rightly entitled. The characteristics he gives for the genus are simple, excellent, and those he attributes to the subclass, division, subdivision are no less so. They are as follows:

2nd *Subclass*: the lower part of the leg without feathers, or several toes joined by a wide membrane (both are present here);

Drawing of the albatross described by Péron and caught on 14 January 1801 at latitude 30° South and longitude 13° 30' West of Paris. Charles-Alexandre Lesueur or Nicolas-Martin Petit. Muséum d'Histoire naturelle, Le Havre – no. 79 046.

1st *Division*: three toes in front; one toe or no toe behind (the last case is present here);

1st *Subdivision*: Front toes completely joined by a wide membrane.

Waterbirds
22nd Order: Hooked Bill
Genus 79: Albatross: Diomedea

Large, strong, sharp bill, ending in a big hook. The openings of the nostrils, situated at the end of a small longitudinal tube; each foot with only three toes.

Indeed, these characteristics are no less true than they are simple; if those pertaining to species are equally well defined, there is no doubt that the work of the French scholar is greatly superior to the *Systema Naturae*, even in terms of accuracy. Unfortunately, I do not have Lacépède's ornithology[40] in order to determine whether in the latter case as well he is superior to Linnaeus, but I am all the more inclined to think so, given that the marvellous sagacity, the delicate and exquisite judgement and the profound erudition of my estimable professor are just as well known to me. Yet, whatever the case may be, it remains a source of regret that, by adopting the concise, urgent style of the scholar, he did not seek to produce a work which, if it were more portable, less dense, than his magnificent history of birds, would have, if not replaced, at least been on a par with Linnaeus' work. In the meantime, this is the description that the latter gives of the Albatross, a description whose great accuracy I acknowledge, but about which we can make some useful observations.[41]

Order 3. Anseres or Geese

Bill: smooth, covered with an epidermis, enlarged at the tip;

Webbed Feet: with webbed *toes* joined by a membrane; short, compressed legs;

Body: heavy, with tough skin, very large feathers;

Food: from the water: plants, fish, molluscs;

Nest: most often on land; the mother rarely feeds its young; frequent *polygamy*;

Analogous: to mammals, of the order of *Belluae*.

Genus 71. Diomedea: Albatross.

Diomedea. Rostrum rectum: maxilla superiore apice adunca, inferiore truncata. *Nares* ovatæ, patulæ, prominulæ, laterales. *Lingua* minima.[42] *Pedes* tridactyli.[43]	*Diomedea. Bill* straight: *mandible*, upper, hooked at the tip, lower, truncated. *Nostrils*: openings, oval, thick,[44] slightly prominent, lateral. *Tongue*: very small. Feet: with three toes.

The characteristics of the species are no less accurate in Linnaeus;[45] they are as follows:[46]

Diomedea exulans alba, dorso alisque nigro-lineatis, rostro luteo, pedibus incarnatis, remigibus nigris, cauda plumbea, rotundata.	Diomedea *exulans* white; back and wings with kinds of black lines (see below); yellow bill; flesh-coloured feet; black remiges; tail: dull grey colour, rounded.

Observations

Linnaeus accepted two other subspecies of Diomedea *exulans*, which he designated by the following characteristics:

ß. Diomedea *exulans, fusca,* supra in nigrum colorem vergens, rostro rubro apice nigricante, lanugine cinerea, versus caput albida.	ß. Diomedea exulans brown, bordering on black on the upper part; bill: red[47] and slightly blackish at its tip; soft feathers: ash-coloured and whitish towards the head.

The 2nd subspecies is the one he designates by the name of:

γ Diomedea alba, interscapulio, remigibus rectricibusque ex fusco nigricantibus, capite sommoque collo intense stramineis, mandibula superiore alba vel rubicunda, inferioris rubræ carina alba.	γ Diomedea white, but the space between its shoulders, its remiges and rectrix feathers a blackish brown; the head and upper part of the neck dark brown; the upper mandible white, or reddish; the carina of the lower mandible white, although the rest of the mandible itself is red.

Could it not be that the subspecies[48] are so many varieties of the same species,[49] order Diomedea exulans alba itself? Indeed these are only based on shades of more or less dark colours, and less on age, the sex of the individual; the climate of the place where it was caught; the exact time of the year when it was shot; all of which can be the cause of more or fewer variations for many reasons. I was all the more inclined to share that opinion in that the very individual that we had caught provided us with a few facts that were liable to confirm it. Indeed, those black lines that Linnaeus designated as a characteristic do not yet exist; but you can already see the first indications of these lines in the ash-grey zigzags running in a transversal direction in relation to the animal's back. The same can be said of the yellow bill he gives as a characteristic. The bill of our individual is a definite matt white. Yet we should not conclude from this that the characteristic indicated by Linnaeus is wrong,[50] for when it is examined carefully against the light you can easily perceive a nuance of light yellow, which, despite not being even more visible, nonetheless exists, and is no doubt only awaiting

Drawing of one of three albatrosses caught on 16 February 1801 at latitude 33° South and longitude 38° East of Paris (southern Indian Ocean). Charles-Alexandre Lesueur or Nicolas-Martin Petit. Muséum d'Histoire naturelle, Le Havre – no. 79 045

favourable circumstances, such as age, time of year, etc, for this to be stated more strongly, especially in the first case, for I have no doubt, as I shall soon prove, that our individual is a young animal. The same can be said of the colour of the feet, which he says to be flesh-coloured, for those of our bird barely displayed a very light pinkish shade at the time we shot it, a shade which, even after desiccation and exposure to the air, had almost entirely diasappeared. But this shade alone is sufficient to establish the truth of this characteristic. However, the same remark can easily apply in the case of older individuals, as with geese (Anser olor), in the order of which Diomedea is included by Linnaeus. These are far from having a lead-grey colour, as Linnaeus indicates, but some ash-grey markings show clearly enough that it must take on a more distinct grey colour with age.

From these different remarks I feel bound to conclude:

1° that the two subspecies I have just mentioned could definitely be mere varieties of the 1st order of Diomedea *exulans alba*;

Diomedea species, Drake Passage Atlantic Ocean, January 2006.

2° that the individual in our possession is very young, and the suspicion that these differences in colouring had already aroused in me has just been confirmed by my esteemed colleague, Citizen Maugé, who had assured me, when preparing this animal, that its tender flesh and the ease with which he operated on it left no doubt as to its youth, all the more so because those older specimens in the Museum indeed displayed the characteristics assigned by Linnaeus. This observation, which may be of no importance, proves that sometimes we need to put away our books and refer solely to nature itself.

Now let us see what the *Systema Naturae* has to say about the habits and dispositions of this bird:

Diomedea exulans alba habitat in mari, tum intra tum extra tropicos, frequens ad caput bonæ spei, circa finem Julii in Camtschatcæ littore marique hanc Asiæ partem et Americam separante numerosissima, magnitudine inter cygnum anseremque media, frequentius cygno major, 2 pedes 9 pollices, 3 pedes 6 pollices ad 4 usque pedes longa a *Falconibus* et Catarrhacte perquam infestata, voracissima, *salmonum* turmis in fluviorum ostiis, *triglis* volitantibus, a *coryphœna* exagitatis, aliisque piscibus, quos marìs accolis prænunciat, inhians, quos integros et immensa copia devorat, ut adscendere eorum pondere cohibeatur, quamvis alias altissime volet, molluscis etiam viditans; in Americæ australis littore Septembris fine nidum in tellure ex terra stuit rotundum, pedem 1-3 altum, ovaque ponit numerosa, edulia, albumine in calore non coeunte, anserinis majora, 4½ pollices longa, alba, versus finem magis obtusum obsolete maculata; vox asini; rostro mordicus se defendit: Caro dura; Camtschadali intestini partem inflatam retibus suis appendunt, alarum ossa sugendo tabaci fumo, aciothecæ, et carminando, quod lini vices iis supplet, gramini adaptant.

Rostrum fulcatum, *sordide flavum*, aciebus duabus palati argutissimis, cultriformibus, versus basin rostri longitudinalibus, in mandibulam inferiorem inciduis; nares a basi remotæ, e fulco rostri emergentes, quasi tubuli compressi, brevissimi; vertex ex pallide cinereo fuscus; dorsum versus uropygium nigro-maculatum; alæ longissimæ angustissimæ; remiges primariæ 9 nigræ, scapis supra intense flavis, extima longissima, reliquis subito decrescentibus, rectrices breves, 14; pedes incarnati aut spadecei unguibus obtusis, membrana connectente fusca.

The white albatross *exulans* lives at sea; it can be found both in the tropics and beyond; it is commonly found in the vicinity of the Cape of Good Hope[51] and in very great numbers towards the end of July on the shores of Kamchatka and in the seas separating this part of Asia from the Americas. In terms of size this bird is midway between the swan and the goose. It is larger than the swan and its length varies from two feet nine inches to three feet six inches and even four feet. Its enemies are *falcons* and *crested penguins*; it is extremely voracious, and feeds particularly on salmon, pursuing its large schools up into the mouths of rivers; it also follows the *flying fish* being pursued by the bands of *sea bream* whose arrival it announces to the inhabitants of the seashore; it not only devours these animals whole, but it swallows them in such prodigious quantities that this weight it carries in its body can sometimes prevent it from flying, even though, at other times, it can rise up to very great heights.[52] It also feeds on molluscs. On the shores of South America, towards the end of September, it constructs its nest of soil on the seashore; in this nest which is round, and from one to three feet high, it lays its eggs in large numbers; they are good to eat, larger than goose eggs, four and a half inches long, white, but more rounded at the tip; they have markings of an unpleasant shade; the remarkable phenomenon with the white of this egg is that it is not liable to coagulate in the heat; the cry of this bird is very similar to the braying of the donkey (see below); it defends itself by biting with its bill.

Grooved bill; dirty yellow; the two rows of the palate very sharp, in the form of knives, longitudinal towards the base of the bill, incidental on the lower jaw; the openings of the nostrils distant from the base, and emerging from the grooves of the bill, like compressed tubes, very short. The top of the head is a pale ash-grey; the back has black markings near the rump, the wings are very long, very narrow; the primary remige feathers are black, and nine in number; their shaft is dark yellow on top; the last one very long; the others decreasing rapidly in length; the short rectrix feathers are 14 in number; their feet flesh-coloured or grey; the nails rounded and the membrane that covers the toes is brown in colour.

Comparative Anatomy

Being convinced that an examination of the intestines of this animal could be of some interest, I requested of my indefatigable colleague Citizen Maugé, who intended to prepare this animal, I requested, as I said, that he give me the viscera of this animal, a request which he granted me with great pleasure. These are the results of my examination, which could never have been as rigorous as it should have been, since it is difficult when doing the anatomy of an animal to identify with precision the relationship of its parts unless one has the entire animal at one's disposal. However, as I focused on the essential objects, I identified several things of the greatest interest. I shall not mention the structural relationships which it has in common with all birds in general and particularly with waterbirds to which it is related by all the general characteristics, like the webbing of the feet, the leg structure, which is usually short, compressed; the extended neck, the position of the centre of gravity, the nature of the feathers of the down, etc, etc, the form of the bill, etc. Two principal objects caught my attention: the animal's voice and its digestive system.

Voice of the Albatross

The cry of this animal, says Linnaeus, resembles the braying of the donkey: *Vox asini*. As I was sure that the trachea would present some particular arrangement, I removed it entirely, along with the larynx and everything up to above the bifurcation of the bronchial tubes. It presented me with phenomena that were too far above my knowledge of comparative anatomy for me not to feel incapable of going into the mechanism in a way that would bring me any satisfaction. I thus restricted myself to preserving the larynx and its muscles, the hyoid bone and its muscles, the trachea up to two inches above the division into bronchial tubes and, lastly, a portion of the right bronchial tube itself. These parts are sufficient to give Citizen Cuvier interesting knowledge of the relationship between this physical organisation and the particular cry of the animal.[53]

The same was not true of the digestive system, since many parts were hardly able to be preserved; indeed most of them needed to be examined while they were still very fresh **since** their nature can be readily determined from this; I took the greatest care with this examination, and here are the highly interesting results which it presented to me.

1° *Mastication*: Equipped with a large, strong, long, hooked bill, both mandibles are operated by vigorous muscles. They are of a corneous nature, very dense, very compact and very wide, in the form of a knife; very sharp and arranged in such a manner that [illegible] present a groove and a gutter in a way that **allows the** front part of the upper jaw to [illegible] in the groove of the lower jaw, while, in turn, **the back part of the lower jaw likewise receives the back part of the upper jaw**. This remarkable interlocking arrangement of the two jaws gives them an astonishing strength [illegible] they [illegible] so to speak [four illegible words] which it can at will make slide over one another, rub against one or other [illegible] of its jaws, a very [illegible] arrangement no doubt and very good for fulfilling the aim of the opening, also provides it with the means of grinding very hard food and thus increases the means of existence of this voracious animal . . .

The *pharynx* is so wide it is extremely easy to insert a completely closed fist. The pharynx, I say, displays large and very strong muscles on its upper part and some [illegible] through their almost circular arrangement [two illegible words] to contract this opening and prevent the return of food introduced into the stomach. Nature has taken a second precaution to prevent this reflux of food: this is a bundle of membraneous cartilaginous papillae a few lines long[54] which form a kind of circular extension which [two illegible words] the opening of certain kinds of [illegible], the tips of these papillae being turned towards the inside of the œsophagus so as to prevent the return of food;[55]

Albatross

The liver is bilobate, with a third incomplete subdivision between the two lobes corresponding to the spigelian lobe.[56] The right lobe is much more elongated than the left. The internal substance is a yellowish grey and when one tastes it one experiences a very strong flavour of stiplicity and bitterness.[57] Within can be seen the divisions of the artery and the hepatic veins which are **very grey**.[58]

The opening of the œsophagus, which is so wide that you can easily put your entire arm through it, displays at its upper extremity several packets of muscles designed to contract or dilate its opening at the animal's will independently of this structure to prevent the reflux of the matter which enters it. At its orifice there is a membraneous cartilaginous zone laid out in the form of a circle and presenting more or less the organisation of certain kinds of **dobby**, a large number of small protuberances about two or three lines long with their base turned towards the orifice of the mouth. Independently of this zone, which forms a kind of valve, you can see at about an inch below, descending still further into the pharynx, a large number of these small cone-shaped bumps no doubt intended for the same use. From this spiny circle to the cardia is where the œsophagus seems to begin; it is from 13 to 14 inches long by 8 to 9 inches large. You can easily distinguish three membranes: one which is internal, smooth and apparently containing no mucous glands; the second presents ramifications of quite a large number of arterial and venous vessels; the third, which is external and muscular is a whitish red. You can easily make out the transversal muscular fibres and some longitudinal ones which are finer and also more difficult to see. The small number of glands distributed throughout the pharynx and the œsophagus, the lack of density in its walls, are sufficient proof that it has little of a role to play in digestion. After going through the space we have just indicated, a narrowing marked by a brownish line is a clear enough indication that we have reached the stomach. It has a very large capacity and can be extended by a prodigious amount through the elasticity of its walls. In the upper part its form is more narrow, its middle section is more distended, and it ends abruptly in a pylorus with a diameter of one or two lines at the most, which has quite a large number of mucous glands, two with fleshy fibres. It is about 13 to 14 inches long to 6 to 7 in its middle section. The stomach of such a voracious animal would seem to have to present with great consistency a large number of mucous glands, but this is not the case. Having a consistency that is more or less similar to the œsophagus, it presents the same arrangement for the number of tunics for their distribution. Only in addition, you can see one mucous tunic, although it is quite small and only displays follicles which are barely visible. On the outside a fold of the mesentery provides it with the peritoneal tunic. The muscular tunic is a little stronger, but if the stomach of this animal does not in itself command much digestive strength, nature, which is always wondrous in its operations, has compensated for this:

1° by the necessarily longer time food spends there, time which is determined by the difficulty it has passing back through the œsophagus, according to the distribution we discussed;

2° by the extreme narrowness of the pylorus;

3° by the very distribution of the first parts of the duodenum which, instead of forming a [illegible], as in man, for example, performs a flat circumvolution of a turn and a half on itself, which, by slowing down the flow of matter from the stomach, prolongs the time it spends in this part of the intestinal duct which is closer to the glands of the pylorus and the stomach itself;

4° lastly by the length and by the narrowness of the intestinal canal which is not itself very elongated in its upper sections, it presents a very strong muscular tunic.

NB Blood vessels are also very abundant in this intestinal duct and seem to start from a large trunk, **the means of providing the** mesenteries which themselves are very voluminous and accompanied by *very substantial nerves*.

Intestinal tract 8 feet 4 inches. Four membranes: mucous, membraneous, muscular and peritoneal, medial [illegible] formed by the duplication of the mesentery from which the arteries, veins and fibrous nerves come to establish themselves, **a transfer which** is very pronounced; **the longitudinal ones are insensitive, especially** the muscular tunic and muscular one which is very remarkable. By reducing its thickness and density, the intestinal canal keeps on becoming wider and thinner. These circumvolutions have the particular feature of almost adhering to one another. I found nothing particular in the stomach that appeared to me to be lumbrici.[59]

The intestinal duct[60] which I had only measured in [illegible] ends soon after going for another **8 4½ 12½ inches**[61] in a much larger bulge which is equivalent to the **cecum**, but without having its valves. The gall bladder, which is thin, elongated, contains a small quantity of a yellowish green bile which is **extremely** bitter and intolerable. In the folds of the mesentery is the pancreas, which is a thin, very elongated body of a very firm consistency; it is about 6 to 7 inches long.

The last sections of the intestinal duct are extremely thin and fragile, and add four and a half feet to the length of the intestinal duct.

```
 8.4
 5.6
   8
15.6
```

Natural History

Ornithology
Diomedea exulans: Albatross
24 Nivôse Year 9 [14 January 1801]

For a few days the appearance of several birds, and especially those belonging to that species known by the name of gannet (Sula – Lacépède), some petrels (Procellaria), gave us a clear enough indication that we were finally approaching land. This morning we were at 33° latitude and 14° longitude.

Document 2[62]

3rd Order: Anseres or Geese
Characteristics of the Order

Bill: smooth, covered with an epidermis, enlarged at the tip;
Webbed Feet: with webbed toes joined by a membrane;
Legs: compressed, short;
Body: heavy, with tough skin, very large feathers; **becomes rancid**;
Food: from the water: plants, fish, molluscs, etc;
Nest: most often on land; the mother rarely feeds its young; frequent polygamy;
Analogous: to mammals, of the order of *Belluae*.

Genus 71: Diomedea
Characteristics of the Genus

Diomedea. Rostrum rectum: maxillâ superiore apice aduncâ, inferiore truncatâ.
Nares ovatœ, patulœ, prominulœ, laterales.
Lingua minima.
Pedes tridactili.

Straight bill. Upper mandible hooked at the tip; lower bill truncated.
Openings of the *nostrils* oval, thick, slightly prominent, lateral.
Tongue very small.
Feet with three toes.

Speciei caracteres Diomedea exulans *alba*, dorso alisque nigro-lineatis, rostro luteo, pedibus incarnatis, remigibus nigris, cauda plumbea, rotundata.	Characteristics of the species Diomedea exulans *white*, the back and wings with kinds of blackish transversal lines; yellow bill; flesh-coloured feet; black remiges; tail: dull grey colour, rounded.
Synonymies As there is very little difference between those I have given opposite in French, or even, to put it more clearly, between these and the Latin that I have just translated, it would serve no purpose to repeat them. I shall limit myself to observing that Linnaeus distinguishes three varieties of *Diomedea exulans*, namely, *exulans alba*, *exulans fusca*, *exulans alba* with a very brown head and neck. Perhaps this division does not [illegible] varieties that depend on age, sex or the time of year when the animal was caught.	Synonymies[63] *Diomedea* with **pinnate** wings; feet of equal **height**, with three toes. Sist. nat. XII. 1. p. 214. n. I. Diomedea *Albatrus*. P̶a̶l̶ Pallas. Spic. zool. 5. p. 28. *Tohaiki* Steller. Hist. Camtschatc. p. 154[64] *Albatros*. Edw. av. t. 88. Grew. mus. t. 6. f. 1. Briss. av. 6. p. 126. n. 1. Buffon hist. nat. des oiseaux. 9. p. 339. t. 24. pl. enlum. n. 237. Man of War bird. Albin. av. 3. t. 81. Wandering Albatros. Arct. zool. 2. p. 506. n. 423. Lath. Syn. III. I. p. 304. n. 1.

Document 3[65]

Albatross

As the ribs are very long and the tendons are muscles **of the grand** pectoral which appears trifurcated or at least lateral parts of the [illegible] from which seem to originate three small portions of muscle which combine to increase its action, as I say, these small muscles which [illegible] to [illegible] the arm [illegible] and the **body** are obliged to carry their action very far. **Nature**, to make them stronger, has distanced them from the centre of the joint by means of a kind of rod situated on the outside tuberosity of the humerus and, in the joint of this bone with the cubitus and the radius, another kind of bony cartilaginous rod intended to serve both as a kind of pulley block and as a means of increasing the power to keep it away from the centre of movement and have it act at the tip of a much greater lever, is continuous with the joint itself, by means of very thick and strong ligaments, one of which will attach it to the external tuberosity of the humerus and the other to the base of the [illegible].

The pectoral muscles are all the weaker in that the animal is in the class of those animals where they are the most voluminous and in which their particularly large size should mean that their organs have greater development. Not only are the pectoral muscles weak, but those which are arranged so as to bring the arm back alongside the body of the animal are likewise very weak. Their thin, flattened tendons are very long and are quickly separated from the muscular body, and since, according to what we have already said, and, despite the arrangement that we mentioned and which favoured the adhesion of the pectoral muscles, which through their adhesion to the upper part of the carpal bones are arranged so as to move it onto the forearm, it follows that [illegible] the entire apparatus for flight in this animal is excessively weak. The length of its wings, the weakness of all of the muscles arranged so as to make them work, the length of these [illegible] themselves, everything contributes, with the weight of the animal, and especially the narrowness of its wings, everything contributes to making flight very imperfect, and this does not support Linnaeus, who claims that, for the beginning of flight, it is less a question of a lack of wind, as people have said, that means one can manage to catch them on the water, or at least come as close to them as one would like. He attributes this phenomenon to the imperfection of flight in this animal which, barely capable of [illegible] when its stomach is empty, necessarily becomes incapable of it when it has filled its enormous stomach with food.

The sternal rib which is so strong in birds is only prominent here in the front part and then in a manner infinitely less than in other birds and particularly in birds of prey; in the upper part it keeps expanding and becomes barely visible in the back part.

This weakness of the wings and everything linked to the flight system provides an even stronger contrast with the large size of the animal because it has thighs of enormous size surrounded on all sides by very strong, large muscles which meant that nature destined it to swim rather than to fly.

Behind the clavicle lurks a large bundle of antagonistic muscles of the pectorals which consequently are designed to keep the arms away from the body of the animal while the former bring it closer. Nature uses the clavicle like a pulley which serves to give direction to movement.

Immediately after opening the white **line** one finds an immense cavity in which can be seen floating freely, forced forward by the diaphragm [illegible] by a [illegible] by the same diaphragm which not only does not adhere to the ribs but also leaves a great empty space between them no doubt intended for the development of the lungs which are **far behind**. This huge cavity contains:

1° only [illegible] and, on the right, the liver [illegible] a beautiful grey brownish colour and of very pleasant appearance; the right lobe which is flattened, elongated and much less voluminous than the left, seems to be laid on, and adhering to the peritoneum. The vessels of one can clearly be seen [illegible] with those of the other, or rather, **they are the same**.

2° Immediately above and on the same right side is the portion of the vesicle which [illegible] the liver, which is cylindrical and of a dark brown greenish colour, the portion which [illegible] the liver is barely more than three inches long.

3° To the left and immediately above the lower edge of the left lobe is the stomach, which [illegible] the diaphragm; below can be seen the narrowing [illegible] by the [illegible] this stomach, which has a white, slightly pinkish colour and is covered by a kind of [illegible] which, instead of being free and floating as it is in other animals, is immediately attached to the stomach and that forms, so to speak, the outer wall. In this kind of **pylorus** [illegible] an enormous quantity of blood vessels; this stomach and the intestinal tract, which only contain a little food, are far from occupying the entire capacity of the abdomen, but if you consider the elongated form, the [illegible], the strong and numerous wrinkles that it presents at the same time in the [illegible], above all, if you consider the frightful quantity of food that this voracious animal can ingest, you must agree that when, instead of being empty, it is full of food, [illegible] the empty space of the abdomen ... The stomach when it is thus empty has a cylindrical, elongated shape which is about an inch and a half, two inches in diametre by four to five inches in length. It then narrows practically all at once and forms the pylorus which is very narrow and immediately folds back on itself to form the [illegible] that can be seen [illegible] above the peritoneum.
4° Immediately above the bile duct is the pancreas, which is oblong, a clear white in colour, and very intimately linked to, and even continuous with, the bile duct.
5° [illegible] the left lobe of the liver which alone is free. You can see [illegible] that the left lobe not only adheres but even penetrates the partition which separates them inside a second cavity formed by a double fold of the peritoneum in which we have observed: (i) the entire right lobe of the lung which did not simply adhere, as we first thought, but which was lodged entirely between the two **parts** of the peritoneum, or rather laid onto the front of [illegible] and [illegible] of a fold in the peritoneum which was adhering to it only in the place where it pierced the membrane.

Notes

1. Antoine-Laurent de Jussieu, 'Notice sur l'expédition à la Nouvelle-Hollande entreprise pour des recherches de Géographie et d'Histoire naturelle', *Annales du Muséum national d'Histoire naturelle*, vol. 5, 1804, pp. 1–11; Georges Cuvier, 'Rapport fait au gouvernement par l'Institut Impérial sur le Voyage de Découvertes aux Terres Australes', *Procès-verbaux des séances de l'Académie, Classe des Sciences physiques et mathématiques*, vol. 3 (séance du lundi 9 juin 1806), 1807, pp. 363–367.
2. Marie Joseph Louis Alard, *Éloge historique de François Péron, redacteur du voyage de découvertes aux terres australes, lu à la Société Médicale d'émulation de Paris, séant à la Faculté de médecine, dans la séance du 6 mars*, Paris: Imprimerie de L.-P. Dubray, 1811; Maurice Girard, *François Péron, naturaliste, voyageur aux Terres Australes: sa vie, appréciation de ses travaux, analyse raisonnée de ses recherches sur les animaux vertébrés et invertébrés, d'après ses collections déposées au Muséum d'Histoire naturelle*, Paris: Baillière; Moulins: Énaut, 1856.
3. To give but the example for ornithology, see Jacqueline Bonnemains and Claude Chappuis, 'Les oiseaux de la collection C.A. Lesueur du Muséum d'Histoire naturelle du Havre (dessins et manuscrits)', *Bulletin trimestriel de la Société géologique de Normandie et des Amis du Muséum du Havre*, vol. 72, fasc. 1–2, 1985, pp. 25–78.
4. Jacqueline Goy, *Les Méduses de Péron et Lesueur: un autre regard sur l'expédition Baudin*, Paris: Éditions du CTHS, 1995, p. 31; Michel Jangoux, 'François Péron: l'émergence d'un naturaliste', *Une petite ville, trois grands hommes. Actes du colloque de Cérilly, 15–16 mai 1999*, Moulins: Pottier, 2000, p. 139.
5. Michel Jangoux, 'François Péron', p. 140, gives a summary of the reasons why Péron's work was not completed and why his papers for so long had the status of 'neglected archives'.
6. For a summary of the nature and extent of Péron's papers held in the Lesueur Collection at Le Havre, see the article by Gabrielle Baglione and Cédric Crémière in this volume.
7. Goy, *Les Méduses*; Gabrielle Baglione, Cédric Crémière, Jacqueline Goy and Stéphane Schmitt, *Méduses-Jellyfish*, Paris: MkF Editions, 2014.
8. Michel Jangoux, 'L'expédition du capitaine Baudin aux Terres australes: les observations zoologiques de François Péron pendant la première campagne (1801–1802)', *Annales du Muséum du Havre*, no. 73, 2005, pp. 1–35.
9. This questionnaire was first published in its entirety in an article by Alphonse Milne-Edwards and Émile Oustalet, 'Note sur l'émeu noir (*Dromaeus ater V.*) de l'île Decrès (Australie),' *Bulletin du Muséum d'Histoire naturelle*, vol. 5, 1899, pp. 206–214.
10. The expedition conducted by Joseph Billings between 1785 and 1794 in the North Pacific was commissioned by Catherine the Great and collected a wealth of documentation in terms of cartography, ethnography and the natural sciences.
11. The unpublished notes on the albatross written by François Péron and held in the Lesueur Collection of the Le Havre Museum correspond to three separate documents in dossier 79 and are numbered as follows: 79 089-1, images A-J; 79 089- 2, image A; 79 090, images A-B.
12. For details of Péron's initiation during the early stage of the voyage, see Jangoux, 'François Péron', p. 145.
13. Péron makes copious use of Linnaeus' *Systema naturae*, which we know, from various sources, was on board both ships on the Baudin expedition. Bory de Saint-Vincent, in his *Voyage dans les quatre principales îles des mers d'Afrique, fait par ordre du gouvernement pendant les années neuf et dix de la République (1801 et 1802)*, Paris: F. Buisson, 3 vols, 1804, vol. 1, p. 9, specifies that this was the 13th or Gmelin edition: Johann Friedrich Gmelin, *Systema naturae per regna tria naturae, secundum classes, ordines, genera, species, cum characteribus, differentiis,*

synonymis, locis. Editio decima tertia, aucta, reformata, Leipzig: Georg Emanuel Beer, 1789–1790. Baudin on the *Géographe* mentions using Linnaeus to identify a specimen that the zoologists had collected: Nicolas Baudin, *The Journal of Post Captain Nicolas Baudin, Commander-in-Chief of the Corvettes* Géographe *and* Naturaliste, translated by Christine Cornell, Adelaide: Libraries Board of South Australia, 1974, p. 73. Indeed, Péron's zoological observations reveal that he was continually referencing Linnaeus' work during the voyage (see Jangoux, 'L'expédition du capitaine Baudin', p. 5).

14 Jangoux, 'L'expédition du capitaine Baudin', p. 5.
15 It can be compared to a completed ornithological description Péron submitted to his commander on 11 May 1801. See Jacqueline Bonnemains (ed.), *Mon voyage aux Terres Australes: Journal personnel du commandant Baudin*, Paris: Imprimerie nationale, 2000, pp. 207–218.
16 Joseph Philippe François Deleuze, *Notice historique sur M. Péron*, Paris: Imprimerie de A. Belin, 1811, pp. 3–4.
17 Louis Audiat, *F. Péron (de Cérilly), sa vie, ses voyages et ses ouvrages*, Moulins: Énaut, 1855, p. 19.
18 Girard, *François Péron*, p. 19.
19 Audiat, *F. Péron de Cérilly*, pp. 21–22.
20 *Ibid.*, pp. 27–28.
21 Edward Duyker, *François Péron, an Impetuous Life: Naturalist and Voyager*, Melbourne: The Miegunyah Press, 2006, pp. 41–42.
22 *Ibid.*, pp. 45–46.
23 Justin J.F.J. Jansen, 'Towards the resolution of long-standing issues regarding birds collected during the Baudin expedition to Australia and Timor (1800–1804): specimens still present, and their importance to Australian ornithology', *Journal of the National Museum (Prague), Natural History Series*, vol. 186, 2017, pp. 51–84.
24 See Camille Limoges, 'Louis-Jean-Marie Daubenton', in Charles C. Gillispie (ed.), *Dictionary of Scientific Biography*, vol. 15, supp. 1, New York: Charles Scribner's Sons, 1978, pp. 111–114; Yves Laissus, 'Les cabinets d'histoire naturelle', in René Taton, (ed.) *Enseignement et diffusion des sciences au XVIIIe siecle*, Paris: Hermann, 1964, pp. 659–712.
25 Jangoux, 'L'expédition du capitaine Baudin', p. 5.
26 François Péron, *Voyage de découvertes aux Terres Australes, exécuté par ordre de Sa Majesté l'Empereur et Roi, sur les corvettes le* Géographe *et le* Naturaliste *et la* goëlette le Casuarina *pendant les années 1800, 1801, 1802, 1803, et 1804, Historique*, vol. 1, Paris: Imprimerie impériale, 1807, p. 42.
27 Max V. Vinarskiĭ, 'The fate of subspecies category in zoological systematics. 1. The History', *Zhurnal Obshchei Biologii*, vol. 76, no. 1, 2015, pp. 3–14.
28 Plumage B in Derek Onley and Paul Scofield, *Albatrosses, Petrels and Shearwaters of the World*, Oxford: Princeton Field Guides, 2007, pp. 34–35.
29 Plumage F, in Onley and Scofield, *Albatrosses*, pp. 34–35.
30 Justin J.F.J. Jansen, *The Ornithology of the Baudin Expedition (1800–1804)*, Grave, The Netherlands: Privately published, 2018, pp. 306–308.
31 See William Young, *The Fascination of Birds: From the Albatross to the Yellow Throat*, New York: Dover Publications, 2014.
32 The ornithological documents that follow are all written in François Péron's hand. These documents, the first of which has been given the number '1506' by Péron, have been faithfully transcribed from the original French and translated into English. No corrections or revisions have been made to the information provided, so as to represent exactly what Péron described. Where Péron has underlined words, we have italicised them, as is the custom. Any inconsistencies in italicisations or other forms of presentation are thus Péron's. The albatross that Péron describes in these papers is likely to be the best known and largest albatross, the Wandering Albatross or great albatross (*Diomedea exulans*).

However, since this is now considered to comprise at least six separate species, all very similar in appearance, the species Péron describes cannot be identified with absolute certainty and, in the southern Atlantic, where the specimen was collected, the Tristan Albatross (*Diomedea dabbenena*) is a possible alternative.

33 The document that follows corresponds to the contents of MHNH CL 79 089-1. All of the documents relating to the albatross have been transcribed and translated into English by Jean Fornasiero and John West-Sooby, with the assistance of Gabrielle Baglione, and reproduced with the kind permission of the Muséum d'Histoire naturelle of Le Havre.

34 This no doubt represents the Cape Gannet, *Morus capensis*.

35 This must be the bird mentioned by other members of the expedition. It is described by Baudin as being shot on 14 January 1801 and its skin given to Maugé for preparation (Baudin, *Journal*, p. 74). In Baudin's fair copy of his journal, further details are given of the bird and its dissection. See Bonnemains (ed.), *Mon voyage*, p. 136. The bird is also mentioned in a second-hand account on 22 January 1801 as having been shot by René Maugé (Bory de Saint-Vincent, *Voyage*, vol. 1, p. 132). This albatross was collected roughly between Saint Helena and Cape Town.

36 This name was introduced in Lacépède's *Tableau des sous-classes, divisions, sous-divisions, ordres et genres des oiseaux*, Paris: Plassan, 1799. This rare work went through several editions but was later reproduced as *Vue générale des progrès de plusieurs branches des sciences naturelles depuis la mort de Buffon, pour faire suite aux Œuvres complètes de ce grand naturaliste*, par M. le comte de Lacépède, Paris: Rapet, 1818, where the gannet appears as '97. Fou. *Sula*', p. 85.

37 Swedish naturalist Carl Linnaeus (1707–1778), published the first edition of his *Systema Naturae* in 1735. It was the tenth edition of his work which was considered the most influential since it marked the beginning of zoological classification. It is in this tenth edition that he published the name of *Diomedea exulans*. See Linnaeus, *Systema naturae per regna tria naturæ, secundum classes, ordines, genera, species, cum characteribus, differentiis, synonymis, locis*, Stockholm: Salvius, 1758, vol. 1, part 2, p. 132. However, the name subsequently applied to various taxa of great albatrosses. This issue was only recently resolved by Richard Schodde, Alan J.D. Tennyson, Jeff G. Groth, Jonas Lai, Paul Scofield and Frank D. Steinheimer, 'Settling the name *Diomedea exulans* Linnaeus, 1758 for the Wandering Albatross by neotypification', *Zootaxa*, vol. 4236, no. 1, 2017, pp. 135–148.

38 See note 32. Either the Wandering Albatross *exulans* or the Tristan Albatross, *Diomedea dabbenena*.

39 Péron's error: Linnaeus was Swedish.

40 When Péron refers to a major and bulky work by Lacépède as either *Ornithologie* or *Histoire des Oiseaux* (*History of Birds*), he is perhaps referring to the 9 volumes devoted to birds that were published as part of Buffon's encyclopædic work (Georges-Louis Leclerc, comte de Buffon, *Histoire naturelle, générale et particulière, avec la description du Cabinet du Roi*, Paris: Imprimerie royale, 10 vols, 1749–1804), and which appeared as *Histoire naturelle des oiseaux*, Paris: Imprimerie royale, 1771–1786. Although Lacépède was not listed as the editor of the *Histoire naturelle des oiseaux*, he was a contributor to this series. The albatross is discussed in the ninth volume. See Buffon, *Histoire naturelle des oiseaux*, vol. 9 (vol. 24 of *Histoire naturelle, générale et particulière*), Paris: Imprimerie royale, 1783, pp. 339–349.

41 In the descriptions of the albatross that follow, Péron has indeed copied out the Latin texts that appear in the *Systema Naturae*, and translated them into French. However, Péron was not referencing the tenth edition of Linnaeus' *Systema Naturae* in which the species was first named (1758, p. 132). The edition he used was the 13th edition: Johann Friedrich Gmelin, *Systema Naturae*, Leipzig: Georg Emanuel Beer, vol. 1, part 2, 1789. Gmelin, for his part, had taken his description from John Latham, *A General Synopsis of Birds*, London: Leigh and Sotheby, vol. 3, part 1, 1785, pp. 304–308. To reflect the source text that Péron actually consulted

we have given the Latin text as it appears in the Gmelin edition, thus correcting the odd inaccuracy in Péron's transcription. We have indicated in footnotes where Gmelin's text differs from Linnaeus' tenth edition.

42 This detail, which is included in the Gmelin edition (1789), was not in the original description by Linnaeus (1758).

43 As per previous note.

44 Péron has given 'épaisses' ('thick') as a translation of 'patulæ'. 'Évasées' ('flared') would have been a more accurate description of the nostrils.

45 Péron is repeating Gmelin's description here (Gmelin, *Systema Naturae*, 1789) and not Linnaeus' original description (*Systema Naturae*, 1758, p. 132). The same is true for all following references in this document that Péron makes to Linnaeus' text.

46 Exceptionally, in this table, Péron placed the Latin text in the right hand column. In order to maintain consistency with all of the other tables, we have placed the Latin text on the left and the translation on the right.

47 Great albatross bills are pink, never red, nor are they yellow when fresh.

48 Linnaeus (*Systema Naturae*, 1758) and subsequently Gmelin (*Systema Naturae*, 1789) had only the category of variety (*varietas*), which had no precise and unambiguous definition. See Vinarskiĭ, 'The fate of subspecies category', p. 395. Péron was thus among the few people who used the term 'sous-espèce' (subspecies) for zoological purposes at that time, as Vinarskiĭ has stated in 'The fate of subspecies category'.

49 Not only are various larger albatrosses included, but the various ages of albatrosses are not excluded either (at least 5 years are needed for the bird to grow into an adult).

50 Linnaeus (*Systema Naturae*, 1758, p. 132) did not derive his original description of *Diomedea exulans* from specimens but based it on three earlier anecdotal and illustrated accounts by: Nehemiah Grew, *Musaeum Regalis Societatis. Or a Catalogue & Description of the Natural and Artificial Rarities belonging to the Royal Society and preserved at Gresham College*, London: W. Rawlins, 1681; Eleazar Albin, *A Natural History of Birds*, London: W. Innys and J. Brindley, vol. 3, 1738; George Edwards, *A Natural History of Birds*, London: College of Physicians, 1747.

51 Péron's note: 'This is also where we found it on 14 January [1801], at [blank].'

52 Péron's note: 'Would this not be the reason why ours could not fly away; it regurgitated as well huge amounts of non digested remains of squid tentacles …'

53 It is unknown whether the body parts were ever made available to Georges Cuvier.

54 The French *ligne* or Paris line was 1/12 of the French *pouce* (inch) and about 1.06L.

55 Péron's description ends abruptly at the bottom of this page (image 79 089-1 Fr). It is followed by a page bearing only the title 'Albatross' (image 79 089-1 Fv) and a new descriptive section focusing on the liver and œsophagus, etc (images 79 089-1 Gr *et sqq.*).

56 This page, which corresponds to image 79 089-1 Gr, does not directly follow on from the description that ends on 79 089-1 Fr. It contains large sections that have been crossed out. These crossed out passages will be given in this and subsequent notes. The first such passage corresponds to the first paragraph on the page and is as follows: Larynx 19 inches long and presenting several sinuosities; Trachea formed of cartilaginous armour that is almost continuous, leaving only very small membraneous intervals between sections. When it reaches the level of the sternum, it divides into two principal branches which, through a large number of ramifications, will be distributed into the trachea of the two lungs.

57 A sentence, as follows, is crossed out: Then, in the inner part of the two principal lobes, can be found the **undivided** ligament.

58 A sentence, as follows, is crossed out, as is the next paragraph: There can also be seen some branches of the hepatic canal. The heart, in the form of a pyramid, is dense, compact; the ~~right~~ left ventricle of a lesser capacity but a greater density than the right. In the left one, you can see meaty ridges as in mammals.

59 The following sentence is entirely crossed out, and the rest of the paragraph has a cross drawn through it. The entire text omitted by Péron is as follows: The lungs [illegible] extremely [illegible] spongy like those of all birds [illegible] distributed in two lobes almost equal in size. [illegible] quite remarkable and which can explain why the cry of these animals is so unpleasant, is the distribution of the latter parts of the bronchi, which in their front portion, which is joined by their membrane as in other birds, forms kinds of partitions separated from one another and almost rounded in shape and which, being separated by small sections of ligamentary hoops, create the impression of so many vocal cords that can greatly modify the modulations of the air passing through them.

60 It is difficult to determine exactly what Péron intended to be crossed out on the first half of this page (image 79 089-1 Ir). On the one hand, slanted lines across the page indicate he wished to omit the first half of the page entirely; on the other, horizontal crossings-out indicate clearly that he wished to omit certain words. In the interest of clarity, the first half of the page is given below, as having been omitted, along with the crossed-out words and phrases within the text itself: Their testicles, which are two in number as in other birds, have nothing particular about them except their rather considerable size, which, although the animal is very young, are at least as big as those in man. The kidneys situated below have the usual form of these organs and go from. They are voluminous, receive very large arteries and end in quite a large artery. The pancreas which is less flattened and has the form The **uniform** which forms the pancreatic duct, which in merging with the hepatic canal, contributes to the formation of the choledochal duct which opens into the intestinal duct.

61 These figures seem to refer to the calculation at the end of the paragraph.

62 This second document is MHNH CL 79 089-2.

63 Péron has copied this entire set of bibliographic references from Gmelin (*Systema Naturae*, 1789). In addition to the *Systema Naturae* (Sist.nat.), these are: Peter Simon Pallas, *Spicilegia zoologica: quibus novae imprimis et obscurae animalium species iconibus, descriptionibus atque commentariis illustrantur*, vol. 1, fasc. 5, Berlin: Gottlieb August Lange, 1769, 'Diomedea Albatrus', pp. 28–32; Steller (see following footnote); Edwards, *A Natural History of Birds*, 'The Albatross', pt. II, no. 88; Grew, *Musaeum Regalis Societatis*, 'The Head of the Man of War; called also Albitrosse', part 1, sect. IV, ch. III, pp. 73–74; Mathurin-Jacques Brisson, *Ornithologie, ou, Méthode contenant la division des oiseaux en ordres, sections, genres, especes & leurs variétés*, Paris: Cl. Jean-Baptiste Bauche, vol. 6, 1760, n° 1: 'Albatrus', pp. 126–128; Buffon, *Histoire naturelle des oiseaux*, vol. 9 (vol. 24 of *Histoire naturelle, générale et particulière*), 'L'Albatros. (a)', pp. 339–349; Albin, *A Natural History of Birds*, vol. 3, 'The Bill of the Man of War Bird', no. 81; Thomas Pennant, *Arctic Zoology*, vol. 2, *Class II, Birds*, London: Henry Hughs, 1785, no. 423: 'Wandering Albatross', pp. 506–508.

64 Details of the original Russian edition of the work of Georg Wilhelm Steller and his description of the albatross, as reported by Stepan Kracheninnikov, as well as details of the French edition indicated by Péron, are as follows: Stepan Kracheninnikov, *Opisanie zemli Kamcatki*, Saint Petersburg: Academy of Science, 2 vols, 1755; *Histoire et description du Kamtchatka*, French translation by M. de Saint-Pré, Amsterdam: M.M. Rey, 2 vols, 1770, vol. 2, *Du Tchaika ou de l'Hirondelle de mer ou Cormoran*, pp. 261–264. Steller referred to the species he sighted as 'Tchaika' or 'Tchaiki' in the plural and Péron seems to be simply repeating the spelling he saw in the Gmelin text.

65 This document is MHNH CL 79 090.

Part 4

François Péron's Fellow Voyagers

Chapter 12

Jacques Félix Emmanuel Hamelin: A Reluctant Scientific Voyager?

Jean Fornasiero

Of the officers and midshipmen who accompanied Nicolas Baudin on his voyage to the Southern Lands, Emmanuel Hamelin, the commander of Baudin's consort ship the *Naturaliste*, is one of the happy few to have survived the adventure with a heightened reputation in both moral and professional terms, for, as his biographers assert, he managed his difficult assignment with courage and skill. Nicolas Baudin himself would not have disagreed: on many occasions he reported favourably on the conduct of his second-in-command. In the years following the return of the expedition, Hamelin continued to be well regarded by his superiors, with promotion following promotion. He eventually rose to the rank of Rear Admiral and to the position of Director of the Mapping Division, after obtaining all manner of distinctions and titles.[1] If we list other attributes commonly cited by his biographers, those of ardent patriot, or bold and wily combatant, we can understand why they deemed him a 'celebrated navyman'.[2]

If Hamelin owed his good reputation in the first instance to his service as a scientific voyager – the appointment which led to his promotion to post-captain – his situation stood in complete contrast to that of his commander, who was enduringly and harshly rejected by the scientific and naval establishments as a consequence of the same voyage.[3] While Baudin's disgrace has increasingly claimed the attention of historians such as Jean-Luc Chappey, who have articulated the political and institutional causes behind it,[4] Hamelin's role has so far received much less attention. Given that the biographical notices on Hamelin were written for the most part in the nineteenth century, and that even the most recent biography predates the current renewal of research on the Baudin voyage, it is more than timely to cast a fresh eye over the life and times of this key player. Fortunately, there exists a wealth of resources that allow us to garner further insights into Hamelin's character and motivations.[5] For his 1962 biography, Jean-Paul Faivre made a noted foray into the then underused archives of the French navy, demonstrating how the journals from the Voyage to the Southern Lands and documentation from other marine archives could assist in identifying certain traits of the man and in providing explanations of puzzling incidents that occurred during the expedition. However, the judgements Faivre derives from his research are not always convincing. For example, he chooses to explain away the 'pettiness' of character that he perceives in Hamelin by invoking 'the mores of the day' rather than examining how this trait may have played into Hamelin's ultimate survival.[6] Faivre also praises Hamelin's 'bluntness of speech' and refers to the impossibility of imposing silence on this plain-speaking naval man.[7] Yet, on one important matter – the disgrace of Nicolas Baudin – Hamelin chose to hold his tongue. As we know, the refusal to speak can be an ambivalent gesture, but in this case Faivre suggests that Hamelin was inspired by the noble motive of refusing to join Baudin's detractors.[8] Would it not have been a clearer sign of Hamelin's strength of character if he had used his famous outspokenness to express his opinion of Baudin one way or the other?[9]

From this brief survey of the existing record, we can see that the Rear-Admiral's portrait could indeed benefit from a little light and shade. The marine records of the Baudin expedition, as Faivre demonstrates, are a valuable tool, but the sheer vastness, geographical spread and sometimes illegible nature of the archival material relating to the expedition have meant that its full value has taken time to be realised. New research conducted by scholars such as Jacqueline Bonnemains, Frank Horner and Michel Jangoux has repeatedly demonstrated the usefulness of these documents, while exponentially heightening their visibility.[10] To make sense of Hamelin's actions and his role during the voyage, the primary documents remain his own journal,[11] those of the officers and midshipmen of the *Naturaliste*[12] and the journals of the commander, Nicolas Baudin.[13] However, the lesser known papers of those members of the scientific team who spent time under Hamelin's command also constitute precious unpublished resources,[14] as do

Hamelin's personal naval file and correspondence.[15] Two studies have amply demonstrated the uses to be made of this documentation when it comes to reviewing the personality and the reputation of Hamelin. In 1993 William P. Helling was the first to affirm not only that 'the myth about Hamelin's faultless conduct must be discarded', but also that the records reveal 'a different man from the accepted image'.[16] He based his assessment of Hamelin's 'unpredictable behaviour' largely on Baudin's journals and those of Hamelin's officers and midshipmen, concluding that many of the navigational delays around which Baudin's bad reputation was constructed could be imputed to Hamelin. In 2004 Michel Jangoux published an extract from Hamelin's journal and quoted from a range of other documents in order to examine a key episode in the Baudin voyage: the surprise departure of Hamelin from Port Jackson, prior to the imminent arrival of his commander.[17] By comparing Hamelin's own explanation of his decision with those given by his staff, Jangoux suggested that the captain had contrived to extricate himself from a subordinate position that he could no longer tolerate, while giving his superiors the impression that he had remained faithful to his orders and his mission. This explanation indeed takes much of the mystery out of Hamelin's decision: understood as a way to end his contribution to the expedition without endangering his future career, this becomes an action that speaks more of self-interest than of dedication to his mission – as Helling has clearly demonstrated.[18]

For both historians, Hamelin's loyalty as a subordinate can be called into question. It is true that Baudin's own purpose was eventually served by the return to France of the *Naturaliste*, the very outcome that Hamelin had, for his own reasons, sought to achieve. By retrospectively granting Hamelin's wish, Baudin was able to reshape the expedition and fulfil his mission to greater effect.[19] No trace, however, of a similar desire to enhance the outcomes of the voyage can be discerned in Hamelin's decision to depart: his reasons are not clearly explained in his journal nor to his staff. Does this mean that the notion of loyalty, which for Hamelin's early biographers summed up in a single trait the character of their subject, may be irrelevant? Historian Geoffrey Ingleton was certainly of that view. He did not hesitate to dismiss Hamelin's reputation for loyalty by identifying in the captain of the *Naturaliste* not only a hint of cruelty but also a fundamental disloyalty, which he illustrates by evoking his unkind and deceptive treatment of Matthew Flinders during the latter's captivity on Mauritius.[20] Ingleton's example thus points, like Jangoux's, to a moment when Hamelin showed little deference to others. By abandoning the *Géographe*, Hamelin demonstrated loyalty neither to his commandant, his own subordinates or scientific team, nor to the mission of scientific exploration itself. Could his decision be construed, not just as a sign of his fatigue with a difficult voyage, but as a disavowal of the commander himself? From a further survey of documents relating to his life and times, we shall seek an answer to this question which, as we have seen, is crucial to our understanding of the voyage's ultimate fate and the reputations of both navigators.

We should state from the outset that our aim is not to establish a systematic comparison with his commandant, since we already have at our disposal several important contributions on that topic that bring clarity to the debate: for example, they allow us to refute Faivre's assertion that Hamelin was 'more respectful of science and scientists' than his commander[21] or that Hamelin was better at managing his ship than Baudin.[22] There is thus little to be gained by returning to this well-trodden ground. Of more interest is the task of analysing Hamelin's actions in and for themselves. We should recall that the moral and professional superiority commonly attributed to Hamelin over Baudin constitutes one of the myths that have been woven around the voyage and that continue to problematise its historiography. So let us start by focusing on Jacques Félix Emmanuel Hamelin himself, as revealed in his own writings and in those of his companions.

From all accounts, Hamelin was a proficient naval officer, whose discipline and physical courage consistently earned him good reports and the esteem of his superior officers.[23] In case they had not noticed, he was not averse to pointing out his qualities to his superiors: namely, his fighting spirit, his toughness and his devotion to the needs of navy and nation.[24] In a letter discovered by Faivre, young Hamelin announced his intention to go without part of his rations in the name of the Republic:

> I can assure you that since I have been at sea, and although possessing a large appetite, I have almost never

> eaten my 18 ounces of biscuit; [...] I strongly urge you to revoke your decree, in the knowledge that myself and my brothers the *sans-culottes*, who make up the crews, will be amply provided for with 18 ounces a day. I am sending back to the canteen in advance the 6 ounces that I acknowledge as surplus to my needs.[25]

It is hardly surprising that, once he had risen to the rank of commander, he would expect his subordinates to display the same qualities. However, those who accompanied Hamelin on the voyage to the Southern Lands did not see eye to eye with him on the question of reduced rations. This is precisely where the captain of the *Naturaliste* incurrred accusations of inhumanity and even cruelty from his officers and midshipmen. Their complaints were directed equally at the quality of the food supplied and at the captain's refusal to provide it in sufficient quantity. As Sub-Lieutenant Jacques de Saint-Cricq noted, when Hamelin informed him of his decision to leave Port Jackson without obtaining sufficient supplies for the crossing to Mauritius:

> I reminded Captain Hamelin that one does not place a crew on half rations except in very grave circumstances, and that I even believed that humanitarian concerns prevent the adoption of such a measure when there is a port to leeward.[26]

For midshipman François-Désiré Breton, who put it more bluntly, Hamelin was a 'hard and cruel man', in particular for refusing to have supplies sent out to sailors whose dinghy had overturned.[27] This same midshipman added that Hamelin was a 'despicable man who economises on his crew's food and who would make them eat grass if he could'.[28]

If such grievances are not necessarily of major significance on a long sea voyage where privations are common, we can nonetheless see, in the light of these examples, that Faivre is in error when he affirms that 'nowhere do we find, among the officers or the savants, the slightest trace of any animosity towards Hamelin'.[29] This was not the case, as we have seen, with the officers, since Saint-Cricq complained of his commander's decisions on a regular basis. If we add to the mix the comments of midshipmen such as Breton, the level of animosity appears even higher. The scientists likewise had some substantial accusations. Faivre himself notes that the astronomer Pierre-François Bernier expressed a highly negative opinion of Hamelin. He attempts to get around the difficulty by suggesting that Bernier's remark was an aberration.[30] Yet Bernier gave substance to his criticism by subsequently requesting a transfer from the *Naturaliste* to the *Géographe* and asserting in his private journal that he preferred Baudin's openly tough manner to the deceptive behaviour of Hamelin. And he was not the only one to express his thoughts on what he considered to be Hamelin's duplicitous nature. The detailed comments made by another member of the *Naturaliste*'s scientific staff are in complete conformity with Bernier's opinion that Hamelin's so-called 'gentle and sociable' disposition was a mere façade.[31] Zoologist Stanislas Levillain relates the events that occurred on 5 August 1801 during a shore expedition on Middle Island (Peron Peninsula) in Shark Bay. Levillain's account begins with a protest against Hamelin's decision to head out on a long excursion without ensuring that his team was supplied with sufficient food and water, but his story ends with a completely different accusation:

> It is inconceivable that a leader can be so thoughtless in the way he conducts his excursions. A poor wretch of a sailor, who was a respectable man, covered in wounds he had incurred in the service, and who had a limp, was one of our party and he could not keep up with us. The unfortunate man soon became exhausted and since he could no longer go on, well, our smooth, honey-tongued captain called him the lowest of the low, and in the cruellest manner, because he could not walk.[32]

Since this is the only occasion on which Levillain, a self-effacing and gentle man, berates Hamelin or anyone else, his accusation of inhumane conduct is of real interest and gives added weight to the criticism made by Bernier. It casts in a crude light the other uses to which Hamelin put his frankness and physical courage: they appear to have given him a licence to insult those less fortunate and less powerful than he. Moreover, the comments of Bernier and Levillain overlap. Far from being aberrations, the anecdotes they relate thus show that the feelings of animosity Hamelin inspired in the scientific staff were entirely unrelated to the eternal dissatisfaction of sea-travellers with their diet; Bernier's and Levillain's criticisms of their leader point to their perception of fundamental harshness and dishonesty. Further, the traces of malevolence and crudeness which they detected in Hamelin correspond exactly to the characteristics of which his naval staff complained in an even more pointed way.

Indeed, the officers and midshipmen of the *Naturaliste* repeatedly expressed their disgust with the 'coarse words' or the 'gross errors' of Hamelin.[33] They even threw in accusations of dishonesty, with Breton showing no hesitation in declaring that Hamelin was involved in ignoble trafficking:

> During our stay in Port Jackson Captain Hamelin behaved in a manner unworthy of a French officer. [...] He had many exchange items taken to his lodgings in Sydney and he traded them there for potatoes and pumpkins that the inhabitants brought to him. This illicit trading, which is shameful for an officer, and especially the officer who is in command of a vessel and who represents the French Government, caused problems between Captain Hamelin and the unfortunate deportees who were exchanging their vegetables for tools. And Magistrate Harris was obliged to make the peace. Captain Hamelin had such a good reputation in Sydney that one day, when I was dining in town, a lady asked me whether he sold women's shoes.[34]

It must be admitted that the absence of repercussions to this affair considerably attenuates the gravity of Breton's allegations. We should also acknowledge that Breton's demotion during the Port Jackson stay was not unrelated to the opinion he then held of his commanding officer. Yet, the fact remains that the accepted representation of Hamelin as a man held in great esteem by his entire staff is a little too good to be true, especially in the harsh environment of a long sea voyage.

When we consult Hamelin's journal alone, we note that few traces remain of his quarrels with his officers or midshipmen; it is through their journals, not his, that we learn of the existence of different causes of dissatisfaction. This absence of negative reporting on Hamelin's part, or his unwillingness to put the contents of such disputes in writing, can no doubt be explained both by the captain's wish to give his superiors a good impression of the atmosphere on board the *Naturaliste* and by the lack of importance that this hardened officer attached to routine incidents of this type. Yet the complaints about Hamelin are frequent enough to make us wary of the idea that there was an extraordinary loyalty that bound him to his officers and naturalists. When Hamelin does choose to write of his displeasure, it is usually in response to issues with seamanship rather than manners. As a result, his complaints concern his crew more than they do his officers. His intolerance of those sailors he considered unfit for service at sea is pronounced, his punishments swift and severe.[35] His tendency to protect those who were of good family contrasts with his treatment of the crew, as we have seen in the example provided by Levillain.

The captain reserved his finer feelings for his family and for his 'dear' and 'precious' lieutenant Milius[36] – but as he eventually had a spectacular falling out with Milius, with no explanation provided in his journal, we are again entitled to question the constancy of Hamelin's attachment. One scientist of whom he took great care, however, was Jean-Baptiste (Théodore) Leschenault, the botanist, who agreed to transfer to the *Naturaliste* after the desertion of the majority of its scientific team at Mauritius. Leschenault was unstinting in his praise of Hamelin, whom he deemed to be both helpful to him in his work and 'an officer full of zeal for the important mission for which he was responsible'.[37] During the first campaign, which extended from Mauritius to the *Naturaliste*'s false departure from Port Jackson, and which corresponded to Leschenault's time on board his ship, Hamelin was indeed bent on showing his interest in the tasks of the scientific voyager and did all he could to facilitate them, especially for a noble and educated young man such as Leschenault, who enjoyed the esteem and protection of Antoine-Laurent de Jussieu, director of the Paris Museum and enthusiastic sponsor of the voyage. Leschenault in fact noted that Hamelin's kind attentions were reserved for those naturalists whose 'honest and irreproachable conduct' merited his esteem.[38] This implication of two types of treatment for the naturalists resonates in no small way with the portrait of a two-faced Hamelin traced by other voyagers.

However, that Hamelin's initial response to his role of scientific voyager was one of enthusiasm and pride is not in doubt. When, during the stopover at Mauritius, he realised the extent of the honour and responsibility bestowed upon him as a leader of a scientific voyage, he was both apprehensive of the scope of the geographical survey required and determined to do his duty.[39] The journals of his fellow travellers contain numerous passages recording Hamelin's desire to advance the cause of science, thereby corroborating Leschenault's assessment. Hamelin himself also commented in some detail on incidents where specimens had been collected and observations made, as in the case of the encounters with native peoples at Geographe Bay.[40] In Shark Bay, the discovery made by the chief helmsman of the *Naturaliste* produced a reaction that provides ample proof of Hamelin's honour and zealous commitment to his role:

> The chief helmsman gave me his report on what he had been able to see relating to the tides and brought me a flattened pewter plate bearing the inscription made by the navigator of the *Eendracht* and which was left on (Dirk) Hartog Island in 1616, and the inscription engraved below in 1697 by Vlamingh, commander of the *Geelvinck*. He found this kind of medallion on the NE point, where it lay at the foot of a post (now rotten) to which it had once been nailed. I had a copy of it made that was the same size as the plate. [. . .] If this inscription had still been attached to the post, I would have considered it a crime on the part of the chief helmsman to have laid a sacrilegious hand on it in order to tear it down, but as he found it on the ground, exposed to the risk of being buried there by its own weight, I was grateful to him for

having brought it on board. I ordered the chief carpenter to prepare immediately a post on which I shall have it securely nailed and I shall send him out to plant it on the very spot where it was placed 181 years ago by the Dutch navigator. It seems to me that such monuments should always be treated with the same respect.[41]

On this occasion, Hamelin's patriotism, which could have impelled him to claim this treasure for France – as it would drive Louis Freycinet to commit this 'sacrilege' some years later – yielded to a sentiment that was even stronger, the duty to his mission and his sense of belonging to an international community of navigators.

For the expedition's first campaign (from Mauritius to Port Jackson), despite the grumblings of his companions on the *Naturaliste*, Hamelin remained fully focused on his role, working in accordance with his instructions and with the objectives of his commander, as he assiduously fulfilled his charting duties and collected specimens with his men. Once he reached Port Jackson, his attitude changed. Nicole Starbuck has examined in great detail how Hamelin's enthusiasm for collecting specimens waned at this point, as he appeared convinced that the expedition had now ended.[42] The strength of the anti-British feelings that Hamelin expressed when engaged in the war against the English, both before and after the voyage to the Southern Lands, also leads us to suggest that it was during his stay at Port Jackson that the neutrality required of a scientific voyager became too much to bear for the vigilant patriot who had, in his early career, shown a real taste for combat. His hasty departure from Port Jackson can thus be partly explained by the realisation that his nation had lost a valued colonial prize to its ancestral enemy. One of the officers of the *Naturaliste*, Jacques de Saint-Cricq, expressed this feeling with clarity:

It can thus be said that we were beaten in every domain! Discoveries and settlements! The English reached the south-west coast before we did, will survey the Gulf, and will establish settlements with impunity in the places we discovered![43]

There is additional evidence of Hamelin's reaction to this loss at the hands of the British, since he wrote a separate report on Port Jackson that was intended for his superiors and the government.[44] Further, Hamelin's refusal in later years to visit Matthew Flinders – a representative of the British Government and a rival in the discovery of the Southern Lands – during Flinders' imprisonment on Mauritius[45] is not particularly surprising if we place it in the context of his wounded national pride. Could the lack of interest he showed in defending the reputation of Nicolas Baudin also be explained by the disappointment he felt when their voyage was judged a failure by their government? If this hypothesis seems plausible, it is because the sentiment that inspired Hamelin's most passionate speeches was his love of country rather than any political allegiance. His lack of support for Napoleon during the Hundred Days provides evidence either of the lack of political conviction of the former republican or of his opportunism.[46]

Times had certainly changed when Hamelin was confronted with those dilemmas. France was at war with England and he had enthusiastically rejoined what he saw as the good combat. After the collapse of his allegiance to the objectives of scientific voyaging, he embraced the French navy with such zeal that one could postulate that it was precisely this renewed commitment that prevented him from showing solidarity towards his former companions. Did he fear that he might one day experience, as they had, the worst fate of all: being reviled by one's superiors and either removed from active service or designated a scapegoat?

If there is any doubt about the extent of Hamelin's commitment to combat, we dispose of other sources of documentation which are particularly revealing on that point. There are numerous letters in Hamelin's personal navy file in which he expressed his impatience to return to active duty,[47] especially in the war against the English, whom he described as his 'born enemies'.[48] Moreover, this same file provides evidence that, whatever the theatre of war and right to the very end of his active career, Hamelin displayed his customary zeal and passion when doing battle with this enemy.[49] His zeal – or over-zealousness – was even brought to the attention of the British newpapers, which featured the capture by him of the English colony of Tappanooly in Sumatra on 10 October 1809.[50] According to the reports, Hamelin not only destroyed the colony, but was also brutal and coarse in his behaviour towards the English ladies whom he had taken prisoner.[51] Naturally, as Faivre points out, there was some exaggeration and hypocrisy involved in the reaction of the British press to such incidents of war – offences of which no warfaring nation was innocent.[52] Nevertheless, if we recall the charges of uncouth behaviour that Hamelin's own officers made against him – bearing in mind that they were probably much less sensitive than the ladies in question – and knowing the hatred that Hamelin felt for his 'born enemies' as well as his tendency to over-zealousness, it is not completely improbable that, on this occasion, Hamelin may have shown either his contempt or the hardheartedness of which his fellow voyagers to the Southern Lands had complained – especially if we consider that the capture of Tappanooly and the destruction of an English colony might have compensated in some way for the humiliation that Hamelin had suffered at the thought that the English had beaten the French to the discovery and colonisation of New Holland.

At this point, we might ask the question as to whether Hamelin had merely adopted the appearance of the scientific voyager, rather than embracing its essential substance. As a young man, he had shown a strong republican ethic before lending his support to the Napoleonic wars of conquest, in an understandable attempt to stay in tune with the rapidly changing times. In then accepting a scientific mission, he may have adopted a role to which he was temperamentally unsuited. His impetuous nature did not always sit well with the patience and application required of the philosophical traveller, as the desertions or dissatisfaction of his naturalists may imply. Nor did he completely understand the role required of an 'Observer of Man'. We have only to hear the words on slavery that Hamelin wrote while in Mauritius to be persuaded that his erstwhile republicanism may have corresponded to a career path rather than to a firm adoption of an ethics of egalitarianism :

> The colony is happy and peaceful, its happiness will only be complete when it is certain that the French Government will be wise enough never to attempt to proclaim the law of 16 Pluviôse here.[53] May the First Consul give them that assurance and he will find them to

> be faithful colonists who will forever hold France and her interests dear to their hearts. They should be sent money and a few hundred soldiers to protect them from attacks by the English, whose predatory actions they really fear.
>
> I shall leave it to Mr. Baudin to inform the Minister of his way of thinking on the colony; this is mine, no commissaries, whatever you do, no commissaries.[54]

Not only did Hamelin have friends in the colony who may have influenced his thinking, but he was still too comfortable in his former role as a slave-trader to allow himself to rethink his relationship to the 'other', as his role of 'Observer of Man' required. His commitment to colonial interests certainly stands in stark contrast to Baudin's famous words on colonialism and the rights of natural man.[55] Exclaim as he may that his dearest wish was to protect the 'natives' from bloodshed, Hamelin remained incapable of accepting the indigenous women of Australia as human beings in the fullest sense:

> The youngest were the prettiest, two were not bad, but not one of them was beautiful. As I have sailed for many years along the African coast, I am qualified to express my opinion on what is a beautiful or an ugly negress and I hope that no-one will suspect that the reason why I do not find them attractive is the difference in colour between them and myself.[56]

Indeed, he had earlier distinguished himself by announcing that he was leaving civilisation and his beloved family in order to encounter the 'stupid thieving inhabitants of New Holland and the South Sea Islands'.[57] In his attitudes, he was, of course, no different from most of his contemporaries, or most of his companions on the voyage, but such attitudes nonetheless give us a glimpse of that 'narrow-minded man' whom Marine Minister Denis Decrès[58] had detected in him in the early days of his career and who remained unreconstructed by his role as observer of Man, a role he may have learnt by heart, but had not taken to heart.

In conclusion, Hamelin gives the appearance of an accidental scientific traveller. Circumstance and career opportunities thrust him into the role as they had led him to other roles in different phases of his career. That he survived every twist and turn in the troubled times he traversed speaks volumes for his tenacity, even while lingering doubts must remain about the loyalty he showed his companions along the way. It is impossible to overlook Hamelin's tendency to place his loyalty to the State or to his own interests above the duties of friendship or simple humanity. As a result, we can no longer accept, as Faivre did, that Hamelin's careerist moments can be entirely redeemed by acts of greatness nor that his careerism was a minor element of his character that can be attributed to the 'mores of the day'.[59] If we accept that an obstinate careerism defines the man, this explains not only his constant requests for titles and promotions, but also the episodes that were once deemed a mystery or an aberration. They reveal the self-interest and even a certain hardheartedness that lay hidden beneath his 'mild and amiable' exterior. Moreover, this image of Hamelin as an accidental scientific voyager, ready to abandon the cause in case of conflict of interest, does not simply provide explanations for certain historical events, it also allows glimpses into his true nature.

By placing Emmanuel Hamelin's ambition at the centre of his preoccupations, we finally come to see in this 'celebrated navyman' the man himself, and even the naively enthusiastic and energetic man who was appreciated by Nicolas Baudin and who was grateful for Baudin's kindness and understanding when he almost broke ranks in Port Jackson. If he abandoned Baudin's cause in later years, despite Baudin's support for him, there is no evidence of spite or malevolence on Hamelin's part, rather the silence of a prudent man seeking to save what he could from the wreckage. For the careerist trait does not come with the usual attendant flaws in Hamelin's case: he had no conspiratorial tendencies, no vengeful desires. He simply followed his own path, oblivious to distractions. His attention was focused on his current superiors; his official papers were thus written with the intention of demonstrating his know-how or showing off his merits, rather than confounding his rivals. It is not the least of the paradoxes in the history of the Baudin expedition, which abounds in paradoxes, that it should be precisely within these official papers and through the discourse of the faithful servant of the State that the man revealed himself in all of his foibles.

In the pages of his journal and in the correspondence that we have just examined – those pages in which Emmanuel Hamelin was seeking to present himself as an exemplary mariner – he did end up painting a faithful portrait of himself, in spite of himself: as a man faithful only to himself, as a careful man whose horizons did not extend beyond his own chosen world. Far be it from him to caress any lasting aspirations to the difficult and thankless role of philosophical voyager or explorer of worlds unknown. The small world of the French navy was vast enough for him.

Notes

1. Contre-amiral, Baron de l'Empire, croix de Saint Louis, grand officier de la Légion d'honneur: these are just some of his most prestigious titles. See Jean-Paul Faivre, *Le Contre-amiral Hamelin et la marine française*, Paris: Nouvelles éditions latines, 1962, pp. 55, 95, 96, 137.
2. The expression is Admiral Victor-Guy Duperré's, in a document dated 23 April 1839 that is to be found in Hamelin's Dossier personnel, housed in the Service Historique de la Défense, Archives centrales de la Marine à Vincennes, CC^7 Alpha 1146/22. All translations of archival documents in this chapter are my own.
3. Jean Fornasiero and John West-Sooby, 'Doing it by the Book: Breaking the Reputation of Nicolas Baudin', in Jean Fornasiero and Colette Mrowa-Hopkins (eds), *Explorations and Encounters in French*, Adelaide: University of Adelaide Press, 2010, pp. 135–164.
4. Jean-Luc Chappey, 'Le capitaine Baudin et la Société des observateurs de l'homme. Questions autour d'une mauvaise réputation', in Michel Jangoux (ed.), *Portés par l'air du temps: les voyages du capitaine Baudin*, special number of *Études sur le XVIIIe siècle*, vol. 38, 2010, pp. 145–155.
5. These include the journals of Baudin's voyage to the Southern Lands which are to be found in the Archives Nationales de France (ANF), série Marine, 5JJ, but other major resources, including journals, scientific papers and iconography, are to be found in the Muséum national d'Histoire naturelle, Paris (MNHN), and the Lesueur Collection of the Muséum d'Histoire naturelle in Le Havre (MHNH CL).
6. Faivre, *Le Contre-amiral Hamelin*, p. 172.
7. *Ibid.*, p. 172.
8. *Ibid.*, p. 54.
9. Faivre's position is that Hamelin's behaviour towards his commander was exemplary, both when he praised him in his journal and when in later years he refused to join Baudin's detractors. This seems to presuppose that Baudin was guilty as charged. In fact, given what we now know of the systematic campaign of vilification waged against Baudin, it could be argued that Hamelin's silence has no particular merit: if he praised Baudin for his kindness, could this not be simply because such praise was due? If he remained silent about Baudin in later years, could this not simply be in his own interests as a career officer to avoid drawing attention to his connection to a figure held in such contempt? In any case, the plain speaking which Faivre lists as a dominating trait is singularly absent.
10. Jacqueline Bonnemains, Elliott Forsyth and Bernard Smith, *Baudin in Australian Waters. The Artwork of the French Voyage of Discovery to the Southern Lands*

1800–1804, Melbourne/New York: Oxford University Press, 1988; Frank Horner, *The French Reconnaissance: Baudin in Australia 1801–1803*, Carlton: Melbourne University Press, 1987; Michel Jangoux, *Le Voyage aux Terres Australes du commandant Nicolas Baudin: Genèse et préambule (1798–1800)*, Paris: Presses de l'Université Paris-Sorbonne, 2013.

11 Only extracts from Hamelin's journal – those relating to the Baudin expedition's stay in Sydney – have been published to date. See Michel Jangoux, 'La première relâche du *Naturaliste* au Port Jackson (26 avril–18 mai 1802): le témoignage du capitaine Hamelin", *Australian Journal of French Studies*, vol. 41, no. 2, 2004, pp. 126–151. The manuscript of Hamelin's journal is held in the Archives Nationales de France, série Marine, 5JJ 41, 42.

12 In particular the journals of midshipman first class François-Désiré Breton (ANF, série Marine, 5JJ 57), sub-lieutenants Jacques de Saint-Cricq (ANF, série Marine, 5JJ 48) and François Heirisson (ANF, série Marine, 5JJ 56).

13 There are two versions of Baudin's narrative: his journal (ANF, série Marine, 5JJ 36–39 and 40^A) and the fair copy (ANF, série Marine, 5JJ 35, 40^B, 40^C, 40^D). The first version has been published in English translation by Christine Cornell, *The Journal of Post Captain Nicolas Baudin, Commander-in-Chief of the Corvettes* Géographe *and* Naturaliste, Adelaide: Libraries Board of South Australia, 1974 (2nd ed., 2004); the second has been published by Jacqueline Bonnemains (ed.), *Mon voyage aux Terres Australes: Journal personnel du commandant Baudin*, Paris: Imprimerie nationale, 2000.

14 See Stanislas Levillain, Journal, MHNH CL, 07 008; Levillain, Journal, ANF, série Marine, 5JJ 52; Pierre-François Bernier, ANF, série Marine, 5JJ 24; J.-B. Leschenault, 'Lettre à A.-L. de Jussieu, 11 novembre 1802', MNHN, Fonds Phanérogamie, published in Viviane Desmet and Michel Jangoux, 'Un naturaliste aux Terres australes: Jean-Baptiste Leschenault de La Tour (1773–1826)', in Jangoux (ed.), *Portés par l'air du temps*, pp. 226–230.

15 For example, Hamelin's Dossier personnel.

16 William P. Helling, 'Redistributing the blame: Baudin's voyage to the Australian seas', *The Great Circle*, vol. 15, no. 2, 1993, p. 132.

17 Jangoux, 'La première relâche du *Naturaliste* au Port Jackson'.

18 Helling, 'Redistributing the blame', p. 122.

19 See Nicole Starbuck, *Baudin, Napoleon and the Exploration of Australia*, London: Pickering and Chatto, 2013.

20 Geoffrey C. Ingleton, *Matthew Flinders, Navigator and Chartmaker*, Guildford: Genesis Publications, 1986, p. 198.

21 Faivre, *Le Contre-amiral Hamelin*, p. 54. Jacqueline Goy also rejects the idea that Hamelin handled his team of scientists more skilfully than Baudin; she points out that the desertions at Île de France were much greater among the savants of the *Naturaliste* than among those from the *Géographe*. See *Les Méduses de Péron et Lesueur: un autre regard sur l'expédition Baudin*, Paris: Éditions du CTHS, 1995, p. 19. See also Chapter 2 in this volume, note 16.

22 Faivre, *Le Contre-amiral Hamelin*, p. 35. Horner (*The French Reconnaissance*, p. 350) offers a strong defence of Baudin's health record.

23 For Marine Minister Forfait's opinion of Hamelin, see Faivre, *Le Contre-amiral Hamelin*, p. 32. See also the descriptions of his 'tireless enthusiasm', of the naval combats in which he 'covered himself in glory', and his qualities as a 'skilled seaman', to be found in the notice on him in *Fastes de la Légion-d'Honneur*, Paris: Au bureau de l'administration, vol. 5, 1847, p. 439.

24 Dossier Hamelin. See, for example, document 5, in which Hamelin writes to the Minister to request his transfer to La Hougue: 'if you do not envisage that I can be useful at Brest, please issue me the order to go there [La Hougue] instead to put my life at risk'. In document 100, Hamelin stresses that he has 'often saved from imminent danger my vessel and my crew'.

25 Faivre, *Le Contre-amiral Hamelin*, p. 16.
26 Saint-Cricq, Journal, 5 Floréal Year 9 (25 April 1801).
27 Breton, Journal, 6 Floréal Year 9 (26 avril 1801). Heirisson's journal entry for 6-7 Floréal Year 9 (26–27 April 1802) also emphasises the disgust and indignation that this decision by Captain Hamelin inspired in him.
28 Breton, Journal, 6 Floréal Year 9 (26 April 1801).
29 Faivre, *Le Contre-amiral Hamelin*, p. 37.
30 *Ibid.*, p. 38.
31 *Ibid.*, p. 38.
32 Stanislas Levillain, Journal, MHNH CL, 07 008, entry of 17 Thermidor (5 August 1801).
33 In his journal entry dated 16 Prairial Year 10 (5 June 1802), Breton noted that he feared being grossly insulted by his captain; Heirisson mentioned the coarse language the captain used when speaking to him, in spite of his own courtesy (28 Floréal Year 9 [18 May 1802]); Saint-Cricq stressed the incompetence and obstination of his superior officer (entry dated 29 Ventôse Year 10 [20 March 1802], for example).
34 Breton, Journal, 28 Floréal Year 9 (18 May 1801).
35 Faivre affirms a propos of any statements that Hamelin made in his journal about his officers that these 'contrast by their impartiality with the sarcastic tone employed almost invariably by Baudin' (*Le Contre-amiral Hamelin*, p. 36). While Hamelin did indeed make relatively neutral comments on his officers in his writings, we should also note that his journal is not of the same nature as Baudin's, in which a narrative unfolds that encompasses all the aspects of the voyage, including tense social interactions. More concise and more focused on practical details, more of an officer's record than a narrative, Hamelin's journal mentions neither the interpersonal conflicts nor the altercations he had with members of the staff of the *Naturaliste*. And yet, these conflicts definitely existed because the officers discussed them. On the other hand, the judgements Hamelin made of the sailors he deemed useless (for example, the entries of 19–20 Brumaire Year 9 [10–11 November 1800] or 30 Vendémiaire–1 Brumaire Year 9 [22–23 October 1800]) show that his attitudes were not very different from Baudin's, but that his punishments were often more severe.
36 Hamelin speaks of Milius in this manner when he believes him to be lost during the exploration of Rottnest Island and the surrounding area. In his journal entry dated 29–30 Prairial Year 9 (18 June 1801), Hamelin wrote:
At this moment I would give half, what am I saying, all that I possess on board to see the return of these brave men, among whose number, taking my anxiety to the limit, are Brèvedent du Bocage, my relative, and lieutenant Milius with whom I have been associated for several years and whose moral qualities and talents make him more dear and more valuable to me with every passing day.
37 Jean-Baptiste Leschenault, 'Lettre à A.-L. de Jussieu, 11 novembre 1802', cited in Viviane Desmet and Michel Jangoux, 'Un naturaliste aux Terres australes', p. 229.
38 *Ibid.*
39 Hamelin, Journal, entry of 5–6 Floréal Year 9 (25–26 April 1801).
40 See for example the entry in his journal for 15–18 Prairial Year 9 (4–7 June 1800).
41 Hamelin, Journal, 5–6 Thermidor Year 9 (24–25 July 1801).
42 Nicole Starbuck, 'Constructing the "Perfect" Voyage. Nicolas Baudin at Port Jackson, 1802', PhD thesis, University of Adelaide, 2010, Part 1, Chapter 3.
43 Saint-Cricq, Journal, 11 Pluviôse Year 11 (31 January 1803).
44 Nicole Starbuck, 'Constructing the "Perfect" Voyage', pp. 76–77, reminds us that 'listed amongst the various papers and charts that were returned to France was a document entitled "Notes sur les établissements des Anglais dans la mer du sud, par Hamelin", now to be found in his 'Lettres, journaux et papiers', ANF, série Marine, 5JJ 24.

45 Ingleton, *Matthew Flinders*, pp. 367–368, reproaches Hamelin with having Thomi Pitot inform Flinders that the French had respected Flinders' nomenclature in the official account of the expedition by François Péron (*Voyage de découvertes aux Terres Australes*, Paris: Imprimerie impériale, 1807). Ingleton is very critical of this untruth and of the lack of consideration that this showed for Flinders.
46 Or, once more, of his inherent lack of loyalty. See Faivre, *Le Contre-amiral Hamelin*, p. 139.
47 Hamelin, Dossier personnel. See, for example, letters dated 13 Prairial Year 6 (1 June 1798) and 31 August 1831 (written more than thirty years apart), in which Hamelin, true to himself, declared that he was 'dying to fight' and remained 'ever ready to march'.
48 Hamelin, Dossier personnel, letter dated 11 Thermidor Year 7 (29 July 1799).
49 See, for example, in Hamelin's Dossier personnel, his letter to the Minister dated 9 Ventôse Year 13 (28 February 1805): 'all my life I shall do everything in my power to uphold the Glory of our armed forces.'
50 Faivre, *Le Contre-amiral Hamelin*, pp. 85–86.
51 This story is repeated in the influential work on the Royal Navy of this period by William James, *Naval History of Great Britain 1793–1827*, London: Richard Bentley, 6 vols, 1837. In volume 5, on page 295, another example of Hamelin's cruelty is given, relating to the surrender of an English officer in 1810.
52 Faivre, *Le Contre-amiral Hamelin*, p. 86.
53 The law of 16 Pluviôse Year 2 (February 1794) decreed the abolition of slavery in the First French Republic.
54 ANF, AJ 15/569, Dossier Baudin, letter from Hamelin to Citizen Le Comte, his brother-in-law, written at Mauritius and dated 26 Ventôse Year 9 (17 March 1801).
55 Jean Fornasiero (ed. and trans.), *Reflections of a Philosophical Voyager. Letter from Nicolas Baudin to Philip Gidley King, 24 December 1802*, Adelaide: Friends of the State Library of South Australia, 2016.
56 Hamelin, Journal, 12–13 Pluviôse Year 10 (1–2 February 1802).
57 Hamelin, Journal, 5–6 Floréal Year 9 (25–26 April 1801).
58 Faivre, *Le Contre-amiral Hamelin*, p. 59.
59 *Ibid.*, p. 172.

Chapter 13

A Scientific Voyager in Limbo: Théodore Leschenault's Return to Imperial France

Paul Gibbard

Théodore Leschenault de la Tour,[1] the chief botanist of the Baudin expedition, arrived back in France more than three years after his colleagues had sailed into Lorient aboard the *Géographe*. Suffering from illness, Leschenault had left the expedition at Timor in mid-1803 and spent several years on an odyssey through the Dutch East Indies before taking a ship from Batavia to Cayenne and Philadelphia, and finally reaching the French coast in July 1807. On arrival in Paris he found himself deeply in debt and with few prospects. He set about writing letters to the government, seeking remuneration and employment. To his signature he often added the epithet '*naturaliste voyageur*' – but what did this mean? He was no longer employed by the state as a naturalist and his travels had come to an end. It was a reference to his past which he hoped would carry weight when negotiating his future. In a period when naturalists were often amateurs rather than professionals, it was not clear what career avenues lay open to Leschenault, despite all the extraordinary experience he had gained as a botanist while voyaging in the southern hemisphere. As a returning scientific traveller, Leschenault struggled to secure his financial position and his professional status under the First Empire – and in this he was not unique. His former colleague François Péron and others found themselves facing similar battles under a government whose interests had turned away from global exploration towards the consolidation of its Continental empire. It was a period of upheaval also among French scientific institutions, as new structures of power and influence developed, and Leschenault, as an outsider to these, was obliged to try different strategies and exploit various personal connections in an attempt to gain payment for his arrears of salary, obtain compensation for his collections of natural history, and, ultimately, find employment once again as a government botanist.

In early nineteenth-century France there was no clear path available to young men wishing to pursue a career in botany. Few science degrees were awarded at this time, and botany was usually studied at university as part of a medical degree. Leschenault developed his interest in plants, as many others did, while enrolled at medical school: he attended university in Paris, and undoubtedly followed botanical courses at the Museum of Natural History.[2] In any case, once a student had gained expertise in this area, very few paid positions were open to candidates at the universities and other institutions – and connections were often more important than qualifications. Prestigious positions at the Museum tended to be dominated by certain families:[3] members of the Jussieu family, for example, had filled positions as professors or demonstrators of botany at the Jardin du Roi and, subsequently, the Museum, for almost a century, and had the power to appoint subordinates in the field.[4] It was important, therefore, for aspiring botanists to cultivate the patronage of powerful figures – and indeed Leschenault had succeeded in gaining the endorsement of Antoine-Laurent de Jussieu for his application to join the Baudin expedition. Leschenault continued to enjoy support from Jussieu after his return to France, but it is not clear whether he ever solicited Jussieu for a botanical appointment.

Leschenault's most pressing concern on his arrival back in France, after an absence of six years and eight months, was his deep indebtedness. Although he had been housed and aided at times by acquaintances he had made in the Dutch East Indies, such as Nicolaus Engelhard, the governor of the north-east coast of Java, who took a keen interest in the sciences, he had nevertheless had to borrow large sums of money from creditors, amounting to around 10,000 francs in total – equivalent to more than two years of Leschenault's salary as a botanist. One of the first steps Leschenault took to address his predicament was, on 27 August 1807, to write to a friend at the Ministry of the Interior asking whether any positions were available. He supplied references attesting to his conduct 'during the stormy period of revolution', cited his experience in 'diverse branches of administration' prior to the Baudin expedition, and concluded with a plea that his addressee be 'sensitive to [his] friend's painful situation'.[5]

A second letter, written in the following week, confirms Leschenault's lack of funds. His cousin Jean-Baptiste-Antoine Leschenault du Villard had appealed to him to return from Paris to their home town of Chalon-sur-Saône to resolve some financial problem in which Théodore's younger brother had embroiled himself. Théodore wrote from Paris on 2 September 1807: 'The sacrifices that I am making are the only ones that my present position allows. If certain promises made to me are kept, perhaps I will be able to do more subsequently'. He was, he explained, unable to come down to help in person, as it might adversely affect his prospects: 'I cannot in truth anticipate exactly when I will be able to go to Chalon although I strongly wish it, but if I left Paris at this moment I would perhaps suffer the greatest loss as a result.'[6]

In Paris, Leschenault was not only engaged in searching for a new position; he was also seeking payment for his arrears of salary and for the collections of natural history he had brought back. The day after his arrival in France, Leschenault had written to Jussieu describing the collections he had made in the environs of Java, Cayenne and Philadelphia:

> My collections consist of a herbarium of 900 plant species, 130 species of stuffed birds (around 20 species are from Cayenne or the United States – I acquired them during my passage to Philadelphia), two species of quadruped, 200 species of insect, most of which are butterflies, 30 species of snakes in arrack, some fishes and molluscs, several skeletons of animals, two stone statues found in the ruined temples in the interior of Java.[7]

The professors at the Museum were eager to acquire his collections, and composed a report on them for the Minister of the Interior, Emmanuel Crétet. On 14 October 1807, this highly favourable report, compiled by Jean-Baptiste Lamarck, René Louiche Desfontaines and Georges Cuvier, was read at a meeting at the Museum. They concluded by urging Crétet to acquire the collections, as they would constitute 'a very important and very necessary addition' to the Museum.[8] They also indicated that the collections contained anthropological objects that could embellish the Musée Napoléon and the Bibliothèque Impériale. In their argument, the professors sought to characterise Leschenault's work in the Dutch East Indies not as a private venture, but as a continuation of the Baudin expedition:

> In the light of this account, you will no doubt be of the view, as we are, that M. Leschenault honourably carried out the mission entrusted to him by the government, on the recommendation of the Institute and the Museum.
>
> The sojourn that he was obliged to make in Java, subsequent to the illness which had kept him in Timor, considerably increased the usefulness of this last expedition in terms of natural history, introducing us to the productions of this great island where other naturalists of the expedition did not go ashore.[9]

By making this argument, the professors suggested that they were not seeking to buy a private collection, but were simply exerting their right to receive the final collections of the Baudin expedition. The compensation they sought for Leschenault was not in the nature of a purchase price, but was instead linked to his role in the expedition: they suggested firstly that he receive a backdated payment of salary to cover the period from when he ceased to receive his expedition salary up to the time he arrived back in France, and secondly a pension similar to those granted the previous year to François Péron and Charles-Alexandre Lesueur.

The government had in fact been very slow to compensate the members of the Baudin expedition who had returned to France aboard the *Naturaliste* and the *Géographe* in 1803 and 1804 respectively. It had taken until 1806 for the Ministry of the Navy and Colonies to resolve the question of back pay and table money for those returnees.[10] In addition, in 1804 members of the Museum and the Institute of France had lobbied the Ministry of the Navy in an attempt to secure a further six years' scientific employment for Leschenault, Péron and Lesueur following their return, but had not met with success.[11] It was only on 4 August 1806 that Napoleon approved a decree awarding Péron and Lesueur pensions of 2,000 francs and 1,500 francs respectively. After Leschenault's return, the professors of the Museum sought to obtain similar compensation for him.

The professors sent their report on Leschenault's collections to Crétet on 24 October 1807, and Crétet seems to have been sympathetic towards Leschenault's predicament. Just over a week later, on 2 November, the minister put the professors' requests before the emperor. Napoleon was amenable to the first of them, and in a decree signed on 3 November 1807 awarded Leschenault a pension of 1,800 francs, to be paid from the budgets of the Minister of the Interior and the Minister of the Public Treasury 'as reward and compensation for the collections he made during his trip to Java, and which he has deposited with the Museum of Natural History'.[12] Although happy to contribute to Leschenault's pension, Crétet did not believe that the large back payment of salary requested had anything to do with his ministry: he believed that this was the responsibility of the Ministry of the Navy. The sum Leschenault was claiming was very large: around four years' salary while he travelled in the Dutch East Indies and subsequently, in addition to whatever part of his salary had not been paid during his travels with the Baudin expedition between October 1800 and June 1803. Given that Leschenault had been recruited for the expedition on a salary of 4,200 francs, a back payment covering the entire six years and eight months that Leschenault had been away would have been in the order of 28,000 francs. Crétet gained Napoleon's consent for the matter to be referred to the Ministry of the Navy.

After learning of these decisions, Leschenault wrote to Crétet on 16 November 1807 to express his concern. As he pointed out, the professors in their report had not indicated that a pension alone was adequate compensation for his collections: 'the payment of my salary up until my return is rightfully requested by them, without which my collections of natural history cannot be claimed by the government'. Furthermore, as he explained:

> Your Excellency, I have the most urgent need for this payment, to satisfy the debts of honour that I was obliged to contract for my requirements over the course of seven years' absence, during which time I had no means apart than those that I procured at my own liability.[13]

Leschenault asked Crétet to pursue the matter with the Ministry of the Navy and sought advice on how he himself should proceed. He concluded by warning Crétet that any further delay might prove deleterious to the state of preservation of his collections.

Crétet acted immediately on receipt of Leschenault's letter, and on 18 November 1807 sent a letter to Denis Decrès, the Minister for the Navy, in which he explained the situation:

> His Majesty deigned, in a decree of the 3rd of this month, to grant the first part of these requests, awarding a pension to M. Leschenault, but he considered that the second part, which is to say, that concerning the payment of the arrears of salary due to him, should be examined by Your Excellency. I am fulfilling the intentions of His Majesty by informing Your Excellency of the claim that M. Leschenault is renewing in this regard.

Crétet was careful to emphasise that the decision came from Napoleon rather than from himself, and went on to extol Leschenault's character and the contribution that Leschenault had made to science during his travels.[14] The question of Leschenault's salary had become a subject of ministerial wrangling.

The Ministry of the Navy was slow in dealing with the matter. It was more than three months later, on 24 February 1808, that Decrès wrote back to Crétet, acknowledging the delay but stating that he could not accede to Crétet's request in full, as 'the rules observed in my department for the acquittal of expenditure do not allow me the means'.[15] According to Decrès, from the moment that Leschenault left the *Géographe* in Timor on 2 June 1803, he was no longer acting under orders from the Ministry of the Navy. In the absence of any official gazetting or special orders being issued by the navy, Leschenault could not be paid a salary for his 'private voyage' in the Dutch East Indies. And, Decrès commented further: 'the work undertaken by M. Leschenault after disembarkation is foreign to the assignment he was given by the Navy, and was directed towards making observations in the realm of science, particularly natural history'.[16] This is of course a surprising remark on Decrès's part, as Leschenault had been employed on the Baudin expedition precisely for that purpose. Decrès proposed that his Ministry should pay Leschenault's wages and table money only up to the moment he left the Baudin expedition, while the Ministry of the Interior should pay any remuneration for Leschenault's subsequent travels.

The Ministry of the Navy informed Leschenault of this decision, which caused him great despair. Rather than choosing to battle with the Ministry, Leschenault adopted another tactic. On 4 March 1808 he wrote a long and impassioned letter to Crétet imploring him instead to entreat Napoleon directly for the arrears of salary for the period June 1803 to July 1807. He headed the letter accordingly with the word 'petition'. His stay in the Dutch East Indies was not undertaken by choice, he explained, but was rather 'an enforced stay': at first, he had been ill, and then, when recovered, he had found it impossible to find a neutral ship to take him home. So he had resolved to make the best of it, and to continue his scientific work while stranded in the region. In Java there was no French agent to turn to for help, and so he had had to spend his own money or borrow from acquaintances made there. Now he was struggling to repay his creditors. These worries were taking a toll on his health: 'The delay I am experiencing is as detrimental to me as it is wearying to my sensibility'. Leschenault made a highly emotional plea in his attempt to convince Crétet:

> Seven years of voyaging completed with honour, accompanied by innumerable dangers and privations; fascinating collections of natural history successfully brought back to France through all the hazards of a long journey and the continual concern that I might see the fruits of my labour carried off by the enemies of my nation; the deposition of these collections at the Museum of Natural History; the reports made on my behalf; two-fifths of a modest fortune consumed by my voyages; the best years of my life spent on investigations having a general utility; these are the grounds, Your Excellency, on which I call for prompt justice.[17]

This appeal seems to have moved Crétet, as on 9 March 1808 he submitted the requested petition to Napoleon.

In a three-page report, Crétet argued strongly that Leschenault deserved to receive back-pay for the period June 1803–July 1807. He set out the reasons which Decrès had given for refusing to pay this sum, and criticised Decrès's logic on two counts: firstly, 'that the attached commission which M. Leschenault received expressly states that he is attached to the expedition *as a botanist*',[18] and secondly, that Leschenault was forced to leave the expedition due to illness. In other words, during his travels in the Dutch East Indies Leschenault was simply continuing the scientific work he had been commissioned to do for the navy, and that, furthermore, although he had left the expedition, he had not in fact left the service.

To support Leschenault's case further, Crétet described the costs which Leschenault had incurred and explained the financial predicament in which his family found itself:

> his stay on Timor and Java, his illness, his return, the acquisition and transportation of the collections that he brought back, cost him considerable sums, for which he has incurred debts; [...] his formerly wealthy family was ruined by the Revolution; [...] the four years' salary that he was to draw amounted to a sum of 16,800 francs.

And to this, Crétet added a further pragmatic observation: 'I do not have in my ministry's budget any funds applicable to this type of expenditure'. Appealing to Napoleon's wisdom and kindness, Crétet reflected on whether 'one can leave this young man weighed down by the debts he contracted', and concluded by entreating Napoleon to place at his disposal 'whatever sum [His Majesty] would judge suitable'.[19]

Leschenault was kept informed of the steps that Crétet was taking in his interests, but was deeply concerned that the machinery of state was moving slowly. So he wrote again to Crétet on 18 March 1808, augmenting the sentimental appeal that he had used in his previous letter with precise details about the extent of his debts and his increasingly precarious legal position. The reason for Leschenault's desperation was now clear: he had refinanced his debts in November, and payment of these new debts had fallen due at the end of February:

> I still owe a little over 10,000 francs, the sum total of two promissory notes in favour of Messieurs Van-Neck and Sarwell, one for 1,080 piastres, the other for 850 piastres. In order to honour these two bills which fell due last November, I was obliged to take out loans; these later liabilities were payable at the end of February, and it is only because of the assurance I gave that I would soon be able to clear my debts that proceedings against me have not yet been brought. I am being pressed more and more urgently to settle; I have no source of funds other than the payment of my salary.[20]

Meanwhile the emperor responded to Crétet's petition by asking to have a valuation made of Leschenault's collections. Crétet duly passed this request on to the professors at the Museum on 26 March 1808.[21] It seemed that Leschenault would no longer have to pursue the Ministry of the Navy over his disputed salary claim, but might instead receive a special payment, directly related to the value of his collections.

The professors charged their colleague at the Museum, the assistant-naturalist Louis Dufresne, with drawing up the valuation of Leschenault's collections. Dufresne found this to be a difficult task because, as he explained, 'most of the items which make up this collection being new, one can only allot them an arbitrary value, which could only be truly assessed if private collectors were to offer a competing price'.[22] Nevertheless, he examined and placed a valuation on each group of specimens – mammals, birds, skeletons, oviparous quadrupeds, reptiles, shells, insects, botanical samples and mineralogical objects. He estimated that the bird specimens were the most valuable, worth 6,000 francs in total (noting incidentally that half of them had already been given to the empress Joséphine). The next most valuable group, at 5,000 francs, was a 'magnificent collection of insects and butterflies, consisting of 714 specimens, all in the most beautiful state of preservation; a very large number of them do not feature in the collections of the Museum'.

When all the categories were added together, the value of Leschenault's collections was 18,700 francs. Dufresne completed his report on 4 April 1808 and the professors sent it through to Crétet on 8 April 1808, urging the minister to consider Leschenault not 'simply as a merchant, but as a man given an assignment by the government, with the assurance of a fixed salary as long as his assignment should last'.[23] Unfortunately for Leschenault, after this communication between the Museum and the Ministry of the Interior, the matter seems to have languished – no doubt because the French administration at this time was preoccupied with the invasion of Spain. Napoleon left Paris for Bayonne in April and was absent from the capital through most of the summer as he oversaw the usurpation by his brother Joseph of the Spanish crown. Napoleon returned to his palace at Saint-Cloud in mid-August, after the French had suffered several disastrous defeats on the Iberian peninsula and Joseph had had to flee Madrid.

As Napoleon travelled north from Bordeaux to Paris through Rochefort and Nantes in early August 1808, Leschenault renewed his own campaign. The botanist adopted a different strategy now, and sought to resolve his case with the help of his influential friend Nicéphore Niépce, from whom he had borrowed money. From Chalon-sur-Saône, on 9 August 1808, Leschenault wrote once more to Crétet:

> Family matters have forced me to leave Paris and will keep me away for another month. You were kind enough, Your Excellency, to promise that, on His Majesty the Emperor's return, you would seek a conclusion to my affairs.[24]

Leschenault informed Crétet that he had given Niépce legal authority to obtain the money due to him from the government: 'I have the honour to inform you, Your Excellency, that I have authorised M. Niépce to collect what is owed to me. M. Niépce is one of my creditors.' Niépce was later to achieve fame as the inventor of photography, and in this period was working with his brother Claude on the development of the first combustion engine, which they called the pyreolophore. Niépce had in fact begun corresponding with the previous Minister of the Interior, Jean-Baptiste Nompère de Champagny, in November 1806, as he sought to secure a ten-year patent for their engine, which was granted by Napoleon on 20 July 1807.[25] After Champagny moved to the Ministry of Foreign Relations in August 1807, Niépce addressed his letters to the new Minister of the Interior, Crétet. Although he was eight years younger than Niépce, Leschenault must have become acquainted with the future inventor while they were children. The family homes of Niépce and Leschenault were situated several streets apart in the centre of Chalon-sur-Saône, in the rue de l'Oratoire and the rue Saint-Antoine respectively, and both their fathers were lawyers and *conseillers du roi*.[26]

Leschenault sent his letter to Crétet via Niépce, who was then in Paris, Niépce enclosing it with a letter of his own dated 15 August 1808 and addressed to the minister. Niépce, in his letter, explained to Crétet that any financial help given to Leschenault would also benefit Niépce himself:

> I join him in entreating [Your Excellency] to obtain for him what he claims. As far as my interests are concerned, I would be greatly obliged to you, having lent him quite a considerable sum on his arrival back in Paris to pay off the debts that he had been obliged to contract during such a long journey. As he is my compatriot, I hastened to come to his aid in the expectation that he would swiftly receive what he is owed. I implore you therefore, Your Excellency, to continue your kindness towards him and seek settlement from His Majesty the Emperor of what he claims. I would be highly grateful to you, as I find myself in the deepest difficulty, having waited patiently until now in the hope of receiving present payment. I hope thus to rely on your kindness to come to our aid and help us out of this predicament. As he informs you, he has authorised me to act on his behalf. I will show proof of this to you when you request it.[27]

The implication of the letters written by the two Chalonnais men to Crétet was that Leschenault's continuing debts were causing financial problems for one of France's most promising inventors, which they no doubt felt added weight and urgency to Leschenault's claim.

Leschenault also received assistance from another quarter at this time. The Prussian naturalist Alexander von Humboldt, who had chosen to reside in Paris despite the fact that France was at war with Prussia, sent a letter to Crétet on 5 August 1808 concerning the evaluation of Leschenault's collections. In it he heaped praise on the scientific work done by Péron and Leschenault, while reserving criticism for Baudin. He concluded by stating to Crétet: 'Fortunate are those savants who, on returning to their homeland, find in Your Excellency a protector and a father'.[28] Leschenault and Humboldt had in fact been in contact prior to this point about scientific matters. Leschenault had written to Humboldt describing a custom followed by certain Javanese women, who ate a type of red clay which was toasted and consumed as an appetite suppressant. Humboldt reproduced this letter, which was dated 15 May 1808, in his *Tableaux de la nature* (1808).[29]

The combined support of Niépce and Humboldt seems to have effected what Leschenault alone had not been able to bring about: a resolution to his petition. On 17 August 1808, a 'Note for His Majesty the Emperor and King' was drafted by functionaries at the Ministry of the Interior, which reproduced details from Dufresne's assessment of the collection, including his valuation of 18,700 francs, and alluded to Leschenault's debts of 10,000 francs. It seems that a decision was taken by Crétet to offer Leschenault the lower amount, as on 20 August a functionary asked in an internal note: 'From what fund may we draw the sum of 10,000 francs requested by His Excellency in favour of M. Leschenault'?[30] Another functionary replied on the verso that the sum fell under chapter 6 of the budget, entitled 'Encouragements', though it would be up to the minister to decide whether the more suitable article was 'Assistance and pensions for men of letters and artists', or 'Encouragement to agriculture', adding: 'Both appear to contain enough funds in the year to afford 10,000 francs above anticipated expenditure'. On 24 August the note for Napoleon was redrafted, and referred firstly to Leschenault's debts of 10,000 francs, and only secondly to Dufresne's larger figure of 18,700 francs, with its author emphasising that the latter estimation 'cannot be precise, as it does not relate to objects which are familiar or widely sold'.[31] The note concluded: 'I am honoured to propose a draft decree granting M. Leschenault the sum of 10,000 francs which he requires to clear the debts he was obliged to contract in the Indies'. Crétet was effectively deflecting a possible implication of Napoleon's that Leschenault be paid on the basis of the collection's worth, and Crétet instead advised a smaller sum which would clear Leschenault's debt to Niépce.

On 28 August 1808 an imperial decree was issued by Napoleon at Saint-Cloud, bringing to a close bureaucratic negotiations that had dragged on for more than a year. It stated:

> Article 1
>
> M. Leschenault, naturalist, who took part in the expedition to the southern lands, is granted a sum of 10,000 francs as compensation for the illness he contracted during the expedition and for the collections of items of natural history which he brought back to our museum at the *Jardin des plantes*.
>
> Article 2
>
> This sum will be paid under chapter 6 of the budget for 1808, the article concerning assistance and pensions for men of letters and artists.[32]

It was signed by Jean-Pierre de Bachasson, comte de Montalivet, in the absence of Crétet, who would resign from his position due to ill health the following year, in August 1809, and die several months after that. Of the three sums that had been discussed – 18,700 francs (the value of Leschenault's collections), 16,800 francs (equivalent to four years' back pay) and 10,000 francs (his debt) – Leschenault received the lowest. But Crétet had certainly been far more sympathetic to his cause than Decrès at the Ministry of the Navy. In fact, in an obituary which appeared in *Le Moniteur* on 2 December 1809, Crétet was praised not just for the public works he had overseen as minister, but also because: 'He welcomed and supported savants and artists'.[33]

After securing remuneration from the government in 1808, Leschenault continued to struggle financially for a further eight years. If was only after the fall of Napoleon and the restoration of the monarchy that he received his second professional appointment as a botanist, and was sent in 1816 to the recently recovered territory of Pondicherry in India to collect botanical specimens for the Museum. From 1816 onwards he bore the title *naturaliste du roi* ('naturalist to the king'), and was able to draw a salary for his work in this position. During the period 1808 to 1816, however, Leschenault pursued a number of different projects without great financial reward. He applied himself to writing up accounts of his travels in the Dutch East Indies along with some of his scientific observations relating to that region and Australia. He published articles in the *Annales du Muséum d'Histoire naturelle* on three different topics in 1810 and 1811: on the properties of poisons he had experimented with in Java; on the vegetation of New Holland; and on the acidic qualities of the crater lake of Mt Ijen in east Java. He published two further articles in 1811 in Conrad Malte-Brun's *Annales des voyages* on his travels in Timor and Java. There is no indication that Leschenault ever sought to publish a comprehensive description of the plants he had discovered during his travels in the southern lands – but in any case the appearance of Robert Brown's *Prodromus Florae Novae Hollandiae et Insulae Van Diemen* in 1810 would have rendered a large part of such a project redundant.[34]

Leschenault's struggles to obtain remuneration from the Ministries of the Interior and the Navy may have emphasised to him the importance of obtaining support from influential figures. He seems to have maintained good relations with his mentor Jussieu, who occasionally employed him for odd jobs. In June 1809, for example, Jussieu sent Leschenault out to the Vaux-de-Cernay, around 50 kilometres to the south-west of Paris, to scout for a property for purchase. Leschenault reported back to him:

> It is with much regret that I inform you that my search has been fruitless. Only one property is for sale in Cernay (around one league from here), but the price being asked is 160,000 francs. [...] I am very sorry that there is nothing for sale, as the countryside would have greatly pleased you. Your map of the environs of Paris did not mislead you about the beauty of the area.[35]

Jussieu also seems to have introduced Leschenault to the circle of Constance, comtesse de Salm, a celebrated author who was married to the botanist Joseph Maria Franz Anton Hubert, comte de Salm-Reifferscheidt-Dyck. Leschenault attended her salons at the rue du Bac in Paris, which were frequented by scholars, scientists, writers and composers, including Jussieu himself, Humboldt and the botanist Augustin Pyramus de Candolle.[36] Leschenault sought to cultivate his friendship with Constance de Salm, corresponded with her during the course of 1811 while he was away from Paris, and in this period even entertained hopes of marrying her daughter Clémentine.[37]

Leschenault pursued several different money-making projects between 1809 and 1814. With the linguist and translator Louis-Mathieu Langlès, who also attended Salm's salon, he prepared a French-Malay dictionary, based on the study he had made of the languages he encountered during his travels in the Dutch East Indies. He submitted a draft of it to the Imprimerie Nationale in June 1811, for which he was paid the first third of the promised fee of 2,000 francs. However, the project was never completed: in the wake of Napoleon's fall from power, a new Imprimerie Royale replaced the old government publisher and Leschenault's project was cancelled. In 1810 Leschenault also sought to sell to the government two large and ancient Hindu statues carved out of lava which he had taken from a temple in Java. He offered them first to the empress Joséphine, but after keeping them for a time at the Château of Malmaison, she returned them to Leschenault on the grounds that she did not have the funds to purchase them in her household budget.[38] Baron Vivant Denon then sought to buy the statues for the Musée Napoléon (the Louvre), of which he was director, and the purchase – for a sum of 6000 francs – was concluded in March 1811.

Leschenault had some success also in his applications for government jobs. In May 1811 he visited Nicolas Fauchat, the head of the Second Division at the Ministry of the Interior, where they discussed the possibility of Leschenault being appointed an inspector of merino rams. The opportunity had arisen as Napoleon was keen to ensure that the prized merino sheep which had been brought back to France after the invasion of Spain in 1808 were properly tended in their new pastures. Obliged to wait for the minister's return to hear the decision,

Leschenault reflected ironically: 'One does not become a shepherd or a professor as easily as one might like'.[39] Leschenault was appointed to the position of inspector on 22 July 1811 for the southern region between Puy-de-Dôme and the eastern Pyrénées. He complained about the poor salary he received, 2,400 francs, with an additional 1,200 francs travelling expenses, but tried to maintain a sense of perspective:

> in time it will perhaps be possible for me to set my sights on the position of inspector general, and then this job will have been worth the effort. It was essential for my future that I got hold of something. The government does not abandon those whom it employs.

Towards the end of August he set out on horseback for the south, and in the autumn travelled widely in that region inspecting flocks of sheep:

> despite the bad roads and bad inns, I have travelled more than 100 leagues in the department of Corrèze, and will soon have covered as many in the department of Cantal. I have criss-crossed them in every direction, talking pastures and flocks, and am none too happy with the way these innocent sheep are treated.[40]

He detailed his findings in a report for the Minister of the Interior, who was apparently pleased with his work. It seems that Leschenault continued in this role for at least two years, and in 1813 the Imprimerie Impériale published his short pamphlet entitled *Notice sur l'épizootie qui a régné en 1812 sur les troupeaux à laine des départements méridionaux de l'Empire*.

By late 1813 Leschenault was seeking different work. On 7 November 1813 he wrote once more to the Ministry of the Interior, this time offering to contribute to what remained to be published of the official account of the Baudin expedition, the *Voyage de découvertes aux Terres Australes*. The first volume of the historical account written by François Péron had appeared in 1807, and two parts of the *Atlas* in 1807 and 1811 (attributed to Lesueur and Nicolas Petit, and to Louis Freycinet, respectively).

However, Leschenault's offer was not taken up, even if Louis Freycinet later included Leschenault's article on the vegetation of New Holland as Chapter 38 in the second volume of the historical account (1816).[41] Then, some time in the spring of 1814, perhaps in the wake of Napoleon's first abdication, Leschenault wrote once more to the Ministry of the Interior, requesting that he be considered for the position of administrator of the domain of Rambouillet, which sheltered a valuable flock of merino sheep. Leschenault does not seem to have been successful in this instance either, but, under the newly restored monarchy, was appointed in June 1814 as a functionary at the Bureau of Agriculture, where he worked as a *rédacteur*, a position which entailed writing letters and reports.[42]

The fall of Napoleon had the unexpected and indirect effect of securing Leschenault's career as a botanist. The Treaty of Paris of 30 May 1814, which ended the war between France and the Sixth Coalition, stipulated the return to France of her former possessions in India. In May 1816 two vessels, the *Amphitrite* and the *Licorne*, set out from France carrying the new governor-general for the French colonies in India along with a large number of other administrators, and Leschenault sailed with them in his new capacity as *naturaliste du roi*. Based in Pondicherry for the following six years, Leschenault established a botanical garden there and explored southern India and Ceylon, sending collections of specimens back to the Museum at regular intervals. On his return to France in 1822 he was named a chevalier of the Legion of Honour in recognition of his scientific work. For ten years, between 1807 and 1816, Leschenault had struggled to forge a career for himself and had signed pleading letters to the government with the epithet '*naturaliste voyageur*', a title that referred to a salaried position that he had lost. In First Empire France, there were few opportunities for scientific travellers with his experience – Napoleon had no further interest in funding expeditions to distant parts of the globe and concentrated instead on securing Continental territories. Leschenault was restricted in that period to trudging through muddy rural regions of France as a government inspector of merino sheep – a far cry, he felt, from the pioneering scientific work he had done in the southern hemisphere. With the restoration of the Bourbon monarchy and the resumption of France's colonial aspirations, Leschenault found himself in favour once more, and was able to resume his scientific travelling. In India, Leschenault often signed himself '*naturaliste du roi*': this indicated to his readers that, after long years of struggle, he had recovered his status as a professional naturalist. Although the term '*voyageur*' had disappeared from the title he chose to use, he was in fact on the move again.

Notes

1. Jean-Baptiste Louis Claude Théodore Leschenault de la Tour (1773–1826), known as Théodore.
2. See Edward Duyker, *François Péron, an Impetuous Life: Naturalist and Voyager*, Melbourne: The Miegunyah Press, 2006, p. 50.
3. See Dorinda Outram, 'Politics and vocation: French science, 1793–1830', *British Journal for the History of Science*, vol. 13, no. 1, 1980, p. 29.
4. On the Jussieu family, see Emma C. Spary, *Utopia's Garden: French Natural History from Old Regime to Revolution*, Cambridge: Cambridge University Press, 2000, pp. 39–42.
5. Leschenault to the Ministry of the Interior, 27 August 1807, Archives Nationales de France (ANF), série F, Versements des ministères et des administrations qui en dépendent, AF/F/1d II/L/16.
6. Théodore Leschenault de la Tour to Jean-Baptiste-Antoine Leschenault du Villard, 2 September 1807, private collection. I am grateful to François Broch d'Hotelans Leschenault du Villard for allowing me to consult this letter.
7. Leschenault to Antoine-Laurent de Jussieu, 17 July 1807, cited by Viviane Desmet and Michel Jangoux, 'Un naturaliste aux Terres australes: Jean-Baptiste Leschenault de la Tour (1773–1826)', in M. Jangoux (ed.), *Portés par l'air du temps, les voyages du capitaine Baudin*, special number of *Études sur le XVIIIe siècle*, vol. 38, 2010, p. 231.
8. Copie de l'extrait du registre des délibérations de l'Assemblée administrative des professeurs du Muséum d'Histoire naturelle. Séance du 14 octobre 1807, ANF, AF IV/953, dossier 190.
9. Copie de l'extrait du registre, ANF, AF IV/953, dossier 190.
10. See Frank Horner, *The French Reconnaissance: Baudin in Australia 1801–1803*, Carlton: Melbourne University Press, 1987, p. 322.
11. See Horner, *The French Reconnaissance*, p. 329.
12. Extrait des minutes de la secrétairerie d'État, ANF, F 17/3979, dossier 14.
13. Leschenault to Emmanuel Crétet, Minister of the Interior, 16 November 1807, ANF, F 17/3979, dossier 14.
14. See Crétet to Decrès, 18 November 1807, ANF, F 17/3979, dossier 14.
15. Decrès to Crétet, 24 February 1808, ANF, F 17/3979, dossier 14.
16. *Ibid.*
17. Leschenault to Crétet, 4 March 1808, ANF, F 17/3979, dossier 14.
18. Crétet, 'Rapport à Sa Majesté l'empereur et roi', 9 March 1808, ANF, AF IV/956, dossier 56.
19. *Ibid.*
20. Leschenault to Crétet, 18 March 1808, ANF, F 17/3979, dossier 14.
21. See Crétet to the administrators of the Museum of Natural History, 26 March 1808, cited by Michel Jangoux, *Le Voyage aux Terres Australes du commandant Nicolas Baudin: Genèse et préambule (1798–1800)*, Paris: Presses de l'Université Paris-Sorbonne, 2013, p. 210.
22. Louis Dufresne, 'Aperçu sommaire de la valeur des objets d'histoire naturelle rapportés par M. Leschenault en 1807', dated 4 April 1808, ANF, F 17/3979, dossier 14.

23 Georges Cuvier and Louis Nicolas Vauquelin to Crétet, 8 April 1808, ANF, F 17/3979, dossier 14.
24 Leschenault to Crétet, 9 August 1808, ANF, F 17/3979, dossier 14.
25 See Manuel Bonnet and Jean-Louis Marignier, *Niépce: correspondance et papiers*, Saint-Loup-de-Varenne: Maison Nicéphore Niépce, 2003, p. 201.
26 See Victor Fouque, *La Vérité sur l'invention de la photographie: Nicéphore Niépce, sa vie, ses essais, ses travaux, d'après sa correspondance et autres documents inédits*, Paris: Librairie des Auteurs et de l'Académie des Bibliophiles; Chalon-sur-Saône: Librairie Ferran, 1867, pp. 16, 21–22, and Gilbert Prieur, 'Jean-Baptiste Leschenault de la Tour (1773–1826): naturaliste et voyageur chalonnais', *Mémoires de la Société d'Histoire et d'Archéologie de Chalon-sur-Saône*, vol. 41, 1971, p. 130.
27 Joseph Nicéphore Niépce to Crétet, 15 August 1808, ANF, F 17/3979, dossier 14.
28 Alexander von Humboldt to Crétet, 5 August 1808, ANF, F 17/3979, dossier 14.
29 Leschenault, 'Sur l'espèce de terre qu'on mange à Java: extrait d'une lettre de M. Leschenault, botaniste de l'expédition aux terres australes, à M. de Humboldt', in Alexander von Humboldt, *Tableaux de la nature, ou considérations sur les déserts, sur la physionomie des végétaux, sur les cataractes de l'Orénoque*, trans. J.B.B. Eyriès, Paris: F. Schœll, 2 vols, 1808, vol. 1, pp. 209–211.
30 Note on Leschenault's payment, Ministry of the Interior, 20 August 1808, ANF, F 17/3979, dossier 14.
31 Note on Leschenault's payment, Ministry of the Interior, 24 August 1808, ANF, F 17/3979, dossier 14.
32 Extrait des minutes de la secrétairerie d'État, 28 August 1808, ANF, F 17/3979, dossier 14.
33 Nicolas Fauchat, Obituary of Emmanuel Crétet, comte de Champmol, *Le Moniteur Universel*, 2 December 1809, cited in *Nouvelles Littéraires et Politiques*, 3 December 1809, p. 2.
34 See Jean Fornasiero, Peter Monteath and John West-Sooby, *Encountering Terra Australis: The Australian Voyages of Nicolas Baudin and Matthew Flinders*, Kent Town: Wakefield Press, 2nd edition, 2010, pp. 346–348.
35 Leschenault to Jussieu, 1 June 1809, Muséum national d'Histoire naturelle, Paris, Fonds Jussieu, ms Per. K130 (6).
36 See Ellen McNiven Hine, *Constance de Salm, her influence and her circle in the aftermath of the French Revolution: 'A Mind of No Common Order'*, New York: Peter Lang, 2012, p. 115.
37 See Constance de Salm to Antoine Barbier, 18 September 1820, Toulon, Bibliothèque de la Société des Amis du Vieux Toulon et de sa Région (BSAVT), Fonds Salm, correspondence of Constance de Salm.
38 See 'Rapport présenté au Ministre de l'Intérieur', 21 May 1810, ANF, F 17/1539, dossier 2.
39 Leschenault to Constance de Salm, 28 May 1811, BSAVT, Fonds Salm, correspondence of Constance de Salm.
40 Leschenault to Constance de Salm, 21 August 1811, BSAVT, Fonds Salm, correspondence of Constance de Salm.
41 François Péron clearly saw Leschenault as a threat to his own position and did his best to ensure he was not given a role in preparing the other volumes of the *Voyage*. Péron was indeed quite scathing about Leschenault's ability to act as his successor. See the chapter by Jean-Luc Chappey in this volume.
42 ANF, AF V/*/2 and F 17/1539.

Chapter 14

An Emotional Voyager: Stanislas Levillain (1774–1801), Trainee Zoologist on the Baudin Expedition

John West-Sooby

When the Baudin expedition left Le Havre on 19 October 1800, it carried an impressive contingent of no less than 22 naturalists and artists – 24, if we count the two young artists Baudin hired to illustrate his personal journal, Nicolas-Martin Petit and Charles-Alexandre Lesueur. Included in this complement of *savants* were five zoologists: Désiré Dumont and Jean Baptiste Bory de Saint-Vincent, who were assigned to Baudin's consort ship the *Naturaliste*; and René Maugé, François Péron and Stanislas Levillain, who travelled with the commander on the *Géographe*. Much has been written, and justifiably so, about François Péron's zoological work, which was wide-ranging and included ground-breaking studies of marine life, conducted in partnership with the young artist Lesueur. The focus on Péron is also understandable given the central position he came to occupy as the expedition's chronicler and spokesman. However, as a result of the attention paid to Péron and Lesueur, the scientific contribution made by the other zoologists is often marginalised or neglected in the historiography of the Baudin expedition. In the case of Dumont and Bory de Saint-Vincent, there is admittedly not much to tell, as both abandoned the expedition at the Île de France (Mauritius) on the outward journey – though Bory did leave a record of his scientific activities in an account of his travels during and after his time on the Baudin expedition, which he published in 1804.[1] The marginal status of Levillain and Maugé in most accounts of the voyage and its scientific achievements is, on the other hand, less easy to accept.

One obvious explanation is that they both had the misfortune to die relatively early during the expedition, succumbing to diseases contracted during the fateful first stopover in Timor following the exploration of the western Australian coast – Levillain at sea on 23 December 1801, Maugé in Tasmania on 20 February 1802. This left Péron as the last zoologist standing. Their curtailed participation in the expedition, however, did not prevent Maugé and Levillain from making a significant and crucial contribution to its scientific work – not just in western Australia and Timor, but during the long sea voyage from France, which was in itself particularly productive in terms of the study of marine life. As Levillain recorded, it was he and Maugé who invented the 'kind of small fine-meshed pouch with a long wooden handle' that enabled them to catch 'everything that swam alongside' the ship during the passage down the Atlantic and across the Indian Ocean.[2] The references in Levillain's scientific notes to the sketches made by Lesueur also suggest that he played the role of mentor for the young artist early in the voyage.[3] Just as pertinently, we know that François Péron was sometimes less than scrupulous in acknowledging the work of his fellow zoologists, recognising Maugé's tireless efforts but otherwise paying him and Levillain scant attention in his official account of the voyage.[4] He even went so far as to deprive them of their achievements – crossing out Maugé's name on documents recording his collections or discoveries, and replacing it with his own or that of his friend Lesueur, as Michel Jangoux has demonstrated.[5] It is important to note in this respect that, despite Péron's superior formal education, he was very much a novice in terms of field work when he left France, and learned a great deal during the outward journey from the example set by Maugé and Levillain. The practical expertise of Maugé and Levillain and their previous experience of scientific voyaging – on Baudin's *Belle Angélique* voyage to the West Indies in 1796–1798 – placed them at a distinct advantage. The dominant position that Péron came to acquire during the course of the expedition and subsequent to it should not, therefore, be allowed to cast a shadow over the work of his two fellow zoologists, who worked diligently and with discernment up until their untimely deaths.

Recent studies have begun to shed light on the role played by some of the lesser-known figures of the Baudin expedition's scientific staff – the botanists André Michaux[6] and Jean-Baptiste (Théodore) Leschenault de La Tour,[7] for example, and the geographers Charles

Boullanger and Pierre Faure.[8] Michel Jangoux, in particular, has provided an excellent account of the work conducted by the three zoologists and four botanists who remained with the expedition following its stopover at Mauritius.[9] The aim here, then, is to contribute further to the task of drawing these neglected figures out of the shadows by taking one of their number, Stanislas Levillain, and examining his status as a scientific voyager – that is to say by considering his scientific credentials while at the same time attempting to bring to life the human qualities and frailties he displayed during the course of the voyage.

Little is known of Levillain's early life. As recorded in two short biographical notices by Édouard Vuacheux (1905) and André Maury (1954), Levillain was born in Le Havre on 21 April 1774, the son of a sea captain.[10] His father later died at sea, as did Stanislas's older brother. From an early age, Stanislas took an interest in natural history and in 1793–1794 he donated his collections to the local authorities in response to a decree by the National Convention regarding public education – a sign, perhaps, of his pride in what he had collected and of his civic spirit. Levillain was also an excellent hunter and had a gift for taxidermy. As Michel Jangoux suggests, it was possibly these talents and a certain local notoriety that led to him being recruited for a scientific voyage to the West Indies that left Le Havre in September 1796 under the command of Nicolas Baudin.[11] Levillain embarked on the *Belle Angélique* with the status of 'amateur d'histoire naturelle' and effectively served his apprenticeship as a naturalist-collector working alongside the employees of the Museum who had been appointed to this expedition: the zoologist René Maugé, the botanist André-Pierre Ledru, and the gardener Anselme Riedlé. During the voyage, he also served as Baudin's secretary. Levillain must have performed his duties to the captain's satisfaction, as Baudin's journal of the voyage does not record any moment of displeasure with respect to him. On the other hand, neither did he earn the praise of his commander, who was, in contrast, fulsome in his appreciation of the 'zeal and indefatigable activity' of Ledru, Maugé and the 'peerless' Riedlé.[12] This narrative silence on Baudin's part is intriguing. It might suggest that Levillain was perceived as a rather colourless character whose qualities of hard work and loyalty could not wholly compensate for a tendency to self-effacement – an image that his journal of the subsequent voyage to the Southern Lands would seem to belie. On the other hand, it may simply be the case that, because Levillain was recruited locally at Le Havre and was not an employee of the Museum, Baudin did not expect him to play a leading part and felt under no obligation to report on his activities to the authorities in Paris or record them in his journal. Levillain's role as the commander's secretary could also have contributed to the perception that he was 'part of the furniture'. A note in Ledru's published account of the voyage attests to the contribution Levillain made in observing and collecting molluscs, in company with Baudin and Maugé.[13] The director of the Paris Museum, Antoine-Laurent de Jussieu, also recorded in a note that 'Citizen Villain' had greatly contributed to the collection of animals and especially insects through his 'care and research'.[14] Otherwise, there is no other textual evidence of his activities during the *Belle Angélique* voyage.

What is certain is that, in 1800, two years after the return to France of the *Belle Angélique*, Levillain volunteered for the voyage to New Holland and was successful in gaining appointment as a trainee zoologist, with Baudin's support. And as was the case for the *Belle Angélique* voyage, he was again to serve as the commander's secretary. From this we can safely surmise that the working relationship between Baudin and Levillain was a good one. It is significant, given Baudin's subsequent reputation as a poor leader of men and an enemy of science, that both Maugé and Riedlé also signed up for the expedition to the Southern Lands. Ledru likewise volunteered, but withdrew from the expedition two months before its departure because, as Jussieu, reported, 'being an only son, he was unable to resist the tears of his elderly and infirm mother, to whom his departure would have come as a mortal blow'.[15] With the exception of Ledru, then, Baudin was in a sense getting the band back together.[16]

For this expedition to the Southern Lands, there is more documentary evidence available to testify to Levillain's work and character, beginning with his own journals and notes. One version of his journal is to be found in the Archives Nationales de France, with another slightly longer and more detailed version of the same text held in the Lesueur Collection at the Museum of Natural History in Le Havre.[17] The Lesueur Collection also holds various scientific notes and sketches by Levillain, as does the

National Museum of Natural History in Paris. Of further interest, in terms of documentation, is the report Levillain provided on the shipwreck of the *Naturaliste*'s longboat north of the Swan River entrance (17 June 1801), which is included in the journal of that ship's captain, Emmanuel Hamelin. This is significant in that it differs in crucial aspects from the account of the officer in charge of the longboat, Pierre-Bernard Milius.

Levillain's journal begins on 25 April 1801, date of the expedition's departure from Mauritius, where three days earlier he had transferred from the *Géographe* to the *Naturaliste* to compensate for the withdrawal from the expedition of Dumont and Bory. It ends on 20 September 1801 as the *Naturaliste* approached Timor, where it was reunited with the *Géographe* from which it had been separated in a storm in Geographe Bay some three months earlier. His journal therefore recounts the journey across the Indian Ocean to the first landfall at Cape Leeuwin and traces the exploration of the western coastline of New Holland, with particularly detailed accounts of the time spent in Geographe Bay and Shark Bay. Levillain's journal and notes constitute a valuable source of information on the peoples and the fauna of coastal western Australia. They also shed fresh light on some of the key historical events that unfolded during the French exploration of this area. The following analysis will thus look firstly at what these documents reveal about Levillain's contribution to the scientific work of the expedition, and then at his personal reactions to some of the more dramatic events that marked this period of the voyage.

In terms of his scientific work, the portrait of Levillain that emerges from his writings is that of a diligent collector and observer. While at sea, during the crossing from Mauritius to New Holland, he was ever alert to opportunities for collecting molluscs or capturing birds, for example. He was very pleased to gather from the sea two specimens of sea cucumber and marvelled at their extraordinary weight.[18] When Maugé called over from the *Géographe* to show him two Cape Petrels he had caught, Levillain asked the crew of the *Naturaliste* to rig some lines so that he could try to catch some himself.[19] There were various species of petrels following the ships at that point. To his frustration, however, the birds did not take the bait. He put this lack of success down to the speed of the ship, which was sailing at seven knots. A few days later, he took advantage of a moment of calm to try to collect some molluscs, but 'could not satisfy [his] curiosity as nothing passed by the ship'.[20] His frustration continued when the expedition finally reached New Holland: at a mere eight leagues from the shore, he found only one cuttlefish bone, one plant and one mollusc.[21] His first shore excursion in Geographe Bay brought him hope that he might use his hunting skills to collect some of the many magnificent birds that the men from the *Géographe* reported having sighted, but as he wrote, 'either because it was too late or for some other reason, we had no luck'.[22] Levillain nevertheless carefully noted the marine and plant life he found on the shore, and commented on the arid nature of the forest, where all the trees seemed to have been affected by fire. This, he observed, 'together with the solitude of this place, makes for a very sad spectacle'.[23] He found signs of animal life, but his dog could find nothing. He heard birds, but could not get close enough to shoot any. One detail that caught his eye was the way in which trees had been hollowed out by fire to provide shelter for the natives. He was also struck by a grass tree, whose resin was of a bright red colour, and by a particularly large anthill, both of which he drew in the margin of his journal. Otherwise, though, this first contact with Australia was characterised by absence: 'insects appear to be scarce here, so that during our entire excursion we saw nothing but solitude and Nature in its primitive state'.[24]

This was hardly an auspicious beginning to his scientific exploration of Australia, but things soon took a turn for the better. Over the following days, Levillain recorded the collection a number of useful specimens: a small crab and a highly interesting starfish, several rather curious marine plants, a number of seashells and urchins, a crow, various brightly coloured parrots and several hawks, and a 'charming red fish' caught by one of the gunners, and which he drew, he says, 'as well as I could'.[25] Levillain participated in a number of other shore parties which allowed him to pursue his natural history collecting. During one such expedition, in the area around Rottnest Island, the longboat in which he was sailing was shipwrecked – on present-day Cottesloe Beach, according to Leslie Marchant.[26] It was here that necessity led him and his companions to try eating some indigenous nuts that they thought resembled chestnuts, but which caused them to be violently ill, Levillain coughing up the equivalent of two glassfuls of blood. As Frank Horner has noted: 'The "chestnuts" they had eaten were evidently kernels from the cone of the macrozamia plant, which the Aborigines eat only after leaching out the poison. Vlamingh's men and Flinders' men made the same mistake, and so did La Pérouse's in Botany Bay.'[27] Levillain had earlier been part of a shore party that had encountered some members of the local Wardandi tribe in Geographe Bay. On that occasion, Levillain and his companions came upon a woman and a man on the beach with whom they were keen to interact. Despite their careful approach, however, the man fled, leaving the heavily pregnant woman on her own. Levillain describes this scene in some detail in his journal, recording that he gave the woman an empty bottle and offering a description of the Aborigines he had seen in which he distinguished them from the 'negroes' of Africa.[28] While natural history was his primary occupation, Levillain was dutiful, like the other scientists and officers, in recording his impressions of the native people he encountered.

Following its explorations of Rottnest Island and the adjacent mainland, the *Naturaliste* sailed north and anchored in Shark Bay, where Levillain again had the opportunity to reflect on the local inhabitants. He described in some detail the abandoned dwellings they found on Peron Peninsula and speculated about the objects that were lying around. During an encounter with some Aborigines, midshipman Brüe attempted to establish contact using a puppet. To his surprise one of the men responded by lunging at his stomach with a firebrand, causing a painful burn. Levillain concluded that either the puppet display had upset the man in some way or else he was just a nasty character.[29]

In terms of natural history, the number and range of specimens Levillain collected in Shark Bay was particularly impressive. These included a yellow and black sea snake which, despite his own skills in taxidermy, he decided to ask the pharmacist François Colas to help him prepare, noting that, 'on your own, it is a considerable amount of work'.[30] Levillain made the most of this prolonged stay in Shark Bay to pack his specimens in crates in order to preserve them for the Museum. He records packing in one large crate a great variety of objects: a dozen white hammer oysters, six or seven types of clam, various colourful bivalves, sponges, land and sea snakes, a large black petrel, four Cape

Petrels, several cormorants, two oyster catchers, various mussels, a large and well-preserved gastropod mollusc commonly known in French as the *couronne d'Éthiopie* (the *Melo aethiopica* or crowned baler), and 'many other species'.[31] Levillain made some quite accomplished sketches of several of these animal specimens, though their value in terms of scientific study is limited because of the lack of anatomical detail.[32] Levillain was not entirely alone in his natural history pursuits. He reserved praise in his journal for his captain, Emmanuel Hamelin, who showed 'the greatest zeal for natural history' and who collected 'two magnificent starfish'.[33] Others on board the *Naturaliste* may also have contributed to the collection. When we consider, however, that the mineralogist Bailly was the only other naturalist on board this ship, the collection compiled by Levillain becomes even more noteworthy. Despite his 'trainee' status, then, there is no doubt that Levillain can be considered to be a scientific voyager – in the mould of the astute traveller-collector that was favoured by Baudin and by leading savants such as Georges Cuvier.

A clear sign of the value of Levillain's collection is provided by Baudin himself. When the expedition arrived in Tasmania following the stopover in Timor and the subsequent death of Levillain, Hamelin sent the young zoologist's collection over to the *Géographe* for safekeeping. Baudin took one look at what was sent over and immediately realised that all the valuable items had been either stolen or sold with Levillain's personal effects after his death. He ordered Hamelin to recover all the specimens, and by the end of the day the collection was duly restored.[34]

Levillain himself would have been quite distressed to know that the results of his hard work had been put in such jeopardy. As his journal reveals, and as Michel Jangoux has observed, Levillain was a highly emotional traveller who was of a naturally melancholy temperament.[35] Despite his enthusiasm for collecting, he frequently found the exploration of western Australia to be a source of gloom and despair. His first impression of New Holland, as the expedition approached Cape Leeuwin, was that it could not possibly be inhabited, given its desolate nature.[36] His description of the coast north of Rottnest Island was equally negative: 'this section of coastline is awful and is as depressing as the coasts we have just visited, nothing but sand dunes and bare ground'.[37]

Several days later the air became heavy and Levillain complained of headaches, which he put down to his state of *ennui*.[38] Having passed the Abrolhos, he once again found the coast to be desolate and arid. The arrival of the *Naturaliste* in Shark Bay did little to lift his spirits. He writes that the sight of Dirk Hartog island, for example:

> produced in my soul a desolation that I cannot express [...]. For more than two leagues inland it is covered in fine white sand with miserable little trees that suffer from want of water and a few plants here and there that are in the same situation. In short it seems as though this island is destined to be eternally deserted.[39]

Levillain does occasionally express his appreciation of the spectacle of nature – in particular the beauty of the sunsets and sunrises – but his overwhelming feeling during his time in western Australia is that of desolation.

One word which occurs with great regularity in Levillain's journal is the adjective 'impatient'. This can be the sign of his enthusiasm or excitement – he is 'impatient' to make landfall, for example, and when they sight land he is 'impatient' to spend some time on shore: 'we are truly impatient to set foot on this land, especially this part of it which, as far as we can tell, has never been visited before'.[40] More often, however, this term is used to express his fear and apprehension regarding the fate of his comrades. When 19 men from the *Géographe* are left stranded on shore in Geographe Bay, Levillain reports that everyone on board the *Naturaliste* was 'highly impatient' to receive news of them; at 9.30 at night they thought they could see some lights heading towards the *Géographe* and were 'highly impatient' to have confirmation of this, but at that very moment they heard 'a loud voice which seemed to emerge from the water' and which made everyone's 'blood turn'. In the event, it was his own ship's jolly boat, which had been sent to help the stranded men and was just returning. This had the effect of jolting them all out of their 'panic and anguish'.[41] Levillain's account of the ensuing exploration of the western Australian coast is punctuated by references to his 'impatience' to be reunited with the *Géographe*, from which the

Naturaliste had become separated during a storm in Geographe Bay. When the *Naturaliste* arrived in Shark Bay and he was sent to Dirk Hartog Island, he soon became 'impatient' to see the boat Hamelin had promised to send two days later to collect him and his companions, as they were not well equipped with supplies, and 'moreover, the fear of a change in the weather made me reflect on the predicament we would be in if we could not get back to the ship'.[42] In circumstances such as these, Levillain was also inclined to implore the intervention of the Almighty. The inclement weather and persistent strong swell near Rottnest Island produced this exasperated outburst: 'We have not had two consecutive days of tranquillity, there is always some new source of trouble. Dear God, watch over us, we have great need of it!'[43] The continued uncertainty regarding the fate of the *Géographe* likewise led him to invoke the Lord: 'Oh God, no news of the *Géographe*. What anxiety consumes us!'[44]

This anxiety is in fact a sign of Levillain's deep sense of attachment to his fellow travellers. It is clear from his journal, and from the few comments others made about him, that Levillain had a great capacity for friendship and was frequently emotional when his comrades were in difficulty. When a rocket signalled that the stranded party in Geographe Bay had been found, he noted that this caused him 'the greatest pleasure – a pleasure which we surely all share; the sentiments of friendship are most keenly felt in such moments of anxiety'.[45] He was yet to learn that the rescue operation had cost the life of a seaman, Timothée Vasse, who was carried off by a wave and was drowned. A loss of another kind produced a particularly heartfelt outpouring of grief. Levillain's emotional investment in his relations with others extended to his dog, Kismy. In Geographe Bay, Levillain obliged Lieutenant Milius by lending him his dog for a shore party, but this decision proved fateful:

> My poor dog Kismy [...], my most faithful friend for whom my attachment is without question, became frightened by the waves and would not let them catch him to put him in the boat. In the end they had to leave him. Alas, I cannot hold back my tears – my old and faithful friend – you have to have had a pet such as this to feel the pain one feels when one is deprived of an animal to which one has become attached!!![46]

It then struck him that the loss of his dog would have grave practical consequences, but he immediately lapsed back into personal lamentations:

> This is a considerable loss in many respects, particularly for zoology, for how can we catch quadrupeds without a dog, how can we retrieve game from the marshes, how can we retrieve one of these birds that fall into the water. Alas, it seems to me that I can hear the plaintive howling and calls of that poor animal. May nature show him the means of existing by hunting for his own account or by seeking to befriend some gentle savage. This poor animal was loved by everyone on board and was so gentle that the entire crew adored him. I can no longer speak of him . . . my eyes are once more filled with tears and I can no longer see to continue writing. This is the first time I've become attached to an animal, and how miserable I now am!!![47]

Little wonder that the visit to Geographe Bay left such bitter memories for him. As he noted on leaving it: 'We have lost in this bay one man [Vasse], one longboat, in equipment three anchors, a dredge and three grapnels, all sorts of weapons – and a dog. It was high time to leave.'[48]

It is difficult to imagine that such an emotional character could go unnoticed on board a ship over an extended period. It is interesting to find, however, that Levillain's travelling companions said little about him in their journals. This might indicate that he kept his emotions to himself and went about his work in a quiet and modest manner. On the other hand, most officers considered their journal a place for noting essential navigational information and few of them devoted much time or space to recounting events of a more personal nature. The botanist Leschenault noted that Levillain was a man of 'excellent company and infinitely gentle manners'.[49] Baudin, who felt the loss of this loyal companion from the *Belle Angélique* voyage very keenly, wrote that he had 'a gentle, affable nature and came from good society'.[50] François Péron, in the official account of the voyage, likewise noted that he 'possessed an extremely gentle, peaceful nature which endeared him to all his companions.'[51] Levillain's own journal suggests that he indeed enjoyed excellent relations with the other expeditioners, his generosity of spirit leading him to consider them all as his friends. Here is what he had to say, for example, about his transfer from the *Géographe* to the *Naturaliste* just before the departure from Mauritius:

> I introduced myself to all the officers of the *Naturaliste* who paid me the most flattering compliments, and I could see that they were sincere (about my arrival on board their ship). From that moment I told myself that I might be leaving friends behind, but I have the hope of making new ones, and that is surely a pleasant and flattering perspective for such a long campaign.[52]

This sense of fraternity and solidarity was no doubt the result of Levillain's naturally friendly and generous disposition, but it is worth remembering that these were also key principles of the recent Revolution, which broke out when Stanislas was at the impressionable age of 15. His voyage with Baudin on the *Belle Angélique* would have reinforced the values of fraternity and cooperation. As demonstrated in a recent study, that expedition was a true republican voyage, both in its conception – the instructions written by Jussieu regarding natural history insisted strongly on the principles of collaboration and equality – and in its conduct – all the naturalists worked side by side, frequently with the captain, as peers with no sense of hierarchy to disturb their relations.[53] Evidence that Levillain had retained this spirit of cooperation and fraternity during the voyage to New Holland can be found in his own journal, where on several occasions he expressed his solidarity, not just with the officers and his scientific colleagues, but with the sailors as well. During the storm in Geographe Bay which separated the two ships, all on board the *Naturaliste* decided to put their shoulder to the wheel and Levillain was full of praise for everyone concerned:

> We owe a tribute of praise to our officers and Captain, all of whom in these difficult circumstances showed the

greatest composure, foresight and courage one could desire. Our position was desperate and critical, almost all the junior officers and the crew were quite anxious, and there was indeed good reason to be concerned. We all worked to manoeuvre the ship, which greatly pleased our sailors.[54]

Levillain again showed his understanding of the feelings and needs of the sailors in Shark Bay when he was being taken back to the ship after spending several days on Dirk Hartog Island: 'they stopped to do some fishing on the way, which greatly tried my patience, given my desire to return on board, but the well-being and health of the crew demanded it. This just consideration therefore comforted me in my impatience.'[55] In similar spirit, he was highly critical of his captain, Hamelin, for making a group of men (which included himself) undertake an arduous hike under the burning sun: 'it is inconceivable that a leader could be so thoughtless'. He was particularly shocked when Hamelin berated a sailor whose injured leg made it impossible for him to keep up: 'That poor wretch was exhausted and could not go on. Well, our unctuous and honey-tongued captain treated him like the lowest of all men, in the most dreadful and cruel manner, because he could not walk.'[56] The sarcasm evident in this comment suggests that Levillain's relationship with Hamelin was far from an easy one. Conversely, his indignant reaction to this incident highlights a deep empathy for his fellow travellers, including the humble sailors. This sense of solidarity was no doubt a manifestation of his generous and emotional nature; the prevailing republican values and his experience on the *Belle Angélique* could only have reinforced in him those inclinations.

What the records reveal, then, is that Levillain performed his duties with great zeal and dedication and made a significant contribution to the scientific results of the Baudin expedition. He may not have had the education of some of the other scientists on board, but his practical experience and commitment put him in the category of those whose endeavours, in Baudin's words, were 'work and not wit', in contrast to the savants, who had a propensity to write long reports that were 'all wit and no work'.[57] As a scientific voyager, Levillain was a dutiful traveller-collector whose efforts significantly enhanced the collections of the Museum. More than this, however, and contrary to the impression we might gain from the lack of commentary on him in the journals of his companions, it is clear that he brought colour and character to the voyage. He displayed in particular a gift for dramatic narrative in his account of the expedition up to the point of his untimely death. He was indeed an emotional traveller who was prone to great highs and lows, but whose sense of camaraderie was unfailing. In true republican spirit, Stanislas Levillain was the quintessential fraternal voyager.

Notes

1   Jean-Baptiste Bory de Saint-Vincent, *Voyage dans les quatre principales îles des mers d'Afrique, fait par ordre du gouvernement, pendant les années neuf et dix de la République (1801 et 1802), avec l'histoire de la traversée du capitaine Baudin jusqu'au Port-Louis de l'Île Maurice*, Paris: Chez F. Buisson, 3 vols, 1804, vol. 1. Bory's life and work more generally have attracted a certain amount of scholarly attention, a recent example being Hervé Ferrière's book-length study deriving from his doctoral thesis, *Bory de Saint-Vincent: L'évolution d'un voyageur naturaliste*, Paris: Éditions Syllepse, 2009. The motivations behind the criticisms of Baudin's leadership contained in Bory's 1804 publication have been discussed at length by scholars of the Baudin expedition. See Frank Horner, *The French Reconnaissance: Baudin in Australia 1801–1803*, Carlton: Melbourne University Press, 1987, pp. 126–128; Jean Fornasiero and John West-Sooby, 'Doing it by the Book: Breaking the Reputation of Nicolas Baudin', in Jean Fornasiero and Colette Mrowa-Hopkins (eds), *Explorations and Encounters in French*, Adelaide: University of Adelaide Press, 2010, pp. 135–164 (see especially pp. 142–145).
2   Stanislas Levillain, 'Descriptions 7 à 13 bis', Muséum d'Histoire naturelle, Le Havre, Collection Lesueur (MHNH CL), dossier 14 040. Unless otherwise indicated, translations of French sources are my own.
3   A point highlighted by Jean Fornasiero in the catalogue she and Vivonne Thwaites produced for the 2010 exhibition 'Littoral' that was shown in Hobart and Burnie. See Jean Fornasiero, 'Charles-Alexandre Lesueur: An Art of the Littoral', in Vivonne Thwaites and Jean Fornasiero (eds), *Littoral*, Adelaide: 5 Star Print, 2010, p. 16. In a letter to his father, Lesueur wrote that one of his duties was to help the commander's secretary (Levillain). Charles-Alexandre Lesueur to his father, 24 April 1801, MHNH CL, dossier 63 016.
4   In recording his death, Péron noted that Maugé's 'character' and 'devotion to the success of the expedition' made him 'universally regretted'. François Péron (continued by Louis Freycinet), *Voyage of Discovery to the Southern Lands*, Adelaide: The Friends of the State Library of South Australia, translation of the second edition (1824) by Christine Cornell, 2 vols, 2006/2003, vol. 1, p. 219.
5   Michel Jangoux, 'L'expédition du capitaine Baudin aux Terres australes: les observations zoologiques de François Péron pendant la première campagne (1801–1802)', *Annales du Muséum du Havre*, vol. 73, 2005, pp. 1–35.
6   Régis Pluchet, 'En marge de l'expédition vers les Terres australes: Un portrait du botaniste André Michaux', in Michel Jangoux (ed.), *Portés par l'air du temps: les voyages du capitaine Baudin*, special number of *Études sur le XVIIIe siècle*, vol. 38, 2010, pp. 187–201. Michaux left the expedition at Mauritius on 20 April 1801, during the outward journey, which explains the marginal status attributed to him in the title of Pluchet's study.

7   Viviane Desmet and Michel Jangoux, 'Un naturaliste aux Terres australes: Jean-Baptiste Leschenault de La Tour (1773–1826)', in Jangoux (ed.), *Portés par l'air du temps*, pp. 225–232. See also Paul Gibbard's chapter in this volume and his on-line essay 'Théodore Leschenault de la Tour, Botanist of the Baudin Expedition', Western Australian Museum web site: http://museum.wa.gov.au/fc/aos/pg, 2016.
8   Dany Bréelle, 'Les géographes de l'expédition Baudin et la reconnaissance des côtes australes', in Jangoux (ed.), *Portés par l'air du temps*, pp. 213–223.
9   Michel Jangoux, 'Les zoologistes et botanistes qui accompagnèrent le capitaine Baudin aux Terres australes', *Australian Journal of French Studies*, vol. 41, no. 2, 2004, pp. 55–78. For a good account of the background of the scientists recruited for the expedition, see Horner, *The French Reconnaissance*, pp. 70–78, and Michel Jangoux, *Le Voyage aux Terres Australes du commandant Nicolas Baudin: Genèse et préambule (1798–1800)*, Paris: Presses de l'Université Paris-Sorbonne, 2013, Chapitre V.
10 Édouard Vuacheux, 'Quelques renseignements sur le voyageur naturaliste Stanislas Levillain (1774–1801)', *Bulletin du Muséum d'Histoire naturelle de Paris*, vol. 11, 1905, pp. 136–138; André Maury, 'Un naturaliste voyageur havrais du 18e siècle, Stanislas Levillain (1774–1801)', *Bulletin de la Société Géologique de Normandie*, vol. 44, 1954, pp. 20–27.
11 Michel Jangoux, *Le Voyage aux Terres Australes*, p. 251.
12 Nicolas Baudin, *Journal du voyage aux Antilles de* La Belle Angélique *(1796–1798)*, édition établie et commentée par Michel Jangoux, Paris: Presses de l'Université Paris-Sorbonne/Académie royale de Belgique, 2009, pp. 298 and 484, respectively.
13 André-Pierre Ledru, *Voyage aux îles de Ténériffe, la Trinité, Saint-Thomas, Sainte-Croix et Porto-Ricco* [sic], *exécuté par ordre du gouvernement français, depuis le 30 septembre 1796 jusqu'au 7 juin 1798, sous la direction du capitaine Baudin, pour faire des recherches et des collections relatives à l'histoire naturelle; . . . par André-Pierre Ledru*, Paris: Arthus Bertrand, 2 vols, 1810, vol. 1, p. 186.
14 Jussieu, Note, Archives Nationales de France (ANF), AJ 15/569, fol. 370. Quoted in Jangoux, *Le Voyage aux Terres Australes*, p. 251.
15 Jussieu to Pierre Forfait (French Minister of Marine and the Colonies), 19 Thermidor Year 8 (7 August 1800), ANF, série Marine BB4 997, (1), 74. Quoted in Frank Horner, *The French Reconnaissance*, p. 73.
16 We know that Baudin would have preferred to limit the scientific staff to just such a small group of experienced collectors for the voyage to the Southern Lands, but the authorities decided otherwise.
17 Levillain, Journal, ANF, série Marine 5JJ 52 (commences on 4 June 1801); Levillain, Journal, Muséum d'Histoire naturelle, Le Havre, Collection Lesueur (MHNH CL), dossier 07 008 (commences on 25 April 1801).
18 Levillain, Journal, MHNH CL, entry dated 15 Floréal Year 9 (5 May 1801).
19 Levillain, Journal, MHNH CL, 24 Floréal Year 9 (14 May 1801).
20 Levillain, Journal, MHNH CL, 1 Prairial Year 9 (21 May 1801).
21 Levillain, Journal, MHNH CL, 7 Prairial Year 9 (27 May 1801).
22 Levillain, Journal, MHNH CL, 11 Prairial Year 9 (31 May 1801).
23 *Ibid.*
24 *Ibid.*
25 Levillain, Journal, MHNH CL, 14 Prairial Year 9 (3 June 1801).
26 Leslie Marchant, *France Australe: A Study of French Explorations and Attempts to Found a Penal Colony and Strategic Base in South Western Australia 1503–1826*, Perth: Artlook, 1982, p. 168.
27 Horner, *The French Reconnaissance*, p. 170. See also Marchant, *France Australe*, p. 169.
28 Levillain, Journal, ANF, 16 Prairial Year 9 (5 June 1801).
29 Levillain, Journal, ANF, 21 Thermidor to 16 Fructidor Year 9 (9 August to 3 September 1801).

30 Levillain, Journal, MHNH CL, 4 Thermidor Year 9 (23 July 1801).
31 Levillain, Journal, MHNH CL, 5 Thermidor Year 9 (24 July 1801).
32 MHNH CL, dossier 07 009. In addition to his natural history drawings, Levillain sketched the French observatory camp in Shark Bay as well as the Aboriginal huts the French found nearby. When considered side by side, these sketches present a poignant contrast.
33 Levillain, Journal, MHNH CL, 5 Thermidor Year 9 (24 July 1801).
34 Baudin to Hamelin: 'I write to tell you that upon making an inventory and general inspection of the objects of curiosity and Natural History collected and assembled by Mr. Levillain, we were most astonished to find nothing but things of little value, very common and worthless. We know, however, that he had a fairly large number of shells, which Citizen Maugé, the zoologist-in-chief, took the trouble to look after and which he put into a separate box in the chest in which there were, and still are, the valueless things that have been left. As the chests were immediately and firmly sealed, there seems to us to be no doubt that since his death, somebody on board has opened them without your knowledge and taken things that belong incontestably to the Government. I ask you, therefore, to make a thorough search to find what is missing and to give me the names of the perpetrators of such an offence.' *The Journal of Post Captain Nicolas Baudin, Commander-in-Chief of the Corvettes* Géographe *and* Naturaliste, translated by Christine Cornell, Adelaide: Libraries Board of South Australia, 1974, p. 330.
35 Jangoux, 'Les zoologistes et botanistes', p. 59.
36 Levillain, Journal, MHNH CL, 9 Prairial Year 9 (29 May 1801).
37 Levillain, Journal, ANF, 9 Messidor Year 9 (28 June 1801).
38 Levillain, Journal, ANF, 16 Messidor Year 9 (5 July 1801).
39 Levillain, Journal, ANF, 2–4 Thermidor Year 9 (21–23 July 1801).
40 Levillain, Journal, MHNH CL, 9 Prairial Year 9 (29 May 1801).
41 Levillain, Journal, MHNH CL, 18 and 19 Prairial Year 9 (7 and 8 June 1801).
42 Levillain, Journal, ANF, 3 Thermidor Year 9 (22 July 1801).
43 Levillain, Journal, ANF, 26 Prairial Year 9 (15 June 1801).
44 Levillain, Journal, ANF, 20 Thermidor Year 9 (8 August 1801).
45 Levillain, Journal, ANF, 18 Prairial Year 9 (7 June 1801).
46 Levillain, Journal, ANF, 19–23 Prairial Year 9 (8–12 June 1801).
47 *Ibid.*
48 *Ibid.* The same comment in the Lesueur Collection manuscript is punctuated with exclamation marks.
49 Théodore Leschenault, Journal, ANF, série Marine, 5JJ 56, p. 130.
50 Baudin, *Journal*, p. 288.
51 Péron, *Voyage of Discovery*, vol. 1, p. 172.
52 Levillain, Journal, MHNH CL, 5 Floréal Year 9 (25 April 1801).
53 See Jean Fornasiero and John West-Sooby, 'Voyages et déplacements des savoirs. Les expéditions de Nicolas Baudin entre Révolution et Empire', *Annales historiques de la Révolution française*, vol. 385, no. 3, 2016, pp. 23–46.
54 Levillain, Journal, ANF, 19–23 Prairial Year 9 (8–12 June 1801).
55 Levillain, Journal, ANF, 4 Thermidor Year 9 (23 July 1801).
56 Levillain, Journal, ANF, 18 Thermidor Year 9 (6 August 1801).
57 Baudin, *Journal*, p. 490.

Chapter 15

Louis Freycinet at Port Jackson: 'Race', Colonialism and the Figure of the French Scientific Traveller, 1802–1839

Nicole Starbuck

The practice of colonial ethnography could brightly illuminate the figure of the scientific traveller. In the field and on the page, it has confronted voyagers such as Nicolas Baudin, François Péron and Louis Freycinet with questions of humanity contextualised directly and deeply in the key, wider elements of scientific voyaging: diplomacy, international politics, colonisation, 'civilisation', and theories and exchanges of knowledge. By comparison with those which occurred 'in nature', colonial encounters were affected more sharply by competing social demands and were more highly and explicitly politicised. This particular type of 'contact zone' could simultaneously highlight key aspects of the scientific traveller's role as well as how those aspects were managed by individual travellers.[1] Would they consider indigenous people who were no longer in a pristine 'state of nature' worthy of ethnographic study? How would they combine observations of the vast array of people who inhabited the colonial space – that is, not only indigenous people, but also colonial authorities, settlers, visiting merchants, whalers and sealers, and perhaps convicts? And to what extent would the colonial context affect their evaluations of 'civilising' potential and 'race'? Their approaches to colonial ethnography revealed much not only about their understanding of human nature but also about who they were as scientific travellers, from the most multi-dimensional perspective.

They also provide prime opportunities for comparison and considerations of change over time, highlighting the contingent nature of voyage ethnography. More so than predominantly indigenous spaces, on which historians of cross-cultural contact and anthropology mainly concentrate,[2] eighteenth- to nineteenth-century colonies were busy global contact zones and regular ports-of-call for scientific travellers. The same voyager might visit one port multiple times over the course of his career and he almost always followed in the footsteps of other scientific voyagers when he stepped ashore there. For example, when they visited and wrote about the British colony of Port Jackson during the early nineteenth century, Baudin, Péron and Louis Freycinet observed the Eora people from diverse perspectives with varied reference to the reports of others and at different stages in the colony's history, from 1802 to 1820. They each mentally removed the garb of 'civilisation' from indigenous bodies and, piece by piece, while considering the fabric and pieces in various lights, put them back to observe how they were worn – where they hung loose, where they clung too tightly, indeed, whether they were worn at all or discarded in disgust. Yet they did so with individual evaluations and varying degrees of attention to each step in the process, to the bodies themselves, and to the various articles of cultural and political dress.

All three sojourned for over five months in colonial Sydney during 1802, midway through Baudin's Australian voyage,[3] and Freycinet returned once more as captain of his own scientific expedition in 1819–1820.[4] In 1839, Freycinet published an extensive, in-depth account of the area's Aboriginal people.[5] Yet, in contrast to the relatively sweeping, brief report produced earlier by Péron and even the unpublished comments by Baudin,[6] Freycinet's contribution to the history of voyage ethnography remains to be explored. Péron's ethnography, published in the official account of the Baudin expedition – the *Voyage de découvertes* – has been credited with playing a significant role in the history of anthropology.[7] Based on strength tests he conducted with a dynamometer as well as other observations concerning physique, character and lifestyle, it is an argument for the superiority of 'civilisation' over the 'natural state'. Colonial spaces played a crucial part in the development of this thesis. Péron concluded that the Aboriginal people of Port Jackson, due to their 15 years in contact with European society, were less 'savage' than the Palawa of Tasmania but markedly more savage than the inhabitants of Timor, which was in its second century of colonisation. This thesis was produced by a scientific traveller keenly engaged in his intellectual and political context. Péron was an ex-soldier of the Revolutionary Wars and a student of Georges Cuvier, professor of comparative anatomy at the Muséum national d'Histoire naturelle and member of the Société des Observateurs de l'Homme. He travelled on the Baudin expedition as a civilian naturalist. If Péron took up the task of publishing and promoting the expedition's results, it was because of a number of factors: the commander himself had passed away, Péron had become the leading naturalist and spokesperson of the expedition, and Napoleon had lost interest in the Australian mission. He finally produced the narrative of the *Voyage*, in 1807, to suit, as Jean-Luc Chappey convincingly argues, the scientific and political climate of the Napoleonic Empire.[8] This representation of the Eora and other indigenous people is a very individual, manufactured work, and is commonly considered a turning point on 'the way to nineteenth-century physical anthropology'.[9] However, its relationship with subsequent French voyage ethnographies and the significance of colonialism to its development remain to be clarified.

In an examination of Péron's work in the context of the emergence of a 'science' of 'race', Bronwen Douglas implies a degree of disconnect between that study published in 1807 and subsequent ethnographies by naval surgeons of the 1820s and 1830s. She points to 'the influx of new empirical knowledge [which] only complicated the difficulties of trying to match received theoretical systems with fleeting observations of baffling human variation or ambiguous affinities and the ambivalent experience of unpredictable local behaviour'.[10] Certainly, the expeditions of Louis de Freycinet (1817–1820), Louis Isidore Duperrey (1822–1825) and Jules Dumont d'Urville (1826–1829 and 1837–1840) encountered a wider range of societies in Oceania than had the Baudin expedition.[11] And the contingent nature of contact experience is always a complicating factor in the production of voyage ethnography.[12] Between any two voyage ethnographers there are also differences in character, education and contemporary politics, culture and science which further blur the boundaries between change and continuity. Yet the application of the figure of the scientific traveller as a frame of analysis, centred on Port Jackson as a common contact zone, does serve to facilitate a comparative study. The legacy of Péron's work in subsequent French voyage ethnographies demands interrogation, for it bears on the significance of that study in the early nineteenth-century history of anthropology while highlighting the role of colonialism – key to Péron's theory as well as other voyagers' ethnographies – in that history.

It is Louis de Freycinet's ethnography, particularly his chapters on the colonial Eora, that provides an apt starting point for such an investigation. True, it was produced by a scientific captain rather than a civilian naturalist like Péron, but that difference is outweighed by other circumstances which tightly draw these travellers' histories together. Freycinet voyaged to Australia with Péron under Baudin (1800–1804). Although he and Péron sailed on different vessels – Freycinet was first-lieutenant aboard the *Naturaliste* then captain of the *Casuarina* while Péron travelled on the *Géographe* – they both spent the winter and spring of 1802 at anchor in Port Jackson. Then back in France, they collaborated to compile the official account of the expedition, with Freycinet publishing the *Navigation et Géographie* volume of the *Voyage de découvertes*.[13] And interestingly, following his own Pacific expedition but before publishing the account of its work, Freycinet produced an edited, second edition of the multi-volume *Voyage de découvertes*.[14] More than any other Pacific voyager, Freycinet had experiences of scientific travel and ethnography that overlapped with those of Péron. He even had privileged insight into Péron's way of thinking about and representing these pursuits, experiences and, specifically, the 'natural history of Man' at Port Jackson.

During his first sojourn in the British colony, with the Baudin expedition, Freycinet made no ethnographic entries in his journal. It was at this point in the voyage that he was transferred from the *Naturaliste* and given command of the *Géographe*'s new consort vessel, the *Casuarina*. His five months at anchor were taken up with preparations for what he called Baudin's 'new voyage'. Under Baudin's guidance, he was now making his transition to becoming a leading figure in scientific travel.[15] Freycinet had joined the French navy as a young adolescent alongside his elder brother Henri in 1793. The boys' aristocratic father had sought to distance them in this way from the violence of the Terror. Although at certain times during the voyage, particularly in its early months, Louis Freycinet had given expression to presumptions of social superiority aboard the

Naturaliste – for example, by demanding a more refined diet for him and his fellow officers than that offered to the crew – he also revealed his republican loyalty when he celebrated France's Fête de la Liberté and attended Freemason meetings in Sydney-Town.[16] By this pivotal point in the voyage and in his career, Freycinet was a self-assured and ambitious scientific traveller – popular among his companions on the expedition, by all reports, as well as with his new acquaintances at Port Jackson, and champing at the bit as Baudin tried to keep a hold on the reins.[17]

The reflective style of Freycinet's ethnographic observations during the first half of the voyage suggests he was a more judicious scientific traveller than he may have seemed at first glance. The Baudin expedition is noted for its exceptional contribution to voyage ethnography. It carried the most specialised directions on anthropological research of any scientific expedition to that point, supplied by the Société des Observateurs de l'Homme.[18] It even carried an 'observer of Man' in François Péron, among an original, unprecedented, tally of 22 natural history staff. In fact, the division of research responsibilities and the share of scientific accountability between naval officers and naturalists was generally unclear. Discord over scientific knowledge on this expedition has been a focus for several scholars.[19] Maritime engineer François-Michel Ronsard, for one, expressed in his journal some contempt for the observations of Péron and his civilian colleagues. 'Nature is so much studied by the educated men', he remarked with some irony, 'the eye of the observer fixes itself with such precision upon each of its secrets that I do not think anything could escape their research'.[20] Yet several of the senior and junior officers regularly recorded their own observations of indigenous life, often in considerable detail. Freycinet, for his own part, described encounters down to the detail of precise movements, responses and spaces. He noted physical features with consideration to culture, and related cultural and social practices to the notion of universal humanity.[21] Moreover, certain comments in his journal suggest a consideration of the territorial rights of those he observed. At Geographe Bay in 1801, he wrote about an Aboriginal man who, at his approach, held his spear aloft and shouted repeatedly 'porai' (water, according to James Cook's vocabulary). It was, Freycinet suggested, 'perhaps a very eloquent speech, no doubt to invite us to return to the water from which we had come and never to settle ourselves upon the land that they inhabited'.[22] Aboard the *Naturaliste*, junior officer Léon Brèvedent shared Freycinet's relatively open-minded approach,[23] but their perspectives stand in contrast to those of their captain, Emmanuel Hamelin – a naval man who regretted on leaving Mauritius that 'the journey [he] was about to commence would take him only to the stupid and thieving inhabitants of New Holland and the South Sea islands'[24] – and of their civilian companion, botanist Théodore Leschenault. Leschenault's journal entries, however, show that he was one of the observers of Man on the expedition who paid the closest attention to indigenous peoples.[25] There is a significant difference even between Louis and his brother, who travelled on the *Géographe*: Henri, for his part, made no ethnographic observations in his journal at all.[26] In contrast, Louis Freycinet clearly saw his role to be not merely that of a naval officer participating in a scientific expedition but also that of a rounded – in the sense of Enlightenment-inspired – scientific voyager.

The matter of Aboriginal 'civilisation' does not feature in Freycinet's Baudin expedition journal, largely because he put his research aside while in the British colony, but it certainly is prominent in the narrative of his later voyage, the *Voyage autour du monde* (1839). Following his account of the *Uranie*'s sojourn at Port Jackson in 1819–1820, Freycinet wrote two separate ethnographic chapters: one entitled 'Concerning the Primitive Peoples of New Holland (at the Time when the English arrived)' and the other 'Present State of the Aboriginal Peoples'. The second of these chapters includes a section entitled 'Digression Concerning the Inhabitants of New Zealand', which looks at Maori who had visited the British at Port Jackson and were experiencing European 'civilising' efforts at home.

Even at that level of overall scope and structure, this approach to the question of 'civilising' processes is markedly different from that taken earlier by Péron in the *Voyage de découvertes*. Péron's single chapter on Man combines observations of people from mainland Australia, Tasmania and Timor, in the course of presenting a specific theory based on an early physical anthropology. It is in the form of a dissertation; in its introduction, for example, he declares: 'Until now [. . .] all means have been lacking to make exact comparisons of the strength of individuals and populations; until now, nobody has carried out a single direct experiment on this subject'.[27] It is by its very nature a comparative piece. In fact, as scholars from George Stocking to Jean Fornasiero and Bronwen Douglas have observed, it is an expression of an emergent nineteenth-century concept of 'race'.[28] 'All of New Holland, from Wilson's Promontory in the south to Cape York in the north', asserts Péron, 'appears to be inhabited by a second race of men, differing essentially from those known up until the present day'.[29] Péron seeks to illustrate this assertion with comparative, physical descriptions of the two Australian 'races'. Of the men of New Holland, for example, he wrote:

> they particularly differ from the latter [the 'Vandiemenites'] in the lighter colour of their skin, the nature of their long, sleek hair and the remarkable shape of their head, which is smaller and somehow flattened towards the crown, whereas that of the Vandiemenites is (by contrast) elongated in the same direction'.[30]

As noted earlier, Péron ranked the people of Tasmania, New Holland, and Timor according to the results of his tests of physical strength, using the dynamometer, from weakest to strongest. The men of New Holland, he concluded, were a little stronger than those of Tasmania, but very much weaker than those of Timor and still far weaker again that those of England or France. His interpretation of these data, taking observations of lifestyle and diet into account, led him to argue that it was the 'wild state in which these people [the Aborigines] still vegetate' that was the 'primary cause of [their] excessive weakness'.[31] 'The advancement of civilisation', he claimed, would 'become the source of both vigour and physical perfection'.[32] Considered in isolation, Péron's dissertation would seem more comparable to the treatise 'On Man' authored by Freycinet's naval surgeons on the *Uranie*, Jean René Quoy and Joseph Paul Gaimard.[33] However, this later work is focused on a particular group of people, the Papuans of the Raja Ampat Archipelago, rather than on comparison of several societies, and it was published in the volume on *Zoologie*, rather than the *Historique* (or narrative) volume of the *Voyage autour du monde*. It was distinctly set apart from the expedition's general ethnographic work and its day-to-day experiences and observations. By contrast, Péron's chapter entitled 'Experiments on the Physical Strength of the Native Peoples of Van Diemen's Land and New Holland and the Inhabitants of Timor' is positioned directly following the chapter devoted to the narration of the Baudin expedition's sojourn in the British colony at Port Jackson. In this narrative space, Péron has inserted a quasi-scientific argument for civilisation; Freycinet, in contrast, following his subsequent visit to the British colony in the *Uranie*, would focus in his account on the effects of colonisation upon Aboriginal life at Port Jackson.

If we look more closely at Freycinet's account of colonisation and the Eora, we see that it bears some similarity in tone to the unpublished observations made by Baudin in 1802. In a letter to Antoine-Laurent de Jussieu, professor of botany at the Muséum national d'Histoire naturelle in Paris, Baudin explained that the English had not yet found a way to keep within the environs of the settlements the Aboriginal people 'who inhabited the land that has been seized'. Most of the Eora, he noted, had 'retreated into the interior to live in their own way'.[34] In a letter to the governor of New South Wales, Philip Gidley King, Baudin criticised the colonists' 'civilising' efforts: he explained that 'the reason they kept their distance from you and your customs stemmed from the idea they formed of the men who sought to live with them'. Baudin added that: 'they could see your plans; however, since they are too weak to resist you, the fear of your weapons has made them leave their land; the hope of seeing them mix with your people is therefore lost and you will soon remain in peaceful possession of their birthright.'[35] Like Freycinet at Geographe Bay during that same expedition, Baudin was acutely conscious of the Aboriginal people's claim to the land. And like Freycinet in his later *Uranie* voyage account, when he contemplated the question of the 'progress' made by the Eora since colonisation, he looked more to the nature of this colonial project itself than to the nature of this people's humanity. Granted, we do not know what type of colonial ethnography Baudin would have published if he had had the chance; still, it is clear that both men were scientific travellers of the type whose ethnographic gaze within the colonial field was relatively widened, driven by general curiosity, and contextualised in the immediate geopolitical interest as well as, at times, scientific or philosophical theory.

In fact, Freycinet introduced his chapter on the 'present state of the Aboriginal peoples' with a question concerning, not stadial theory in general, but the specific circumstance at hand: 'It seems strange to an observer to see that the natives of the south-east part of New Holland live today in a state that is no less barbarous than it was when Europeans landed on these shores for the first time [. . .]. What possible cause could there have been for such singular stability?' He presented two possible answers: 'Is it because the Australian races refuse all social advancement? Or must we, rather, limit ourselves to the notion that effective methods of civilising them were not employed?'[36] Like Baudin, Freycinet was not necessarily opposed to colonisation. But his broader critique took in the process itself as well as the people. And in regard to the people, it focused more on their experience than on their supposed physical, moral or intellectual characteristics. 'The invasion of their soil', Freycinet declared, 'immediately destroyed a most essential part of the means of livelihood of these poor folk'. Moreover, he reflected, 'it could even be said that the fundamental principles of human rights, that in other parts of the world are so vigorously invoked and respected, were, in this place, completely ignored and unscrupulously violated'.[37] That said, Freycinet greatly admired the 'special institution for [. . .] educating and civilising' Aboriginal children which was established by Governor Lachlan Macquarie in 1814.[38] The only reason he believed it failed in the end was because, with Macquarie's retirement from the position of governor of the colony and protector of the institution, the financial and material support fell away.[39] In regard to the students who fled the school and returned to their communities, Freycinet wrote of their 'great love' for 'their own bush-land, for their countrymen, and for their relatives'; they were 'in no way inferior to any of their fellow pupils'. Moreover, he pointed out, the children's parents had encouraged them to leave, and he was 'convinced that not a single pupil would remain in such schools at the end of a fortnight' given such circumstances.[40] A strong sense of cultural relativity underlies this ambiguous yet relatively open-minded view of the 'civilising mission'. And in this, Freycinet's perspective is similar to that of Baudin. In his letter to Governor King, where he pointed to their aversion to colonial society, Baudin remarked that the Aboriginal people of Port Jackson were 'no more uncivilised than your present-day Scottish Highlanders or our peasants of Lower Brittany'.⁴¹ Péron's mind, when he composed his ethnography for the *Voyage de découvertes*, was evidently on the prospects of his own career above all. Yet, for both Freycinet and Baudin, the consideration of human progress in this British colony particularly called to mind comparable circumstances and concerns at home in France and in its empire.

Freycinet's study of the Eora was less tied to observations of bodies, and more concerned about culture, human rights and emotions, than Péron's had been, but the commander did value the observation of physical features. Freycinet himself wrote the ethnographic instructions for his expedition, and there he included 50 questions relating to 'physical constitution'. The expedition's research in this area was to be thorough, involving the collection of data on a variety of physical characteristics: cranial dimensions and facial angles; fertility; childbirth and ageing; disease; and strength. Freycinet instructed his men to use a dynamometer, though, only to test whether they could use the instrument on their subjects, and if so, just to 'record' rather than to analyse the results.⁴² The results were presented in a table and published in the chapter concerning the 'Primitive Peoples' of New Holland,⁴³ but Freycinet treated them rather dismissively. The dynamometer, he noted, 'which recently enabled Péron to present novel and interesting facts concerning the relative strength of different primitive peoples, was used by Gaimard to continue this series of important experiments'. Asserting that 'there is no need to dwell further on such a simple matter', he invited readers to draw their own conclusions from the results.⁴⁴ In fact, this attitude was evidently shared by the surgeon-naturalists Quoy and Gaimard. In their chapter 'On Man' in the *Zoologie* volume, which was based largely on emergent physical anthropology, they made no mention of the strength tests. Like those conducted by subsequent French scientific voyagers as well as sedentary scientists in Paris, the physical analyses Quoy and Gaimard undertook were focused mainly on cranial measurements, which was an aspect of anthropological study that Péron himself had not engaged in. In fact, their collection of bodily measurements more closely resembles that made by Alexandre d'Hesmivy d'Auribeau during the d'Entrecasteaux expedition's 1793 visit to Tasmania.⁴⁵ Moreover, Freycinet's *Voyage autour du monde*, in relation to the indigenous people of Port Jackson and elsewhere in Oceania, generally concentrates on skin colour, hair and bodily proportions when it comes to the physical.[46] The descriptions are typically brief, include attention to variability as well as to natural/unnatural features, and are not linked to moral character or intellectual capacity. Freycinet summarised what he perceived to be the most common physique, with an eye for proportion and muscularity, in accordance with the European ideal. The proportions of the Aborigines of Port Jackson, he wrote, were 'chiefly characterised by largeness of the head, lack of prominence of body muscle, and above all, inconceivably skinny arms, thighs and calves'; however, he added, there were exceptions.[47] He found the hair type of individuals to be fairly consistent in this region: 'invariably black, smooth although wavy'.[48] Yet their skin colour, he observed, varied considerably, 'from light-black to reddish-black and there are many slight variations in tint'. Furthermore, Freycinet also pointed out that their skin colour darkens from childhood to adulthood, which 'is not in any way the result of any one particular act, nor of their dirty living conditions; it springs from a cause that is entirely natural'.[49] These descriptions were far more detailed and nuanced than Péron's had been. In accordance with the purpose of the treatise, the latter were given in a sweeping style (quoted earlier) in order briefly to compare the Aboriginal people of New Holland, taken all together, to those of Tasmania and the people of Timor.[50] That said, in his table of strength-test results, Péron did give a brief description of each individual tested. His purpose there was apparently to imply a link between their 'fierce' or 'savage' state and his claims about their relative physical weakness, for he described several of the men in corresponding terms: 'fierce face', 'hard, fierce features', 'fierce treacherous face', even 'ferocious man'.[51] Remarkably, even though this work directly preceded Freycinet's in the genre of French voyage ethnography on Port Jackson's indigenous people, and despite Freycinet having actually worked both alongside Péron and on the text of the *Voyage de découvertes*, of all the existing publications Freycinet drew upon in relation to this subject, it is Péron's to which he referred the most fleetingly.

The Freycinet expedition's physical descriptions did not venture to a ranking of perceived races, as Péron's analysis closely bordered upon doing. In the early nineteenth century, the modern, supposedly scientific notion of 'race' was still emerging. Polygenist theories were gaining ground but the point of view propounded by the leading thinker in the field, Georges Cuvier, was most representative of the time. In 1817, the same year that the *Uranie* set sail, he wrote: 'Although the human species seems to be unique [...] one notes within it certain hereditary physical features that constitute what we name "races".'[52] The *Voyage autour du monde*, in regard to the people of Port Jackson and elsewhere, presented an ambiguous concept of 'race': one that blurred perceptions of origins, biological and geographic, and of class. Moreover, the term 'race' itself was applied by Freycinet no more frequently than it had been by Péron and still generally in the Enlightenment-era sense of 'varieties'.[53] In his chapter on the 'primitive' – that is, pre-colonial – people of Port Jackson, Freycinet declared that there was 'one single race of Aborigines who everywhere [in Australia] exhibited identical physical and moral characteristics'. He also referred to the Australian Aboriginal people as the 'same *type* of human being', though later seemed to contradict himself when he wrote of the Australian 'races', in the plural.[54] Indeed, Freycinet's discussion of the degrees of similarity and variation among this population did not include categorisation, by comparison to other human groups, nor claims about innate or fixed traits. Like the work produced by Péron, the physical data his men gathered would go toward the development of biological thought about racial difference, which in turn contributed to French colonising projects in Oceania later in the nineteenth century,[55] but the expedition's treatment of race in regard to the Eora was actually less racialist than Péron's. Péron had speculated about these peoples' potential to improve their condition by eventually taking up 'civilised' practices of farming and fixed habitation, but he did so only in an abstract, imaginative, sense. 'Let us suppose for a moment that these deprived children of nature should happen to abandon their fierce, vagabond ways', he declared.[56] Freycinet, for his own part, implied that they had 'civilising' potential due to their intellectual and moral capacities which, he assumed, could be applied to the purpose under suitable European guidance.[57] The commander's ethnography was more engaged in this particular colonial context.

Péron's ethnographic legacy did not have a strong impact on

Freycinet's voyage. In fact, despite the common ground of their beginnings in maritime exploration, Péron and Louis Freycinet each cut quite a different figure as a scientific traveller. Even when they were together on the Baudin expedition, their perspectives on human diversity were markedly different; and, by the time Freycinet led his own ethnographic project 15 years later, they had evidently not grown any closer. By bringing questions of progress, diversity, and colonialism to the fore, and providing an international theatre,[58] the Port Jackson sojourns pushed each man to take a stand as to what type of voyager they were, including, correspondingly, how they understood the study of human nature. While Péron turned from a Rousseauesque belief in the 'noble savage' to faith in the superiority of European society, Freycinet expanded on his notions of human rights and universalism. Moreover, Freycinet's expedition was more strongly influenced by the methods and theories of early physical anthropology, and put them more thoroughly into practice than did Baudin's, yet still gave markedly less value to strength testing. As a scientific traveller himself, Louis Freycinet observed the natural history of Man in a manner far more akin to that of Baudin than to that of Péron. He presented himself, through the expedition's official Port Jackson ethnography, as a reflective French voyager concerned with the nature of humanity in the context of contemporary concerns about civilisation and rights; Péron, for his part, published his ethnographic work within frames of civilisation and power. Indeed, while Péron believed above all that 'natives' *should* be civilised, Freycinet believed they *could* be civilised, and focused on how this might most realistically be achieved.

Notes

1 Mary Louise Pratt, *Imperial Eyes: Travel Writing and Transculturation*, London: Routledge, 1992.
2 See leading historians on French voyage ethnography such as Bronwen Douglas, *Science, Voyages, and Encounters in Oceania, 1511–1850*, Basingstoke: Palgrave, 2014; Jean Fornasiero, 'Deux observateurs de l'homme aux antipodes: Nicolas Baudin et François Péron', Michel Jangoux (ed.), *Portés par l'air du temps: les voyages du capitaine Baudin*, special number of *Études sur le XVIIIe siècle*, vol. 38, 2010, pp. 157–170; Jean Fornasiero and John West-Sooby, 'Cross-cultural Inquiry in 1802: Musical Performance on the Baudin Expedition to Australia', in Kate Darian Smith and Penny Edmonds (eds), *Conciliation on Colonial Frontiers: Conflict, Performance, and Commemoration in Australia and the Pacific Rim*, Abingdon: Routledge, 2015, pp. 17–35; Shino Konishi, *The Aboriginal Male in the Enlightenment World*, London: Pickering and Chatto, 2012; Nicole Starbuck,

'Neither Civilized nor Savage: The Aborigines of Colonial Port Jackson, Through French Eyes, 1802', in Shino Konishi, Alex Cook and Nick Curthoys (eds), *Representing Humanity in the Age of Enlightenment*, London: Pickering and Chatto, 2013, pp. 123–133; Nicole Starbuck, '"Primitive Race", "Pure Race", "Brown Race", "Every Race": Freycinet's Understanding of Human Difference in Oceania', in John West-Sooby (ed.), *Discovery and Empire: the French in the South Seas*, Adelaide: University of Adelaide Press, 2013, pp. 215–244; and Nicole Starbuck, '"Naturally Fearful": Emotion, Race and French–Papuan Encounters, 1818–1830', *The Journal of Pacific History*, vol. 51, no. 4, 2016, pp. 357–374.

3 See Nicole Starbuck, *Baudin, Napoleon and the Exploration of Australia*, London: Routledge, 2013.

4 See Nicole Starbuck, 'Freycinet's Understanding of Human Difference'; Nicole Starbuck, '"Naturally Fearful"'; Nicole Starbuck, '"Race", intimacy and go-betweens in French–West Papuan Encounters', in Tiffany Shellam, Maria Nugent, Shino Konishi and Allison Cadzow (eds), *Brokers and Boundaries: Colonial Exploration in Indigenous Territory*, Canberra: ANU Press, 2016, pp. 38–60; Bronwen Douglas, 'Expeditions, Encounters and the Praxis of Seaborne Ethnography: The French Voyages of La Pérouse and Freycinet', in Martin Thomas (ed.), *Expedition into Empire: Exploratory Journeys and the Making of the Modern World*, Abingdon: Routledge, 2015, pp. 108–126; Bronwen Douglas, 'L'Idée de "Race" et l'expérience sur le terrain au XIXe siècle: science, action indigène et vacillations d'un naturaliste français en Océanie', *Revue d'Histoire des Sciences Humaines*, no. 21, 2009, pp. 175–209.

5 Louis de Freycinet, *Voyage autour du monde: entrepris par ordre du Roi [...] exécuté sur les corvettes de S. M. l'*Uranie *et la* Physicienne, *pendant les années 1817, 1818, 1819 et 1820, Historique*, Paris: Pillet Aîné, 8 vols, 1824–1844, vol. 2, partie II, 1839, pp. 704–795; Louis de Freycinet, *Reflections on New South Wales, 1788–1839*, translated by Thomas Cullity, Potts Point: Hordern House, 2001.

6 George Stocking Jr., 'French Anthropology in 1800', *Isis*, vol. 55, no. 2, 1964, pp. 134–150; Miranda Hughes, 'Philosophical Travellers at the End of the Earth: Baudin, Péron and the Tasmanians', in R.W. Home (ed.), *Australian Science in the Making*, Cambridge: Cambridge University Press, 1988, pp. 23–44; Stephanie Anderson, 'French Anthropology in Australia: The First Fieldwork Report: François Péron's "Maria Island: Anthropological Observations"', *Aboriginal History*, vol. 25, 2001, pp. 228–242; Bronwen Douglas, 'Slippery Word, Ambiguous Praxis: "Race" and Late-18th-Century Voyagers in Oceania', *Journal of Pacific History*, vol. 41, no. 1, 2006, pp. 23–24; Bronwen Douglas, '"Novus Orbis Australis": Oceania in the Science of Race', in Bronwen Douglas and Chris Ballard (eds), *Foreign Bodies: Oceania and the Science of Race (1750–1940)*, Canberra: ANU Press, 2008, pp. 99–155; Fornasiero, 'Deux observateurs de l'homme'; Konishi, *The Aboriginal Male*.

7 François Péron, *Voyage de découvertes aux Terres Australes, exécuté par ordre de Sa Majesté l'Empereur et Roi, sur les corvettes le* Géographe *et le* Naturaliste *et la goëlette le* Casuarina *pendant les années 1800, 1801, 1802, 1803, et 1804, Historique*, vol. 1, Paris: Imprimerie impériale, 1807, pp. 446–484. English translation: François Péron (continued by Louis Freycinet), *Voyage of Discovery to the Southern Lands*, Adelaide: The Friends of the State Library of South Australia, translation of the second edition (1824) by Christine Cornell, 2 vols, 2006/2003, vol. 1, pp. 351–385.

8 Jean-Luc Chappey, 'François Péron et la question de la civilisation aux antipodes', *Annales historiques de la Revolution française*, vol. 375, no. 1, 2014, pp. 139–159.

9 Carol E. Harrison, 'Replotting the Ethnographic Romance: Revolutionary Frenchmen in the Pacific, 1768–1804', *Journal of the History of Sexuality*, vol. 21, no. 1, 2012, p. 59.

10 Douglas, '"Novus Orbis Australis"', p. 116.

11 The Freycinet expedition visited, in Oceania, Western Australia, Timor, the Raja Ampat Archipelago, the Caroline Islands, the Marianna Islands, Hawaii and New

South Wales. The Baudin expedition visited Timor and explored the west, south and south-east of Australia as well as Tasmania.

12 See, for example: Konishi, *The Aboriginal Male*; Douglas, *Science, Voyages, and Encounters*; Nicole Starbuck, 'Ritual Encounters of the "Savage" and the Citizen: French Revolutionary Ethnographers in Oceania, 1768–1803', in Meridee Bailey and Katie Barclay (eds), *Emotion, Ritual and Power in Europe, 1200–1920*, Basingstoke: Palgrave, 2017, pp. 123–144; and Starbuck, '"Naturally Fearful"'.

13 Louis Freycinet, *Voyage de découvertes aux Terres Australes, exécuté sur les corvettes le* Géographe, *le* Naturaliste, *et la goëlette le* Casuarina, *pendant les années 1800, 1801, 1802, 1803 et 1804, sous le commandement du Capitaine de vaisseau N. Baudin, Navigation et Géographie*, Paris: Imprimerie Royale, 1815.

14 François Péron (continued by Louis de Freycinet), *Voyage de découvertes aux Terres australes, fait par ordre du gouvernement, sur les corvettes le* Géographe, *le* Naturaliste, *et la goëlette le* Casuarina, *pendant les années 1800, 1801, 1802, 1803 et 1804, rédigé par Péron, et continué par M. Louis de Freycinet, Seconde édition revue, corrigée et augmentée par M. Louis de Freycinet*, Paris: Arthus Bertrand, 4 vols and Atlas, 1824.

15 See Starbuck, *Baudin, Napoleon and the Exploration of Australia*, pp. 125–136.

16 *Ibid.*, p. 72.

17 *Ibid.*, pp. 125–136.

18 Joseph-Marie Degérando, 'Considérations sur les diverses méthodes à suivre dans l'observation des peuples sauvages', and Georges Cuvier, 'Note instructive sur les recherches à faire relativement aux différences anatomiques des diverses races d'hommes', both reproduced in Jean Copans and Jean Jamin (eds), *Aux origines de l'anthropologie française: les mémoires de la Société des Observateurs de l'Homme en l'an VIII*, Paris: Le Sycamore, 1978, pp. 127–169 and 171–176 respectively. A text by Louis-Jacques Moreau de la Sarthe, previously attributed to Louis-François Jauffret, was also included in these instructions as 'Mémoire sur l'établissement d'un Muséum anthropologique', in Copans and Jamin, *Aux origines*, pp. 187–194. This latter text was published in English translation as 'Considerations to serve in the choice of objects that may assist in the formation of the special museum of the *Société des Observateurs de l'Homme*, requested of the Society by Captain Baudin', in N. Baudin, *The Journal of Post Captain Nicolas Baudin, Commander-in-Chief of the Corvettes* Géographe *and* Naturaliste, translated by Christine Cornell, Adelaide: Libraries Board of South Australia, 1974, pp. 594–596.

19 See, for example, Jean Fornasiero, Peter Monteath and John West-Sooby, *Encountering Terra Australis: The Australian Voyages of Nicolas Baudin and Matthew Flinders*, Kent Town: Wakefield Press, 2004, and Carol E. Harrison, 'Projections of the Revolutionary Nation: French Expeditions in the Pacific, 1791–1803', *Osiris*, vol. 24, no. 1, 2009, pp. 33–52.

20 François-Michel Ronsard, Journal, Archives Nationales de France (ANF), série Marine, 5JJ 28, p. 49.

21 Of a man encountered in south-east Tasmania he wrote: 'This man's ridiculous hairstyle was really laughable. However I noted a strange parallel between him and our "elegant gentlemen" in France who, after having rubbed their heads with a little fat, cover it with flour. On this point there is really little difference between a civilised people and one that is as little civilised as the inhabitants of Van Diemen's Land appear to be. Some might perhaps draw the conclusion that the custom of covering one's head with a little dust is one of the most natural, perhaps even the oldest custom there is.' Louis Freycinet, Journal, ANF, série Marine 5JJ 50, entry dated 24 Nivôse Year 10 (14 January 1802).

22 Louis Freycinet, Journal, ANF, série Marine 5JJ 49, 16 Prairial Year 9 (5 June 1801).

23 Léon Brèvedent, Journal, ANF, série Marine 5JJ 56, 25 Nivôse Year 10 (15 January 1802).

24 Emmanuel Hamelin, Journal, ANF, série Marine, 5JJ 41, 5–6 Floréal Year 9 (25–

26 April 1801).
25 Leschenault, Journal, ANF, série Marine, 5JJ 56.
26 See Henri Freycinet, Journal, ANF, série Marine, 5JJ 34.
27 Péron, *Voyage of Discovery*, vol. 1, p. 352.
28 Fornasiero, 'Deux observateurs de l'homme', pp. 164–165.
29 Péron, *Voyage of Discovery*, vol. 1, 354.
30 *Ibid.*
31 *Ibid.*, p. 369.
32 *Ibid.*, pp. 369–370.
33 Jean René Constant Quoy and Joseph Paul Gaimard, 'De l'homme: observations sur la constitution physique des Papous', in Louis de Freycinet, *Voyage autour du monde, entrepris par ordre du Roi [. . .] exécuté sur les corvettes de S.M. l'Uranie et la Physicienne, pendant les années 1817, 1818, 1819 et 1820*, vol. 2, *Zoologie*, Paris: Pillet Aîné, 1824, pp. 1–11.
34 Nicolas Baudin to Antoine-Laurent de Jussieu, Port Jackson, 20 Brumaire Year 11 (11 November 1802), Museum national d'Histoire naturelle, Bibliothèque Centrale, ms 2082, pièce no. 5.
35 Jean Fornasiero (ed. and trans.), *Reflections of a Philosophical Voyager: Nicolas Baudin to Philip Gidley King, 24 December 1802*, Adelaide: Friends of the State Library of South Australia, 2016, pp. 22–23.
36 Freycinet, *Reflections on New South Wales*, p. 295.
37 *Ibid.*, p. 296.
38 *Ibid.*, pp. 296–297.
39 *Ibid.*, pp. 297–298.
40 *Ibid.*, p. 300.
41 Fornasiero, *Reflections of a Philosophical Voyager*, p. 21.
42 L. Freycinet, 'Copie de la lettre ecrite a Mssr. les officiers militaires, officiers de sante, eleves de la marine et autres personnes appartenant a l'etat major de la Corvette l'*Uranie*, par le Commandant de l'expedition', reproduced in Louis Raillard, Journal, ANF, série Marine, 5JJ 68.
43 Freycinet, *Reflections on New South Wales*, p. 115.
44 *Ibid.*, p. 114.
45 Alexandre d'Hesmivy d'Auribeau, Journal de mer, ANF, série Marine, 5JJ 6. English translation in N.J.B. (Brian) Plomley and Josiane Piard-Bernier, *The General: The Visits of the Expedition led by Bruny d'Entrecasteaux to Tasmanian waters in 1792 and 1793*, Launceston: Queen Victoria Museum, 1993, p. 283.
46 Freycinet, *Reflections on New South Wales*, pp. 106–114. See also, Starbuck, 'Freycinet's Understanding of Human Difference', pp. 215–244.
47 Freycinet, *Reflections on New South Wales*, pp.106–108.
48 *Ibid.*, pp. 111-112.
49 *Ibid.*, pp. 108-111.
50 Péron, *Voyage of Discovery*, vol. 1, p. 354.
51 *Ibid.*, p. 375.
52 Georges Cuvier, *Le Règne animal distribué d'après son organisation: pour servir de base à l'histoire naturelle des animaux et d'introduction à l'anatomie comparée*, Paris: A. Belin, 1817, 4 vols, vol. 1, p. 94.
53 Starbuck, 'Freycinet's Understanding of Human Difference', p. 222.
54 Freycinet, *Reflections on New South Wales*, p. 103, and Starbuck, 'Freycinet's Understanding of Human Difference', p. 224.
55 Martin Staum, 'The Paris Geographical Society Constructs the Other, 1821–1850', *Journal of Historical Geography*, vol. 26, no. 2, 2000, pp. 222–238.
56 Péron, *Voyage of Discovery*, vol. 1, p. 367.
57 Freycinet, *Reflections on New South Wales*, p. 299.
58 Greg Dening, *Performances*, Carlton: Melbourne University Press, 1996, pp. 103–127.

Bibliography

Archival Sources

—— Minutes (*procès-verbaux*) of the committee meetings of the professors of the Muséum national d'Histoire naturelle, Archives Nationales de France, série Muséum, AJ 15.
—— Documentation relating to the payment of Théodore Leschenault, Archives Nationales de France, série F, Versements des ministères et des administrations qui en dépendent, F 17/3979, dossiers 2 and 14.
—— Correspondence of Constance de Salm, Bibliothèque de la Société des Amis du Vieux Toulon et de sa Région, Fonds Salm.
—— Emmanuel Hamelin, Dossier personnel, Service Historique de la Défense, Archives de la Marine à Vincennes, CC^7 Alpha 1146/22.
—— Copie de l'extrait du registre des délibérations de l'Assemblée administrative des professeurs du Muséum d'Histoire naturelle. Séance du 14 octobre 1807, Archives Nationales de France, AF IV/953, dossier 190.
Anon., Letter to the Minister of the Interior (Jean-Pierre de Montalivet), 21 January 1811, Archives Nationales de France, série F, demandes de places, de secours et de pension, F 1dII/P/5 – Dossier Péron.
Bailly, Charles, 'Copie d'une lettre adressée au C. Grégoire', *La Décade philosophique*, IVe trim., Messidor–Fructidor Year 11 (June–September 1803), pp. 120–121; *Le Moniteur Universel*, 22 Messidor Year 11 (11 July 1803).
Baudin, Nicolas, Journal de mer, Archives Nationales de France, série Marine, 5JJ 36–39 and 40^A.
Baudin, Nicolas, Journal ('Journal personnel' or 'Fair Copy'), Archives Nationales de France, série Marine, 5JJ 35, 40^B, 40^C, 40^D.
Baudin, Nicolas, Letter to François Péron, 12 Messidor Year X (1 July 1802), Muséum d'Histoire naturelle, Le Havre, Collection Lesueur, 63 018.
Baudin, Nicolas, Letter to Citoyen Jussieu from Port Jackson, 20 Brumaire Year 11 (11 November 1802), Muséum national d'Histoire naturelle, Bibliothèque centrale, ms 2082, pièce no. 5.
Baudin, Nicolas, Letter to the Minister of Marine, dated 20 Brumaire Year 11 (11 November 1802), Service Historique de la Défense, Archives de la Marine à Vincennes, BB4 995.
Baudin, Nicolas, Letter to the Minister of Marine, Service Historique de la Défense, Archives de la Marine à Vincennes, série Marine, BB4 999.
Baudin, Nicolas, 'État général des objets [...] embarqués sur *Le Naturaliste* [...]', Service Historique de la Défense, Archives de la Marine à Vincennes, BB4 997, folio 143.
Bernier, Pierre-François, Journal, Archives Nationales de France, série Marine, 5JJ 24.
Besson, Alexandre-Charles, 'Observations sur le choix des minéralogistes et leurs recherches pendant le voyage projetté pour la recherche de M. de la Peyrouse, lues à la Société des naturalistes de Paris le 18 fevrier 1791 par M. Besson Sous Inspecteur des Mines et de la Société', Muséum national d'Histoire naturelle, ms 46 (dossier IV).
Breton, François-Désiré, Journal, Archives Nationales de France, série Marine, 5JJ 57.
Brèvedent, Léon, Journal, Archives Nationales de France, série Marine, 5JJ 56.
Crétet, Emmanuel, 'Rapport à Sa Majesté l'empereur et roi', 9 March 1808, Archives Nationales de France, AF IV/956, dossier 56.
Decrès, Denis, Letter to François Étienne de Rosily, Archives Nationales de France, série

Marine, 5JJ 24.
Decrès, Denis, Letter to Charles-Pierre Claret de Fleurieu, Archives Nationales de France, série Marine, 5JJ 24.
Dolomieu, Déodat, 'Notes communicated to the Naturalists [on the] voyage to the South Sea [. . .]', 29 July 1791, Service Historique de la Défense, Vincennes, série Marine, BB4 993.
d'Entrecasteaux, Antoine Raymond Joseph de Bruni, Letter to the Minister of Marine, 13 February 1792, Archives Nationales de France, série Marine, 5JJ 6A.
Fleurieu, Charles-Pierre Claret de, Letter to the Maritime Prefect of Le Havre, Service Historique de la Défense, Vincennes, série Marine, BB2 84, folio 125.
Freycinet, Henri, Journal, Archives Nationales de France, série Marine, 5JJ 34.
Freycinet, Louis, Journal (Baudin expedition), Archives Nationales de France, série Marine, 5JJ 49.
Gicquel, Pierre, Journal, Archives Nationales de France, série Marine, 5JJ 55.
Hamelin, Emmanuel, Journal, Archives Nationales de France, série Marine, 5JJ 41, 42.
Hamelin, Emmanuel, Letter to Baudin, 19 Pluviôse Year 11 (8 February 1803), Service Historique de la Défense, Vincennes, série Marine, BB4 995, folio 363.
Hamelin, Emmanuel, Report addressed to Bertin, Maritime Prefect of Le Havre, Service Historique de la Défense, Vincennes, série Marine, BB4 995, folio 355.
Hamelin, Emmanuel, Lettres, journaux et papiers, Archives Nationales de France, série Marine, 5JJ 24.
Heirisson, François, Journal, Archives Nationales de France, série Marine, 5JJ 56.
d'Hesmivy d'Auribeau, Journal de mer, Archives Nationales de France, série Marine, 5JJ 6.
Jussieu, Antoine-Laurent de, Letter to the Minister of Marine, 3 Fructidor Year IV (20 August 1796), Archives Nationales de France, série Marine, BB4 995, fol. 253 sq.
Jussieu, Antoine-Laurent de, 'Instructions', 28 Fructidor Year IV (14 September 1796), Archives Nationales de France, série Marine, BB4 995.
Ledru, André-Pierre, Letter to Antoine-Laurent de Jussieu, 4 Vendémiaire Year V (25 September 1796), Archives Nationales de France, série Muséum, AJ 15/569, fol. 40.
Leschenault de la Tour, Jean Baptiste Louis Claude Théodore, Journal, Archives Nationales de France, série Marine, 5JJ 56.
Leschenault de la Tour, Jean Baptiste Louis Claude Théodore, Letter to the Ministry of the Interior, 27 August 1807, Archives Nationales de France, série F, Versements des ministères et des administrations qui en dépendent, AF/F/1d II/L/16.
Leschenault de la Tour, Jean Baptiste Louis Claude Théodore, Letter to Jean-Baptiste-Antoine Leschenault du Villard, 2 September 1807, private collection.
Leschenault de la Tour, Jean Baptiste Louis Claude Théodore, Letter to Antoine-Laurent de Jussieu, 1 June 1809, Muséum national d'Histoire naturelle, Paris, Fonds Jussieu, ms Per. K130 (6).
Lesueur, Charles-Alexandre to his father, 24 April 1801, Muséum d'Histoire naturelle, Le Havre, Collection Lesueur, 63 016.
Levillain, Stanislas, Journal, Archives Nationales de France, série Marine, 5JJ 52.
Levillain, Stanislas, Journal, Muséum d'Histoire naturelle, Le Havre, Collection Lesueur, 07 008.
Levillain, Stanislas, 'Descriptions 7 à 13 bis', Muséum d'Histoire naturelle, Le Havre, Collection Lesueur, 14 040.
Ministry of Marine, 'Mémoire pour La Pérouse', Services Historiques de la Défense, Vincennes, série Marine, BB4 992.
Péron, François, Notes and papers, Muséum d'Histoire naturelle, Le Havre, Collection Lesueur, dossiers 07, 09, 12, 14, 19, 21, 22, 65, 79.
Péron, François, Report to Governor Decaen, 20 Frimaire Year XII (12 December 1803), Bibliothèque Municipale de Caen, Papiers Decaen, tome 92. Transcript held in the National Library of Australia, Hélouis transcripts, MS 11/4, File 28, item 2.

Péron, François, 'Mémoire sur les établissements anglais à la Nouvelle-Hollande, à la terre de Diémen et dans les archipels du grand océan Pacifique, Au citoyen Fourcroy, Membre du Conseil d'État', Muséum d'Histoire naturelle, Le Havre, Collection Lesueur, dossier 12.
Pinel, Philippe,'Sur les progrès que la zoologie attend des voyages de long cours', Services Historiques de la Défense, Vincennes, série Marine, BB4 993.
Raillard, Louis, Journal, Archives Nationales de France, série Marine, 5JJ 68.
Reinaud, Report to Denis Decrès, Service Historique de la Défense, Vincennes, série Marine, BB4 995.
Richard, Louis Claude, 'Adresse à la Société d'histoire naturelle de Paris au sujet de l'expédition à la recherche de la Peyrouse, par Richard (17 janvier 1791)', Muséum national d'Histoire naturelle, ms 46 (dossier I).
Riche, Claude-Antoine-Gaspard, Letter to Bruny d'Entrecasteaux, 29 July 1792, Archives Nationales de France, série Marine, 5JJ 6A.
Ronsard, François Michel, Journal, Archives Nationales de France, série Marine, 5JJ 28.
Saint-Cricq, Jacques de, Journal, Archives Nationales de France, série Marine, 5JJ 58.

Printed Sources

—— *Fastes de la Légion-d'Honneur*, Paris: Au bureau de l'administration, vol. 5, 1847.
Anon., 'Émile Guillaumin, *François Péron*', *Bulletin de la Société d'Émulation du Bourbonnais*, vol. 39, 1936, p. 112 (book review).
Alard, Marie Joseph Louis, *Éloge historique de François Péron, redacteur du voyage de découvertes aux terres australes, lu à la Société Médicale d'émulation de Paris, séant à la Faculté de médecine, dans la séance du 6 mars*, Paris: Imprimerie de L.-P. Dubray, 1811.
Albin, Eleazar, *A Natural History of Birds*, London: W. Innys and J. Brindley, vol. 3, 1738.
Anderson, Stephanie, 'French Anthropology in Australia: The First Fieldwork Report: François Péron's "Maria Island: Anthropological Observations"', *Aboriginal History*, vol. 25, 2001, pp. 228–242.
Audiat, Louis, *F. Péron (de Cérilly), sa vie, ses voyages et ses ouvrages*, Moulins: Énaut, 1855.
Bacon, Francis, *The Advancement of Learning*, in Michael Kiernan (ed.), *The Oxford Francis Bacon*, Oxford: Oxford University Press, vol. 4, 2000 – Oxford Scholarly Editions Online, 2012.
Baglione, Gabrielle, Cédric Crémière, Jacqueline Goy and Stéphane Schmitt, *Méduses-Jellyfish*, Paris: MkF Editions, 2014.
Ballantyne, Tony (ed.), *Science, Empire and the European Exploration of the Pacific*, Aldershot: Ashgate, 2004.
Baudin, Nicolas, *The Journal of Post Captain Nicolas Baudin, Commander-in-Chief of the Corvettes* Géographe *and* Naturaliste, translated by Christine Cornell, Adelaide: Libraries Board of South Australia, 1974.
Baudin, Nicolas, *Journal du voyage aux Antilles de* La Belle Angélique *(1796–1798)*, édition établie et commentée par Michel Jangoux, Paris: Presses de l'Université Paris-Sorbonne/Académie royale de Belgique, 2009.
Belin, André, 'André-Pierre Ledru. Sa correspondance à l'occasion d'un voyage aux Canaries et aux Antilles', *La Révolution dans le Maine*, vol. 10, 1934.
Benot, Yves, *La Démence coloniale sous Napoléon*, Paris: La Découverte, 2006.
Bernardi, Georges, 'Insects', in Jacqueline Bonnemains, Elliott Forsyth and Bernard Smith, *Baudin in Australian Waters. The Artwork of the French Voyage of Discovery to the Southern Lands 1800–1804*, Melbourne/New York: Oxford University Press, 1988, p. 217.
Black, Andrew, Jean Fornasiero, Justin Jansen and Philippa Horton, 'The "new and singular" bird of St Peter Island', *South Australian Ornithologist*, vol. 42, no. 1, 2016, pp. 1–10.
Bonnemains, Jacqueline and Claude Chappuis, 'Les oiseaux de la collection C.A. Lesueur

du Muséum d'Histoire naturelle du Havre (dessins et manuscrits)', *Bulletin trimestriel de la Société géologique de Normandie et des Amis du Muséum du Havre*, vol. 72, fasc. 1–2, 1985, pp. 25–78.
Bonnemains, Jacqueline, 'Les Illustrations du livre de bord du capitaine Nicolas Baudin. Répertoire des documents retrouvés', *Annales du Muséum du Havre*, no. 33, 1986, pp. 1–20.
Bonnemains, Jacqueline and Pascale Hauguel (eds), *Récit du voyage aux Terres australes par Pierre-Bernard Milius*, Le Havre: Société havraise d'études diverses, 1987.
Bonnemains, Jacqueline, Elliott Forsyth and Bernard Smith, *Baudin in Australian Waters. The Artwork of the French Voyage of Discovery to the Southern Lands 1800–1804*, Melbourne/New York: Oxford University Press, 1988.
Bonnemains, Jacqueline and Diana Jones, 'Les Crustacés de la collection C.-A. Lesueur du Muséum d'Histoire naturelle du Havre', *Bulletin de la Société géologique de Normandie et des Amis du Muséum du Havre*, vol. 77, 1990, pp. 27–66.
Bonnemains, 'Origine de la collection "Lesueur" du Muséum d'Histoire naturelle du Havre', *Annales du Muséum du Havre*, no. 49, 1995, pp. 1–23.
Bonnemains, Jacqueline (ed.), *Mon voyage aux Terres Australes: Journal personnel du commandant Baudin*, Paris: Imprimerie nationale, 2000.
Bonnet, Manuel and Jean-Louis Marignier, *Niépce: correspondance et papiers*, Saint-Loup-de-Varenne: Maison Nicéphore Niépce, 2003.
Bory de Saint-Vincent, Jean-Baptiste, *Voyage dans les quatre principales îles des mers d'Afrique, fait par ordre du gouvernement, pendant les années neuf et dix de la République (1801 et 1802), avec l'histoire de la traversée du capitaine Baudin jusqu'au Port-Louis de l'Île Maurice*, Paris: Chez F. Buisson, 3 vols, 1804.
Bourguet, Marie-Noëlle, 'La collecte du monde: voyage et histoire naturelle (fin XVIIe siècle – début XIXe siècle)', in Claude Blanckaert *et al.* (eds), *Le Muséum au premier siècle de son histoire*, Paris: Éditions du Muséum national d'Histoire naturelle, 1997, pp. 163–196.
Boyer, Ferdinand, 'Le Muséum d'Histoire naturelle à Paris et l'Europe des sciences sous la Convention', *Revue d'histoire des sciences*, vol. 26, no. 3, 1973, pp. 251–257.
Boyle, Robert, 'General Heads for a Natural History of a Countrey, Great or Small', *Philosophical Transactions*, vol. 1, 1665–1666, pp. 186–189.
Boyle, Robert, *General Heads for the Natural History of a Country, Great or Small, Drawn out for the Use of Travellers and Navigators*, London: printed for John Taylor, 1692.
Brasil, Louis, 'The Emu of King Island', *Emu*, vol. 14, no. 2, 1914, pp. 88–97.
Bréelle, Dany, 'Les géographes de l'expédition Baudin et la reconnaissance des côtes australes', in Michel Jangoux (ed.), *Portés par l'air du temps: les voyages du capitaine Baudin*, special number of *Études sur le XVIIIe siècle*, vol. 38, 2010, pp. 213–223.
Brissenden, Robert Francis; *Virtue in Distress: Studies in the Novel of Sentiment from Richardson to Sade*, London: Macmillan, 1974.
Brisson, Mathurin-Jacques, *Ornithologie, ou, Méthode contenant la division des oiseaux en ordres, sections, genres, especes & leurs variétés*, Paris: Cl. Jean-Baptiste Bauche, vol. 6, 1760.
Broc, Numa, *La Géographie des philosophes, géographes et voyageurs français au XVIIIe siècle*, Paris: Éditions Ophrys, 1975.
Buffon, Georges-Louis Leclerc, comte de, *Histoire naturelle, générale et particulière, avec la description du Cabinet du Roi*, Paris: Imprimerie royale, 44 vols, 1749–1804.
Buffon, Georges-Louis Leclerc, comte de, *Histoire naturelle des oiseaux*, Paris: Imprimerie royale, 10 vols, 1771–1786.
Burkhardt, Jr., Richard W., 'Unpacking Baudin: Models of Scientific Practice in the Age of Lamarck', in Goulven Laurent (ed.), *Jean-Baptiste Lamarck 1744–1829*, Paris: CTHS, 1997, pp. 497–514.
Chappey, Jean-Luc, *La Société des Observateurs de l'Homme (1799–1804). Des*

anthropologues au temps de Bonaparte, Paris: Société des études robespierristes, 2002.

Chappey, Jean-Luc, 'Le capitaine Baudin et la Société des observateurs de l'homme: Questions autour d'une mauvaise réputation', in Michel Jangoux (ed.), *Portés par l'air du temps: les voyages du capitaine Baudin*, special number of *Études sur le XVIIIe siècle*, vol. 38, 2010, pp. 145–155.

Chappey, Jean-Luc, 'François Péron et la question de la civilisation aux antipodes', *Annales historiques de la Révolution française*, vol. 375, no. 1, 2014, pp. 139–159.

Cleland, John Burton, 'The History of Ornithology in South Australia', *Emu*, vol. 36, no. 3, 1937, pp. 197–221.

Collini, Silvia and Antonella Vannoni (eds), *Les Instructions scientifiques pour les voyageurs (XVIIe–XIXe siècle)*, Paris: L'Harmattan, 2005.

Copans, Jean and Jean Jamin (eds), *Aux origines de l'anthropologie française: les mémoires de la Société des Observateurs de l'Homme en l'an VIII*, Paris: Le Sycamore, 1978.

Crosland, Maurice, *The Society of Arcueil: A View of French Science in the Time of Napoleon*, London: Heinemann, 1967.

Cuvier, Georges, 'Note instructive sur les recherches à faire relativement aux différences anatomiques des diverses races d'hommes', reproduced in Jean Copans and Jean Jamin (eds), *Aux origines de l'anthropologie française: les mémoires de la Société des Observateurs de l'Homme en l'an VIII*, Paris: Le Sycamore, 1978, pp. 171–176.

Cuvier, Georges, 'Rapport fait au gouvernement par l'Institut Impérial sur le Voyage de Découvertes aux Terres Australes', *Procès-verbaux des séances de l'Académie, Classe des Sciences physiques et mathématiques*, vol. 3 (séance du lundi 9 juin 1806), 1807, pp. 363–367. Reproduced in François Péron, *Voyage de découvertes aux Terres Australes, exécuté par ordre de Sa Majesté l'Empereur et Roi, sur les corvettes le* Géographe *et le* Naturaliste *et la goëlette le* Casuarina *pendant les années 1800, 1801, 1802, 1803, et 1804, Historique*, vol. 1, Paris: Imprimerie impériale, 1807, pp. i–xv.

Cuvier, Georges, *Le Règne animal distribué d'après son organisation*, Paris: Deterville, 4 vols, 1817.

Cuvier, Georges, *Mémoires pour servir à l'Histoire et à l'Anatomie des Mollusques*, Paris: Deterville, 1817.

David, Andrew, Felipe Fernández-Armesto, Carlos Novi and Glyndwr Williams (eds), *The Malaspina Expedition 1789–1794*, London: The Hakluyt Society, 3 vols, 2001–2004.

Degérando, Joseph-Marie, 'Considérations sur les diverses méthodes à suivre dans l'observation des peuples sauvages', reproduced in Jean Copans and Jean Jamin (eds), *Aux origines de l'anthropologie française: les mémoires de la Société des Observateurs de l'Homme en l'an VIII*, Paris: Le Sycamore, 1978, pp. 127–169.

Degérando, Joseph-Marie, *The Observation of Savage Peoples by Joseph-Marie Degérando*, translated by F.C.T. Moore, London: Routledge and Kegan Paul, 1969.

Deleuze, Joseph Philippe François, *Notice historique sur M. Péron*, Paris: Imprimerie de A. Belin, 1811. English translation, 'Historical Eulogy of François Péron', in François Péron (continued by Louis Freycinet), *Voyage of Discovery to the Southern Lands*, Adelaide: The Friends of the State Library of South Australia, translation of the second edition (1824) by Christine Cornell, 2 vols, 2006/2003, vol. 1, pp. lxv–lxxxiii.

Denby, David J., *Sentimentalism and the Social Order in France 1760–1820*, Cambridge, New York: Cambridge University Press, 1994.

Dening, Greg, *Performances*, Carlton: Melbourne University Press, 1996.

Descartes, René, *Principia Philosophiae*, Amsterdam: Ludovicum Elzevirium, 1644.

Desmet, Viviane and Michel Jangoux, 'Un naturaliste aux Terres australes: Jean-Baptiste Leschenault de La Tour (1773–1826)', in Michel Jangoux (ed.), *Portés par l'air du temps, les voyages du capitaine Baudin*, special number of *Études sur le XVIIIe siècle*, vol. 38, 2010, pp. 225–232.

Douglas, Bronwen, 'Slippery Word, Ambiguous Praxis: "Race" and Late-18th-Century Voyagers in Oceania', *The Journal of Pacific History*, vol. 41, no. 1, 2006, pp. 1–29.

Douglas, Bronwen, 'Seaborne Ethnography and the Natural History of Man', *The Journal of Pacific History*, vol. 38, no. 1, 2008, pp. 3–27.

Douglas, Bronwen, '"Novus Orbis Australis": Oceania in the Science of Race', in Bronwen Douglas and Chris Ballard (eds), *Foreign Bodies: Oceania and the Science of Race (1750–1940)*, Canberra: ANU Press, 2008, pp. 99–155.

Douglas, Bronwen, 'L'Idée de "Race" et l'expérience sur le terrain au XIXe siècle: science, action indigène et vacillations d'un naturaliste français en Océanie', *Revue d'Histoire des Sciences Humaines*, no. 21, 2009, pp. 175–209.

Douglas, Bronwen, *Science, Voyages, and Encounters in Oceania, 1511–1850*, Basingstoke: Palgrave, 2014.

Douglas, Bronwen, 'Expeditions, Encounters and the Praxis of Seaborne Ethnography: The French Voyages of La Pérouse and Freycinet', in Martin Thomas (ed.), *Expedition into Empire: Exploratory Journeys and the Making of the Modern World*, Abingdon: Routledge, 2015, pp. 108–126.

Duchet, Michèle, *Anthropologie et histoire au siècle des Lumières*, Paris: Albin Michel, 1971.

Dunmore, John, *French Explorers in the Pacific*, Oxford: Clarendon, 2 vols, 1965–1969.

Dunmore, John (ed.), *The Journal of Jean-François de Galaup de la Pérouse*, London: Hakluyt Society, 2 vols, 1994–1995.

Duyker, Edward, *François Péron, an Impetuous Life: Naturalist and Voyager*, Melbourne: The Miegunyah Press, 2006.

Edwards, George, *A Natural History of Birds*, London: College of Physicians, 1747.

Faivre, Jean-Paul, *Le Contre-amiral Hamelin et la marine française*, Paris: Nouvelles éditions latines, 1962.

Fauchat, Nicolas, Obituary of Emmanuel Crétet, comte de Champmol, *Le Moniteur Universel*, 2 December 1809.

Ferrière, Hervé, *Bory de Saint-Vincent: L'évolution d'un voyageur naturaliste*, Paris: Éditions Syllepse, 2009.

Finnegan, Diarmid A., 'The Spatial Turn: Geographical Approaches in the History of Science', *Journal of the History of Biology*, vol. 41, no. 2, 2008, pp. 369–388.

Flinders, Matthew, *A Voyage to Terra Australis: Undertaken for the Purpose of Completing the Discovery of that Vast Country, and Prosecuted in the Years 1801, 1802 and 1803, in His Majesty's Ship the* Investigator, 2 vols and Atlas, London: G. and W. Nicol, 1814.

Fornasiero, Jean, Peter Monteath and John West-Sooby, *Encountering Terra Australis: The Australian Voyages of Nicolas Baudin and Matthew Flinders*, Kent Town: Wakefield Press, 2004 (revised edition 2010).

Fornasiero, Jean, 'Charles-Alexandre Lesueur: An Art of the Littoral', in Vivonne Thwaites and Jean Fornasiero (eds), *Littoral*, Adelaide: 5 Star Print, 2010, pp. 17–19.

Fornasiero, Jean and John West-Sooby, 'Doing it by the Book: Breaking the Reputation of Nicolas Baudin', in Jean Fornasiero and Colette Mrowa-Hopkins (eds), *Explorations and Encounters in French*, Adelaide: University of Adelaide Press, 2010, pp. 135–164.

Fornasiero, Jean, 'Deux observateurs de l'homme aux antipodes: Nicolas Baudin et François Péron', in Michel Jangoux (ed.), *Portés par l'air du temps: les voyages du capitaine Baudin*, special number of *Études sur le XVIIIe siècle*, vol. 38, 2010, pp. 157–170.

Fornasiero, Jean and John West-Sooby, 'The Acquisitive Eye? French Observations in the Pacific from Bougainville to Baudin', in John West-Sooby (ed.), *Discovery and Empire: The French in the South Seas*, Adelaide: University of Adelaide Press, 2013, pp. 69–97.

Fornasiero, Jean and John West-Sooby, *French Designs on Colonial New South Wales*, Adelaide: Friends of the State Library of South Australia, 2014.

Fornasiero, Jean and John West-Sooby, 'Cross-cultural Inquiry in 1802: Musical Performance on the Baudin Expedition to Australia', in Kate Darian Smith and Penny Edmonds (eds), *Conciliation on Colonial Frontiers: Conflict, Performance, and Commemoration in Australia and the Pacific Rim*, Abingdon: Routledge, 2015, pp. 17–35.

Fornasiero, Jean (ed. and trans.), *Reflections of a Philosophical Voyager. Letter from Nicolas Baudin to Philip Gidley King, 24 December 1802*, Adelaide: Friends of the State Library of South Australia, 2016.

Fornasiero, Jean, Lindl Lawton and John West-Sooby (eds), *The Art of Science: Baudin's Voyagers 1800–1803*, Mile End: Wakefield Press, 2016.

Fornasiero, Jean and John West-Sooby, 'Voyages et déplacements des savoirs. Les expéditions de Nicolas Baudin entre Révolution et Empire', *Annales historiques de la Révolution française*, vol. 385, no. 3, 2016, pp. 23–46.

Fouque, Victor, *La Vérité sur l'invention de la photographie: Nicéphore Niépce, sa vie, ses essais, ses travaux, d'après sa correspondance et autres documents inédits*, Paris: Librairie des Auteurs et de l'Académie des Bibliophiles; Chalon-sur-Saône: Librairie Ferran, 1867.

Freycinet, Louis, *Voyage de découvertes aux Terres Australes, exécuté sur les corvettes le Géographe, le Naturaliste, et la goëlette le Casuarina, pendant les années 1800, 1801, 1802, 1803 et 1804, sous le commandement du Capitaine de vaisseau N. Baudin, Navigation et Géographie*, Paris: Imprimerie Royale, 1815.

Freycinet, Louis de, *Voyage autour du monde: entrepris par ordre du Roi [. . .] exécuté sur les corvettes de S. M. l'Uranie et la Physicienne, pendant les années 1817, 1818, 1819 et 1820, Historique*, Paris: Pillet Aîné, 8 vols, 1824–1844.

Freycinet, Louis de, *Reflections on New South Wales, 1788–1839*, translated by Thomas Cullity, Potts Point: Hordern House, 2001.

Gaillard, Jean, 'Gasteropods', in Jacqueline Bonnemains, Elliott Forsyth and Bernard Smith (eds), *Baudin in Australian Waters. The Artwork of the French Voyage of Discovery to the Southern Lands 1800–1804*, Melbourne/New York: Oxford University Press, 1988, pp. 209–213.

Gascoigne, John, *Encountering the Pacific in the Age of Enlightenment*, Cambridge: Cambridge University Press, 2014.

Geoffroy Saint-Hilaire, Étienne, 'Mémoire sur les espèces du genre *Dasyure*', *Annales du Muséum national d'Histoire naturelle*, vol. 3, 1804, pp. 353–363.

Gibbard, Paul, 'Théodore Leschenault de la Tour, Botanist of the Baudin Expedition', Western Australian Museum web site: http://museum.wa.gov.au/fc/aos/pg, 2016.

Girard, Maurice, *François Péron, naturaliste, voyageur aux Terres Australes: sa vie, appréciation de ses travaux, analyse raisonnée de ses recherches sur les animaux vertébrés et invertébrés, d'après ses collections déposées au Muséum d'Histoire naturelle*, Paris: Baillière; Moulins: Énaut, 1856.

Gmelin, Johann Friedrich, *Systema naturae per regna tria naturae, secundum classes, ordines, genera, species, cum characteribus, differentiis, synonymis, locis. Editio decima tertia, aucta, reformata*, Leipzig: Georg Emanuel Beer, vol. 1, 1789–1790.

Goy, Jacqueline, *Les Méduses de Péron et Lesueur: un autre regard sur l'expédition Baudin*, Paris: Éditions du CTHS, 1995.

Grew, Nehemiah, *Musaeum Regalis Societatis. Or a Catalogue & Description of the Natural and Artificial Rarities belonging to the Royal Society and preserved at Gresham College*, London: W. Rawlins, 1681.

Hahn, Roger, 'Scientific Careers in Eighteenth-Century France', in Maurice Crosland (ed.), *The Emergence of Science in Western Europe*, London: Macmillan, 1975, pp. 127–138.

Hansen, Lars *et al.* (eds), *The Linnaeus Apostles: Global Science and Adventure*, Whitby: IK Foundation, 8 vols, 2007–2012.

Harrison, Carol E., 'Projections of the Revolutionary Nation: French Expeditions in the Pacific, 1791–1803', *Osiris*, vol. 24, no. 1, 2009, pp. 33–52.

Harrison, Carol E., 'Replotting the Ethnographic Romance: Revolutionary Frenchmen in the Pacific, 1768–1804', *Journal of the History of Sexuality*, vol. 21, no. 1, 2012, pp. 39–59.

Horner, Frank, *The French Reconnaissance: Baudin in Australia 1801–1803*, Carlton: Melbourne University Press, 1987.

Hughes, Miranda, 'Philosophical Travellers at the End of the Earth: Baudin, Péron and the Tasmanians', in R.W. Home (ed.), *Australian Science in the Making*, Cambridge: Cambridge University Press, 1988, pp. 23–44.

Humboldt, Alexander von, *Tableaux de la nature, ou considérations sur les déserts, sur la physionomie des végétaux, sur les cataractes de l'Orénoque*, trans. J.B.B. Eyriès, Paris: F. Schœll, 2 vols, 1808.

Ingleton, Geoffrey C., *Matthew Flinders, Navigator and Chartmaker*, Guildford: Genesis Publications, 1986.

James, William, *Naval History of Great Britain 1793–1827*, 6 vols, London: Richard Bentley, 1837.

Jangoux, Michel, 'Les astérides (échinodermes) des Terres australes ramenées par l'expédition Baudin', *Bulletin de la Société géologique de Normandie et des Amis du Muséum du Havre*, vol. 71, 1984, pp. 25–56.

Jangoux, Michel, 'Echinoderms', in Jacqueline Bonnemains, Elliott Forsyth and Bernard Smith (eds), *Baudin in Australian Waters. The Artwork of the French Voyage of Discovery to the Southern Lands 1800–1804*, Melbourne/New York: Oxford University Press, 1988, pp. 221–232.

Jangoux, Michel, 'François Péron, l'émergence d'un naturaliste', *Une petite ville, trois grands hommes: Actes du colloque de Cérilly, 15–16 mai 1999*, Moulins: Pottier, 2000, pp. 137–152.

Jangoux, Michel, 'Les zoologistes et botanistes qui accompagnèrent le capitaine Baudin aux Terres australes', *Australian Journal of French Studies*, vol. 41, no. 2, 2004, pp. 55–78.

Jangoux, Michel, 'La première relâche du *Naturaliste* au Port Jackson (26 avril–18 mai 1802): le témoignage du capitaine Hamelin", *Australian Journal of French Studies*, vol. 41, no. 2, 2004, pp. 126–151.

Jangoux, Michel, 'L'expédition du capitaine Baudin aux Terres australes: les observations zoologiques de François Péron pendant la première campagne (1801–1802)', *Annales du Muséum du Havre*, vol. 73, 2005, pp. 1–35.

Jangoux, Michel, Christian Jouanin and Bernard Métivier, 'Les animaux embarqués vivants sur les vaisseaux du voyage de découvertes aux Terres australes', in M. Jangoux (ed.), *Portés par l'air du temps, les voyages du capitaine Baudin*, special number of *Études sur le XVIIIe siècle*, vol. 38, 2010, pp. 265–282.

Jangoux, Michel, *Le Voyage aux Terres Australes du commandant Nicolas Baudin: Genèse et préambule (1798–1800)*, Paris: Presses de l'Université Paris-Sorbonne, 2013.

Jansen, Justin J.F.J., 'Towards the resolution of long-standing issues regarding birds collected during the Baudin expedition to Australia and Timor (1800–1804): specimens still present, and their importance to Australian ornithology', *Journal of the National Museum (Prague), Natural History Series*, vol. 186, 2017, pp. 51–84.

Jansen, Justin J.F.J., *The Ornithology of the Baudin Expedition (1800–1804)*, Grave, The Netherlands: Privately published, 2018.

Jones, Diana, 'Crustaceans', in Jacqueline Bonnemains, Elliott Forsyth and Bernard Smith (eds), *Baudin in Australian Waters. The Artwork of the French Voyage of Discovery to the Southern Lands 1800–1804*, Melbourne/New York: Oxford University Press, 1988, pp. 218–220.

Jussieu, Antoine Laurent de, 'Notice sur l'expédition à la Nouvelle Hollande entreprise pour des recherches de Géographie et d'Histoire naturelle', *Annales du Muséum national d'Histoire naturelle*, vol. 5, 1804, pp. 1–11.

Kilani, Mondher, *L'Invention de l'autre. Essais sur le discours anthropologique*, Lausanne: Payot, 1994.

Kingston, Ralph, 'A not so Pacific voyage: the "floating laboratory" of Nicolas Baudin', *Endeavour*, vol. 31, no. 4, 2007, pp. 145–151.
Konishi, Shino, *The Aboriginal Male in the Enlightenment World*, London: Pickering and Chatto, 2012.
Kracheninnikov, Stepan, *Opisanie zemli Kamcatki*, Saint Petersburg: Academy of Science, 1755, 2 vols. French translation by M. de Saint-Pré, *Histoire et description du Kamtchatka*, Amsterdam: M.M. Rey, 2 vols, 1770, vol. 2, *Du Tchaika ou de l'Hirondelle de mer* ou *Cormoran*.
Kury, Lorelaï, 'Les Instructions de voyage dans les expéditions scientifiques françaises (1750–1830)', *Revue d'histoire des sciences*, vol. 51, no. 1, 1998, pp. 65–92.
Lacépède, Bernard, *Tableau des sous-classes, divisions, sous-divisions, ordres et genres des oiseaux*, Paris: Plassan, 1799.
Lacépède, Bernard, 'Mémoire sur plusieurs animaux de la Nouvelle Hollande dont la description n'a pas encore été publiée', *Annales du Muséum national d'Histoire naturelle*, vol. 4, 1804, pp. 184–213.
Lacépède, Bernard, *Vue générale des progrès de plusieurs branches des sciences naturelles depuis la mort de Buffon, pour faire suite aux Œuvres complètes de ce grand naturaliste*, Paris: Rapet, 1818.
Laissus, Yves, 'Les cabinets d'histoire naturelle', in René Taton, (ed.) *Enseignement et diffusion des sciences au XVIIIe siecle*, Paris: Hermann, 1964, pp. 659–712.
Lamarck, Jean-Baptiste, 'Sur deux nouveaux genres d'insectes de la Nouvelle Hollande', *Annales du Muséum national d'Histoire naturelle*, vol. 3, 1804, pp. 260–265.
Lamarck, Jean-Baptiste, 'Sur une nouvelle espèce de trigonie et une nouvelle espèce d'huître découvertes dans le voyage du capitaine Baudin', *Annales du Muséum national d'Histoire naturelle*, vol. 4, 1804, pp. 351–359.
Lamarck, Jean-Baptiste 'Mémoire sur deux espèces nouvelles de volutes des mers de la Nouvelle Hollande', *Annales du Muséum national d'Histoire naturelle*, vol. 5, 1804, pp. 154–160.
Lamarck, 'Rapport sur la collection d'histoire naturelle du citoyen Baudin', in André-Pierre Ledru, *Voyage aux îles de Ténériffe, la Trinité, Saint-Thomas, Sainte-Croix et Porto-Ricco* [sic], *exécuté par ordre du gouvernement français, depuis le 30 septembre 1796 jusqu'au 7 juin 1798, sous la direction du capitaine Baudin, pour faire des recherches et des collections relatives à l'histoire naturelle; . . . par André-Pierre Ledru*, Paris: Arthus Bertrand, 2 vols, 1810, vol. 2, pp. 297–303.
Lamarck, Jean-Baptiste, 'Tableau des espèces du genre *Conus*', *Annales du Muséum d'Histoire naturelle*, vol. 15, 1810, pp. 29–40, 263–292, 422–442.
Lamarck, Jean-Baptiste, 'Description du genre Porcelaine (*Cypraea*) et des espèces qui le composent', *Annales du Muséum d'Histoire naturelle*, vol. 15, 1810, pp. 443–445.
Lamarck, Jean-Baptiste, 'Suite du genre Porcelaine', *Annales du Muséum d'Histoire naturelle*, vol. 16, 1810, pp. 89–114.
Lamarck, Jean-Baptiste, 'Suite de la détermination des mollusques testacés', *Annales du Muséum d'Histoire naturelle*, vol. 16, 1810, pp. 300–328, and *Annales du Muséum d'Histoire naturelle*, vol. 17, 1811, pp. 54–80, 185–222.
Lamarck, Jean-Baptiste, *Histoire naturelle des animaux sans vertèbres*, Paris: Deterville, 7 vols, 1815-1822.
Lamarck, Jean-Baptiste, *Nouveau Dictionnaire d'Histoire naturelle*, Paris: Deterville, nouvelle édition, 36 vols, 1816–1819.
Latham, John, *A General Synopsis of Birds*, London: Leigh and Sotheby, vol. 3, part 1, 1785.
Latour, Bruno, *Science in Action. How to Follow Scientists and Engineers through Society*, Cambridge, Mass.: Harvard University Press, 1987.
Laubriet, Pierre, 'Les Guides de voyages au début du XVIIIe siècle et la propagande philosophique', *Studies on Voltaire and the Eighteenth Century*, vol. 32, 1965, pp. 269–325.
Leask, Nigel, 'Darwin's "Second Sun": Alexander von Humboldt and the Genesis of *The*

Voyage of the Beagle', in Helen Small and Trudi Tate (eds), *Literature, Science, Psychoanalysis, 1830-1970: Essays in Honour of Gillian Beer*, Oxford: Oxford University Press, 2003, pp. 13–36.

Ledru, André-Pierre, *Voyage aux îles de Ténériffe, la Trinité, Saint-Thomas, Sainte-Croix et Porto-Ricco* [sic], *exécuté par ordre du gouvernement français, depuis le 30 septembre 1796 jusqu'au 7 juin 1798, sous la direction du capitaine Baudin, pour faire des recherches et des collections relatives à l'histoire naturelle; . . . par André-Pierre Ledru*, Paris: Arthus Bertrand, 2 vols, 1810.

Lesueur, Jean-Baptiste, *Notice sur l'Expédition française aux Terres australes, ordonnée en l'an VIII, et exécutée par les deux corvettes de l'État, le* Géographe *et le* Naturaliste, *parties du port du Havre le 17 Brumaire, An IX*, Brochure in-8°, Rouen: Imprimerie des Arts, 1804. Copy held in the National Library of Australia, MS 7445.

Licoppe, Christian, *La Formation de la pratique scientifique*, Paris: La Découverte, 1996.

Limoges, Camille, 'Louis-Jean-Marie Daubenton', in Charles C. Gillispie (ed.), *Dictionary of Scientific Biography*, vol. 15, supp. 1, New York: Charles Scribner's Sons, 1978, pp. 111–114.

Linnaeus, Carl, *Systema naturae per regna tria naturae, secundum classes, ordines, genera, species, cum characteribus, differentiis, synonymis, locis*, Stockholm: Salvius, vol. 1, 1758.

Livingstone, David, *Putting Science in its Place*, Chicago and London: University of Chicago Press, 2003.

Macleod, Roy and Philip F. Rehbock (eds), *Darwin's Laboratory: Evolutionary Theory and Natural History in the Pacific*, Honolulu: University of Hawaii Press, 1994.

Marchant, Leslie, *France Australe: A Study of French Explorations and Attempts to Found a Penal Colony and Strategic Base in South Western Australia 1503–1826*, Perth: Artlook, 1982.

Marchant, Stephen and Peter Higgins (eds), *Handbook of Australian, New Zealand and Antarctic Birds*, Melbourne: Oxford University Press, vol. 1, 1990.

Martin, Roger (ed.), 'Le Rêve australien de Napoléon. Description et projet secret de conquête française', *Revue de l'Institut Napoléon*, vol. 176, no. 1, 1998, pp. 4–187.

Maupertuis, Pierre Louis Moreau de, *Œuvres*, Lyon: J.M. Bruyset, 4 vols, 1756.

Maury, André, 'Un naturaliste voyageur havrais du 18e siècle, Stanislas Levillain (1774–1801)', *Bulletin de la Société Géologique de Normandie*, vol. 44, 1954, pp. 20–27.

McNiven Hine, Ellen, *Constance de Salm, her influence and her circle in the aftermath of the French Revolution: 'A Mind of No Common Order'*, New York: Peter Lang, 2012.

Métivier, Bernard, 'Lamellibranchs', in Jacqueline Bonnemains, Elliott Forsyth and Bernard Smith (eds), *Baudin in Australian Waters. The Artwork of the French Voyage of Discovery to the Southern Lands 1800–1804*, Melbourne/New York: Oxford University Press, 1988, p. 214.

Métivier, Bernard, 'Lamarck et les mollusques de l'Expédition de Découvertes aux Terres australes', in M. Jangoux (ed.), *Portés par l'air du temps, les voyages du capitaine Baudin*, special number of *Études sur le XVIIIe siècle*, vol. 38, 2010, pp. 253–264.

Michaelis, Johann David, *Fragen an eine Gesellschaft Gelehrter Männer, die auf Befehl Ihro Majestät des Königes von Dännemark nach Arabien reisen*, Frankfurt am Main: Johann Gottlieb Garbe, 1762.

Michaelis, Johann David, *Recueil de questions, proposées à une société de savants, qui par ordre de Sa Majesté danoise font le voyage de l'Arabie*, Frankfurt am Main: Johann Gottlieb Garbe, 1763.

Milne-Edwards, Alphonse and Émile Oustalet, 'Note sur l'émeu noir (*Dromaeus ater V.*) de l'île Decrès (Australie)', *Bulletin du Muséum d'Histoire naturelle*, vol. 5, 1899, pp. 206–214.

Milius, Pierre Bernard, *Pierre Bernard Milius, Last Commander of the Baudin Expedition: The Journal 1800–1804*, translated and annotated by Kate Pratt, edited by Peter Hambly, Canberra: National Library of Australia, 2013.

Moreau de la Sarthe, Louis-Jacques, 'Mémoire sur l'établissement d'un Muséum anthropologique', reproduced in Jean Copans and Jean Jamin (eds), *Aux origines de l'anthropologie française: les mémoires de la Société des Observateurs de l'Homme en l'an VIII*, Paris: Le Sycamore, 1978, pp. 187–194.

Müller, Johannes and Franz Hermann Troschel, *System der Asteriden*, Braunschweig: F. Vieweg und Sohn, 1842.

Mundle, Rob, *Dampier, the Dutch and the Great South Land*, Sydney: HarperCollins Publishers Australia, 2015.

Onley, Derek and Paul Scofield, *Albatrosses, Petrels and Shearwaters of the World*, Oxford: Princeton Field Guides, 2007.

Ord, George, 'A memoir of Charles Alexander Lesueur', *American Journal of Sciences and Arts*, 2nd series, vol. 8, 1849, pp. 189–216.

Osborne, Michael, 'Applied Natural History and Utilitarian Ideals: "Jacobin Science" at the Muséum d'Histoire naturelle, 1789–1870', in Bryant Ragan and Elizabeth Williams (eds), *Re-creating Authority in Revolutionary France*, New Brunswick: Rutgers University Press, 1992, pp. 124–126.

Outram, Dorinda, 'Politics and vocation: French science, 1793–1830', *British Journal for the History of Science*, vol. 13, no. 1, 1980, pp. 27–43.

Outram, Dorinda, 'New Spaces in Natural History', in Nicholas Jardine, James A. Secord and Emma C. Spary (eds), *Cultures of Natural History*, Cambridge: Cambridge University Press, 1996, pp. 249–265.

Pallas, Peter Simon, *Spicilegia zoologica: quibus novae imprimis et obscurae animalium species iconibus, descriptionibus atque commentariis illustrantur*, vol. 1, fasc. 5, Berlin: Gottl. August. Lange, 1769.

Pawson, David, 'The Western Australian psolid holothurian *Ceto cuvieria* (Cuvier)', *Journal of the Royal Society of Western Australia*, vol. 54, 1971, pp. 33–39.

Pennant, Thomas, *Arctic Zoology*, vol. 2, *Class II, Birds*, London: Henry Hughs, 1785.

Péron, François, 'Observations sur l'anthropologie, ou l'histoire naturelle de l'homme, la nécessité de s'occuper de l'avancement de cette science et l'importance de l'admission sur la flotte du Capitaine Baudin d'un ou plusieurs naturalistes spécialement chargés des recherches à faire sur cet objet', Paris: Stoupe, 1800. Reproduced in Jean Copans and Jean Jamin (eds), *Aux origines de l'anthropologie française: les mémoires de la Société des Observateurs de l'Homme en l'an VIII*, Paris: Le Sycamore, 1978, pp.177–185.

Péron, François and Charles-Alexandre Lesueur, 'Observations sur le tablier des femmes hottentotes', *Magasin encyclopédique*, vol. 3, 1805, pp. 195–197.

Péron, François, 'Réponse de M. Péron aux observations de M. Dumont sur le "Tablier des femmes hottentotes"', *Magasin encyclopédique*, vol. 5, 1805, pp. 298–310.

Péron, François, 'Notice d'un mémoire sur les animaux observés pendant la traversée de Timor au Cap Sud de la Terre de Van Diémen', *Bulletin des Sciences, Société philomathique de Paris*, vol. 3, no. 95, 1805, pp. 269–270.

Péron, François, *Voyage de découvertes aux Terres Australes, exécuté par ordre de Sa Majesté l'Empereur et Roi, sur les corvettes le* Géographe *et le* Naturaliste *et la goëlette le* Casuarina *pendant les années 1800, 1801, 1802, 1803, et 1804, Historique*, vol. 1, Paris: Imprimerie impériale, 1807.

Péron, François and Louis Freycinet, *Voyage de découvertes aux Terres Australes, Historique*, vol. 2, Paris: Imprimerie royale, 1816.

Péron, François (continued by Louis de Freycinet), *Voyage de découvertes aux Terres australes, fait par ordre du gouvernement, sur les corvettes le* Géographe, le Naturaliste, *et la goëlette le* Casuarina, *pendant les années 1800, 1801, 1802, 1803 et 1804, rédigé par Péron, et continué par M. Louis de Freycinet, Seconde édition revue, corrigée et augmentée par M. Louis de Freycinet*, Paris: Arthus Bertrand, 4 vols and Atlas, 1824.

Péron, François and Louis Freycinet, *Voyage of Discovery to the Southern Lands*, translation of the second edition (1824) by Christine Cornell, Adelaide: The Friends of the State Library of South Australia, 2 vols, 2006/2003.

Plomley, N.J.B. (Brian), *The Baudin Expedition and the Tasmanian Aborigines, 1802*, Hobart: Blubberhead Press, 1983.

Plomley, N.J.B. (Brian) and Josiane Piard-Bernier, *The General: The Visits of the Expedition led by Bruny d'Entrecasteaux to Tasmanian waters in 1792 and 1793*, Launceston: Queen Victoria Museum, 1993.

Pfennigwerth, Stephanie, 'New Creatures Made Known: (Re)discovering the Extinct King Island Emu', MA thesis, University of Tasmania, 2010.

Pfennigwerth, Stephanie, 'New Creatures Made Known: Some Animal Histories of the Baudin Expedition', in John West-Sooby (ed.), *Discovery and Empire: The French in the South Seas*, Adelaide: University of Adelaide Press, 2013, pp. 171–213.

Pluchet, Régis, 'En marge de l'expédition vers les Terres australes: Un portrait du botaniste André Michaux', in Michel Jangoux (ed.), *Portés par l'air du temps: les voyages du capitaine Baudin*, special number of *Études sur le XVIIIe siècle*, vol. 38, 2010, pp. 187–201.

Pratt, Mary Louise, *Imperial Eyes: Travel Writing and Transculturation*, London: Routledge, 1992.

Prieur, Gilbert, 'Jean-Baptiste Leschenault de la Tour (1773–1826): naturaliste et voyageur chalonnais', *Mémoires de la Société d'Histoire et d'Archéologie de Chalon-sur-Saône*, vol. 41, 1971.

Quoy, Jean René Constant and Joseph Paul Gaimard, 'De l'homme: observations sur la constitution physique des Papous', in Louis de Freycinet, *Voyage autour du monde, entrepris par ordre du Roi [. . .] exécuté sur les corvettes de S.M. l'Uranie et la Physicienne, pendant les années 1817, 1818, 1819 et 1820*, vol. 2, Zoologie, Paris: Pillet Aîné, 1824, pp. 1–11.

Regourd, François and James McLellan, *The Colonial Machine: French Science and Overseas Expansion in the Old Regime*, Turnhout: Brepols Publishers, 2012.

Reidy, Michael S., Gary Kroll and Erik M. Conway, *Exploration and Science. Social Impact and Interaction*, Santa Barbara: ABC Clio, 2007.

Richard, Hélène, *Le Voyage de d'Entrecasteaux à la recherche de Lapérouse*, Paris: Éditions du CTHS, 1986.

Rousseau, Jean-Jacques, *Discours sur l'origine et les fondements de l'inégalité parmi les hommes*, Amsterdam: Marc Michel Rey, 1755.

Sankey, Margaret, 'François-Auguste Péron: le mythe de l'homme sauvage et l'écriture de la science', *Cahiers de sociologie économique et culturelle*, vol. 9, 1988, pp. 37–46.

Sankey, Margaret, Peter Cowley and Jean Fornasiero, 'The Baudin Expedition in Review: Old Quarrels and New Approaches', *Australian Journal of French Studies*, vol. 41, no. 2, 2004, pp. 4–14.

Sankey, Margaret, 'Les premiers contacts: Les Aborigènes de la Nouvelle Hollande observés par les officiers et les savants de l'expédition Baudin', in Michel Jangoux (ed.), *Portés par l'air du temps, les voyages du capitaine Baudin*, special number of *Études sur le XVIIIe siècle*, vol. 38, 2010, pp. 171–185.

Schodde, Richard, Alan J.D. Tennyson, Jeff G. Groth, Jonas Lai, Paul Scofield and Frank D. Steinheimer, 'Settling the name *Diomedea exulans* Linnaeus, 1758 for the Wandering Albatross by neotypification', *Zootaxa*, vol. 4236, no. 1, 2017, pp. 135–148.

Sloan, Phillip, 'The Gaze of Natural History', in Christopher Fox, Roy Porter and Robert Wokler (eds), *Inventing Human Science. Eighteenth-Century Domains*, Berkeley: University of California Press, 1995, pp. 112–151.

Sloan, Phillip, 'Natural History, 1670–1802', in Robert Olby, Geoffrey Cantor, John Christie and Jonathon Hodge (eds), *Companion to the History of Modern Science*, London: Routledge, 1996, pp. 295–313.

Sloan, Phillip, 'Natural History', in Knud Haakonssen (ed.), *The Cambridge History of Eighteenth-Century Philosophy*, Cambridge: Cambridge University Press, 2 vols, 2006, vol. 2, pp. 903–938.

Spary, Emma C., *Utopia's Garden: French Natural History from Old Regime to Revolution*,

Cambridge: Cambridge University Press, 2000.
Spate, Oskar, 'Ames damnées: Baudin and Péron', *Overland*, no. 58, 1974, pp. 52–57.
Starbuck, Nicole, 'Constructing the "Perfect" Voyage. Nicolas Baudin at Port Jackson, 1802', PhD thesis, University of Adelaide, 2010.
Starbuck, Nicole, *Baudin, Napoleon and the Exploration of Australia*, London: Pickering and Chatto, 2013.
Starbuck, Nicole, 'Neither Civilized nor Savage: The Aborigines of Colonial Port Jackson, Through French Eyes, 1802', in Shino Konishi, Alex Cook and Nick Curthoys (eds), *Representing Humanity in the Age of Enlightenment*, London: Pickering and Chatto, 2013, pp. 123–133.
Starbuck, Nicole, '"Primitive Race", "Pure Race", "Brown Race", "Every Race": Freycinet's Understanding of Human Difference in Oceania', in John West-Sooby (ed.), *Discovery and Empire: the French in the South Seas*, Adelaide: University of Adelaide Press, 2013, pp. 215–244.
Starbuck, Nicole, '"Naturally Fearful": Emotion, Race and French–Papuan Encounters, 1818–1830', *The Journal of Pacific History*, vol. 51, no. 4, 2016, pp. 357–374.
Starbuck, Nicole, '"Race", intimacy and go-betweens in French–West Papuan Encounters', in Tiffany Shellam, Maria Nugent, Shino Konishi and Allison Cadzow (eds), *Brokers and Boundaries: Colonial Exploration in Indigenous Territory*, Canberra: ANU Press, 2016, pp. 38–60.
Starbuck, Nicole, 'Ritual Encounters of the "Savage" and the Citizen: French Revolutionary Ethnographers in Oceania, 1768–1803', in Meridee Bailey and Katie Barclay (eds), *Emotion, Ritual and Power in Europe, 1200–1920*, Basingstoke: Palgrave, 2017, pp. 123–144.
Staum, Martin, 'The Paris Geographical Society Constructs the Other, 1821–1850', *Journal of Historical Geography*, vol. 26, no. 2, 2000, pp. 222–238.
Stocking, Jr., George, 'French Anthropology in 1800', *Isis*, vol. 55, no. 2, 1964, pp. 134–150.
Stresemann, Erwin, 'Type Localities of Australian Birds collected by the "Expedition Baudin" (1801–1803)', *Emu*, vol. 51, no. 1, 1951, pp. 65–70.
Tulard, Jean, 'Claret de Fleurieu: conseiller d'État et sénateur', in Ulane Bonnel (ed.), *Fleurieu et la marine de son temps*, Paris: Éditions Economica, 1992, pp. 311–316.
Van Strien-Chardonneau, Madeleine, *Le Voyage de Hollande: récits de voyageurs français dans les Provinces-Unies, 1748–1795*, Oxford: Voltaire Foundation, 1994.
Vinarskiĭ, Max V., 'The fate of subspecies category in zoological systematics. 1. The History', *Zhurnal Obshchei Biologii*, vol. 76, no. 1, 2015, pp. 3–14.
Vuacheux, Édouard, 'Quelques renseignements sur le voyageur naturaliste Stanislas Levillain (1774–1801)', *Bulletin du Muséum d'Histoire naturelle de Paris*, vol. 11, 1905, pp. 136–138.
West-Sooby, John, 'Baudin, Flinders and the Scientific Voyage', in Serge M. Rivière and Kumari R. Issur (eds), *Baudin-Flinders dans l'océan Indien, Voyages, découvertes, rencontre/Travels, Discoveries, Encounter*, Paris: l'Harmattan, 2007, pp. 179–194.
Whittell, Hubert Massey, *The Literature of Australian Birds*, Perth: Paterson Brokensha, 1954.
Young, William, *The Fascination of Birds: From the Albatross to the Yellow Throat*, New York: Dover Publications, 2014.

Contributors

Gabrielle Baglione is Curator of the Lesueur Collection at the Muséum d'Histoire naturelle of Le Havre, France.

Andrew Black was awarded the Medal of the Order of Australia (OAM) in 2000 for his contributions to Medicine, in particular epilepsy, and to Conservation, the Environment and Ornithology. He is an Honorary Research Associate at the South Australian Museum.

Jean-Luc Chappey is Professor of the History of Science at the Université de Paris 1 Panthéon-Sorbonne.

Cédric Crémière is an independent researcher. He was Director of the Muséum d'Histoire naturelle of Le Havre, France, from 2005 to 2019.

Jean Fornasiero is Professor Emerita of French Studies at the University of Adelaide and a Fellow of the Australian Academy of the Humanities.

John Gascoigne is Emeritus Professor of History at the University of New South Wales and a Fellow of the Australian Academy of the Humanities.

Paul Gibbard is Senior Lecturer in French Studies at the University of Western Australia.

Philippa Horton was Collection Manager in Ornithology at the South Australian Museum from 1984 to 2019. She is now an Honorary Research Associate at the Museum.

Michel Jangoux is a specialist of marine biology and of the history of maritime exploration, and is Emeritus Professor at the Université Libre de Bruxelles and at the Université de Mons, Belgium.

Justin Jansen is an Honorary Research Associate in the Department of Vertebrates within the Naturalis Biodiversity Center in Leiden, Netherlands.

Stephanie Pfennigwerth is Exhibitions Curator at the Museum of Australian Democracy at Old Parliament House, Canberra.

Margaret Sankey is Professor Emerita of French Studies at the University of Sydney and a Fellow of the Australian Academy of the Humanities.

Nicole Starbuck is a Research Fellow at Flinders University and an Honorary Associate Investigator with the Australian Research Council Centre of Excellence for the History of Emotions.

John West-Sooby is Emeritus Professor of French Studies at the University of Adelaide.

Index

A

Advenier, Alexandre Philippe: 15, 20
Alard, Marie Joseph Louis: 7, 64, 220, 242
Albin, Eleazar: 238, 245, 246
Amourette, Geneviève: 70
Anderson, Stephanie: 315
Argentin, Jean-Marc: 70
Arra-Maïda: 82
Audiat, Louis: 243

B

Bacon, Francis: 28–30, 37
Baglione, Gabrielle: 242, 244
Bailey, Meridee: 316
Bailly, Joseph Charles: 25, 120, 135, 137, 150, 293
Ballantyne, Tony: 111, 121
Ballard, Chris: 315
Banks, Joseph: 11, 14, 25, 29, 128, 198, 216
Barbier, Antoine: 285
Barbier, Vinard: 149
Barclay, Katie: 316
Barré de Saint-Venant, Jean: 58
Bauche, Jean-Baptiste: 246
Baudin, Thomas Nicolas: *Belle Angélique* voyage, 4, 15–17, 20, 21, 287–289, 297; 'Baudin expedition' to the Southern Lands, 1, 11, 18, 23, 35, 40, 53, 69, 89, 100, 107, 157, 180, 181, 184, 222–224, 267, 268, 270, 286, 288, 304; instructions, 21, 23, 34, 42, 109, 146; financial arrangements, 131, 270–273; natural history, 33, 78, 129, 130, 138–145, 166, 169, 175, 181, 182, 187, 188, 191, 192, 195, 196, 220, 270, 286, 298; anthropology, 34, 42, 99, 302, 303, 305, 306, 309–311, 314; fate of collections, 157, 166, 169, 175, 199, 200, 270; Sydney sojourn, 77, 125, 181, 251, 303, 305, 309; Baudin's views on colonialism, 261, 309–311; Baudin's reputation, 2, 3, 5, 91, 99, 138, 139, 249–252, 259, 278, 289; his relations with officers, 91, 106, 125, 249, 262, 306; relations with scientists, 3–5, 15, 23, 91, 99, 100, 111, 250, 254, 288, 289, 296; relations with Péron, 2, 4, 5, 23, 78, 92, 105, 106; views on scientific work, 15–17, 22, 35, 293, 298; correspondence, 126, 130, 146, 147, 309, 310; other writings, 1, 70, 90, 92, 111, 250, 251, 309; reports to Baudin, 181, 183, 195; expedition journals, 92, 130, 250, 307; Baudin's death, 1; his place in history, 2; Baudin as scientific voyager, 1, 2, 4, 5, 15, 16, 45, 91, 305, 314; voyage account, 282, 303, 309; legacy of expedition, 41; Baudin Legacy project, 70
Beauharnais, Joséphine de: 80, 130, 139, 140, 142, 149, 173, 275, 281
Beautemps-Beaupré, Charles-François: 138
Belin, André: 150, 243, 317
Benot, Yves: 64
Bernardi, Georges: 164, 177
Bernier, Pierre-François: 25, 254, 255, 264
Bertin, Charles-Henri: 128, 149
Besson, Alexandre-Charles: 19, 26
Billings, Joseph: 221, 242
Billiore, Jim: 149
Bissy, Frédéric: 25, 138, 150

Black, Andrew: 217
Blanckaert, Claude: 24, 63
Boddaert, Pieter: 187
Bonald, Louis de: 50
Bonaparte, Mme – see Beauharnais
Bonaparte, Napoleon: 11, 12, 16, 36, 80, 89, 91, 109, 121, 259, 270–274, 276–279, 281, 283, 304
Bonnel, Ulane: 149
Bonnemains, Jacqueline: 7, 26, 38, 70, 83–85, 87, 88, 93, 101, 157, 158, 164, 176–179, 220, 242–244, 250, 263, 264
Bonnet, Manuel: 285
Bory de Saint-Vincent, Georges Jean-Baptiste Marcellin: 4, 7, 25, 41, 63, 91, 101, 157, 158, 164, 176–179, 220, 242–244, 250, 263, 264
Bougainville, Hyacinthe de: 126, 147, 151
Bougainville, Louis Antoine de: 3, 7, 11, 31
Bouguer, Pierre: 13
Boullanger, Charles Pierre: 25, 120, 288
Bourguet, Marie-Noëlle: 24, 63
Boyer, Ferdinand: 64
Boyle, Robert: 12, 24
Brasil, Louis: 113, 122
Bréelle, Dany: 300
Breton, Gérard: 70
Breton, François-Désiré: 126, 147, 151, 253–255, 264, 265
Brèvedent du Bocage, Léon: 127, 149, 265, 307, 316
Brissenden, Robert Francis: 116, 122
Brisson, Mathurin-Jacques: 246
Broc, Numa: 37
Broca, Paul: 39
Broussonet, Pierre Marie Auguste: 17, 25, 139
Brown, Anthony J.: 88

Brown, Robert: 280
Brüe, Joseph Louis Michel: 126, 148, 151, 292
Buffon, Georges-Louis Leclerc, comte de: 30–33, 37, 48, 59, 64, 223, 238, 244, 246
Burkhardt, Richard: 121, 170, 175, 178, 179
Burton, Tom: 217
Bustaret, Claire: 70

C

Cadzow, Allison: 315
Cagnet, Jean François: 25
Candolle, Augustin Pyramus de: 281
Carteret, Philip: 108
Cassini, Jacques: 14
Catherine the Great: 242
Chappey, Jean-Luc: 2, 6, 7, 26, 38, 63, 64, 103, 249, 263, 285, 304, 315
Chaptal, Jean-Antoine: 129, 130, 139, 149, 150
Chappuis, Claude: 242
Charpentier, Julie: 141, 144, 150
Chateaubriand, François-René de: 50
Chaussier, François: 222
Chemnitz, Johann Hieronymus: 17, 25
Cleland, John Burton: 217
Coat, G.: 70
Colas, François: 292
Collini, Silvia: 24
Collins, David: 17, 25
Commerson, Philibert: 11
Conway, Erik M.: 37
Cook, Alexander: 315
Cook, James: 3, 11, 14, 25, 28, 29, 31, 77, 108, 306
Cooper, Daniel: 113, 117, 221
Copans, Jean: 26, 39, 63, 64, 101, 102, 316

Cornell, Christine: 6, 26, 37, 64, 101, 120, 121, 217, 243, 264, 299, 301, 315, 316
Corvisart des Marets, Jean-Nicolas: 222
Coulomb, Charles-Augustin: 63
Couture, Joseph Victor: 126, 148
Cowley, Peter: 6
Crémière, Cédric: 242
Crétet, Emmanuel: 269, 271–279, 284, 285
Crosland, Maurice: 24, 121
Cullity, Thomas: 315
Curthoys, Nick: 315
Cuvier, Georges: 5, 11, 12, 15, 17, 18, 21, 23, 26, 34, 44, 59, 60, 62–64, 90, 101, 108, 112, 113, 120, 121, 167–169, 177, 178, 220, 223, 232, 242, 245, 269, 285, 293, 304, 313, 316, 323

D

Dampier, William: 136, 150
Darian Smith, Kate: 314
Darwin, Charles: 18, 25, 28, 31
Daubenton, Louis Jean-Marie: 33, 223, 243
Daudin, François Marie: 185
David, Andrew: 37
Decaen, Charles-Mathieu-Isidore: 36, 38, 88
Decrès, Denis: 131, 138, 145, 147, 149, 261, 272–274, 279, 284
Degérando, Joseph-Marie: 21, 26, 34, 38, 44, 46, 64, 90, 101, 316
Deleuze, Joseph Philippe François: 106, 110, 115, 116, 120–122, 140, 150, 243
Delisse, Jacques: 25
Denby, David J.: 118, 119, 122
Dening, Greg: 317

d'Entrecasteaux, Antoine Raymond Joseph de Bruni: 18–22, 26, 32, 33, 35, 107, 218, 311
Depuch, Louis: 25, 121, 126, 137, 148
Descartes, René: 30, 31, 37
Deschamps de Pas, Louis Auguste: 20, 35, 38
Desfontaines, René Louiche: 150, 269
Desmet, Viviane: 264, 265, 284, 300
d'Hesmivy d'Auribeau, Alexandre: 311, 317
Dolomieu, Déodat: 32, 37
Douglas, Bronwen: 59, 65, 304, 308, 314–316
Drapiez, Auguste: 192
Duchet, Michèle: 64
Dufresne, Louis: 140, 145, 150, 173, 174, 275, 276, 278, 284
Dufresne, Mme: 141, 150
Duméril, André Marie Constant: 60, 62
Dumont, Charles: 88
Dumont, Désiré: 25, 286, 290
Dumont d'Urville, Jules: 304
Dunmore, John: 37, 120
Duperré, Victor-Guy: 263
Duperrey, Louis Isidore: 304
Duval Dailly, Étienne: 126, 148
Duyker, Edward: 70, 120–122, 218, 219, 222, 243, 284

E

Edmonds, Penny: 314
Edwards, George: 245, 246
Engelhard, Nicolaus: 268

F

Fabert (seaman): 148
Fabricius, Johan Christian: 17, 25, 155, 156, 158, 162, 163, 176, 177

Faivre, Jean-Paul: 149, 250, 252–254, 260, 262–266
Fauchat, Nicolas: 281, 285
Faujas de Saint Fond, Barthélemy: 142, 150
Faure, Pierre Auguste: 25, 120, 288
Fernández-Armesto, Felipe: 37
Ferrière, Hervé: 299
Finnegan, Diarmid A.: 12, 24
Fleurieu, Charles-Pierre Claret de: 130, 138, 145, 146, 148–151
Flinders, Matthew: 14, 36, 53, 76, 80, 88, 97, 252, 259, 266, 292
Forfait, Pierre-Alexandre-Laurent: 7, 109, 121, 264, 300
Fornasiero, Jean: 6, 7, 24, 63, 65, 87, 88, 121, 148, 217, 218, 244, 263, 266, 285, 299, 301, 308, 314–317
Forsskål, Peter: 14, 158
Forster, Georg: 31, 59
Forster, Johann Reinhold: 31, 198
Forsyth, Elliott: 38, 176–178, 263
Fouque, Victor: 285
Fourcroy, Antoine-François de: 40, 42, 51, 54, 63, 173, 222
Fox, Christopher: 38
Freycinet, Louis-Claude de Saulses de: 6, 26, 37, 63, 64, 91, 92, 99, 101, 102, 120, 151, 177, 180, 181, 217, 218, 258, 282, 283, 299, 302–317
Freycinet, Louis-Henri de Saulses de: 91, 99, 101
Furneaux, Tobias: 108

G

Gaillard, Jean: 170, 178
Gaimard, Joseph Paul: 184, 308, 311, 317
Gall, Franz Joseph: 44
Garnier, Michel: 25
Garnot, Prosper: 186
Gascoigne, John: 14, 24
Geoffroy Saint-Hilaire, Étienne: 60, 62, 139, 140, 142, 150–152, 171–173
Gibbard, Paul: 300
Gicquel, Pierre: 138, 139, 150
Gillispie, Charles C.: 243
Girard, Maurice: 220, 242, 243
Giraud, Antoine: 126, 148
Gmelin, Johann Friedrich: 87, 185, 186, 242, 244–246
Godin, Louis: 13
Goffman, Erving: 111
Gould, John: 185, 188, 193, 198, 200
Goy, Jacqueline: 70, 85, 87, 88, 220, 242, 264
Gray, George Robert: 187
Grégoire, (Abbé) Henri Jean-Baptiste: 46, 58, 135, 150
Grew, Nehemiah: 238, 245, 246
Groth, Jeff G.: 244
Guichenot, Antoine: 25, 114, 120
Guillaumin, Émile: 106, 120

H

Haakonssen, Knud: 37
Hahn, Roger: 24
Hallé, Jean-Noël: 47, 222
Hamelin, Jacques Félix Emmanuel: 121, 125–131, 140, 146–150, 249–266, 290, 293, 295, 298, 301, 307, 316
Hansen, Lars: 24
Harris, John: 255
Harrison, Carol E.: 37, 315, 316
Hauguel, Pascale: 87, 88
Heirisson, François Antoine Boniface: 126, 151, 264, 265
Herbst, Johann Friedrich Wilhelm: 158
Higgins, Peter: 218

Home, Roderick Weir: 315
Hooke, Robert: 12
Horner, Frank: 6, 7, 88, 102, 120, 121, 250, 264, 284, 292, 299, 300
Horton, Philippa: 217
Hughes, Miranda: 315
Humboldt, Alexander von: 18, 25, 31, 278, 281, 285

I
Ingleton, Geoffrey C.: 251, 252, 264, 266
Issur, Kumari R.: 6
Itard, Jean-Marc Gaspard: 51

J
James, William: 266
Jamin, Jean: 26, 39, 63, 64, 101, 102, 316
Jangoux, Michel: 6, 7, 22, 24–27, 64, 70, 87, 88, 102, 103, 148, 150, 177, 178, 220, 242, 243, 250–252, 263–265, 284, 287, 288, 293, 299–301, 314
Jansen, Justin J.F.J.: 87, 189, 217, 218, 243
Janszoon, Willem: 218
Jardine, Nicholas: 23, 37, 121
Jauffret, Louis-François: 3, 7, 26, 316
Jones, Diana: 157, 158, 176
Joséphine – *see Beauharnais*
Josse (novice): 148
Jouanin, Christian: 150
Jurien de la Gravière, Pierre Roch: 107
Jussieu, Antoine-Laurent de: 3–7, 20–24, 26, 33, 38, 129, 130, 138, 149, 150, 220, 242, 257, 264, 265, 268, 269, 280, 281, 284, 285, 289, 297, 300, 309, 317

K
Kéraudren, Pierre-François: 61, 63, 106, 115, 120, 122
Kiernan, Michael: 37

Kilani, Mondher: 63
King, Philip Gidley: 309, 310
Kingston, Ralph: 2, 6, 7
Kleinne, Valentin: 149
Koken, Phil W.: 191, 195
Konishi, Shino: 314–316
Kracheninnikov, Stepan: 246
Kroll, Gary: 37
Kuhl, Heinrich: 186
Kury, Lorelaï: 24

L
Labillardière, Jacques-Julien Houtou de: 20, 182, 200, 218
Lacépède, Bernard Germain de: 113, 145, 151, 174, 196, 211, 223, 225, 226, 236, 244
La Condamine, Charles Marie de: 13
Lai, Jonas: 244
Laissus, Yves: 243
Lalande (or Delalande), Adrien-Alexis: 141, 150
Lalande (or Delalande), Pierre-Antoine: 141, 150
Lamanon, Robert de: 33, 37
Lamarck, Jean-Baptiste: 3, 7, 121, 143, 145, 150–153, 156–158, 163, 164, 167, 169, 170, 173, 175–179, 223, 269
Lange, Gottlieb August: 246
Langlès, Louis-Mathieu: 281
La Pérouse, Jean-François de Galaup de: 7, 18, 19, 32, 33, 35, 292
Lasalle: 134
Lassus, Pierre: 222
Latham, John: 184–188, 200, 244
Latour, Bruno: 30, 37
Latreille, Pierre-André: 143, 151, 156, 162, 163, 176, 177
Laubriet, Pierre: 24
Laurent, Goulven: 121, 178

Laurillard, Charles Léopold: 168
Lawton, Lindl: 88
Leask, Nigel: 18, 25
Le Bas de Sainte Croix (or Sainte Croix Lebas), Alexandre: 127, 138, 149, 150
Lebrun, Louis: 25
Ledru, André-Pierre: 6, 7, 15, 21, 26, 138, 150, 288, 289, 300
Leroy, Alphonse: 222
Léry, Jean de: 115
Leschenault de la Tour, Jean-Baptiste Louis Claude Théodore: 25, 60, 62, 102, 120, 135, 256, 257, 264, 265, 267–285, 287, 296, 300, 301, 317
Leschenault du Villard, François Broch d'Hotelans: 284
Leschenault du Villard, Jean-Baptiste-Antoine: 269, 284
Lesueur, Charles-Alexandre: 5, 11, 18, 25, 60–63, 70, 76, 80, 83–85, 87, 88, 90, 93, 102, 108, 153, 155, 158, 164–166, 168, 170, 171, 173–175, 177–182, 184, 187–190, 192–194, 196, 198, 199, 217, 218, 226, 229, 270, 282, 286, 287, 299
Lesueur, Jean-Baptiste: 38
Levillain, Stanislas: 15, 16, 22, 25, 76, 88, 96, 102, 129, 138, 181, 218, 221, 254–256, 264, 265, 286–301
Lichtenstein, Martin Hinrich Carl: 185
Licoppe, Christian: 63
Limoges, Camille: 243
Linnaeus, Carl: 13, 14, 24, 25, 29, 33, 158, 185, 202, 203, 207, 225–230, 232, 238, 239, 242–245
Livingstone, David: 112, 114, 115, 122
Louvigny (clandestine passenger): 149
Lucas (lieutenant): 149
Lund, Anders Jahan: 158

M

Macleod, Roy: 37
Maclure, William: 168
Macquarie, Lachlan: 310
Magallon de la Morlière, François Louis: 127
Malaspina, Alejandro: 29, 30, 37
Malouet, Pierre-Victor: 58
Malte-Brun, Conrad: 280
Marchant, Leslie: 291, 300
Marchant, Stephen: 218
Marignier, Jean-Louis: 285
Martin, Roger: 63, 70, 87
Maugé, René: 4, 15, 16, 21, 22, 25, 88, 129, 135, 138, 142, 153–155, 181, 217, 221, 230, 232, 244, 286–290, 299, 301
Maupertuis, Pierre Louis Moreau de: 13, 14, 32, 37
Maurouard, Jean-Marie: 126, 147, 151
Maury, André: 288, 300
McLellan, James: 23
McNiven Hine, Ellen: 285
Meares, John: 108
Merlot (slave): 25
Métivier, Bernard: 150, 169, 170, 176, 178
Michaelis, Johann David: 14, 24
Michaux, André: 25, 287, 299
Milbert, Jacques Gérard: 25, 80, 87
Milius, Pierre-Bernard: 77, 87, 88, 256, 265, 290, 295
Milne-Edwards, Alphonse: 122, 242
Milne-Edwards, Henri: 158, 176
Mirbel, Charles-François Brisseau de: 130, 139, 149
Montalivet, Jean-Pierre de Bachasson, comte de: 65, 279
Monteath, Peter: 285, 316

Moore, Francis Charles Timothy: 26, 64, 101
Moreau, Charles: 126, 151
Moreau de la Sarthe, Louis-Jacques: 316
Mrowa-Hopkins, Colette: 6, 263, 299
Müller, Johannes: 168, 178
Mundle, Rob: 218

N
Napoleon – *see Bonaparte*
Neufchâteau, François de: 54
Niebuhr, Carsten: 14
Niépce, Joseph Nicéphore: 276–279, 285
Nompère de Champagny, Jean-Baptiste: 276
Nordblad, Erik Anders: 24
Novi, Carlos: 37
Nugent, Maria: 315

O
Onley, Derek: 243
Ord, George: 178
Osborne, Michael: 38
Oudinot, Pierre: 145, 151
Oustalet, Émile: 122, 242
Outram, Dorinda: 23, 24, 37, 111, 121, 122, 284

P
Pallas, Peter Simon: 158, 238, 246
Pawson, David: 178
Pelletan, Philippe: 222
Pennant, Thomas: 17, 25, 246
Péron, François: war service, 110, 201, 304; scientific training and patronage, 5, 11, 17, 33, 47, 90, 108, 113, 210, 211, 216, 221–223, 287; range of interests, 76, 77, 93; role and work on voyage, 1, 2, 5, 6, 11, 17, 18, 23, 76, 78, 91, 94, 97, 104, 105, 107, 110–112, 125, 153, 155, 164, 165, 167–170, 180, 221, 286, 287, 305; attitude to scientific work, 22, 23, 33, 78, 85; relations with Baudin, 2–5, 23, 45; relations with Lesueur, 80, 84, 93, 108; sensibility, 94–96, 99, 115, 117–119; concern for his collections, 60–63, 171, 173, 174; manuscripts, 69–72, 75, 76, 78, 79, 83, 86, 87, 89, 92–99, 101, 181–184, 189, 190, 194, 220, 223; author of voyage account, 1, 2, 33, 41, 49, 51, 80–83, 90–95, 98–100, 112, 180, 181, 196, 198, 282, 296, 304, 307, 309, 312; narrative strategies, 42–46, 49, 50, 52, 83, 85, 99, 100, 105, 106, 108, 113–120, 311; as 'observer of man', 37, 39, 40, 42–48, 54, 55, 59, 76, 77, 90, 100, 303–309, 311–314; on 'civilisation', 46, 47, 49–51, 309, 313, 314; on colonisation, 51–55, 57, 58, 77; as political analyst and patriot, 36, 52, 53, 77, 78, 109–111; as ornithologist, 180–201, 221, 223–226; post-voyage scientific work, 78, 80–84, 152, 155, 166, 167, 173–176, 267, 270, 287; career management, 4, 5, 17, 18, 23, 41, 43–45, 75, 80, 83, 91, 92, 100, 111, 113; reputation, 5, 41, 59, 106, 108, 120, 220, 278, 286; as scientific voyager, 2, 5, 18, 54, 58, 97, 112, 302, 314; death, 18, 91, 92, 106, 174
Petit, Nicolas-Martin: 11, 25, 80–82, 87, 90, 114, 226, 229, 282, 286
Petitjean, Anne-Sophie: 102
Petitjean, Pierre-Lazare: 102
Peyrilhe, Bernard: 222
Pfennigwerth, Stephanie: 122
Philippe, Daniel: 217

Piard-Bernier, Josiane: 317
Picquet, Antoine Furcy: 106, 110
Picton, Thomas: 16
Pinel, Philippe: 37, 222
Pipelet, Clémence ('Clémentine'): 281
Pitot, Thomi: 266
Plomley, Norman James Brian: 87, 317
Pluchet, Régis: 299
Pommel (novice): 148
Pontoppidan, Erik: 186
Porter, Roy: 38
Pratt, Kate: 88
Pratt, Mary Louise: 25, 314
Prieur, Gilbert: 285

Q
Quoy, Jean René Constant: 184, 308, 311, 317

R
Ragan, Bryant: 38
Raty, Laurent: 217
Ravelet, Monsieur: 78
Régnier, Edmé: 39, 47
Regourd, François: 23
Rehbock, Philip F.: 37
Reidy, Michael S.: 37
Reinaud (acting prefect): 131
Renould, Jean Bertrand: 149
Richard, Hélène: 19, 26
Richard, Louis Claude: 19, 26, 222
Riche, Claude: 20, 26
Riedlé, Anselme: 4, 15, 16, 22, 25, 129, 133, 138, 288, 289
Rivière, Serge M.: 6
Ronsard, François-Michel: 150, 306, 316
Rosily, François Étienne de: 131, 146, 149

Rousseau, Jean-Jacques: 99, 102, 314

S
Sabatier, Raphaël: 222
Saint Cricq, Jacques de: 126, 131, 134, 147, 149, 253, 258, 264, 265
Saint-Pré, Jean de: 246
Salm, Constance Marie de Théis, comtesse de: 281, 285
Salm-Reifferscheidt-Dyck, Joseph Maria Franz Anton Hubert Ignaz, comte de: 281
Sankey, Margaret: 6, 54, 64, 87, 102, 103
Sarwell, Monsieur: 275
Sautier, Antoine: 25, 129, 138
Schmidt, Frédéric-Chrétien: 17, 25
Schmitt, Stéphane: 242
Schodde, Richard: 244
Scofield, Paul: 243, 244
Secord, James A.: 24, 37, 121
Shaw, George: 17, 25
Shellam, Tiffany: 315
Sloan, Phillip R.: 37, 38
Small, Helen: 25
Smith, Bernard: 38, 176–178, 263
Solander, Daniel: 11, 14, 29
Spary, Emma C.: 24, 37, 121, 284
Spate, Oskar: 6
Spöring, Herman: 11, 14
Starbuck, Nicole: 258, 264, 265, 314–317
Staum, Martin: 317
Steinheimer, Frank D.: 244
Steller, Georg Wilhelm: 238, 246
Stocking, George: 308, 315
Stresemann, Erwin: 217
Swainson, William John: 195

T

Taillefer, Hubert Jules: 107, 126
Tate, Trudi: 25
Taton, René: 243
Tennyson, Alan J.D.: 244
Thomas, Martin: 315
Thomson, James: 126, 128, 148, 149
Thouin, André: 54, 129–131, 134, 135, 139, 149, 174
Thwaites, Vivonne: 88, 299
Troschel, Franz Hermann: 168, 178
Truffet, Valentin: 15
Tulard, Jean: 149

V

Vancouver, George: 108
Van-Neck, Monsieur: 275
Vannoni, Antonella: 24
Van Strien-Chardonneau, Madeleine: 64
Vasse, Timothée: 295, 296
Vauquelin, Louis Nicolas: 285
Verne, François: 116
Vieillot, Louis Jean Pierre: 184, 187, 193
Vinarskiĭ, Max V.: 243, 245
Vince (seaman): 148
Virey, Jean-Joseph: 58
Vivant, Dominique, Baron Denon: 281
Vlamingh, Willem Hesselsz de: 257, 292
Vuacheux, Édouard: 288, 300

W

Wailly, Pierre-François de: 145, 151
Wallis, Samuel: 108
West-Sooby, John: 2, 6, 7, 24, 63, 87, 88, 121, 122, 176, 244, 263, 285, 299, 301, 314–316
Whittell, Hubert Massey: 217
Williams, Elizabeth: 38
Williams, Glyndwr: 37
Witt, Gerrit Frederikszoon de: 218
Witt, Willem de: 218
Wokler, Robert: 38

Y

Young, William: 243

Encountering Terra Australis

Jean Fornasiero, Peter Monteath, and John West-Sooby

Encountering Terra Australis traces the parallel lives and voyages of the explorers Flinders and Baudin, as they travelled to Australia and explored the coastline of mainland Australia and Tasmania. Unusually, the book takes its lead from the voyages of Baudin, rather than Flinders, providing a rather different interpretation than those presently circulating. Furthermore the authors have worked using their own totally fresh translation of Baudin's journals, sourcing original accounts including material which has never before been available in English.

Winner of the Frank Broeze Maritime History Prize.

The First Wave

Edited by Gillian Dooley and Danielle Clode

The European maritime explorers who first visited the bays and beaches of Australia brought with them diverse assumptions about the inhabitants of the country, most of them based on sketchy or non-existent knowledge, contemporary theories like the idea of the noble savage, and an automatic belief in the superiority of European civilisation. Mutual misunderstanding was almost universal, whether it resulted in violence or apparently friendly transactions.

Written for a general audience, *The First Wave* brings together a variety of contributions from thought-provoking writers, including both original research and creative work. Our contributors explore the dynamics of these early encounters, from Indigenous cosmological perspectives and European history of ideas, from representations in art and literature to the role of animals, food and fire in mediating first contact encounters, and Indigenous agency in exploration and shipwrecks.

The First Wave includes poetry by Yankunytjatjara Aboriginal poet Ali Cobby Eckermann, fiction by Miles Franklin award-winning Noongar author Kim Scott and Danielle Clode, and an account of the arrival of Christian missionaries in the Torres Strait Islands by Torres Strait political leader George Mye.

Alas, for the Pelicans!

Edited by Anne Chittleborough, Gillian Dooley,
Brenda Glover, and Rick Hosking

In 1802 a Frenchman and an Englishman famously encountered each other off the southern shores of 'Terra Australis'. The voyages of discovery of Nicolas Baudin and Matthew Flinders opened the way for the increasingly rapid invasion and colonisation of the Australian continent. This collection of essays, images and poems examines some of the cultural contexts of their voyages and the ramifications of their discoveries over the ensuing years. Flinders himself poignantly noted that the arrival of Europeans in the waters surrounding Kangaroo Island also heralded the passing of what he romantically termed the golden age of the pelicans.

'There are four small islands in the eastern branch [of Nepean Bay]; one of them is moderately high and woody, the others are grassy and lower; and upon two of these we found many young pelicans unable to fly ... Alas, for the pelicans! Their golden age is past; but it has much exceeded in duration that of man.' – Matthew Flinders, *A Voyage to Terra Australis*

The Art of Science

Edited by Jean Fornasiero, Lindl Lawton, and John West-Sooby

It was one of the most lavishly equipped scientific expeditions ever to leave Europe. At the dawn of the nineteenth century, French navigator Nicolas Baudin led two ships carrying 22 scientists and more than 230 officers and crew on a three-and-a-half-year voyage to the 'Southern Lands', charting coasts, studying the natural environment and recording encounters with indigenous peoples.

Inspired by the Enlightenment's hunger for knowledge, Baudin's expedition collected well in excess of 100,000 specimens, produced more than 1500 drawings and published the first complete chart of Australia.

Baudin's artists, Charles-Alexandre Lesueur and Nicolas-Martin Petit, painted a series of remarkable portraits of Aboriginal people and produced some of the earliest European views of Australian fauna. An integral part of the French scientific project, these exquisite artworks reveal the sense of wonder this strange new world inspired.

Wakefield Press is an independent publishing and
distribution company based in Adelaide, South Australia.
We love good stories and publish beautiful books.
To see our full range of books, please visit our website at
www.wakefieldpress.com.au
where all titles are available for purchase.
To keep up with our latest releases, news and events,
subscribe to our monthly newsletter.

Find us!

Facebook: www.facebook.com/wakefield.press
Twitter: www.twitter.com/wakefieldpress
Instagram: www.instagram.com/wakefieldpress

www.ingramcontent.com/pod-product-compliance
Lightning Source LLC
Chambersburg PA
CBHW021817300426
44114CB00009BA/214